W9-CHA-705

BORN AT THE RIGHT TIME

DOUG OWRAM

Born at the Right Time:
A History of the Baby-Boom Generation

UNIVERSITY OF TORONTO PRESS
Toronto Buffalo London

Toronto Buffalo London
Printed in Canada

ISBN 0-8020-5957-0 (cloth)

Printed on acid-free paper

Canadian Cataloguing in Publication Data

Owram, Douglas, 1947–
Born at the right time : a history of the baby-boom generation

Includes index.
ISBN 0-8020-5957-0

1. Baby-boom generation – Canada. 2. Canada – Social conditions – 1945–1971.* 3. Canada – Civilization – 1945– . I. Title.

FC89.09 1996 971.064 C96-931036-6
F1021.2.09 1996

University of Toronto Press acknowledges the financial assistance to its publishing program of the Canada Council and the Ontario Arts Council.

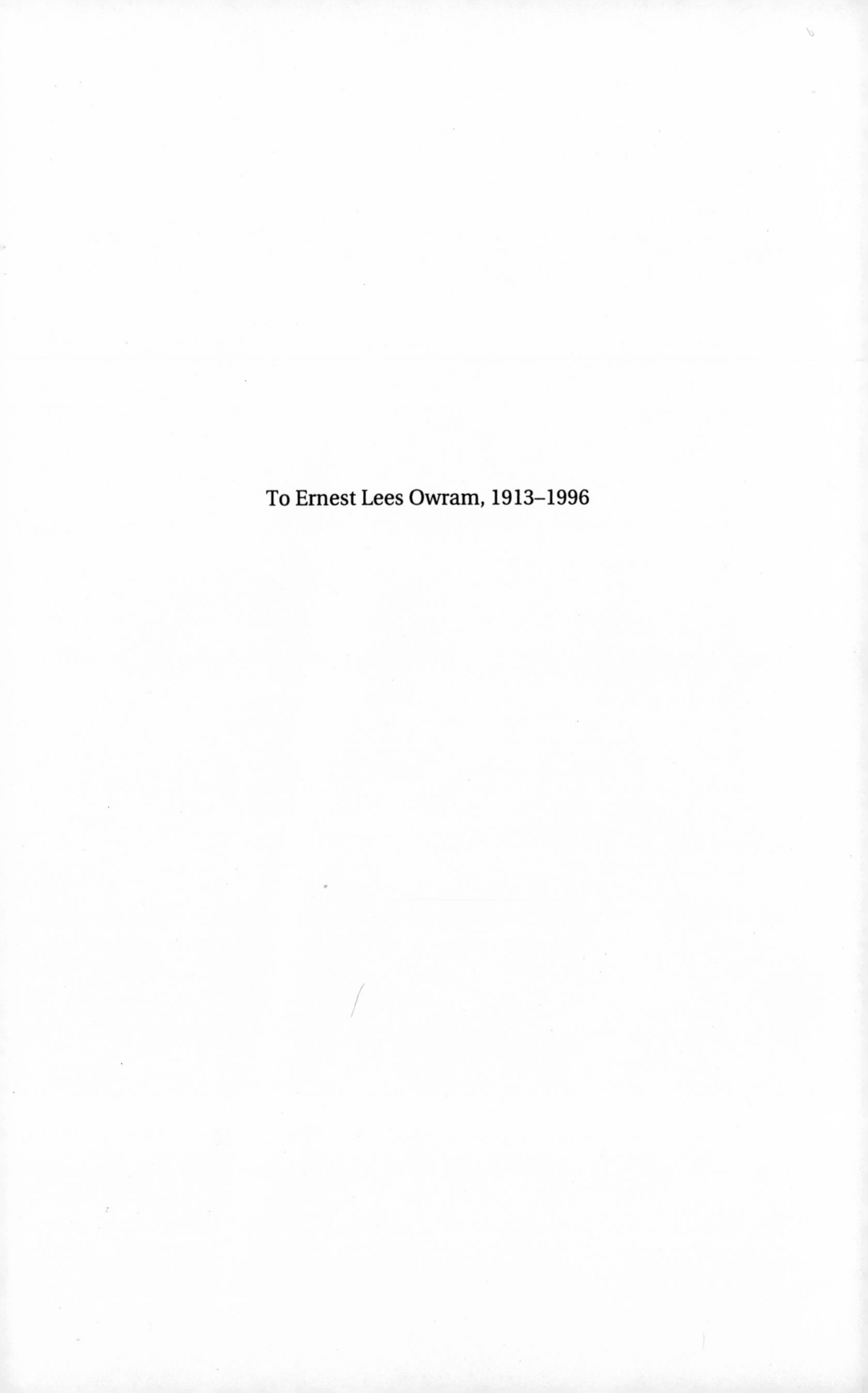

To Ernest Lees Owram, 1913–1996

Contents

Preface

The greater the proportion of young people the greater the likelihood of cultural and political change.

Herbert Moller, 1968[1]

This book is a biography of the first twenty-five years of a generation. It is also one perspective on an era in Canadian history. Each generation has a story to tell, but it is actually relatively rare in history that people think of themselves in terms of generational identity, and rarer still when it can be said that children and adolescents had a defining influence on the history of the larger society that surrounds them.

Both situations existed in this quarter-century. From the time the baby boom was born, it was extraordinarily powerful and, from a young age, it thought of itself as a group distinct from previous generations. This power and sense of self, which makes the baby boom a worthy subject, stems from three historical forces.

Its influence began with its size. From a low of 227,000 live births in the mid-1930s, the number of Canadian babies born each year rose to 343,504 by 1946, and to a peak of 479,000 by the later 1950s. Then the birth rate collapsed. By 1967, Canada's centennial year, the number of births was down by more than 100,000 annually, and by the mid-1970s, the birth rate per capita was less than half of what it had been at the height of the boom. As several writers have noted, baby boom was followed by baby bust. The changing numbers of births, both relative and absolute, created the force of the generation, as the baby-boomers came to overshadow the smaller generations that preceded and succeeded them. As the boom generation moves through the life cycle, its sheer size has forced society to adapt. In the apt words of American historian Landon Jones, it is 'the pig in the python,' distending society as it passes along.[2]

The baby boom was also a fortunate generation, and this good fortune increased its influence. Few generations grew up in such prosperous times. The quarter-century after the Second World War brought the Western world some of the most sustained economic growth in history. People – both parents and children – went from year to year expecting things to improve. Although occasional recessions caused worry, and many individual lives did not reflect the prosperity of the times, this good fortune was broadly based. A growing economy, an improving set of government social programs, and a wide dispersion of wealth meant that the average Canadian citizen benefited. As a result the baby-boomers became the best-fed, best-educated, and healthiest generation in Canadian history. Boomers did not have to struggle for survival and could afford to worry less about economic security. Thus, the generation could turn its attention to its own sensibilities. The boomers' sense of self was due, in no small part, to the fact they had the luxury of being free to think about such things.

Finally, though, much of the myth, and hence the power, of the baby boom lies in its connection with the fabled decade of the 1960s. Hippies and dope, free love, flower power and women's liberation, Vietnam, the Kennedys and Trudeau, university protest, and the Beatles – the decade has few rivals as an age of change and excitement. Even the roar of the 1920s is muted in comparison. Much of the turmoil of the 1960s was identified with youth. Here was a generation that, according to the rhetoric of the time, was about to transform Western society. Here was a group with so much confidence in itself, with so many idealistic expectations, with so much impatience in its rhetoric that it denied the force of history. For boomers, the past simply had to give way to the future. This perception of change was the final, and probably the crucial link in the myth of the baby boom. For here was power and good fortune asserting itself as a historical force. Here, for those who were a part of it, was confirmation of both the uniqueness of the generation and its meaning. This was a historical moment so powerful that a quarter-century later its events were still legends – witness Woodstock 2 or the triumphant 1994–5 Voodoo Lounge tour of the Rolling Stones.

To these three historical forces – numbers, affluence, and the link to a turbulent decade – it is possible to add a fourth, more controversial factor. The baby-boomers have generated almost continuous controversy from the time that Doctor Spock decided they should be treated gently. Psychiatrists, lay and professional, have argued about the generation's collective mental state. Marshall McLuhan, Canada's famous communications theorist of the 1960s, saw them as a special television generation: 'When the present TV generation, aged 15 and down, reaches the job plateau the prayer mat will succeed the Cadillac.'[3] Baby-boomers themselves were far from immune to claims about their uniqueness: This was the generation that proclaimed the 'age of Aquarius,' a 'revolution,' and a mistrust based purely on age (never trust anyone over thirty). In all of this is an implicit, and often explicit, claim that the baby-boomers were different, not just in terms of opportunity and numbers, but in character as well. That qualitative difference led to expectations that they would have a special effect.[4]

What that difference means in moral, ethical, or historical terms is even more controversial. This fact was brought home to me forcefully a few years ago while I was teaching a senior seminar on postwar Canada. One of the topics was 'The Sixties' and to open discussion I asked the class, largely infants in the sixties, to give their image of that decade. The answer was unremittingly hostile – dirty hippies, dope freaks, and whining. The reaction surprised me at the time and I was tempted to dismiss it as aberrant. I have long since learned that it wasn't. Instead, these students were expressing a theme that has, in recent years, become a stock-in-trade of magazine articles, newspaper columns, and television specials – Generation X versus the baby boom.

Undoubtedly such themes are played up for the sake of a good story. Undoubtedly as well, as other students have noted, the whole idea of Generation X has been siezed by baby-boomers, who so instinctively think in terms of generations. Yet beneath the hype is a point of some interest. Many of its non-members dislike the baby boom. The composite accusation – given no attempt to discriminate between truth and fiction – would run something like this: Here is the spoiled generation who had it all. They obtained the best jobs; ran up the government debt; and now sit astride career paths in corporations, education, and government. They will perch there for another ten to twenty years and, by the time they leave, a whole generation (our famous Xers) will have been sacrificed. Even then, if they can, they will probably use their massive numbers to ensure that pensions remain healthy, and thus an increasing burden on the smaller workforce that follows them.

On the cultural level – the accusation would continue – the baby-boomers have been equally selfish. Their music, their style of dress, and their interests have overshadowed society. When they were young, society was interested in young things. Now that they are middle-aged, society has little interest in or time for the concerns of youth. Indeed, at the extreme, the accusations edge towards notions of intergenerational warfare. As one Generation Xer said bitterly, 'We are the most aborted generation in history!' All of this is instructive. The very fact that we are continuing to discuss issues along generational lines reflects the powerful hold the baby boom has had on the latter half of the twentieth century.

THE INTENTION OF THIS BOOK IS TO TRY TO UNRAVEL some of the myth and history surrounding the life of the baby-boomers from their beginning, at war's end, to the end of the sixties. It is, in other words, the story not of a generation's life but of its youth. My intention is to follow the generation's creation of its own identity and its assertion of a place in history. For though they will remain the pig in the python until old age begins to remove them, the baby-boomers laid their claim upon history even before they became adults. Indeed, it seems likely that the great historical moment of the baby boom occurred before those on its leading edge had reached their mid-twenties. Of course, individual boomers will go on to high office and great achievement. However, as a generation, the baby boom in middle age seems a much less forceful or purposeful group than it did before it had fully matured.

The purposes of this book shaped its structure. The best approach to examining the history of a generation is through the study of history as a life cycle. Accordingly, the early part of this work explores the world of childhood and the family life that surrounded it. Toys and school, parental rules and the family home were the world of these children. Later, of course, their world broadens. Adolescence brings wider horizons and new interests. Home and neighbourhood begin to diminish in importance, superseded by the opposite sex and the clothes, music, and culture of the peer group. High school and, far more than ever before, university become the centre of life. Outside issues intrude, and personal and political experimentation sets in. I have tried to capture these shifts by focusing on the particular events that dominate given periods of the baby boom's life cycle. Fortunately, the generation's tremendous influence also means that these issues tended to be predominant for society as a whole. Thus one of the side-effects of this life-cycle approach is to convey some sense of the main concerns of the quarter-century.

Still, the use of generation as a primary category of organization, as with any other, such as gender, class, or ethnicity, forces a degree of generalization. In what follows, I attempt to re-create some of the primary interests of baby-boomers without pretending that everyone in the generation can be captured in such a story. Practicality required that I concentrate on the mainstream of the generation rather than the margins. As a colleague of mine aptly put it, this is history from the middle out. The very poor, the very remote, certain ethnic communities had a very different experience and, just as they did not fully participate in the generational sense of self, so they are not fully part of this story. Nor, for that matter, are the very rich or those who, for whatever reason, did not become tied into the broad youth world of the postwar years.

My research quickly exposed one other problem. What is the real baby boom? Demographically there are minor disputes. Did it end in 1962 or 1964? Did it begin in 1945 or 1946? I argue here that demographically the baby boom runs from 1946 to 1962, but that is not the real issue. The real problem is that these dates are not all that meaningful historically. First, much of the story of the baby boom is that of adjustment to a giant change in the number of children being born. The baby boom is, to use a somewhat less graphic metaphor than the pig, a shock wave. As its front edge arrived at a point in the life cycle – kindergarten, high school, university, the job market – it forced tremendous adjustments to the relevant parts of society and, over the next few years, adaptations were made. By the time the later half of the baby boom arrived at any point in the life cycle, the social system had already regained a relatively steady state. The next dramatic change, indeed, comes in the wake of the boomers, when the last of them pass through and the relevant social institution has to reverse itself.

Second, if the notion of a generation is to have meaning, it has to be more than a statistical bulge. As one of the foremost generational historians of the United States put it, a generation is 'an age group shaped by history.'[5] The historian of the tragic generation which headed into the First World War made the point that 'generations are made not born.'[6] Perhaps the most famous of the sociological theorists of generations, Karl Mannheim, agreed, albeit in somewhat more ponderous language: 'We shall therefore speak of generation as an actuality only where a concrete bond is created between members of a generation by their being exposed to the social and intellectual symptoms of a process of dynamic de-stabilization.'[7]

As shock wave or as a shared historical experience, the baby boom does not run from 1946 to 1962. Those on the sharp upward curve of births created the shock-wave effect. Those who were children in the 1950s and grew through teenage years to adulthood in the 1960s and early 1970s can lay some claim to the shared historical moment. Those who came later shared neither in the shock-wave effect nor in the cultural influence of the baby boom. They would come to adulthood after prosperity had passed and after many of the best positions had been taken. If you were born in 1960, in other words, you are more likely a Generation Xer in outlook and experience, whatever the demographers may say. Conversely, the late war babies were eighteen years old when Kennedy was shot, and in their early twenties at the height of the counter-culture. Indeed, these demographic pre-boomers were often, by virtue of their advanced age, in the forefront of many of the boom-associated activities of the decade. As a historical rather than a purely demographic phenomenon, therefore, it seems reasonable to say that in cultural terms the baby boom was born sometime between the late war and about 1955 or 1956.[8]

There was another restriction that developed during my research, a matter not so much of choice but of practicality. The worlds of anglophone and francophone youth were linked after the war, but both the rhythms and the perspectives were, to use a word currently in vogue, 'distinct.' The obsession with independence, the revolt against religion, the differing demographics of francophone Quebec meant that one could not recount a story of 'the' baby boom that encompassed French and English equally. By necessity, therefore, the story of the francophone generation is told here only in so far as it was a part of the larger national story. I cannot pretend, however, that this book has anything other than an English-Canadian perspective or focus.

I said at the beginning that this was not only the story of a generation but a perspective on an era. For I believe that the baby boom was so powerful that it did much to shape the history of the era. Certainly, at the very least, this book is an attempt to relate the experiences of a generation to its impact on society. Economics, politics, education, and family life would all have been considerably different without the vast demographic upsurge of births after the Second World War.

Acknowledgments

This has been a massive project, and it could not have been completed without considerable help. The Social Sciences and Humanities Research Council gave me a grant, which facilitated archival travel and provided for research assistance. That research assistance, in the person of David Kales, was invaluable for the work on aspects of the 1940s and 1950s. Others were involved in later stages of the project. Rob Ferguson helped me with material on Ontario schools; Philip Massolin, Eric Gormley, Heather Rollason, and others undertook specific research assignments funded through the university. The University of Alberta was also generous in its grant of a McCalla Professorship, which provides a year's teaching relief. The bulk of this book was written during that time. A university that believes in research and gives it support is an invaluable asset.

I woud also like to recognize the usual efficient and able people at the University of Toronto Press. Gerry Hallowell has been enthusiastic about the book from the beginning. Laura Macleod was equally supportive and helpful in answering an author's random and sundry questions. When she left, Rob Ferguson took over the task of working on the manuscript. Beverley Beetham Endersby did a wonderful job of copy-editing, pointing out inconsistencies, infelicities, and questionable citations. My thanks to them all. Finally, Deborah and Kristine – one a baby-boomer and the other part of the new 'millennial' generation – were patient as always with my obsession with writing.

Average Canadian housewife, 1950 – mother, baby, and an abundance of consumer goods. The picture says much about the postwar ideal of a happy life and women's role in it.

Don Mills Shopping Centre, 1957. Although the early shopping centres were uninspiring, they became an essential part of the baby-boomer's culture.

The Grange School, late 1950s. The baby boom spawned thousands of new schools with plans that varied little from region to region.

By 1967, protests against the Vietnam War had a wide base of support on campuses across Canada. This one was in Edmonton, 1967.

Occupation of the UBC Faculty Club, 1968. Part party, part protest, such scenes were a common aspect of university life by the late 1960s.

The New Left Caucus invades the freshman dinner, University of Toronto, 1969. Such high-profile events raised the NLC to a dominant position in new left politics in the late 1960s.

Mackay Street, Montreal. Print-outs litter the street in the aftermath of the Sir George Williams 'Computer Riot.'

The police move in to quell student unrest at Loyola College, 1970. Such scenes were common to many Canadian campuses.

Hare Krishna, UBC, 1970. An age of romanticism spawned numerous religious cults.

BORN AT THE RIGHT TIME

1

Home and Family at Mid-Century

So much for predictions! The Dominion Bureau of Statistics commissioned Enid Charles, a well-known British demographer, to assess the implications of the 1941 census.[1] For Charles, the striking thing about that census was the steady decline in the Canadian birth rate. In the dry and unemotional language of the social scientist, Charles struck a warning note: In a land with so many resources, the Canadian population was in danger of failing even to reproduce itself. In 1941 the Canadian population figure was just over 11.5 million. Using the best demographic projections available, Charles predicted that by 1971 that figure would reach only 13.5 to 14 million. The longer term was even bleaker. 'A projection of the fertility and mortality trends of 1921–1939 into the future indicates that the rate of natural increase will decline. If the trend towards smaller families continues, and no large-scale immigration occurs, the population will reach a maximum of about 15 million towards the end of the century, and thereafter will begin to decline.'[2]

Publishing can be a slow process. Charles's study wasn't released until 1948, and by then her projections had been reduced to nonsense. Within a year the population would reach the figure projected for 1971; within three years it would surpass the number predicted for the end of the century! It is not that Charles was a bad demographer; she had used all the standard methods in producing her estimates. It was that the public wasn't following the rules. After showing a trend towards a lower birth rate for three-quarters of a century, the pattern had changed. Even as the demographers pondered over the gloomy scenarios of an ageing society, the men and women who had lived through war and depression set out in unprecedented numbers to have children.

With the advantage of hindsight, it is easy to see that there were fore-warnings of the boom. The war years had brought a steady increase in the number of Canadian babies born each year (see figure 1.1). Likewise, the crude birth rate (the ratio of numbers of babies born annually to the total-population figure) increased from approximately twenty per thousand through the later 1930s to twenty-four per thousand by mid-war, at which point it seemed to level off. But wartime was an economic and social anomaly in so many ways that Charles, as well as most others who noticed such things, assumed that this blip in the birth rate was just another war-induced event. Presumably, when the anomaly came to an end, the birth rate would resume its long-term decline.

That, obviously, isn't what happened. In many of the victorious countries, the end of the war brought an upsurge in births. In four countries, however – Canada, the United States, New Zealand, and Australia – there was an unprecedented increase in the birth rate that lasted long beyond the immediate postwar years.[3] In Canada the number of babies born went up from just over 300,000 at war's end to 372,000 by 1947, and to more than 400,000 by 1952. It would be 1966 before the number of children born fell below 400,000 again. The change in the birth rate was even more dramatic. From a figure of 24.3 per thousand population in 1945, it soared to 28.9 in 1947. Not until 1963 did it again fall to the 24 range.

This, then, was the baby boom. The years when that birth rate went well above twenty-four per thousand population, though that measurement is inexact, provide convenient dates by which to define the era. In Canada, therefore, the baby boom began in 1946, peaked in terms of absolute numbers in 1959, and ended by 1962. The births in those seventeen years have been among the most potent forces shaping Canadian cultural, political, and economic life ever since. The first half of this generation, born between 1947 and the mid-1950s, brought about an especially turbulent time. After years of an ageing society, institutions weren't prepared for the needs and demands this shock wave of children would create.

Data like these give something of the dimension of the baby boom but cannot convey the way in which, from the beginning, the boom changed the nature of day-to-day life. Women married between the ages of twenty and twenty-four were, by mid-century, waiting less than two years before having their first child. By the mid-1950s their younger sisters were waiting only 1.5 years.[4] The generation emerging

FIGURE 1.1
Live Births as a Percentage of Those in 1940

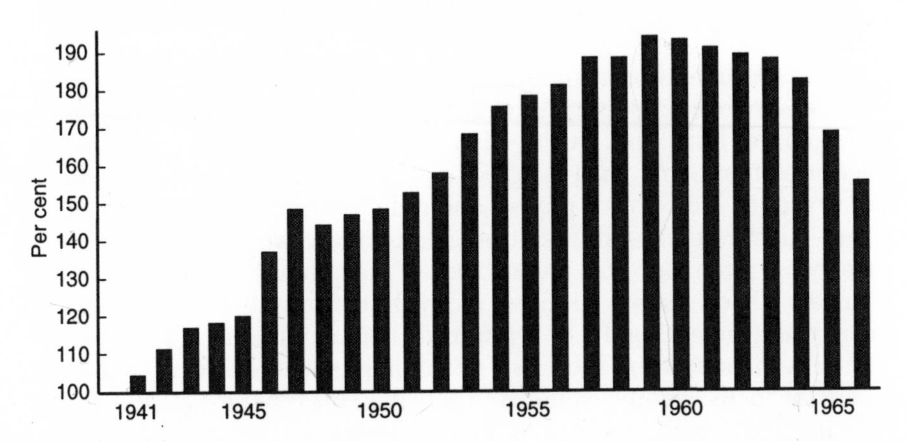

Source: F.H. Leacy, *Historical Statistics of Canada*, 2d ed. (Ottawa 1983), tables B1–14

from war and depression not only were marrying earlier but were having their children younger than had their predecessors. They were joined by those who had been married before the war but who deferred having children until war's end. The fertility rate for women aged thirty to thirty-five went from 120 per thousand before the war to more than 150 per thousand in 1947. Society seemed to revolve around babies. One in five women between the ages of twenty and twenty-nine gave birth in any given year through the late 1940s and early 1950s. Sometimes it seemed that everybody was pregnant or had a new baby.

Babies became the predominant topic of conversation. Columns of advice, fiction, and advertisements were aimed at families with infants. Articles either extolled the wonder of it all – 'Born to Mr and Mrs Canada 300,000 Babies' – or provided tales aimed at the parents of young children.[5] More and more baby-food, diaper, and baby-powder ads appeared. Life insurance companies were especially quick to capitalize on the new responsibilities of young fathers. 'Security – the Birth Right of Children,' said the timely 1947 Sun Life advertisement. 'Children think only of today; it is for you to think of their tomorrows.'[6] Automobile companies, which had previously tended to target young couples with their ads, now featured whole families. The media, in turn, was reflecting the interests of society. For people between the ages of twenty and thirty-five, babies were the topic of the day. Indeed, as magazine surveys consistently showed, girls, starting at about age fifteen, were increasingly focused on the prospect of marriage and children.

This attention raises an interesting question. The high marriage rate, the reasonable prosperity, the desire for home and stability – all affected the birth rate. But to what degree did people have children because other people had children? Certainly the childless couple was an object of criticism or pity second only to unmarried individuals.[7] The young mother who wasn't pregnant within two or three years of marrying often became the subject of neighbourhood gossip and friendly advice. Even without such direct pressures, the drive to pregnancy and parenthood was reinforced by the simple fact that, especially in the sprawling suburbs surrounding the larger cities, children were the focus of conversation and activity. This is not to say that people had children just to belong to a community. It does imply, however, that everything they saw around them made having children seem the natural and proper thing to do. Experts reinforced this tendency. The marriage manuals in particular emphasized the importance of children to a marriage: 'Children give life new meaning, a new focal point, a new frame of reference, a new perspective.' Moreover, just as marriage lengthened life expectancy, so children lengthened the marriage. Children 'are a guarantee of married happiness,' said one writer. 'The divorce rate of childless couples is several times that of couples with children,' concluded another.[8]

To understand why society suddenly focused on children, we have to understand the parents, for they not only brought the new generation into the world but also instilled primary social and cultural values. And the parents came from a generation that was as unique as the baby boom itself. Indeed, of the many ironies in the history of the baby boom, the most prominent is that it, a generation which so often scorned the ideals of family and home, was descended from a generation that valued home so much. The parents of the baby boom were more likely to marry, married earlier, divorced more rarely, and had a more unabashed pride of ownership than their parents or children. They operated by a code of family values that was firm and surprisingly uniform. At the centre of a web of social and familial values were the children themselves. This social structure was neither an accident nor, even in the child-oriented twentieth century, normal. Rather, the baby boom's unique place and unique influence drew directly from parental hopes and fears.

THE HOPES AND THE FEARS OF THE BOOM'S parents were the product of the terrible war that had so recently ended in victory. For if you had asked Canadian soldiers or war workers what they were fighting for, not against, in the Second World War, odds are they would have answered: 'Home.' The idea of home, really an emblem for a million personal recollections of friends, family, and normal daily activities, seemed much more immediate and emotionally meaningful than abstract concepts like democracy, or faraway places like Poland. Government agencies and the popular press both sensed this. In fiction, magazine articles, poems, and newspaper stories, the vision of 'home' was re-created with hundreds of variations. Coca-Cola ads showed returning soldiers and sailors coming back into the embrace of the family. Automobiles were portrayed as being built 'by home-loving, home-owning craftsmen.'[9] The short fiction that abounded in magazines and newspapers built its themes around the maintenance or renewal of home. Most potent of all were the songs. The lyrics of period pieces like 'Sentimental Journey,' 'Don't Sit under the Apple Tree,' and 'I'll Be Seeing You' asserted the poignancy of separation and the desire for reunion, home, and the return of loved ones.

The idea of home was flexible, and that was part of its appeal. To the soldiers overseas, home meant the return to family, friends, and civilian life, a sense captured in a short story of the time: 'Dick Bannerman closed his eyes. It was over for him – at last –, the waiting. He was leaving for home in two days. Home! he held the word within him until it began to expand and blossom with a ripe rich fullness he could hardly contain.'[10] For those who remained in Canada, 'home' was shorthand for the notion of reunion with loved ones, with the idea that relationships put on hold could soon resume. It was depicted in advice to young women on how to handle that 'long dreamed of moment when that man's here again, when you cease to carry the torch alone.'[11] It also took on material meanings, as the consumption of household items became associated with intimacy, romance, and the fulfilment of dreams. People selling everything from stoves to mouthwash tried to associate their products with an idealized image of home. Community Silverware, aiming squarely at concepts of romance, marriage, and the establishment of all the trappings of home, was especially blatant, running a series of ads that unabashedly made silverware a necessary adjunct to home life. 'Joy ... Joy ... Joy! The sun and the moon and the stars. The big shining world with a white fence around it. There's a great day coming. When HE'S BACK HOME FOR KEEPS.'[12]

Home life is a repository of special meaning and special values for every generation. Yet the one that came of age in the years surrounding the Second World War was special. This generation, comprising more than a quarter of the Canadian population, could scarcely remember a time in which home life had not been threatened. First there had been the Great Depression, affecting the ability of their parents to provide comfort and affecting as well their own future possibilities. Throughout the 1930s politicians and economists watched the skies for signs of improvement. The reality was, however, that the 1930s saw a lower standard of living overall than had the 1920s. For many families it brought unrelieved disaster. Lifelong jobs were lost. Farms were buried under dust storms. People migrated from region to region in search of work. Others doubled up, grandchildren growing up in their grandparents' house and newly married couples living at home because they couldn't afford a place of their own. For tens of thousands in the 1930s, home was a makeshift thing, subject to the vicissitudes of the economy and never quite what their parents had hoped for.

The gloom of the 1930s was at odds with the mythology of the North American experience. This was supposed to be the new world, the land of opportunity, where an open frontier and waves of immigrants promised growth and development. There might be bad years or individual setbacks, but Canadians and Americans both had grown accustomed to the idea that each succeeding generation would live a better material life than its predecessor. Yet for those born in the teens or twenties, this promise had been elusive.

The war ended the Depression, but it further disrupted lives. More than a million individuals, mainly those who came of age in the Depression, joined the military.[13] As many as 350,000 of them were stationed overseas at the height of the war.[14] Roughly speaking, this meant that half the male population of military age was in uniform at some point during the war, and nearly a third of them served overseas at one time or another. Military age was also marrying and child-rearing age. Thus, these people who, in other times, could have expected to be forming families were instead bivouacked in England, patrolling the North Atlantic, or, later in the war, fighting their way through Italy and France.

Some were already married when the war began. Others got married in haste when war was declared. The marriage rate increased by a third between 1938 and 1940.[15] The war meant that couples who had barely had time to adjust to married life now had to live apart, put their lives on hold, and wonder whether their relationship would survive the distance. For some, periods of leave or a home posting might allow at least intermittent contact. For many others, however, especially in the case of troops posted to England from 1939 on, there were six long years in which husbands and wives, or sweethearts, waited anxiously for the end to come. For all, the separation brought with it the constant fear that it might be permanent. For the 55,000 who died in the war and for those who loved them, the dream of home was shattered.[16]

The war also disrupted the lives of those on the home front. The Second World War, even more than the Great War, affected all Canadians. The entire industrial and resource capacity of Canada was involved, and life changed in thousands of small and not so small ways as the economy and society moved to a war footing. The face of the workforce altered dramatically as thousands of women moved into office and factory positions previously held by men. There had always been women who worked outside the home, of course, but the numbers during the Second World War were unprecedented – up to 1.2 million women worked at any one time, a participation rate of nearly 33 per cent. This increase had many effects – on women, on social attitudes, on children. Along the way, however, it also further disrupted the traditional concept of home and family. For the war, which had already taken husbands and fathers overseas in large numbers, brought into the factories and bureaucracies large numbers of women who, before the war, would normally have remained at home – middle-class housewives and mothers.[17] Traditional family patterns were thus further disrupted. With many fathers overseas large numbers of women had to face raising children alone. These same women, moreover, often had to make arrangements with relatives, friends, or, as the war went on, the government-supported day-care systems, to leave their children as they went off to work. Throughout the war, social workers and psychologists fretted about a generation of children raised in a haphazard manner.

Even the money that Canadians were now earning was of limited use. After years of making do because money was scarce, Canadians now had to make do because goods were unavailable. This was a total war, and the industrial capacity of Canada was directed towards military necessities. By 1941 production of a wide range of appliances was restricted in order to reserve metals for the war effort. Refrigerators, vacuum cleaners, washing machines, and a host of other goods virtually disappeared from the market. Automobile production ground to a halt as factories turned to the production of military vehicles. Even if you could find a car, its use was severely restricted by a shortage of tires and by gasoline rationing. The average Canadian was allowed only 120 gallons of gasoline per year by 1943. Nor were alternatives without their problems. Taxis were restricted to operations within fifteen miles of their home base, and even travel by public buses was restricted to a round trip of no more than fifty miles.[18]

It wasn't just the big, expensive goods; for somebody trying to raise a family, the small things probably brought the war home more emphatically than did the dearth of cars and refrigerators. Rationing of sugar, butter, coffee, tea, and meat severely restricted the family diet. Prohibitions on the import of canned fruit made tomato juice the vitamin-C source of necessity for most. Shopping became a matter, not of what you could afford, as it had been in the Depression, but of what you could find. 'Shopping is becoming more and more like a treasure hunt,' wrote one woman in 1943. 'Someone tells someone else that there is kleenex on sale at a drug store and the rush is on. Within a couple of hours stocks are cleaned out. Women with babies are finding shopping particularly difficult. Wool for knitting them clothes can only be got occasionally and it is difficult, sometimes impossible, to buy flannelette. Stores have to be gone over with a fine tooth comb in order to scratch up a few diapers.'[19]

Worst of all was the housing. The attachment of this generation to their homes and gardens became a source of criticism, even derision, by the 1960s. Given their experiences, this attitude was hardly reasonable. To put it simply, they grew up and came to adulthood at a time when Canadian housing was in an abysmal state. Construction has always been extremely sensitive to economic downturn, and it is hardly surprising, therefore, that construction collapsed in 1929–30. Even after halting recovery began in other areas of the economy towards the end of the 1930s, construction remained sluggish. Throughout the decade there were fewer houses being built than families being formed. In other words, the availability and, given the absence of repairs, the quality of Canadian housing were in decline. A good many children and adolescents growing up in the 1930s lived in crowded, run-down conditions. Hundreds of thousands of families could not afford to own or rent their own place and had to share with others. Newly married couples found themselves forced either to live apart or to share quarters with parents. It was estimated that, by the beginning of the Second World War, more than a million Canadians lived in residences with less than one room per person.

The war only worsened the situation. Building materials were diverted to the war effort, and thus the new prosperity did not rekindle housing starts. It was mid-war before building permits reached the numbers of the later 1920s. Much more than that was needed, however, for the war created tremendous new pressures. Thousands of Canadians moved to take advantage of desirable jobs in war industries or government. Urban centres gained at the expense of rural areas or smaller towns, but not equally. The bulk of the jobs were created in a few large cities. Montreal, the 'golden horseshoe' from Oshawa to Hamilton, Vancouver, Halifax, and Ottawa became magnets that drew thousands. Those that went found jobs more readily than they found accommodation. By mid-war a survey of 'ordinary' rental housing in Toronto discovered that just short of half was overcrowded, much of it badly so.[20] Newspapers were full of 'apartments wanted' ads, and key money, under-the-table kickbacks, and similar devices were common. So, too, was makeshift housing. Toronto put up temporary accommodation around city parks. Other cities experimented with quonset huts, rudimentary shelters, and even, in some cases, tent cities. Looking at the longer term, the Dominion government strengthened its support of home ownership with a new National Housing Act in 1944. At the same time it recognized the emergency faced in the short term and actually made it illegal to move to Victoria, Vancouver, Ottawa, Hull, Toronto, or Montreal unless you could prove to government that there was a wartime need for you to do so.[21]

The efforts were insufficient. Years of depression slump and wartime boom had taken their toll. For many the plight of crowding and long-distance commuting turned to desperation, especially when young children were involved. 'For countless numbers of children,' lamented a postwar Commission on Youth, 'home was a dilapidated makeshift dwelling, hopeless as far as healthful living was concerned, where life was insecure, and days were anxious. Lowered self-respect, poor health, anxiety, strained family relationships, lack of privacy – these were the consequences of poor housing that often created the juvenile delinquent.'[22]

The idea of home thus had very powerful connotations by the end of the war, ranging from material comfort to renewed relationships, to peace itself. Underlying it all was a search for stability on the part of a generation that had known nothing but instability. The home, coming home, and the formation of the family as a point of reference in an unstable world merged into one vision. For soldiers overseas, according to one editorial, there was a growing recognition of the values of Canadian home life. 'They felt a growing desire to give similar advantages to children of their own.' The war had been fought for the values of the family. 'Christian and democratic countries have made no mistake in emphasizing the value of family and home life. Individuals who exemplify the art of being in a family circle are better fitted thereby for usefulness in larger spheres and for gaining the secret of true happiness.'[23]

Such a romanticized and idealized vision of family was a natural human reaction to years of disruption. It was strengthened, though, because this was a society that placed a high premium upon marriage and family. Though family has always been central to social institutions, during the fifteen years or so after the Second World War the values of marriage and family were exalted to new levels. The young adults of the 1940s were the most domestically oriented generation of the twentieth century. When an American sociologist attempted, two years after the war, to set out what he termed the 'major cultural configurations of North American society,' he focused above all on marriage. 'Marriage,' he concluded, 'is a dominating life goal, for men as well as women ... Nearly all persons marry who are physically and mentally capable of contracting marriage.'[24] All the evidence indicates that he was correct.

Marriage and family was the young adult's route to respectability. This message was reinforced by social psychologists, politicians, and religious leaders. Those who did not marry were the subject of suspicion, for they were, in a sense, deviant in terms of cultural norms. There might be valid reasons, experts opined, for choosing not to marry, but when those reasons were listed, the image of social failure or hidden forces came through loud and clear. American Henry Bowman was the author of a number of manuals on building a successful marriage that were popular in both Canada and the United States. To him there was no doubt that failure to marry was proof of personality problems. The 'immature person,' 'the narcissist,' 'the predator,' those who are 'victims of parent fixation,' and those with deep inferiority complexes fail to marry, concluded Bowman.[25] Another book was even less subtle. *Why Are You Single?*, published in 1949, opened with a plea for 'sympathetic awareness' of the 'forgotten class,' the unmarried adult. That one phrase set the tone of the book. The unmarried were afflicted, like the victim of disease or mental illness. People who were single had been victims of 'psychological maladjustment,' and those who would learn from this book must undertake an 'inner change' if they are to make it to the altar.[26] There then followed a series of articles by medical and social 'experts' who talked about such things as 'the problem of bachelors and spinsters' and the possibility that 'deep seated neurosis' was creating an aversion to marriage. As one marriage expert candidly put it, 'Society looks askance at those who do not marry.'[27]

Such messages indicate just how pervasive the culture of marriage was at mid-century. 'Expert' opinion was reinforced, at the least subtle level, by advertisers. Product after product told consumers that what they wanted, or should want, was to be married, and that this or that product would help them. An amazing number of products could, with a little imagination, be associated with a successful marriage. Advertisers of soap, feminine-hygiene products, and mouthwash were especially forceful in making the link. 'She's Engaged! She's Lovely! She Uses Ponds!' said one soap commercial. 'Another man just slipped through my fingers,' lamented one lonely heart. 'Might not be so serious if it had happened just one time ... but when it happens time and time again – better check up. Something's wrong! Very often the trouble is bad breath.'[28] The main goal of youth was to get married. The main goal of adults was to stay happily married.

Marriage and married life also dominated the fiction of the day. Canada's two most popular magazines both regularly ran short stories. Amid such regular mystery fare as 'Murder in Mukluks,' there were inevitably stories about seeking marriage or coping with married life – 'He was a man in a hurry ... but that didn't seem a good reason why he should walk into her life on Tuesday and expect to marry her next Thursday.' A forgettable piece of fiction published in *Chatelaine* in 1948 had the lead-in 'When a conventional young man goes berserk it's a clever girl who gives him just enough rope for the marriage knot.'[29]

Though marriage was a dual decision, everybody acted as if it was the particular interest and goal of the female. The majority of products whose advertising was built around marriage either were explicitly for female use or targeted women consumers. The short fiction was aimed pretty much exclusively at a female readership. When, towards the end of the war, the well-known women's magazine *Chatelaine* established a set of 'teen councils' to get in touch with the female youth of Canada, it found that these girls were overwhelmingly oriented towards marriage. 'We all hope to marry in our early twenties,' reported the Winnipeg council, 'and have two to four children.' In Toronto a post-secondary council heard an argument from one student that higher education was dangerous because it lessened the opportunities for marriage. The others protested – but not because they were uninterested in marriage. 'Our varsity group – no one of whom really looked like a fugitive from a permanent twosome – were all amused that college life interfered with romance. Broader contacts, more interesting men, more preparation for becoming an alert, interesting wife.' There might well be a job in their future, but there was certainly expected to be a husband. A Queen's student article agreed, noting that a BA made a woman more eligible for marriage.[30] As one youthful woman put it in 1946, 'Every normal girl rather hopes to get married, doesn't she?'[31] After describing his treatment of two female patients, a male psychologist concluded without a trace of doubt that they really wanted 'what every woman wants: a house, a husband, children.'[32]

If they really did want such things, they had better not wait too long. In the postwar years the 'ideal' age for marriage advocated by the manuals was twenty to twenty-five for a woman and three or four years older for a man. Yet the insecurities mounted with each year, especially for women. By age twenty-three, the experts said, it was time to worry. 'If you are more than 23 years old ... perhaps you have begun to wonder whether Mr. Right would ever come along,' opined one book.[33]

For men the issue of marriage was more problematic. On the one hand, the longing for home and security was as much a part of the soldier's vision of the future as it was the woman's back in Canada. Yet two popular attitudes created a different perspective on the act of marriage for men. The first was that marriage was, however inevitable, the end of financial freedom since paycheques and financial decisions would be bound in by family responsibilities. Whereas women had financial reasons to pursue marriage, men had at least a rhetorical tradition of 'freedom' from responsibility. This financial relationship between the sexes extended to the biological arena as well. If women were bound by the domestic instinct, men were by nature free-roaming animals. 'The thought of marriage is natural to a woman; she takes to it as a duck to water; but there is something alien in the idea of marriage to men.' What man really wants to do is 'roam over the earth, [and] to conquer life and women; he is restless, and pursuit of happiness means to him to see new things, new countries, new women.'[34] The Errol Flynn movies which had been so popular in recent years had obviously had their effect!

Still, the responsible male was supposed to overcome such urges. Stereotypes played themselves out in bachelor parties and old jokes, but the need for love and stability is a human instinct and affected men as much as it did women. For those men who might take the stereotype too much to heart, there were always the social pressures of respectability and maturity. Marriage and family were expected. It was even shown that the single male lived a shorter life and had a less successful career than the married male.

The most potent social pressure of all was sex. Marriage confirmed sexual identity and gave sexual fulfilment, since sex outside marriage was still socially condemned, especially within the middle class. Conversely, failure to marry raised doubts about one's sexuality. This was an age in which gender roles were as narrowly defined for men as for women, and those who did not conform were easily branded. Even to the well-meaning amateurs of the YMCA's Canadian Youth Commission, the signs were clear from an early age. 'Prescott,' said one survey report, is a 'tall, slender , delicate lad of 17.' His behaviour told it all, for he did not like sports but did like picnics. He was interested in architecture, and maybe even interior design. He found girls easy to talk to and avoided fights with boys. The conclusion was unmistakable, if not actually stated: Prescott was headed to homosexuality. 'Unless Prescott gets prolonged psychotherapy,' concluded the author, 'his chance of a healthy sex adjustment is poor.'[35]

Given the obsession with sexual roles, it is not surprising that homosexuality was routinely seen as one of the major reasons people failed to marry. And since such people were often thought the victims of 'suppressed' or 'latent' homosexuality, they faced not only suspicion in the eyes of the public, but also doubts in their own minds.[36] There was also the danger that the single person, even if not homosexual to begin with, could become sexually disoriented by having to assume the tasks of both men and women. The image of the fussy old bachelor was a prominent part of the popular writing of the time. This, it should be noted, was not a theme that applied solely to men. Women, it was said, could become 'masculinized' or, alternatively, might already be masculinized.[37] In an age which prized clear-cut sexual differentiation and in which homosexuality was both illegal and socially condemned, such fears were especially powerful incentives to marry.

The personal longing for stability and closeness in the wake of war and depression undoubtedly helped bring about the increase in marriages that was a prelude to the baby boom. So, too, the cult of marriage set out expectations that encouraged large numbers of couples to make a formal commitment. Yet neither of these cultural forces is itself sufficient to explain the exceptional nature of this generation. The First World War generation had seen disruption and, while there was an increase in marriages and births after 1918, it was nothing like what occurred after the Second World War. Nor was the cult of marriage new. In its modern form it had certainly been in place through the Depression and the war itself. Likewise the cult of marriage and the sense of disruption were just as prevalent in Britain as in Canada, and yet the former's marriage and birth rates did not experience anything like the same upheaval. All of this is to say that expectations of 1945 were perhaps more fragile than might be surmised. What separated the baby-boom countries and the baby-boom years from their counterparts can be found in three specific conditions.

The first of these conditions was the economy. To some extent, the longing for home and family towards the end of the war was tempered by uncertainty about the future. Economists, politicians, and the average person feared that the war was sparking a temporary economic boom brought on by artificial conditions. The end of fighting could lead to a short bout of rapid spending, rising inflation, and then a sharp crash. That, as their parents reminded them, was what had happened in the years after the First World War. It was also what government experts planned for and expected during the war itself.[38] Such economic gloom clashed sharply with the hopes of Canadians for families, homes, and children. For this reason, the Co-operative Commonwealth Federation (CCF), with its promises of social security, rose to new heights of popularity by mid-war. Government also responded with a series of 'social welfare' reports and studies, all of which attempted to find a way to ensure that the end of the war did not bring economic disaster. In the popular press such plans received a great deal of attention.[39]

The crash never came. There was some economic instability in the first couple of years after the war as consumers dashed out to buy goods that weren't yet available in sufficient quantities. As one article said in 1946, 'there is a powerful demand for everything that one can eat, wear, read, repair, drink, ride, and rest in. The nylon line is the symbol of 1946.'[40] Such pent-up demand led to a sharp rise in inflation and government measures to control it. There were also jobs, however, and that was the most important economic indicator in the minds of average Canadians, especially younger ones considering marriage or children. Unemployment remained well under 4 per cent through the postwar period.[41] By 1947 or so, the postwar rush to buy, the resultant inflation, and then the slump in demand, seemed to have been accommodated without any great difficulty. The very fact that there had been so much pessimism at war's end may also have helped. Expectations count for a great deal, and it is probably safe to say that those the public had for the economy were matched or exceeded in every postwar year until well into the 1950s.[42]

The second condition was demographic. That generation of young adults and older adolescents who were considering marriage in the immediate postwar years – born, for the most part, from 1918 to the later 1920s – was large, its birth rate affected by a more modest version of the sense of loss and need for family brought on by the First World War. That factor was reinforced by relative prosperity (at least, after the end of a disastrous 1921 slump). The percentage of women having children during the 1920s was, for at least a short while, as high as it would be during the baby-boom years. This situation stood in sharp contrast to the collapse of birth rates to all-time lows during the Depression. As it was, though, those of marriage age during and immediately after the Second World War were themselves an age bulge in the population.[43]

The third condition was the educational norms of the time; for this generation, early marriage did not disrupt career plans. The great majority of Canadians in the 1940s and 1950s left school between the ages of sixteen and eighteen. Only 6 per cent of Canadians between the ages of eighteen and twenty-four were still in school in 1950.[44] For most people in their late teens and early twenties, therefore, there was no need to delay marriage until an education was finished. This was the last generation for which that would be the case. As higher education became less exceptional, marriages were increasingly delayed until careers could be begun. Fifteen years later, more than 16 per cent of those aged eighteen to twenty-four were in educational institutions. By the mid-1970s, one in five was.[45]

THUS, THE YEARS AFTER THE SECOND WORLD WAR were ripe for a marriage boom, and that increase in marriages established the conditions for the baby boom.[46] With the end of the war, the marriage rate soared. At a low point early in the Depression, the number of marriages had fallen below 65,000 per year, or 5.9 per thousand people. By 1944, the last full year of the war, marriage had recovered to the point where 104,000 couples went to the altar, or 8.5 per thousand. In 1945, however, 11,000 more people were married than in the previous year, and, in 1946, 33,000 more than that. The marriage rate was now nearly 11 per thousand, the highest figure ever recorded. Also, because those of marriageable age represented a relatively large age bulge, more families were formed in 1946 than ever before in Canada.[47]

After 1946 the marriage rate dipped slightly, and then stabilized, but at much higher rates than at any other time in the twentieth century. From the late 1940s through the mid-1950s, the rate of Canadian marriages remained extraordinary. More than a quarter of a million people each year got married, or, to put it another way, between 1946 and 1955 there were more than 1.2 million wedding ceremonies.

Canadians were also getting married earlier. At the beginning of the war, half of the women were married by the age of 23.2 years. The men they married had held out until the positively stately age of 26.4. A decade later the ages had dropped to 22 and 24.8, respectively, and by 1956 to 21.6 and 24.5. Given the normal vicissitudes of courtship, such numbers indicate not only that marriage was a 'major life goal,' but that little time was being wasted in achieving it. Especially for women, the completion of school, engagement, marriage, and, as we shall see, birth of the first child were more or less consecutive events.[48] Of course, as young couples looked around and saw friends and acquaintances 'tie the knot,' as the phrase went, the normal thing was to follow suit. As twentieth-century North Americans, the wartime generation believed firmly that marriage was a matter of individual choice, undertaken for love. Love is an amorphous thing, however, and individual choice was subject to social and peer pressure.

Once the 'bride's great day,' the honeymoon, and the writing of thank-you cards was over, the young couples had to turn their life to what was often referred to as the 'serious business' of marriage. Most couples, if they thought about it at all, probably liked to assume that their marriage either was unique to them or rested upon universal principles of love and support. Neither idea was correct. Though every marriage has its unique aspects, and though there is a timeless quality about love, the family of mid-twentieth-century North America had certain common patterns that were quite specific to that time and place.

Three patterns of family have, in sequence, dominated Canadian society during the twentieth century. The first was the famous or infamous Victorian family. Characterized in people's imagination by a rural setting, large numbers of children, firm religious mores, and a stern patriarchy, this arrangement was already in decline in English Canada by the First World War.[49] In its place emerged a family structure that was adapted more towards an urban–industrial environment. In this family there were fewer children, work was increasingly separated from the home, and the convention of the stern patriarch was replaced by what might best be termed 'constitutional patriarchy,' in which husband and wife were expected to share decisions about the family, though the husband's financial dominance and surviving notions of the head of the house meant that the actual degree of sharing varied considerably. This new family structure significantly enhanced the place of children. As the family decreased in size, more attention and effort were lavished on the individual child. The third prominent family form of the twentieth century is the most recent. Always present as a matter of necessity among the working class, it began to become a form of choice for the middle class towards the end of the 1960s. In this arrangement, both parents work, and child rearing is delegated in part to others.

The two generations represented by parents of the baby boom and the boom children mark the rise and fall of the second family arrangement. At least in English Canada, family size had been declining since the late nineteenth century and, as early as 1921, the birth rate per capita was only half what it had been just after Confederation. By the inter-war period, therefore, the post-Victorian form of family was becoming more and more common. Women of the period, having gained the vote and having played such an important role in the workforce during the First World War, increasingly assumed a more pronounced role in family decision making. The increasingly urban environment separated work from home and left the mother in charge of domestic affairs. The declining number of children, and the decline as well of Victorian religious strictures, meant less discipline and more open affection towards children.[50] Those marrying in the 1940s and early 1950s, therefore, were not really pioneering any new family arrangements. Instead, they made dominant a form that many of them had already seen at home.

Even if home life wasn't a model of the post-Victorian age, those approaching the altar in the wake of the Second World War had nothing to fear, or so they were told. For marriage and married life, the experts agreed, had become much more of a science than it had been for the previous generation. 'The choice of a mate,' said one pair of social scientists, is comparatively easy. 'And it doesn't matter so much just what kind of man he is. If both parties are emotionally educated almost any pair can make a go of it.'[51]

Underlying such naïvety, or perhaps faith, was the tremendous success of the social sciences in achieving an authoritative voice in society. From the 1890s through the 1930s, the social sciences began to appear at, first, American and, then, Canadian universities. They were a part of the challenge the modern concept of science was making to the dominance of a religious viewpoint that stressed faith and the moral authority of the church. The social sciences, in a way, were even more audacious than the pure sciences, for they sought to comprehend and manipulate the most complex of all forces – humanity. Nevertheless, by the time of the Depression, such disciplines as economics had made great strides both in understanding and in the influence they had among the public. In psychology, as we shall see, Freudianism and its offshoot, psychoanalysis, took postwar North America by storm. Dozens of books and articles talked routinely about ego, id, and super-ego with the confidence that any educated member of the public would know, at least vaguely, what such terms meant.[52] Likewise, sociology, anthropology, and other 'sciences of humanity' assumed new confidence and authority in the inter-war period.

Naturally, the social sciences – especially sociology and psychology – soon turned their attention to the family. From the turn of the century, there were growing concerns about the 'training' of mothers. By the 1920s studies were being undertaken from a dozen angles, and some of the classic works on family and community emanate from that era.[53] Perhaps inevitably, such studies soon spawned an offshoot of both psychology and sociology that moved from study and theory to application. In Canada, the 1920s had already seen the intrusion of 'experts' on child care, telling prospective parents how to raise their children.[54]

The most dramatic, and perhaps most peculiar, of these applications was the whole 'marriage education' movement that began in the 1920s in the United States. The courses proved so popular there that they spread across the nation and became a standard part of university curriculum by the later 1930s. Students flocked to these courses wherever they were established, with thousands enrolled at the larger universities. At larger and smaller institutions alike, students exerted continual pressure to increase the size and range of such courses. At several campuses, by the post–Second World War period, there were even 'Departments of Marriage.' From these experts and these courses, there soon developed a national network of marriage and family experts. By 1938 the first national conference on family relations was held in New York City. The next year the *Journal of Marriage and the Family* was established.[55]

In Canada's more conservative educational environment, there was no mass movement towards college marriage courses or departments. The American trend did have an influence, however. The notion of a 'science of marriage' was almost as pervasive as the cult of marriage itself. People like Henry Bowman, head 'marriage instructor' at St Stephen's College; Paul Popinoe, a 'flamboyant' lecturer much sought by the public; American writer on marriage Judson Landis; and Ernest Groves, the founder of the marriage-course movement, became widely known to the general public.[56] Canada also produced its own experts, who were also usually at universities, though in psychology, sociology, or medical departments, and who turned out a stream of publications for magazines and research journals – people like Mary Jukes and Ruth MacLachlan Frank. More than 1,000 books on marriage were produced in North America in the decade after Second World War.[57] The Canadian Youth Commission endorsed sex education for high schools in 1944 as a necessary step towards 'a good family life.'[58]

It is difficult to predict the precise impact of a mass of literature and of the high profile of a number of 'experts.' How many heard them? How many listened? Even the obviously high sales of the more popular books is not conclusive evidence as thousands of copies were undoubtedly purchased in fits of enthusiasm only to lie unread on the shelf. The large sales, the rise of the university courses, and the general popularity of marriage education do tell us something about the accepted norms of the day. The values and ideals of marriage emerging from marriage classes, marriage research, and marriage books were the norms to be emulated and the values to be cherished. More important, in the public's view, these experts offered not just values and ideals, but success. If you conformed to their advice, you would succeed in marriage. If you did not, you would likely fail. Several marriage manuals had 'tests' that engaged couples could take to see if they were suitable for each other.

Several things went into making modern marriage a success.[59] Some were surprisingly old-fashioned, such as the notion that the couple should not come from differing social classes, different ethnic groups, or different religions. In the United States a great deal was also made of the likelihood that cross-racial marriages would fail. Other themes were more modern. Husband and wife were told to make a serious and dedicated attempt to understand the needs and wishes of the other. This was particularly important early in marriage, and marriage counsellors seemed especially fond of the concept of 'marriage adjustment.' People had 'successful' or 'failed' marriage adjustments, and such adjustments, the counsellors warned, involved everything from living together to that most sensitive of all subjects, sex.[60] If adjustment didn't work, however, the ideal could never be achieved, and problems were likely to ensue.

The fine-tuning through adjustment, discussion, and compromise, however, was to be achieved within relatively fixed roles. No amount of discussion seemed to change the fundamental notion that 'biology was destiny.'[61] Women remained in the home. Men worked. At mid-century this ideal was pervasive. Every magazine, every marriage manual, every advertisement, and the entire cultural milieu – from store hours to the absence of such institutions as day-care facilities – indicated a society that assumed the family was based on the single, male wage-earner and the child-rearing, home-managing housewife. This assumption was supported by the vast majority of both men and women, and in many instances social custom was reinforced by law. During the Depression the civil service had prohibited the employment of married women if a man could be found to fill the job. In many provinces school boards prohibited the employment of married women as teachers, even though teaching was a primarily female profession.[62]

Law reflected public attitudes and social values. In recent years feminist scholarship has wrestled with the degree to which biological and/or psychological differences between men and women do or do not predetermine roles. In the 1950s, though, there was still the assumption of what one marriage counsellor called 'an unbridgeable gulf of sex differences.' Men and women were partners, but they approached issues from different bases. 'The world seems different to a woman from what it does to a man. Vocations, clothes, other people, children, reproduction, homes, sex, all appear in different light depending upon whether the frame of reference is masculine or feminine.'[63] From this belief it was a short step to the notion that the specialized roles of the era were not merely custom, though custom was recognized, but natural.

Democracy, personal fulfilment within the family unit, and specialized roles were the social norms shaping the mid-century family. 'Harmony' and 'tranquillity' became watchwords. The proper family functioned according to certain patterns of behaviour. The scientists said so. The bridal magazines said so. The marriage books said so. The advertisers said so.

> Mary Jane, in a crisp house dress kept spotless and unfaded by Lux, has laid out breakfast – everything Beechnut but the eggs. Jim Junior is busily eating up his cereal for the fun of finding Mickey Mouse at the bottom of the dish thoughtfully supplied by the makers of Cream of Wheat. Jim Senior, spruce in an Arrow Collar and fortified by a perfect night's rest under the auspices of the Simmons Bedding Company, is about to make his way to his office to earn the thirty-five dollars a week which are somehow to pay for the hundred dollar radio, the kitchen, the dapper little car, and the self-satisfied look that comes to those who have provided for retirement at fifty-five.[64]

Such passages obviously ridiculed the idea of the perfect family. The point is, though, that circumstances did work to set very high standards for married life. First, the circumstances of war and disruption created a romantic vision of the postwar world, one in which the family would be reunited, or the marriage knot tied. Second, the role of the family was now defined in terms of personal relationships and 'personal fulfilment' rather than economics. Third, the democratic family, with its consultative structures and assumption that husband and wife should be companions as well as partners, raised the stakes still further. People were affected differently by such expectations, of course. But even for those who never opened a magazine article on marriage or never read a book on the subject, the expectations for married life were there. They went into the postwar world determined to overcome the hardships of previous years and to put together the sort of harmonious and stable family that had seemed so remote only a year or so before. They were a bit naïve perhaps, but they were also determined and idealistic.

THE ENTHUSIASM AND HOPE WERE NOT SHARED BY ALL. Throughout the celebrations of domesticity, there was an undercurrent of doubt. As one anonymous writer said in December 1945, 'There is a lovely dream that is shared by very nearly every girl as she approaches womanhood. It is the dream of marrying the man who belongs to her heart, of owning a beautiful home, and rearing lovely, talented children.' In her case it was not to be, however, for the wartime separation between her and her boyfriend caused the relationship to collapse. The marriage, at least with this sweetheart, was never to take place.[65] Stories like this created a sense of empathy, for the other side of hope was fear. Even after the war ended and husbands or boyfriends no longer faced the possibility of death, the fear remained. What would happen as soldiers and home-front women tried to put their lives back together?

After up to six years of separation, it is not surprising that many were nervous about trying to renew their relationship. For thousands of couples at the end of the war, the time apart, aside from occasional leaves, was greater than the time they had been married. For years they had lived separate lives, coped in crisis as best they could, thought of each other, written to each other, or drifted apart. Even for the close marriages and relationships, however, there is ample testimony that the idea of reunion was not only the most important dream of 1945; it was the most terrifying.

The mass of often mediocre short fiction that was a compulsory part of the magazines drummed home the theme of reunion through 1945 and 1946. As seems to be characteristic of this genre, the writing was often pedestrian but its preoccupations reflected the public mood – 'Was this stranger, this hero who had returned from the war, her husband? How could she find in him the old familiar Tom, the man she loved?'[66] At a higher level of popular culture, the great hit movie of 1946–7 was RKO's *The Best Years of Our Lives*, about the return of three American servicemen to middle America and the problems confronting both them and their families. Its hold on the public imagination was reflected in its box-office success and in the nine Academy Awards it was given, including for best actor.[67]

The issues depicted in magazines and on the screen had their origins in reality. The place of the veteran in postwar society has always been a problem. Prior to the twentieth century soldiers were simply returned to civilian life with a small pension or discharge bonus. The consequences, especially after major wars, were considerable hardship and social disruption. At the end of the First World War, practices began to change. The government took steps to assist the soldier in his transition to civilian life, but these came late and were limited. The Second World War learned from the First, however, and, practically from the beginning, government began to plan for the serviceman's return to civilian life. Departments like Pensions and National Health (which in 1944 spun off Veterans Affairs), and special task forces, such as the one on demobilization and re-establishment, spent much of the war on the precise problem of the returning serviceman. By the end of the war, a series of bills had created what became known as 'the Veterans' Charter,' by far the most comprehensive attempt to ease the return of the soldier in Canadian history.

To ease the return, a number of practical steps were taken, as one article put it, 'to ensure that, so far as possible, no man or woman is worse off for having worn the King's uniform.'[68] The returning serviceman was entitled to a discharge bonus, clothes, and free transportation home. These were pretty standard; more significant were benefits for the wounded, provisions for low-cost mortgages, and loans for education. Such measures were important, not only for the people who received them, but for the postwar society on the whole, because they acted as a spur to the economy and thereby assisted in creating the prosperity that was so important to confidence in the postwar years. Certainly the degree of security such actions gave helped families to put their lives back together after the war and, not incidentally, to decide to have children.

There was another issue, more slippery and amorphous than education benefits or discharge allowances – namely, the mental state of the returning soldier. In this area the Second World War really was different from all previous wars, at least in that the issue was recognized to be a serious one. The inter-war years had seen the rise of psychiatry as a legitimate and recognized, though always controversial, profession. In part this professional status was the result of the tremendous impact of Freudian and post-Freudian ideas, though perhaps on the public more than on the practitioners. By the time of the war, psychological issues had gained a sufficient place in both official and public perceptions in both Canada and the United States that the concepts of 'psychological fitness' for duty and such mental difficulties as 'battle exhaustion' were recognized as warranting military medical treatment.[69]

Experts were also concerned with the psychological transition from the military and war to home and civilian life. As the war neared its end, articles on the psychological difficulties of the returned soldier began to appear in medical journals. Even the normal soldier, the psychiatrists warned, faced stress on returning to civilian life. Popular magazines and newspapers picked up the stories and transmitted them in shorter versions to a wider audience. They all carried the same message: The very dreams of home that so affected everybody could create problems. 'During long separation from his own family and civilian friends the soldier usually idealizes them and the home situation out of all recognition,' warned Canada's senior military psychiatrist. 'His return to the reality of his home environment may prove to be difficult and disturbing to him.'[70]

And there were problems. Many had difficulty adjusting to the unregimented life of the civilian. Others felt a tremendous loss of status as they returned from serving in meaningful military roles to uncertainty and unemployment. It was a situation depicted by Hollywood in *The Best Years of Our Lives,* where one of the returning heroes, a decorated air force captain, was a soda-fountain attendant before the war. The woman he had married just before shipping out wants him to continue to wear his uniform and he must grapple with the fact that all his war activities mean little in civilian life. In fact, the return to 'civvy street' was a shock for thousands. Inevitably friends and relatives did the wrong thing. They asked about war experiences when the veteran didn't want to be asked and they kept mum about war experiences when the veteran wanted to talk. If a pattern runs through the reminiscences of returned servicemen, it is the astonishment of seeing day-to-day life roll on. For the soldier back from overseas, one life had ended and another begun. That made even the happiest return a potentially wrenching event: 'But suddenly it was all over. Done and gone forever. We all had lives to begin living and there was no time to think of that wonderful adventure. Now was the time we had to think of. The real adventure was ahead, and I knew I would miss terribly my friends for a while because they were the only friends I had.'[71]

To put a couple or family back together was hard enough. To put it back together while trying to change what had become a way of life was all the more difficult. It is not surprising, therefore, that the first year or so after the war brought many problems – for family members who had to cope with the moody, irritable, and seemingly unappeasable returned serviceman, as well. Wives and girlfriends had to cope with the rumours about those English, Scottish, or French women and what may have happened overseas. Special hatred was reserved for German women, who, lurid stories reported, had set out to seduce your boyfriend or husband.[72]

Peace also presented a dilemma and a change in the way of life for those hundreds of thousands of women who had gone into war work. Everybody was aware that the strong female presence in the workforce, and especially in industry, was a temporary thing. Both social mores, though undermined to a degree by war experience, and the need to find a place for the returning soldiers dictated that the wartime employment of women would end once the war was over. It was legislated, to a degree at least, by the provision that anybody who sacrificed a paying job to join the services had a right to have that job back when he returned.[73] As one teenage girl commented realistically in the spring of 1945, 'We think that the day of the girl in any job a man does will be gone when we're ready to work.'[74] She was right. Between 1944 and 1946 more than 300,000 women, or 25 per cent of the total female workforce, left their jobs either voluntarily or involuntarily. The percentages were undoubtedly greater in the highly paid industrial professions, where so much war work had been concentrated. Not until a full generation had passed would the presence of women in the workforce be as prevalent as it had been during the war.

If the impact of the end of the war upon female workers is clear, the attitude of women towards the postwar shift is harder to discern. Some had never seen work as anything but a temporary thing, a patriotic duty to be borne. For them there was a sense of being 'liberated to the kitchen' at war's end. Part of the cult of marriage, after all, was a belief that work in the home was not only the inevitable but the desirable goal of a woman. 'This is my generation,' said one young female character to her shocked mother. 'Yours earned the right to have a career ... mine earned the right not to have one if we don't want it.'[75] Others, however, deeply resented what was happening. After years of proving they could do the work, they were now being pushed aside.[76] Most probably felt a mixed set of emotions – regret at loss of paycheque and independence, relief at the opportunity to return to a more normal existence.[77] The adjustment from paycheque to domesticity, however, was yet another point of stress in moving from wartime to peacetime.

One year after the end of the war, homecoming seemed a little less glamorous, a little more troublesome. 'In homes across Canada there are tens of thousands of little battles brewing,' concluded one observer. Husbands constantly reminiscing about England or sneaking off to drink with their army buddies created resentment and friction on the part of wives. Wives who had no understanding or interest in hubbie's wartime stories created bitterness and a sense of isolation in the returned soldier. Many wives, in return, missed the financial independence bestowed by war work and faced a husband so wrapped up in his own past that he could or would not see that they, too, had to face change. Home, as the psychiatrists had warned, wasn't the utopia the soldier had dreamed about. 'Canada, this is your nostalgia. It plants aches in the hearts of men and women in homes from Pacific to Atlantic. It makes the men who come back, and the women who waited for them, bitter with resentment.'[78] For many couples the war stretched on as an unbridgeable gulf between them. The years healed the friction for most, but the gap remained of two lives that had gone separate ways, at least for a while.

Reflecting this trend, magazine fiction turned from nostalgia about home to the tensions of return. Most often this tension was set around the wife's decision to retain her, usually interesting, usually white-collar, job. From that point, there were endless variations. Sometimes the husband was supportive, either setting up a two-career family or staying home as a house-husband. In such cases the wife invariably discovered that the role reversal wasn't what she really wanted. It was wrong for 'big, powerful men like Ritchie' to be working at 'niggling domestic chores.'[79] In other cases the husband is emasculated by his working wife and the marriage is threatened unless she leaves work. In still other cases solutions create new problems: The pretty maid hired to care for him (men cannot take care of the home in many stories) becomes a real or imagined love threat. Whatever the variation, the outcome was always the same: The women return home, and they are always ultimately happy and relieved to do so.

The insistence on the importance of traditional gender roles is an extension of the profound insecurity that beset Canadians in these years. Family life, the previous fifteen years had shown, was a fragile thing, and it was made more so by the need for people to adjust to each other after years apart. Yet, for a year or so after the war, things seemed not to be going well. The tensions of reunion and of hasty marriage quickly showed up in separations and divorces. The year after the war established a record not only for marriages but for divorces as well. The next year was even worse. The divorce rate was at an all-time high, both as a percentage of the population and in absolute numbers –

three times what it had been at the beginning of the war. There was a tremendous tide of concern from clergymen, marriage experts, and others about the apparent collapse of the marriage institution.[80] The drive for stability and for family seemed under challenge and, in reaction, the public, men *and* women, generally insisted upon a return to 'traditional values.' The working housewife became a symbol of the wartime and postwar turbulence in family life. She had to return to the home so that the family might return to stability. Most working housewives would have left their jobs anyway, but the shrill insistence that they do so created a lingering resentment that showed up on occasion over the years to come.

It is also important to remember that, even after the great withdrawal of women from the workforce, the idealized image of the 'normal' family was really a middle-class illusion. A large percentage of married women in blue-collar and working-class occupations had always worked, out of necessity. In the inter-war years, for example, approximately 20 per cent of women were engaged in paid labour at any given time. By 1951 this figure had risen to 25 per cent.[81] Thus, the postwar family was not quite what it appeared to be. In one in four families, the wife headed off to work, at least part of the time. This contradiction was noted in various postwar articles, whose tone is revealing. Such stories were of the 'poverty in our midst' variety, pointing out weaknesses in the Canadian ideal of economic opportunity for all – for working women as well as for those who did not work. 'Most [working] mothers realize that they are needed in the home,' the assumption went; in other words, the ideal was unaltered by the statistics.[82] This deviation from social norms whereby the husband 'failed' to provide adequately for his family and the wife 'failed' to provide for her children must have added psychological tension to the marriage of many working couples.

The transition period was soon over. By 1947 many of the hasty marriages had been smoothed out or had broken apart. The divorce rate began to decline. Not until the later 1960s, under a radically different divorce law, would the rate surpass that of 1947. The spate of fictional and non-fictional theorizing about the returning soldier and the working wife soon faded away and, by 1948, were all but gone. Good murder mysteries or traditional romances filled the fiction pages again. Still, the underlying values remained. This generation had fought hard for the idea of home, all the while performing a balancing act with democratic marriage, traditional work roles, and the upheaval of the war years. Home was a fragile concept and always under threat. For better or worse, though, the children of the 1920s put the war behind them and set out to complete the ideal of family and home by having children of their own. As the upheaval of war subsided, the baby boom began.

2

Babies

A great deal should be done to make childbearing more attractive since it is not merely necessary to national survival but one of the strongest factors in marital happiness.

Maclean's, 1947[1]

In the decade between 1946 and 1955, some 3.9 million babies were born in Canada. By 1961 the number had risen to 6.7 million. This generation, which would later assert itself to be distinct from those that preceded it, seemed determined to lay that claim right from the very beginning. Unlike all previous generations of Canadians, the vast majority of baby-boomers were born in the hospital. Home births declined rapidly as urbanization made hospitals accessible, and as medical and public-health authorities stressed the virtues of hospital birth. Only one in five of those mothers entering maternity wards across the country after the war had been born in a hospital. Yet, by the early 1950s, eight out of ten baby-boomers began life under the harsh lights and regimented care of the hospital ward. Towards the end of the boom, the figure would be nine out of ten. In a single generation the nature of birth in Canada had been revolutionized.[2]

The shift to hospitals took birth from the realm of nature to the interventionist world of science. Birth was no longer a family affair but a medical one. Fathers were not permitted in the delivery room, giving rise to the stock comic bit in the early television years showing the nervous father pacing the waiting-room. Even women, for that matter, did not experience the delivery directly – they were usually unconscious.

Anaesthetic was routinely used, even in the case of normal births. As part of the post-natal routine, the newborns were whisked away to a nursery, where the fathers could view them through a window intended both to prevent the spread of germs and to maintain hospital control of the situation. Several hours later, once the new mother had regained consciousness, the child would be taken to her. The routine of visitations with the mother and return to the nursery would continue for much longer than is now common. Even in normal cases mother and child rarely left for home in under a week.[3]

Sometime during that hospital stay, the child was named, a process normally ceremonialized a few months later by a formal christening. Of course, there were always the unusual names – those honouring parents, uncles and aunts, grandparents, and the like. Even so, the names of the baby boom were distinct from those of the preceding and subsequent generations. This was not an age in which parents struck out in bold, new directions for their children. Rather, they chose names from a roster of options clustered around a relatively few favourites from the Bible and, even more popularly, from the pantheon of Hollywood stars. Parents overwhelmingly named their sons John, Michael, James, Robert, David, Thomas, Stephen, Richard, Joseph, William, Charles, or George, and their daughters Linda, Mary, Deborah, Susan, Patricia, Catherine, Margaret, Barbara, Ruth, Ann, or Carol.[4]

Medicine further differentiated this generation from previous ones because it increased survival rates during those critical first weeks and months. Infant mortality in Canada had been declining from the beginning of the century, and, by the 1920s, a new understanding of sanitation procedures, better medicines, and the ability to control or eradicate key childhood diseases had made the first year of life much safer. A slight upswing in infant mortality in the later 1930s did not mark a long-term reversal of the trend and, through the 1940s and into the 1950s, infant mortality rates continued to decline. A child born in 1953 was only one-third as likely to die before the age of one year as was one born in 1921.

As any parent knows, bringing a child home – especially a first child – is an emotional experience somewhere between ecstasy and terror. If anything, this emotion was greater for the generation that had endured the Second World War, who had invested so much in their expectations of the family, and thus in the infant they carried home. The higher the expectations, both personal and societal, the greater the anxiety. What should one do to raise a child correctly? What signs should one watch for that the child was developing properly? Should a smile come by six weeks? When should toilet training be complete? Should the child be talking by age two? What is the best approach to discipline? feeding? sleep? These and a thousand other questions crowd in upon all new parents. For boomers' parents, there were several sources of advice on child rearing, wanted or unwanted. Relatives offered useful or irritating tips. The friend down the street with a child a vast six months older than your own was generous with bits of wisdom. Common sense played a part, of course, especially as the weeks and months passed and the parent (primarily the mother) became more accustomed to those terrifying mood swings that are a part of infancy.

None of this was new. Families had been relying on such advice through the ages. What was new and of increasing influence, however, was the ready availability of professionals: Doctors, child psychologists, public-health nurses, and other experts had, over the past decades, proliferated.[5] Disciplines that barely existed a half-century before were now proclaiming that their theories were the only means by which a parent could possibly raise a child. Hundreds of books, newspaper articles, popular radio shows, and magazine columns popularized versions of the latest research (and guesses) of 'authoritative' researchers who clamoured for attention.

The American doctor Benjamin Spock, the most prominent of them all, sold 4 million copies of his 1945 work, *The Common Sense Book of Baby and Child Care,* within seven years.[6] Eminent Canadian child-theorist William Blatz was able to fill Massey Hall in Toronto for an evening lecture. Educator and child-theorist S.R. Laycock had a regular series of radio broadcasts on the CBC from 1942 on. By the early 1950s his programs had shifted to the new medium of television, where *The Bossy Parent, The Lazy Parent,* and *The Understanding Parent* presented simple dicta about what a parent should or, more often, should not do in raising a child.[7] Like Blatz, he was published in popular magazines and newspapers, and put out his own books. Blatz and Laycock were the two most prominent among a wide range of advisers whose insights were clipped from newspapers, passed by word of mouth, and taught in high-school classrooms and family-studies books.

This is not to pretend that all advice was taken, that parents read every child-rearing manual they bought, or even read at all.[8] Still, such advice did transmit the conventions of the age and the norms that people took as their yardsticks for child rearing. Moreover, this generation of parents was especially susceptible to such cultural norms in that it was the first with practically universal literacy, and with access to instant communication devices like radio and, as the 1950s went on, television. The advice that was out there was, as a result, more readily available. Indeed, for most it was unavoidable. This was also a generation that had high regard for experts, which indicates that such advice might have been taken more seriously than otherwise would have been the case.[9] Therefore, without pretending that the printed record can recapture the individual experience precisely, the pages that follow assume that it can give us an aggregate sense of the values, expectations, and fears of the parents of all those Lindas, Johns, Marys, and Michaels who headed home from the hospital in the decade after the war.

WHAT THE EXPERTS PREACHED was the result of two related intellectual forces. First, through at least the previous two centuries, philosophers, theologians, and social reformers had been debating the relative desirability of a harsh or permissive approach to child rearing. The side one took depended on such sweeping topics as one's view of the nature of evil, of humanity in a state of nature, of the nature of learning and social structure. Was the newborn child essentially innocent or damned by original sin? Was humanity, if left to its own devices, likely to prosper, or did it need firm tutelage to control its emotions and weaknesses? Should society replicate itself from generation to generation, or should it explore new ideas and values? All of these topics had been debated with enthusiasm and fervour. After all, child rearing, more than anything else, is an activity through which the present generation can influence the next.[10]

The debates took many twists and turns. Generally, however, the trend of the prior two centuries had been away from a harsh and punitive view of child rearing and towards a more lenient one. At the extreme one can cite the eighteenth-century views of American divine Jonathan Edwards. Children, he preached, were 'young vipers and (to God) infinitely more hateful than vipers.' This evangelical vision of children as the unredeemed products of original sin was given concrete implication in the maxim of John Wesley that to spare the rod is to spoil the child. It is an adage often hauled out by those who want to show their displeasure with indulged children or indulgent parents. Yet even traditionalists might feel a slight chill on discovering the rest of the passage: 'Break their will betimes, begin this work before they can run alone, before they speak plain, perhaps before they can speak at all. Whatever pain it costs, break the will if you would not break the child ... If you spare the rod you spoil the child; if you do not conquer you ruin him.'[11]

The vision of conquest and use of sheer force to ensure compliance, not to mention the suffering implicit in this passage, is alien to the modern ideals of child rearing. However, the movement from Wesley's ethic to the one that shaped the baby boom came in stages. By the turn of the century, at least in North America, the belief in extreme force had faded and been replaced by a gentler view of the nature of child discipline. Yet this was not a permissive society. Social order was still an imperative, and books like American Emma Holt's *Care and Feeding of Children* (1894) emphasized the importance of a no-nonsense approach to child care. According to her, coddling the child was indulgent. Feeding schedules should be regular, and parents should not give in to crying, even on the part of small infants.[12] Fear of spoiling was still paramount. Children were no longer to be treated cruelly, but they were to be approached sternly.

This intermediate position – consistency and discipline without extreme force – continued well into the twentieth century. By now, however, it was not evangelical religion or Victorian propriety that gave weight to the arguments but, rather, science. The most influential book published between the wars was John B. Watson's 1928 work, *Psychological Care of Infant and Child.* Watson was a behavioural psychologist who argued that the child must be conditioned early to accept social mores and thereby function within society. From that point, much of what he said drew upon Victorian habits dressed in the guise of science. Like Holt, Watson stated that coddling was dangerous and consistency was crucial. Toilet training should be complete by the time the child was little more than a year old.[13] Other books soon followed Watson's lead. In Canada, for example, Dr Helen MacMurchy, Chief of Child Welfare in the Dominion Department of Health, published a series of 'little blue books' that emphasized consistency in the same manner Watson had.[14] Well into the 1930s, science continued to view socialization as something imposed from without. The imposition of proper external behaviour would lead to internal discipline. Moreover, the theme had been dominant for so long that such aspects of it as early toilet training and regular feeding times, among others, had infiltrated society well beyond the loyal readership of Watson,

MacMurchy, or the others. In Britain, for example, the spirit of the age was captured in verse:

Give when his meal hour strikes
Not at any time he likes
And at night no meals are due
Sleep is best for him and you[15]

Watson's book points to the growing influence of psychology on child rearing. Historians of psychology can trace the subject's roots to Aristotelian thought. As a separate discipline, however, psychology emerged with the work of Wilhelm Wundt in late nineteenth-century Germany. By the early twentieth century, it was well established academically and, with the emergence of 'functionalists' and 'structuralists,' was even sufficiently developed by the turn of the century to have schools of debate.[16] In general, however, psychology was in these early stages a rather obscure discipline, confined to academe and interested more in observation than in solution. Then, in 1909, Sigmund Freud published *The Interpretation of Dreams*, which, along with his other writings, revolutionized psychology.[17] As one writer has neatly put it, Freud was one of those very few thinkers who changed, not just a belief or an attitude, but the very way in which we see the world: 'He changed the whole tenor of human thought so that even those who most violently denounce his views attack them in Freudian clichés and with arguments which would have been incomprehensible had he never existed.'[18]

Freud's impact quickly spread from academic to public circles. The First World War, with its mass slaughter, seemed to provide proof of the Freudian assessment of the human mind as beset by irrational, destructive impulses. By the 1920s popular Freudianism, with its emphasis on sexual impulses and hidden desires, was appropriated by an age in the process of shrugging off Victorian attitudes. Talking in terms of ego and id, of the Oedipus complex and the hidden implications of dreams, became a popular activity among the young and well educated. In the 1930s the rise of Hitler provided one more example of the irrational impulse at work and, more directly, brought an exodus of Continental European psychiatrists to the United States, and with them an emphasis on Freudian techniques.[19] By the onset of the Second World War, the discipline of psychology in general, and Freudianism in particular, was sufficiently accepted that both the Canadian and the U.S. military incorporated psychological analysis into their recruiting and medical practices. By the end of the war, Freudianism and its offshoots had reached new heights of influence both within psychological circles and in the popular imagination. As historian William O'Neill recognized, Freudian theory provided 'moral security in an uncertain time.'[20]

Freud's theories emphasized the crucial role of the child's mental development in the whole of life. The rise of Freudianism, therefore, had a tremendous impact upon child-rearing theory. Child-rearing books routinely used a kind of loose Freudianism in describing the stages of development of the preschool child. After the war, Anna Freud, his daughter, published a series of influential works on the wartime experience of British schoolchildren separated from their families.[21] Benjamin Spock was himself trained in the Freudian techniques and employed Freudian assumptions throughout his famous book.[22] In 1950 Erik Erikson published his widely acclaimed *Childhood and Society,* which applied Freudian theory to the development of children's mental state. For Erikson the mental health of the child was the key to understanding the character of the adult and the adult society: 'Every adult, whether he is a follower or a leader, a member of a mass or of an elite, was once a child.'[23]

There was even a specialized journal, *The Psychoanalytic Study of the Child,* founded in New York at the end of the war by a group of Freudians. Articles such as 'Analysis of Psychogenic Constipation in a Two Year Old,' and 'The Problem of Neurotic Manifestations in Children of Pre-Oedipal Age' testify to its Freudian outlook. Not even nursery rhymes could escape the couch. In the 1953 article 'The Tragedy of Humpty Dumpty,' the tale was taken to symbolize to the child 'the second catastrophic trauma' in life (after birth itself), the arrival of a sibling.[24] 'All the King's Horses and All the King's Men – Couldn't Put Humpty Dumpty Back Together Again.'

The American infatuation with Freudianism had its counterpart in Canada. No Canadian university had a program in psychiatry until after the war. Until that time, therefore, Canadians interested in psychiatry attended American universities and brought back with them the fads and enthusiasms from south of the border. At the popular level, Canadians read many of the same child-care books as did Americans, and picked up the popular articles from *Life* magazine, *Reader's Digest, Look,* or *Time* or *Newsweek.* Even if they had religiously stuck with Canadian writers, the same message would have emerged. The casual use of pop psychology is one of the most striking aspects of magazines, newspapers, and books of the period. Discussions of 'mental hygiene,' or 'mental adjustment,' often laced with specific Freudian terminology, were routinely published in the popular press.

There were also resident Canadian Freudians. The best known was Brock Chisholm, who, soon after the end of the war, turned his attention from the returning soldier to the soldier's children. Before long he was enmeshed in controversy, a place he loved to be. Chisholm was an iconoclast by temperament and this trait, as well as his Freudian beliefs, led him to predict dire psychological consequences if parents weren't extremely careful in bringing up their children. Popping up on radio shows, at public talks, and in popular magazines, Chisholm took on some of the dearest-held assumptions of Canadians. His belief that it was dangerous psychologically to tell lies to children even led him, amid cries of outrage, to insist that the Santa Claus myth left a permanent mental scar upon children. One columnist tartly retorted by reassuring children that psychiatrists were a harmless myth so long as you didn't take them too seriously.[25]

Freudianism wasn't the only stream of psychology. Behaviourism, though less influential in the 1940s than it had been in the 1920s, with John B. Watson, or would be in the later 1950s, under the leadership of B.F. Skinner, still claimed many adherents and influenced child-care literature. Also important in Canada was the influence of William Blatz, head of the Institute of Child Study at the University of Toronto. Blatz, born in Hamilton, was a doctor who took advanced training in psychology at the University of Chicago. In the 1920s he returned to Canada and took up a teaching post at the University of Toronto. Blatz achieved considerable publicity as adviser on the Dionne quintuplets in the 1930s and had been sent to assist the British with the traumas faced by children during the Blitz. By the start of the Second World War, he was Canada's best-known child-care expert. Like Chisholm, Blatz also had a flair for publicity. He, too, could be iconoclastic, even outrageous. However, he was more down-to-earth than Chisholm, and his thoughts on child care were popular. At war's end, and well into the 1950s, Blatz was a regular in newspapers, and wrote syndicated columns for several magazines, including *Chatelaine* and *Maclean's*.[26] In little pieces on 'the Nagging Evil' or 'Disciplining Your Child,' he dispensed simple, assured advice to readers.

Though Blatz was careful to pay homage to the great master, he was no Freudian. 'Time marches on,' he said, and Freud's theories had to be updated.[27] Actually it was not a question of time at all, for Blatz, in the tradition of the Chicago school, had never really accepted Freud's theories about the dominant impact of the unconscious. Nor was Freud's view that sex was the all-consuming psychological force a part of Blatz's assessment of mental life. While recognizing the importance of sex, Blatz preferred to treat it as just another 'appetite' – if satisfied, it was quiescent. For Blatz, the key to understanding the mind and the nature of children was not the unconscious drives but the conscious will. People made conscious choices in their lives, and the key to child rearing, therefore, was to ensure that the choices were directed by a mature mind and in a responsible direction.[28]

Blatz or Chisholm, Freud or Skinner – the decade after the war was the age of psychology. The Canadian Youth Commission warned that there was 'an urgent' need for more child psychiatrists in Canada.[29] Pop psychology like Joshua Liebman's *Peace of Mind* and Norman Vincent Peale's *A Guide to Confident Living* made the best-seller lists throughout the later 1940s.[30] One of the box-office hits of 1947 was Joan Crawford's *Possessed*, a psychologically based thriller. In Canada magazines routinely carried articles on the importance of mental hygiene or on the work of psychologists.[31] Canadian poet Earle Birney wrote a poem about overzealous customs officials, entitled 'Masters of the Id,' with the confidence that the allusion would be understood. Pierre Berton wrote 'Phooey on Freud' as a means of relating some funny dream sequences.[32] People praised, challenged, or mocked psychology but, as popular psychologist Eric Fromm commented in 1955, 'there are few subjects [members of the middle class] like so much to talk about.'[33]

The fact that psychology was taken so seriously is more important than the precise influence of any psychological school. In fact, for the general readers, and indeed for many of the family-studies books, child-rearing manuals, and newspaper pieces on children, there was an extremely eclectic mixing of psychological styles. Few espoused a purely Freudian, or for that matter purely anything, approach to analysis or treatment. What is significant is that parents were barraged with the notion that mental health was every bit as important as physical health. People might scorn extreme theories (usually Freudian), but it was hard for them to dismiss the overwhelming chorus of experts telling them about the importance of dealing with the inner turmoil of growth. Every generation has its fears, it concerns, its particular nuances – religious fervour, physical hardship, family breakdown. The baby boom was raised by a generation that would be prosperous, ceremonialize religion, and maintain a degree of stability, but also be beset by a nagging sense of anxiety about that apparently tortured, fragile, and yet crucial vessel – the human mind. It was something the children of the postwar years have carried with them throughout their life.

The fear of mental trauma was increased by the belief that environment, not heredity, was the determining force in shaping character.[34] The influence of environment had never been completely ignored. A good home life, and respectable and decent surroundings, had been seen by Victorian reformers as crucial for the creation of the decent family. Indeed, the major social-reform movement of the pre–First World War era, prohibition, rested on environmentalist assumptions. Removing a deleterious force would create a better home life for children, and thereby enhance their chances of success.

Throughout the twentieth century, therefore, environmentalism had been gaining ground. The rise of the social sciences, including psychology, emphasized the impact of environment upon human activities and attitudes. The increasing democratization of Canadian society brought political challenges to casual assumptions about class. Until the Second World War, though, environmentalism had faced competition from notions that looked to race and heredity. The eugenics movement, for example, believed that scientific breeding and the sterilization of mental defectives could improve the race.[35] The war decided the competition in favour of environmental forces. The public and the experts recoiled before Nazi Germany's argument that a human being's worth was determined by heredity. Current sensibility thus reinforced longer-term trends to assert with little reservation that the child's character was shaped in the crucible of the environment. Overall, concluded Blatz, 'the child inherits very little: the minimum number of organized patterns necessary to maintain life, providing he is well looked after; and consciousness, in which he builds by learning, the edifice of his experience ... In other words, character is acquired.'[36] One could no longer depend on innate character to overcome the psychological bumps and crashes that were part of growing up.

That assumption was made more potent by another. Psychology emphasized, in Anna Freud's words, 'the overwhelming importance of the first five years of life.' The basic attitudes towards society, sexuality, and one's identity were formed in these years.[37] Having rejected the notions of inherited character, or the racialist recapitulation theory, postwar psychology saw the young mind as a blank slate. It was filled with facts and with experiences that not only taught it how to do things, but shaped the relationships of trust or mistrust, sociability or non-sociability, for the future. Moreover, that process of socialization and maturation was constantly portrayed as a tenuous one. Especially in Freudian psychology, there were always new tensions that challenged existing equilibriums. The process of adjustment posed a delicate and ongoing challenge to the child.[38]

Small causes had such big effects. A relatively trivial event, a minor error, early in life, could begin a chain reaction, with ever larger consequences as time passed. 'Many hate our society for wrongs done to them in childhood,' wrote one American expert on child rearing. Marxism had an appeal because it allowed the maladjusted 'to release their hatreds, to liberate their conscience.'[39] Obviously bad upbringings could have disastrous consequences. 'The poorly adjusted child tends to become the ill-adjusted partner in marriage. The partner who is maladjusted in marriage finds it difficult or impossible to be a good parent. Thus the relationship between maladjusted parents and maladjusted children, who in turn become maladjusted parents, is a vicious circle that repeats itself.'[40] To make it worse, a misstep could occur in either direction. A Grade Nine textbook used in Ontario in the late 1950s summed up the narrow path facing the anxious parent. Alcoholism, it said, was rooted in childhood. 'There has been too much pampering, or too much domination. Whatever the cause, the result is a personality with immature development, easily subject to addictions of various sorts.'[41]

The idea that abused children or those without emotional stability have problems as adults is now well accepted. What is striking about the postwar years, however, is that even small, well-intended acts by parents were seen to have the potential to warp a child permanently. Overly rigorous toilet training could create an authoritarian individual. Scheduled feeding could create frustration that would show up in unpredictable ways in later life. A harsh scolding could lead to long-term social maladjustment. Even concerns for safety could be psychologically damaging. If children want to climb trees as a part of their development, argued one manual, it was 'much better that they suffer for a month the inconvenience of a broken limb than that they suffer for life from undeveloped physical powers and immature personalities.'[42] In 1947 *Maclean's* had an article on a hypothetical child, little Eddy who liked to push Mary Jane's face into a puddle. Such apparent antisocial behaviour wasn't really Eddy's fault, however, for his parents repeatedly compared him unfavourably with Mary Jane. His feelings were being hurt! Worse was to come, however. 'If this keeps on, Eddy will grow up feeling inferior – until some day he breaks out and tells the boss to go to the devil or picks a fight with a guy three times his size.'[43] The ego was a fragile thing, and the young ego was especially tender.

Even if the child did not turn into a Communist or a sociopath (they were seen as much the same in this period), there were real dangers lurking for his or her future happiness. This was portrayed dramatically in a 1947 National Film Board production entitled *The Feeling of Rejection*. Its message and its tone neatly captured the idea that a series of small acts in childhood could have long-term effects. The film tells of a twenty-three-year-old unmarried woman named Margaret. To be unmarried at her age was, of course, in itself a danger signal. More immediate, however, were her problems with recurring headaches. She goes, naturally, to a psychiatrist, who discovers that the headaches occur whenever she is reminded of her status as a single woman with a more popular sibling! She is unable to assert herself and is thus bullied into purchasing things by salespeople, and into doing extra work by colleagues. She avoids social events and seems destined for that most horrible of fates, the life of an innocuous, unassertive spinster. The viewer, however, is treated to the psychiatrist's detective work as he retraces Margaret's upbringing. His conclusion: 'Margaret was sheltered too much as a child.' Knowing this, of course, provides the key to recovery. The movie ends with Margaret well adjusted, saying no to salespeople and developing friendships. Could marriage and children, the movie implies, be far away?[44]

Nowhere was the relationship between infant upbringing and later behaviour more anxiety-ridden than in sexual matters. Freudian psychology put tremendous emphasis on early sexual adjustment. The child had to work through its jealousy of the parent of the same sex if it were to achieve a 'normal adjustment' towards the opposite sex at adolescence. The price to be paid for failure was, at best, the inability to form good relationships with the other sex. Prudery, said one *Maclean's* article in 1948, 'is Father to the Pervert.' For 'furtive guilt and anxiety laid up in early childhood' might never be overcome.[45] Even non-Freudian W.E. Blatz saw dangers lurking and laid them all out in a handy chart. Faulty handling of sexual matters in childhood could lead, he wrote, to 'prudery, promiscuity, masturbation, frigidity.'[46] A thin line separated sexual impotence from sexual anarchy.

The obsession with childhood sexual anxiety did not rest solely on the popularity of Freudian theory. Something about the Freudian obsession with sexual identity resonated with the age. Though sexual attitudes of the era have yet to be fully studied, this appears to have been an era of tremendous stress and change in terms of sexual relations. As is discussed in chapter 10, there was anxiety about sexual roles on the part of both men and women.

Such fears had a tremendous impact upon youth culture in the 1950s. More to the point here, however, is that it also had an impact upon child-rearing notions. American novelist Philip Wylie coined the term 'Momism' in the 1942 to refer to a form of overprotective mothering based less on affection than on neurosis. The child, especially the son, who was 'tied to the apron strings' of the mother was being sacrificed by parental selfishness. Mother's hold would prevent normal relations from developing with members of the opposite sex. It was a theme that reappeared time and again in the literature of the 1940s and well into the 1950s.[47] The Canadian Youth Commission in 1947 found the theory a tempting one, as did the White House Conference on Youth in 1950.[48] It fit well with the popular versions of Freudian theory, with the obsessions of the age about sexuality, and with the concerns about women's role in the wake of the Second World War. It was also brought on by affluence. A rising standard of living and a decreasing number of children meant that women could devote a far greater amount of time to the care and raising of the individual child than could their ancestors.[49]

The fascination with psychology led to a great deal of anxiety about the mental state of the child. By itself this said nothing about whether a child's upbringing should be relatively strict or permissive. When psychological theory joined with the longer-run trend of society towards a more permissive upbringing, however, the direction was clear. As one psychologist noted in a 1953 article, both popular and learned literature on child rearing had extracted from Freudian theory in a selective manner. Those portions that emphasized a permissive attitude towards child rearing had been widely accepted; those with different implications had been downplayed. Not only was American child rearing influenced by psychological theory, but psychological theory was being shaped by the assumptions of North America that the child should be raised in a permissive fashion.[50] Thus, psychology proved a potent ally to the underlying trend towards permissiveness. Science could now be employed to demonstrate why older, stricter beliefs should be jettisoned. Previous family practices, and ethnic, class, or community traditions – all had to meet the test of science, and science, echoing society itself, decreed to an unprecedented degree that child rearing was a gentle art.

The chain of argument that underpinned this tenet rested on two points. The first was that the child was by nature good. Children were not, as earlier psychologists had implied, trying from infancy to train you or trick you. Their mistakes, acts of disobedience, and temper tantrums and other outbursts were natural. Children were immature, Blatz emphasized. Of course they would do immature things. 'How parents regard the failures of youth and the way in which they treat them is the significant factor in child training,' he concluded, 'not the making of mistakes.' An American child-expert put this perspective even more succinctly: 'The child himself is not bad, though some of his behavior may be.'[51]

The second point was Freudian in origin. Mental development was an ongoing attempt to deal with inner frustration. The successful resolution of inherent conflict could be achieved only if parents trod a narrow path. On the one side of it lay all the dangers represented by Momism. Excessive intervention could prevent children from achieving their own resolution of conflicts, and thereby prevent successful maturity. Even non-Freudians like William Blatz saw that allowing a child the freedom to make choices, and mistakes, was central to successful child rearing.[52] On the other hand, the freedom for the child must be accompanied by unreserved love and affection. 'Love small children without reservations, and do not be afraid to play with them as much as they want,' said Brock Chisholm. 'Let him know you love him' concluded a *Star Weekly* column.[53] Such affection should never be withdrawn as a disciplinary tactic or as an emotional reaction to some act of disobedience.[54] 'Don't desert your child when he needs you most – when he's wrong. Your child cannot always be right. But let your love for him give him a sense of security so that when he is wrong he will naturally turn to you.'[55]

In a universe of Freudian frustrations and unreserved affection, discipline had a narrowly circumscribed role. Some writers banished it altogether, arguing that it was at most the forceful intervention of a protector, such as when an adult grabbed a toddler to prevent it from wandering on a busy street. Others were more willing to use it as a behaviour corrective, but by any standards the basis was permissive. 'Punishing a child,' wrote one expert, 'scolding him, merely makes him feel inadequate, "bad," "no good".' Such discipline had only negative consequences. Good discipline, in contrast, 'is founded upon encouragement rather than discouragement.'[56] By the mid-twentieth century the long-term swing of the pendulum was complete. From Wesley's dictum of spare the rod and spoil the child, the opposite had now come to be accepted. The baby boom had the good sense to be born at the end of a long cycle towards permissiveness in child rearing.[57]

THIS PERMISSIVENESS SUITED THE POLITICAL climate of the age. Two sequential events, the Second World War and the Cold War, shaped much of the political thinking of the parents of the baby boom. Both Nazi Germany and the Stalinist Soviet Union demonstrated just how fragile democracy could be. Germany, after all, had been democratic in the 1920s and then had rejected it in the 1930s. This was not just a conspiracy of the few but a failure of the multitude. Books like Eric Fromm's *Escape from Freedom* (1941) theorized that Germans deliberately turned their backs on democracy because the demands it made upon them were not a part of their culture or expectations.[58] The fact that a people could renounce democracy for totalitarianism was of special concern in the face of the Cold War. Democracy, recent history seemed to illustrate, could not be imposed from without. It had to be a part of daily life.

Where was that daily life seen in more fundamental form than in the family? Postwar experts insisted that the modern family must reflect the practices and values of a democratic people. The Second World War was 'part of the armed phase of a conflict between two ideologies, between two ways of life – the totalitarian and the democratic,' wrote Henry Bowman in the 1948 edition of his popular marriage manual. 'Marriage and family, too, are caught in the maelstrom. They are passing from a form roughly paralleling dictatorship and government by force to a democratic form of organization.'[59] Byrne Hope Saunders, the editor of *Chatelaine*, warned that families must seek unity and not uniformity if they are to build 'a strong democracy.'[60] Writing in the same year, the Canadian Youth Commission talked about a 'new democratic pattern' of marriage and portrayed it as a part of the Canadian frontier heritage. 'The snows, the winds, the spaces, the woods and rocks of Canada, have made the Canadian family,' the commission opined, and apparently in doing so wore down the patriarchal family of Europe to create the modern democratic society of Canada.[61]

'Successful relationships depend on cooperation, not on dominance or subservience.'[62] This dictum could be followed in many ways. Family budgeting should be joint, as should major planning activities – 'open budgeting ' was how *Chatelaine* referred to it.[63] Many recommended joint bank accounts, but all recommended joint decisions. 'A thoughtful husband,' said Ernest Groves, 'realizes that he is not the only means of support for his family. He knows that he is not giving his money to the family, but is merely doing his part in the cooperative homemaking to which his wife and children are also contributing.'[64] Where the bank accounts were separate, the housewife should have regular and predetermined access to money rather than having to beg her husband for funds for domestic needs. The husband, for his part, should not regard the money as his to be doled out at whim. The same was true for other decisions, whether on children, career, house, or vacations.[65] Older children were expected to be involved in budget decisions. There was a tremendous enthusiasm for 'family councils' which would include children and make each important decision one in which the governed had been participants.[66] Cooperation and openness in family matters was thought fitting for a world order that had come through war in the name of democracy and was increasingly locked into the Cold War.

Democracy depended upon the democratic family, but the family itself depended upon a democratic structure. The role of the family had changed dramatically in the last century. Rural families in a semi–self-sufficient pioneer environment were units of production and consumption. They produced for the outside world, and many of the goods they consumed were made by them. Likewise, many social functions, from care of relatives to education, were family functions. In modern urban and industrialized Canada, however, many of those original family functions had been moved outside the home. Production was long gone. Education was more and more a state responsibility. Consumption increasingly moved to the marketplace as fewer clothes and baked goods were made in the home. Even mutual economic and financial support seemed less relevant at a time when the first great social programs were coming into being.[67]

What then was left for the family? The answer was what the Canadian Youth Commission termed the 'personality function.' Though there were still residual educational and economic roles, the main purpose of the family was 'emotional satisfaction.'[68] Only if the family operated in this fashion 'may each achieve his unalienable right to life, love, and the pursuit of happiness.'[69] The family was, in Freudian terms, the primary force for the integration of the personality and the creation of a mature adult through affection, guidance, and social interaction. This being the case, the family had to rest on affection and respect, for if it did not, it was, in sociological terms, dysfunctional. 'The authoritarian family still exists,' noted psychologist J.D. Ketchum in a 1954 CBC broadcast. 'But it's a real anachronism, and a dangerous one, particularly to the family's own survival.'[70] In modern marriage the whole concept of family had shifted from blood lines and economics to personal fulfilment.

The 'democratic family' thus became much more than a reflection of child-rearing theory. The concept of a relatively non-hierarchical, tolerant, and permissive family structure became a part of the defence of freedom in the face of external threat, part of the very reason for the family to exist. Practically every child-rearing manual published in the 1940s or 1950s contained some reference to this concept. 'Democracy,' said Blatz, 'can survive, not through legislation nor wishful thinking, but only if the integrity of the individual is preserved.' Such integrity could only come from the family, for 'the parent is the keystone of the social structure.'[71] Many works, such as *The Family and Democratic Society* (1943) and *Democracy in the Home* (1954), made this theme central to their very purpose.[72] Like the society, these books argued, the family must presume all members to be of equal worth. Authority in such a relationship was necessarily limited. 'Democracy is built on the worth of the individual and does not condone the right of a group to withhold individual rights, but it does recognize a group authority. As long as the group realizes that what is good for the individual is in turn good for the group and prevents the rights of one from infringing on those of another, its authority is democratic.'[73] The children, according to such doctrines, were more like junior partners than like true subordinates. Their decision-making powers and responsibilities would increase as they grew older, but the right to such powers was never in doubt.

A chain of argument had been developed by experts that went something like this: The events of early childhood are of tremendous importance. Actions taken in those years could determine the long-term happiness and social adjustment of the child. Yet discipline was of limited value. At best it was a form of compass, pointing the child in the right direction. It was not a form of force and, besides, the principle of the democratic family meant that force was an illegitimate means of enforcing rules. Yet if the children went wrong, the fault lay with the parents, for children were not born bad. Books with titles like *The*

Rights of Infants, published in 1943 and reprinted nine times by 1948, or *The Child Is Right: A Challenge to Parents* (1947), were in both title and content among the more clear-cut examples of such thinking. The theme of parental responsibility was not restricted to a few works, however; it echoed through all of the works published in the years surrounding the war. 'Be kind to him in his failures,' wrote Blatz; 'the teaching technique is usually to blame.' S.R. Laycock put it even more bluntly. When it comes to problem children, he said, 'in great part the parents are guilty.'[74]

All of these theories imposed a tremendous burden upon parents. As columnist Max Braithwaite complained, 'psychologists are continually charging that parents are sowing in their helpless offspring the seeds of alcoholism, prostitution, homosexuality and practically every other neurosis in the book.' Until recently, he said, such dangers were unknown, and thus modern parents were under added pressure.[75] He was right. Many experts portrayed the child as emotionally fragile, easily destroyed by the naïve if well-meaning parent. The anxiety they produced in the parent must have destroyed much of their effectiveness as aids in child rearing. What was needed was a book by an expert who could convey the beliefs and assumptions of the age without destroying parental confidence. Such a book could potentially sell in the millions, to the millions of new parents who desperately sought guidelines on everything from getting the two-year-old to sleep to when to take the child to a doctor.

The expert that captured the potential was Dr Benjamin Spock. The book, published at the beginning of the baby boom, was his *Common Sense Book of Baby and Child Care.* The title itself, with its reference to 'common sense,' and the first subheading in the table of contents, 'Trust Yourself,' set out the message that Spock's book conveyed: 'Don't take seriously all that your neighbours say. Don't be afraid to trust your own common sense ... We know for a fact that the natural loving care that kindly parents give their children is a hundred times more valuable than their knowing how to pin a diaper on just right, or making a formula exactly.'[76] Spock himself was an overtrained, repressed child of a strong-willed family. Perhaps it was that experience that allowed him to strike just the right tone for a generation that believed in experts but needed reassurance.

Spock and his followers have sometimes portrayed the book as radical in its challenge to the rigidities of Watson and his followers. Yet by the 1940s the permissive approach to child-rearing was well established. Spock himself acknowledged that the reassurance to parents drew upon similar material in Arnold Gesell and Frances Ilg's 1943 work. Even the organization of his book, with its age-specific references and comments, draws heavily upon their precedent.[77] Nor did Spock challenge the basic doctrines of his colleagues. Indeed, the book is strikingly conventional in the main. The child is assumed to be good or, as Spock put it, 'a reasonable, friendly human being.' Affection is seen as the key, and discipline should be soft to non-existent. 'The desire to get along with other people happily and considerately develops within him, as part of the unfolding of his nature, provided he grows up with loving, self-respecting parents.' Toilet training, progress in eating habits, walking, talking, and all other events marking a young child's development should be left to the child. Nor were parents let off the hook. Lazy children, Spock concluded, were usually that way because their parents had pushed too hard or been too critical.[78]

Such themes had already been stated by Blatz and other experts of the era. The genius of Spock's work, however, is not its revolutionary nature but its conventionality. Spock did not challenge the predominant theories of his age. His battle against Watson was against a straw man, long displaced from the throne by a generation of writers. What Spock did was capture in an especially apt way the hopes and fears of an age. Moreover, he did so in easy-to-read language that, though it conveyed Freudian undertones, kept the more esoteric or controversial Freudian themes well buried within the common-sense text.[79] This book seemed so commonsensical to parents because, to a large degree, it confirmed their own inclinations and the social prejudices and values they had already absorbed. He was also an MD who devoted a good part of his book to the very practical question of childhood diseases, something most child-rearing books did not do.

This was a child-obsessed age, and Spock's assertion of parental competence combined with his acceptance of popular theory meant that his book became one of the most successful of all time, in its first year selling three-quarters of a million copies. Spock became as essential for child-rearing as diapers. Later editions could boast of numbers sold like hamburger chains do – 'More than 28,000,000 copies sold.' Spock himself became a celebrity. Soon he was a regular on the new medium of television. So was his book. When Little Ricky was born on *I Love Lucy* in 1953 (the most-watched show to that point in television history), the book was front and centre as the source of advice for the panicky new parents.[80] Within just a few years Spock and his book had become a cultural landmark.

It has been commonplace to say that the baby boom was raised in permissive fashion. It has been said to be the chief distinguishing mark of the generation and has repeatedly been used to praise or condemn it. What the writings of Spock, Blatz, and all the others indicate, however, is that permissiveness does not tell the whole story. For the permissiveness shown to the children was not matched by a permissive attitude towards parenting. Missteps were so dangerous that parents were confined to narrow, almost doctrinaire approaches to raising their child. Further, this generation of parents put a great deal of value upon the successful family as a mark of personal achievement and as a means of social recognition. For women in particular, well-brought-up children were the equivalent of career success. Failures, or apparent failures, or imagined failures, could thus lead to stress and guilt on the part of parents.

The combination of permissiveness in child-rearing and parental anxiety was nicely illustrated in a National Film Board release from the postwar period entitled *Why Tommy Won't Eat*. In this film a doctor traces a child's eating habits back to infancy. The movement from breast to bottle, to cup, the film warns, should proceed at the child's pace and not at the parents'. At every step 'lots' of approval is important.' If, when the child gets older, it refuses to eat the vegetables, 'don't say anything about it.' The theme is clear. It is usually parents who mess eating habits up.

All of this is a prelude to Tommy, a child of six or so who often refuses to eat what is on his plate. The fault is with the mother. 'You eat the whole plateful or you won't get one bite of dessert ... Perhaps Tommy's mother spoke that way – a permanent battle over food.' The one sentence sums up two of the important themes contained in the film – the parent (usually, though not always, the mother) is to blame, and any attempt to enforce parental will only makes matters worse. The remedy, of course, is expert help. The mother hauls Tommy off to the doctor, who, after an examination, says that Tommy is physically fine. The kindly, white-haired doctor then takes the mother aside and says firmly, 'Mrs Smith, you are the problem – not the boy.' The well-intentioned Mrs Smith then reforms, putting extra effort into making meals attractive and pleasant. The extra work she is forced to do is a form of penitence for past sins. 'She is paying for her mistakes,' intones the film solemnly. 'And Mrs Smith does a lot of thinking. She realizes that she has been tense since he was a baby. She has forced him to eat what she thinks he should eat and has been unresponsive to his feelings. His refusal to eat has been his way of asserting his individuality.'[81]

WHAT DO THE TRENDS OF THE 1940S AND 1950S imply for the experience of the baby-boomers as infants and small children? At the most obvious level, several things are apparent. First, this was the healthiest generation on record. They were more likely to survive the birth process and less likely to die or be disfigured by childhood diseases. True, polio remained as the last great destroyer of children, but that would be eradicated by Salk vaccine after the mid-1950s. Second, those little landmarks that punctuate an individual's progress from infancy to childhood – self-feeding, toilet training, speech, and socialization – were much more likely to be achieved according to the child's schedule than the parents'. Third, in the aggregate this generation was likely to find its transgressions treated indulgently and its demands, temper tantrums, and acts of disobedience tolerated. In other words, permissiveness was more prevalent in the upbringing of this generation than in the previous one.

More important than such concrete detail, however, may be the intergenerational mood that the culture of the age dictated. All of the trends in child rearing and in family attitudes put baby-boomers more at the centre of the family universe than had been the case for any previous generation. Sometimes, in more extreme writings, the children were seen as the only purpose of the family. Freudian psychiatrist Fritz Kahn summed it up in a 1949 article: 'Above all we must learn that parents exist for their children and not children for their parents. The child comes into life as a son or a daughter, but being a son or a daughter is merely a passing phase and not a life duty.'[82] This piece was more blunt than most. The basic message, though, was extremely common: Parents had no long-term claim upon their children. The flow of family duty extended downward to the new generation and not upward to seniority and wisdom.

This tendency was noticed at the time. Several works worried about the tremendous pressures put upon parents who were expected to be everything to their children.[83] Given that these experts shared the same general assumptions about child rearing, however, such warnings did nothing to resolve the problem. The society of mid-century remained a child-centred one, 'filiocentric,' as the sociologists termed it. The child orientation began with the experiences of the parental generation in war and depression and their resultant drive to family formation – to bring stability and a cohesion in a world so frequented by anarchy. It was reinforced by the prosperity that made children economically feasible and by the replication effect which meant, in effect, that the numbers of children around increased the social interest in children and the likelihood that others would follow the social convention of marrying young and having children early.

Finally, the focus on children was reinforced by the experts. As one historian said, 'Child-rearing tracts might be renamed mother-rearing tracts.'[84] The parents were told by the experts, and by the neighbours or relatives who read the experts, what was expected of them. They were to be permissive but were ultimately responsible for their children's outcome. They were to give their children a free hand while ensuring that their attitudes and 'mental hygiene' were healthily directed. 'A conscientious parent, intent upon the task of raising children,' warned Blatz, 'must be moralist, psychologist, educator, philosopher, theologian, physician, nurse, and dietitian in addition to being a father and mother.'[85] The defining of parents by analogy to professional experts says much about the age.

None of this must be overstated. Common sense and personal experience indicate that the generation raising children after the war was not destroyed by the activity. It is a commonplace of child-rearing theory, however, that parents bring up their children according to the parental view of the world. If this is the case, then the word that seems best to describe that world, and to describe as well the way in which the parents of the later 1940s and early 1950s approached their children, was 'fragile.' This fragility was both internal and external. As we have seen, they faced tremendous burdens of high personal and social expectations. Their children and their homes were especially important to them. At the same time they lived in an era when all the cultural norms circumscribed their ability to control those children who lay at the centre of their universe.

The family was fragile in a world that had seen war and depression tear families apart. Prosperity was fragile to a generation emerging from the war and seeking to create that house and white picket fence in the suburbs. The Cold War, especially with the outbreak of the Korean War in 1950, made the world a fragile place. In the United States, the leitmotif of the Cold War and the fear of annihilation did much to shape family values and actions throughout the 1950s.[86] In Canada, the Cold War seems to have been a less dominant force; nevertheless, it was a brooding presence that reminded people that their current situation was tenuous. Changing technology made things worse. The atomic bomb and the development of long-distance bombers meant that for the first time North America was open to direct and sudden attack. Canada, caught geographically between the two superpowers, was likely to be a battle-ground should war break out. 'Someone said: "We mustn't forget that the January 1950 number [of *Chatelaine*] is the first in a new half-century – what's the one thing which concerns everyone?" The argument stopped by sudden consent, for we all recognized what it was! the Atom Bomb. Around the table faces grew somber, as each of us built on the theme of fear.'[87] The world balanced on a series of pin-points – political, economic, psychological, and social. The children must be preserved from the chaos and given security – economic and personal.

3

Safe in the Hands of Mother Suburbia: Home and Community, 1950–1965

It is a spring day in the early 1950s. Two parents, both still in their twenties, and their three-year-old child live in a small apartment in the city. It is clean and decent, but crowded, and promises to be more so with the arrival of a second child in about three months. The weather is pleasant, and the family piles into their Studebaker for a drive. Although the car is a recent purchase, and the Sunday drive still a novelty, marked by a sense of adventure, today the trip also has at least a vague purpose. Recently newspaper advertisements have trumpeted the grand opening of a new subdivision just beyond the city. There will be brass bands, free ice cream, and even 'pretty models.' The couple knows they will need a house soon and that, if they are going to buy anything, it will have to be farther out. As the advertisements told them, a comparable house in the city would cost considerably more. Still, this is an exploratory trip, a drive out to see the sights as much as anything else.

After half an hour's drive (including one wrong turn), they arrive at the tract of new houses carved out of a farmer's field. The land is raw. The bulldozers have left their mark and there is no landscaping. Still, it's a festive occasion. A remarkable number of families have made the trip, and most have young children in tow. Most exciting are the houses. By modern standards they would seem small, uninspired, and very ordinary. To this family and many others, they seem the very picture of the good life, especially when contrasted with the cramped, old-fashioned apartment back in the city. The show models are all bungalows and feature a picture window, modern kitchen with electric fridge and range, and a separate dining 'area.' They are designed on what the salesman terms an 'open plan,' with living-room, dining-room, and kitchen flowing into one another. There are three bedrooms, a basement that could be made into a rumpus-room, and even a built-in play area in the backyard, conveniently located so that mother can watch from the kitchen. It is easy to imagine a cozy furniture arrangement in the living-room. There is a front driveway and carport. Best of all is the large 50-by-110-foot lot. Though it is now just dirt, images of children's playsets, backyard barbecues, 'thick green grass and flowers, all kinds of flowers,' are easily conjured up.

It is also affordable. Recent years have been prosperous, and not only does the husband's job look secure, but the family has hopes for promotions and pay increases. True, the selling price of $12,000 seems steep, but the salesman points out that only 10 per cent down is required and that monthly payments of principal, interest, and taxes amount to $79 – more than the rent for the apartment, but not that much. The dream seems worth the stretch, and what began as a Sunday drive ends up in home-ownership in a new community. Here is the place the children will know as home. Here, largely for the sake of the kids, the family will put down roots in a community of equally rootless people.

THIS IS A FICTIONAL INCIDENT, BUT it is based very closely on reality.[1] In the fifteen years after the war, more than a million Canadians moved to that borderland between city and country, the suburb, which became the symbol of the young postwar family. Scholars descended on suburbs as if they were a strange and previously undiscovered society.[2] Magazines and newspapers of the era were replete with stories of that new curiosity, suburban life. *Maclean's* called it the 'great phenomenon of the twentieth century' as early as 1954. By 1960 *Time* had dedicated a cover to the suburban housewife and ran as a bannered headline 'One-Third of a Nation, U.S. Suburbia 1960.'[3]

Of course, not all postwar families lived in the suburbs. Hundreds of thousands grew up, as had their parents or grandparents, in city homes, rural farmhouses, or small villages. Still, *Maclean's* was right: The suburb was the great phenomenon of the age and came to typify the childhood of the baby-boomer. The rise and triumph of low-density residentially oriented communities was the single most significant urban event of the postwar decades. As one writer has aptly commented, 'If the nineteenth century could be called the Age of Great Cities, post-1945 America would appear to be the Age of Great Suburbs.'[4] In the United States the suburbs grew 8.5 times as fast as the central cities from 1945 through to the end of the 1960s, and by the 1970s more Americans lived there than in either the cities or the countryside. In Canada the trend was the same. The 1961 census noted that the 1950s had brought growth that was consistently higher in the suburban areas than in the cities proper.[5] Communities that hardly existed before the war became major centres of growth for the postwar generation. Places like Scarborough, North York, and Etobicoke in Toronto; Hamilton Mountain or Burlington near Hamilton; Burnaby or North Vancouver in Vancouver; St Laurent or the west-island communities of Pointe Claire and Beaconsfield in Montreal typified the new urban landscape that developed in the postwar drive for the white picket fence and home.

This suburban explosion, nurtured by an ageing housing stock and by the drive to domesticity, occurred because economic conditions were perfect for home-ownership. Interest rates were low, and the government followed up on pre-war precedents by creating the Central Mortgage and Housing Corporation (CMHC) in 1945 and by encouraging banks to move into mortgage lending by the 1950s. A rising standard of living and easy credit meant that the real cost of housing decreased through the 1950s and into the 1960s, before it began to climb again.[6] Everything thus came together – low unemployment, low down-payments, and availability of credit. Canadians built and bought houses at a greater rate than at any time in their history. In 1945 fewer than 49,000 new units were built. By 1947 this figure had climbed to more than 76,000. By the mid-1950s this figure had gone above 100,000, and it climbed to nearly 150,000 by the end of that decade before receding temporarily. The first great impact of the baby boom came from its need to be housed.

In theory the baby boom could have been housed through higher-density construction within city boundaries. That was the pattern in Continental Europe until well into the 1960s. That had never been the North American vision, however, and the white-picket-fence ideal had little to do with apartment living. Instead the generation of Canadians who came out of the war sought out the single-family detached house with a yard of its own. In the 1951–61 period, more than 70 per cent of all new dwellings built were single-family detached homes. Duplexes and row-houses were marginal, important only in Montreal, and apartments remained a small part of the housing industry until well into the 1960s.[7] As a 1958 CMHC report concluded, 'the normal form of dwelling is the detached house with access to a private plot of ground.'[8] With an average lot frontage of fifty feet and all the accompanying sidewalks, streets, and open spaces, the dominance of the single-family detached house made geographic sprawl an inevitable aspect of the postwar housing boom.[9]

Suburbs were not new and they did not originate in Canada. They had evolved as an adjunct to the modern city. Until the Industrial Revolution, the need to have work within walking distance of home meant that even large cities indiscriminately mixed work and residence, wealth and poverty. Until well into the eighteenth century, home and work were often the same place, with family rooms above or behind the shop. Equally, the houses of the rich would abut on narrow lanes or alleys containing the hovels of the poor. Yards were small or non-existent, as the need for access crowded construction together.[10] Wealth and privilege, then, sought to be close to the centre. The fringes of the city were undesirable, straggling outward in a series of shacks or huts to the open fields beyond. This was as true in the new world as in the old. The wealthy in the ante-bellum United States, for example, built row-housing with little or no set-back from the street. The back-yard of even the more respectable home was the site for the outhouse and for casual garbage, and was thus hardly seen as a play or rest area.[11]

By the nineteenth century the rise of the modern middle class shifted the focus of the family from the extended-kinship to the nuclear form. This shift was largely a matter of the way business was done. Familial alliances and the loyalty of blood lines was replaced by an ideal of domesticity, the provision of support and safety to spouse and children. Encouraging this goal was the rise of an evangelical religious ideal that looked to the family as the fount and support of religious and personal morals in the face of a dangerous, even corrupt, outside world. The middle class were, as one historian has written, 'the ideologists of the closed, nuclear family.'[12]

The desire to remove the family from the chaos and temptation of the city came at a time when the city itself provided good reasons for people to think of escape.[13] The explosive growth that industrialism created in urban areas made city centres even more crowded and chaotic than previously. The development of noisy, polluting factories, usually ringing the city centre, made adjacent areas less livable. Finally, the growth and the factories brought a large working class into the cities. Most of the members of this new industrial class walked to work, and therefore were forced into the unsightly brick row-houses that sat alongside the factories, to live amid the noise and pollution and overcrowding that industrialism brought to their cities. Their very presence further encouraged those with greater means to seek an alternative to city life. In London, Manchester, New York, and other great cities of the nineteenth century, the middle class began to leap outward from the city centre, over the factory and working-class areas to new pollution- and noise-free plots outside the city proper – the suburbs.

Changing technology was essential to the rise of the suburb. Nineteenth-century improvements in transportation made successive waves of suburban dispersal more possible. In the first half of the century, there was the omnibus (a horse-drawn public conveyance) and then the horse railway (horse-drawn, but on a streetcar track). Later, the arrival of the railway and the streetcar further reduced commuting time, and therefore encouraged further spread of suburbs. By the beginning of the twentieth century, there were suburbs strung out along railway and streetcar lines around the major cities of both the United States and Great Britain. The term 'suburb' had become commonplace, and developers were planning whole communities to support the continuing urban growth of the industrial era.[14]

Along with the suburban house came the yard. The modern domestic ideal included space, not just within the house, but outside as well. In part, no doubt, this idea derived from the pretensions of would-be landed gentry. In Britain the early London suburbs, populated by well-off merchants, consciously emulated the tone of the country estates of the aristocracy. In the United States, as well, the gentrified ideal encouraged emulation. There was more to it than that, however. The notion of connection to nature, albeit in tamed form, runs through the history of industrial cities. In an almost mystical way, the small yard, and the flower garden or, better yet, the vegetable plot, would preserve the family from the evil effects of the city, both physical and moral.

As cities grew, the desire to preserve contact with the 'natural' world became even more persistent. Thus it was that some of the most shrill anti-urban rhetoric in Canada came in the early twentieth century, just as the nation began to experience urbanization. There were hopeful, often desperate plans to keep people on the farms and away from the temptations of urban life. For those who saw the city as the inevitable centre of growth, schemes were devised to allow cities to expand without becoming more urban. Typical was the idea of well-known British planner Thomas Adams, who came to Canada carrying his message of 'garden cities.' Adams stretched the notion of suburbia to its logical limit, and perhaps beyond. Railways and streetcars meant, according to him, that there was no need for crowded urban conditions. People might work in the city, but their houses would sit on half-acre lots miles from the urban core. Each house would have its own vegetable garden, and this connection with nature would enable all members of the family to escape the worst evils of urban life. Aimed at saving the working class from itself, the garden cities that were actually built appealed to that bedrock of surburbia – the middle class.[15]

Adams's plan depended on railways. A quarter-century later America's most famous architect, Frank Lloyd Wright, looked to the automobile for his vision of urban utopia. This futuristic vision, which he named 'Broadacres,' focused on the idea of extremely low-density development strung out along fast highways. There would, in effect, be no city. Instead, a widely diffused population, and equally diffused shopping and industry, would allow the average family direct access to nature and, if they so wished, a part-time farm of their own. The city and the country would become so intermixed as to be indistinguishable. It was, in a way, the ultimate suburban fantasy.[16]

Over the course of a century, the middle class had changed its view of the home. Proximity to business and the prestige of being at the centre of activity were replaced over the course of a century with a very different ideal. The home was, in the terminology of Christopher Lasch, 'a haven in a heartless world.'[17] Ideal family living for the suburban middle class now included separation – from neighbours, in the form of a single-family detached house; from other classes and ethnic groups, through restrictive covenants and unwritten understandings; from different socio-economic groups, by virtue of the cost of entry into subdivision life. Low density, and the belief in nature, or at least the outdoors, had also given the yard an important role. It was no longer the dumping-ground for refuse and, with the rise of indoor plumbing, less likely to be the site of the privy. Instead, it was the play area for children and the garden area for the hobbyist.[18]

Though very much in this tradition, postwar suburbs were different from those that preceded them. Most important for the purposes of this book, they were not just domestic in orientation but child-centred. Indeed, a new word had to be invented just to describe it. 'It begins with the children,' wrote William Whyte in 1956. 'There are so many of them and they are so dictatorial in effect that a term like filiarchy would not be entirely facetious. It is the children who set the basic design; their friendships are translated into the mother's friendships, and these, in turn, to the family's.'[19] Indeed, 'filiarchy' was not at all facetious and it, and its counterpart, 'filiocentric,' became standard terms among analysts of postwar suburban life. All the evidence confirms the terms' appropriateness. When Toronto sociologist S.D. Clark did his study of suburbs in the early 1960s, he found the parents kept saying that they moved there 'for the kids.' One American wit described suburban life as a place where the mother 'delivers the children once obstetrically and by car forever.'[20] Postwar suburban values thus took the domestic ideal one step farther. The children, always a part of the suburban value system, now moved front and centre.

Postwar experts, whether architects, town planners, or professionals on family development, were practically unanimous in their belief that the suburbs were the best residential destination for a family with children. Winnipeg architect Joseph Kostis reminded readers that the American Public Health Association recommended that houses have a minimum lot of fifty-foot frontage, and said that sixty or seventy feet was preferable.[21] A junior-high text recommended that prospective buyers ask: Is the lot 'big enough to provide ample space for all members of the family to enjoy outdoor living? Sand-boxes, swings, wading pools and junior-size bikes for the little folks?'[22] The house and neighbourhood were as much a part of the nurturing process as was Doctor Spock and a healthy diet. 'Did it ever occur to you,' wrote one child-expert, 'that in a home with young children a place to play is as much their right as a living room is for adult use? It isn't just a matter of amusing the youngsters either. Providing them with a healthful opportunity to play outdoors is a means of teaching them important lessons in social adjustment with their age group, and of challenging young minds to plan and invent and employ their time happily.'[23]

A suburban house assisted in the triumph of the family circle. 'It is in the neighbourhoods,' wrote one American expert on housing and the family, 'that we make friends, build homes, and rear our children; our manner of life influences and is influenced by the neighbourhood.' Given this, the choice of neighbourhood was crucial. 'The neighbourhood considered good by the experts in town and city planning is outside the commercial district and separated from it by a green belt of lawn and trees or farmland. This belt acts as a buffer for the neighbourhood against the noise, dirt, and the intense activity of the commercial and industrial areas of the city. The houses, not necessarily alike in valuation ... are still similar enough to be harmonious. Their placement on lots ensures family privacy but invites neighbourliness.'[24] A Canadian architect agreed that the cities with 'tiny backyards, the contractor's yard, and junk heap are not desirable places for children to play.' Only decentralization and 'adequate garden spaces around each house' seemed to provide a solution – in other words, suburbia.[25] The suburbs were filiocentric because there were so many children, but the reverse was also true: There were so many children in suburbia because their filiocentric parents believed in the suburban domestic ideal.

The flight to the suburbs had much to do with the insecurities of the age. After decades of war and depression, the generation beginning new families had every reason to be worried that its dreams would not be fulfilled. Psychological theories emphasized the fragility of the family and the child-rearing process. The search for security thus became a hallmark of the generation, later much scorned by their offspring, a generation that had not known insecurity. Indeed, security and the search for it is one of the striking themes in the popular literature and advertisements of the day. The ads for everything from baseboard heaters to copper plumbing played up the theme of security for family, and especially for children. The provision of a proper, secure home was not only a postwar dream, but an obligation hammered home from every angle to young parents.

Perhaps fittingly, the mood of the era may have been captured most blatantly by an advertisement for Ford. This full-page ad began by reminiscing about the old days. Nostalgia was deliberately evoked, with drawings of open fire hydrants and a lively urban street scene. Overriding the nostalgia, however, was a darker theme. 'If you were a kid, back around the turn of the century, there wasn't much to do. Maybe you got into trouble.' Trouble was a creature of the physical environment. It 'breeds in slums, or let down neighbourhoods – wherever children are bored or walled in. The trouble came as sure as Saturday night, when the patrol wagon parks, waiting for its first load.' In a few sentences the reader is taken from a moment of urban nostalgia to a reassertion of long-standing North American distrust of the city. There was hope, though. Your children were not doomed. The automobile (Ford) 'broke through the city limits, letting the people out of town into the great green world beyond. The whole population is on the move from the stone and steel of the city toward the fresh air, the light, the trees and living space of the suburbs.' In case the point was missed, a photograph of a spacious, tree-lined suburb was set hard against the urban children playing dangerously on city streets.[26] Suburbia ensured a promising future for children.

THE SUBURBAN EXPLOSION RESHAPED the Canadian urban landscape. For though Canada had suburbs in 1945, it was not yet a suburban nation. Even the largest cities were reasonably compact by modern-day standards. In Toronto, for example, development was continuous for only about three and a half miles in each direction from the downtown core. Except for a narrow strip along Yonge Street, the city began to sputter out above Eglinton, west of Jane and east of Woodbine.[27] In Montreal the degree of suburbanization and urban spread was even smaller, owing to the presence of significant multiple-family dwellings.[28] In most other Canadian cities a three-mile walk from downtown would take you to open countryside.[29]

The relationship between the periphery and the centre was also different. The modern suburb is, as one urban historian has noted, really a technoburb, containing residential, office, and commercial areas.[30] In Canada, in 1945, however, business, including retailing, remained in the centre of the city. The main shopping areas were contiguous with the main office buildings and were usually anchored by the large department stores. In Vancouver, the Hudson's Bay Store and Woodward's occupied downtown locations within a block of each other. In Montreal, Ogilvie's, Eaton's, Morgan's, and Simpson's lined St Catherine Street, providing shoppers with a convenient central location for shopping. During the Christmas season the window displays provided a touch of magic for the young baby-boomers who ventured downtown with their parents. In Toronto, Simpson's and Eaton's faced each other on Queen Street, competing against each other while mutually drawing customers to the area. Most of the important retailing businesses were located within a few blocks of these commercial giants. Suburban shopping was restricted to corner stores; groceries; and that symbol of the future, the automobile dealership.

Likewise, people worked in the downtown area or in the factory areas that ringed it. As late as 1956, for example, estimates put 85 per cent of Metro Toronto jobs in the downtown core.[31] Thus daily access to downtown was an essential part of life. People hopped the streetcar or bus and, given the small size of most Canadian cities, could be downtown within fifteen minutes. For those farther out, such as the residents of Lachine, near Montreal, or Oakville, near Toronto, there were commuter railways.

The older suburbs were configured differently from those of the postwar era. Before the war, car-ownership was far from universal, and therefore commuter access to the railway station or streetcar line was crucial. This necessity limited sprawl. Lot sizes, for example, remained in the neighbourhood of 3,000 square feet, and the communities tended to be strung out, as one historian put it, like beads on a line, along transportation routes.[32] Between railway stations or adjacent to streetcar routes, open fields still existed. The inter-war years, for example, had seen Toronto develop northward along Yonge Street to Finch Avenue, some five miles from downtown. Yet a walk of a few blocks in either direction from the Yonge corridor would have led to open fields.

Residential construction practices also differed. In the early stages of the creation of Canadian suburbs, developers had acquired the necessary permissions, carved the area into lots, and then auctioned off individual parcels to builders or, more likely, families who wished to build. As time went by, municipal demands for services and growing sophistication of builders meant that development included paving, sewers, and street lighting in many subdivisions. Construction in Canada was still low-key in 1945, however. Advertisements were, with a few exceptions, mere classifieds indicating that lots could be acquired. There were no show homes and none of the hoopla that, a few years later, attracted our fictional couple to take their Sunday drive.[33] People bought lots and ordered houses constructed.[34] There were no fully integrated firms that acted as planner, developer, builder, and marketer.

The traditional Canadian world of compact cities and downtown focus was about to be swept away. In two decades the way people worked, lived, and shopped would be changed by the tremendous explosion of suburbia. Initially, however, the demand was much more straightforward. People desperately wanted housing in order to escape the overcrowding of the war years. Moreover, because they were young, they needed relatively cheap housing. In both Canada and the United States, governments, from federal to municipal levels, tried to develop housing policies that would provide quick solutions to the shortage. As late as 1949 observers saw the resolution of the housing crisis as one of the most important tasks remaining from the war years.[35]

The trick for the builder was to put up economical houses as quickly as possible. This combination of quantity and economy created tremendous incentives for the market to innovate. This was especially true south of the border, where economies of scale could be applied more easily. The response came quickly. After the war new building methods and mass marketing did for the subdivision what Henry

Ford's assembly line did for the automobile. Symbolic of this change – indeed, almost synonymous with it – is Levittown; some 17,000 houses quickly put up on farmland on Long Island and selling for under $10,000.[36]

At the time Levittown was extraordinary. Massive in scale and exceptional in the attention it received, the subdivision was a sign of things to come. Here was a large-scale, integrated company that not only developed the land but built the houses. Here was a subdivision comprised solely of single-family dwellings on sixty-foot lots, just as public taste dictated. Here were ruthless economies such as third bedrooms without closets, living-rooms floored with asphalt tile, and carports rather than garages. Here was an enormous enterprise that used all the techniques of advertising to sell to a house-hungry public, including model homes and low down-payments. As well, innovative construction techniques produced houses at a faster rate than ever before. Here, ultimately, was the sort of mass housing that could overcome the dire shortages at the end of the war.[37]

The public responded. The demand for Levitt's houses and for those of his imitators was tremendous throughout the late 1940s and early 1950s. Trips out to new developments became something of a North American pastime. When Levittown first opened, salesmen were selling as many as 1,400 houses a day.[38] In New Orleans, in 1951, a subdivision opened, complete with model homes and houses with a 'fresh contemporary flavor.' Some 25,000 people went through the project on the first day and, within a month, the developer had sold 700 homes.[39] The Levitts moved on from their Long Island project to an even bigger one near Philadelphia, and throughout the nation integrated companies promised Americans that their postwar dreams could indeed be fulfilled in a three-bedroom, 1,100-square-foot bungalow.

Canadian developers lagged a little behind their American counterparts. Essentially, however, trends in Canada followed those in the United States. Similar technological innovations (such as plywood and drywall) made construction cheaper, while the introduction of prebuilt roof trusses sped up construction.[40] Though the industry always had its share of small-time builders, larger firms increasingly played a significant role. Within a few years Canadian developers were also becoming more aggressive in their marketing. As early as 1950, ads with pictures began to appear, featuring, for example, 'Norwood Heights, Vancouver's Newest Subdivision.'[41] It was not really until the mid-1950s, though, that the full range of marketing techniques – large pictures or, more usually, idealized representations of the home, model homes on site, and increasingly detailed descriptions – became normal in Canada:

> New – New
> $12,400 (only $3000 down)
> Big 6-room Bungalows
> Air Conditioning with Oil
> Decorated to your choice
> Coloured Tile Bath
> Open House All Weekend Drop on Out[42]

As time went on, the hype increased. Elizabeth Gardens, near Toronto, for example, advertised that it was a 'spectacular $11,000,000 subdivision near Bronte' with '4 contemporary styles to choose from.' There were also new incentives, like guaranteed trade-ins, free appliances, and free ice cream, and even Trump Davidson's six-piece Dixieland band, at the model homes.[43]

Canadian development paralleled that in the United States in another way. In the early postwar years, a combination of inexperience and greed on the part of both developers and city officials allowed the construction of subdivisions with little social infrastructure. Developers failed to provide parks, shopping amenities, sufficient street lighting, or much of anything else. Municipalities, in their haste, often overlooked the financial burden of everything from garbage collection to schools.[44] As early as 1950, for example, the fast-growing Vancouver suburb of Burnaby was double-shifting many of its schools. Bleary-eyed pupils trudged in for 7:00 A.M.–12:00 P.M. or 1:00 P.M.–6:00 P.M. shifts.[45] And this was before the baby boom even reached school age! Even with the best of intentions and some decent planning, it was hard to keep up. Burnaby saw its civic expenditures more than quadruple in a decade.[46]

There were also aesthetic concerns. E.G. Faludi, one of Canada's leading architects, complained in 1949 that 'acre by acre we are transforming beautiful ravines, fields, parklands, wooded estates into dismal rows of unsightly identical brick strawberry boxes that will be with us for a generation at least.' Modern tract housing built in the late 1940s, he warned, 'represents the end of everything – the end of individuality, beauty, and privacy.'[47]

Faludi had a point, but he was too pessimistic. As time went on there were improvements. Developers were learning by experience and growing through profits into companies better able to understand the complexities of urban planning. Town planners were becoming more experienced themselves, and more determined to ensure that instant slums weren't being built in their municipality. As well, the continuing growth of the Canadian economy meant that the average standard of living improved and people could afford better housing. The relentless drive for economy typical of 1945–55 gave way to a desire for greater space and outward symbols of success: the double garage, the family room, the large kitchen and second bathroom. People still wanted to live in the suburbs, but their expectations were rising.

By the 1950s these changes were beginning to have an effect. In Vancouver, British Pacific properties was marketing a fully integrated community for the relatively affluent in North Vancouver. Just west of Toronto, the eccentric and upscale development of Thorncrest Village opened in 1950, based on the philosophy that 'dogs and kids run free.' It was an island of planning in an as yet largely undeveloped area complete with residents' council and a whole bevy of architectural and landscape restrictions. Faludi was the architect.[48] However, if one subdivision marks the break between the postwar rush and later integrated development, it is the 1954 suburb of Don Mills, in Toronto. Don Mills was, in its way, to be as influential as Levittown was earlier. It set the standards for planned subdivisions, including later developments such as Erin Mills, near Toronto; Kanata, near Ottawa; and Bow River, in Calgary.[49] Within a few years Bramalea construction would draw upon the precedents set by Don Mills to create what it boasted was 'Canada's first satellite city,' near Toronto.[50]

Don Mills succeeded because it learned from the past while introducing new ideas that began the mutation of the traditional suburb into the new technoburb. It was an integrated development, with Don Mills Development Ltd undertaking planning, infrastructure, and actual construction. For Canada it was development on a massive scale, rivalling the original Levittown. Some 3,000 acres of land were developed, and over a few years the population grew to some 35,000 people. The developers understood the notions that made customers look to suburbia – separateness and a sense of connection to nature. The old grid system of streets had fallen out of favour in the postwar years, and Don Mills reflected that. A few major streets ran through the community, but, for the most part, the residential areas were separated from through traffic and given bucolic names like Cottonwood Drive, Broadleaf Road, and Moccasin Trail.[51]

The planners of Don Mills were also innovative, answering many of Faludi's concerns about tract housing. Aimed at a slightly above-average market, the housing was more varied than in many earlier subdivisions. The result, said *Architectural Forum*, was 'some of the best built houses in Canada.'[52] They were also slightly larger, with more amenities than usual. They therefore held their value as Canadians became more affluent through the next years. The most important innovation came in the infrastructure. Drawing upon and extending the experience of various American developments, the company planned, not just for the roadways, but for a whole community. Schools, parks, churches, and that newest of suburban essentials, the shopping centre, were included in the plan. There was even what the promoters termed 'neat and clean' industry clustered at the north end of the development.

Through the 1950s the suburbs continued to spread over the countryside, transforming local ways of work and life with amazing speed. In Ottawa, for example, two census tracts, south of Carling Avenue and west of Maitland, were still largely empty in the mid-1950s. Three thousand people lived either in essentially rural areas or in straggling exurbanite communities. The school system, the roads, the open fields – all testified to a rhythm of life that was distinct from that of the nearby city. Then the developers arrived. In each of the next five years, a population equal in number to the original moved in. Within a decade the population had increased to nearly 25,000, by which time the edge of suburbia had moved on and the population stabilized. Roads were built, the bus systems extended, school boards reorganized, and the urban frontier pushed across one more area of the surrounding countryside. A new expressway, the Queensway, was being constructed to further integrate the communities into the downtown. The same process was under way in scores of communities across the nation. Perhaps, therefore, the frontier metaphor is entirely appropriate. Suburbia spread relentlessly, overwhelmed traditional patterns of trade and social activity, and reshaped the landscape. Also like the frontier, suburbia was moving ever onward, farther outward from the metropolitan centre.

Like the settlement of the frontier, suburban growth transformed the Canadian landscape and the way Canadians lived. Hamilton Mountain, for example, had a population of only 12,000 people at the end of the war. Within seven years it had reached 25,000 and, in another eight, 50,000.[53] The community of Burnaby, outside Vancouver, grew from slightly more than 30,000 people in 1941 to more than 100,000 twenty years later. In Montreal, in 1941, two-thirds of the population lived within 6.5 kilometres of the city centre. 'By 1961 the same population would be spread out over a 13 kilometre radius.'[54]

Nowhere was the suburban frontier expanding more quickly than around Toronto. The wartime boom continued with postwar growth in financial services, government, and secondary manufacturing. As a result the metropolitan area continued to act as a magnet both for immigrants and for Canadians from the rest of the nation. Moreover, unlike in Montreal, the favoured residence in the Toronto area was the single-family detached house.[55] As a result the population spilled over the borders of the city proper and into vast surrounding suburban communities. In 1941, Scarborough, North York, and Etobicoke were settled only in isolated patches and, with a combined population of slightly more than 66,000, were a mere one-tenth the size of the City of Toronto. Then the explosion occurred. North York became the fastest-growing community in Canada, expanding by 1075 per cent from 1941 to 1961. Etobicoke and Scarborough were not far behind and, by the early 1960s, the three suburbs had equalled the population of the City of Toronto.[56] North York was now larger than any Maritime city, and in two decades it had surpassed Quebec City's three and a half centuries of population growth.

Long-standing communities like Long Branch, Mimico, and Weston were swallowed up or transformed beyond recognition. Farther out, the suburban frontier transformed towns. Aurora, twenty miles up Yonge Street, was a small and distinct community of 2,000 people in the early 1950s, and most of its residents worked in the town. Then, in rapid succession in the late 1950s, large-scale tract subdivisions came in – Aurora Heights and Regency Acres. The population of the town quintupled, and the new residents were likely to work in the city but have their focus in town. In little more than a decade, a small town became, in modern parlance, a 'bedroom community.' Scores of communities across the country went through an identical process in the explosive quarter-century after the war.

Such rapid development made work difficult for planners and politicians. The city's population was relatively stagnant, but it possessed the industrial and commercial base that provided work for the burgeoning suburbs. The concentration of jobs in the core created serious traffic problems as suburbanites flooded downtown every morning and left every evening. New expressways like the Gardiner (1954) and the Don Valley (1961) were needed to handle the thousands of commuters coming from ever farther out. The suburbs, for their part, had even greater problems. Huge population increases meant equally huge budget increases, often at a rate that outran revenue. One estimate was that every 100 new families required 2.2 new schoolrooms, 4 new teachers, a police budget increase of $4,510 and fire-department increase of $2,820, 10,000 gallons of additional water each day, and even 0.02 new people on the planning staff.[57] Remember that, between 1941 and 1961, North York added some 63,000 new families!

The result could be overwhelming. It was estimated that, through the early 1950s, Ontario was converting 6,000 to 8,000 acres of farmland into suburban housing every year. More than 8,000 subdivisions were submitted for the approval of the Ontario government in a nine-year period after the war.[58] Sociologist S.D. Clark, writing in 1961, told horror stories of unprepared rural councils outside Toronto welcoming contractors only to discover, after the fact, the true costs of providing services.[59] Municipalities found that old jurisdictions made no sense as the urban population spilled over into surrounding communities. Communities froze development until plans for roads and sewers could catch up with the ambitions of developers.[60] So great was the growth of suburbia that Toronto had to move to an entirely new form of government in 1953, creating Metropolitan Council. Some of the reasons for the new form of government can be demonstrated by the fact that, when the new Metropolitan Toronto Planning Board began work, it found itself swamped by development proposals. Dozens of subdivision plans came forward at each and every meeting, and these were only the contentious ones! Its director, acting in 'non-contentious' cases, was even busier. At one meeting he announced that he had, on their behalf, approved sixty-five subdivision plans.[61]

The cities of Canada were transformed during the childhood years of the baby boom. The old streetcar cities had yielded just as surely as the walking cities before them. In the place of the streetcar and the commuter railway came what social critic and historian Arthur Lower sarcastically termed in 1958 the 'great god CAR.'[62] For, while suburbia was affected by many new technologies – from electric lawn mowers to TV – nothing was as vital to suburbia as the transformation of the automobile into a common possession in the postwar years.

Not that cars were new. Canadians had owned them from the beginning of twentieth century. By the end of the 1920s, there were more than a million automobiles in Canada, and the nation was second only to the United States in per-capita registrations. The automobile was still not something the average Canadian expected to own, but it was becoming more and more a part of daily life for the well-off middle class and above. Then disaster struck. Automobiles, like home-ownership, were another part of the good life put out of reach by depression, and then war. The number of cars in Canada actually decreased during the early 1930s and then, after a slight recovery, declined again during the war as automobile production ground to a halt. By the end of the war, Canada's figure of one passenger car for every ten people was lower than the comparable figure for the end of the 1920s. In other words, though a common sight, the car remained a dream for most Canadians, especially younger ones forming families.[63]

By 1945 that dream of automobile-ownership was probably second only to that of home-ownership in the minds of Canadians. The automobile symbolized the good life, and the freedom of movement it promised served to add some dash to the prevalent domestic ideal. South of the border the automobile had already reached more deeply into the life and psyche of the average American. There were twice as many cars per capita in the United States by the end of the war.[64] Now Canadians began to catch up to their American cousins. Between 1945 and 1952, registrations doubled. As one observer put it: 'it took only seven years to duplicate the motor vehicle production and ownership achievement of the previous forty-five years.'[65] In 1953 the turning-point was reached as more than 50 per cent of Canadian families now owned a car. By 1960 two-thirds of households had a car, and 10 per cent had two or more.[66]

Tremendous emotional and intellectual energy has been focused on the car. It was the symbol of the good life. It was the destroyer of community. Critics complained, then and since, that the 1950s car was ridiculously unsafe, increasingly overpowered, and aesthetically absurd. Certainly anyone who has seen the swept fins of the late-decade Chryslers or who remembers the family V8 engine, with something in excess of 300 horsepower, would tend to agree. It is important to remember, however, that such criticisms did not reflect the public mood of the 1950s. To those who bought cars in the postwar years, the freedom and status ownership conferred was reinforced by the 'exuberance' of design and the excesses of power. Even those who had owned pre-war cars, after all, could justifiably note that the modern car was more powerful, smoother riding, and, best of all for Canada, heated. Moreover, as suburbs spread, the automobile became more and more essential. In other words, if Canadians had a love affair with the automobile in the 1950s (and there is no doubt they did), there were good reasons for it.

Still, it would be silly to pretend that the automobile was popular just because it was practical. In an age that glorified technology, that was still insecure in its new standard of living, that despised the old and embraced modernism, the automobile was technological symbol par excellence – representing security, status, and freedom. Indeed, the appeal of the automobile was that it neatly combined the two deeply entrenched characteristics of the age – faith in technology, and insecurity. On the one side, the car was the primal example of mass modernism, with hydro-glide transmissions, swept-fin styling, an abundance of chrome, and a new and 'better' model every October. Advertisers deliberately associated it either with technology, evoked by such names as Strato-Chief and Rocket '88, or with luxury, in such names as Bel Air and Parisienne. At the same time the purchase of the car was very much a part of the drive to home and family. 'Give your family Big Car Dependability,' counselled one Chevrolet ad, with a picture of parents and two children cruising along an open road.[67] The suburb and the car became intermingled as symbols of success and of a security desperately sought in the postwar years. Thus it was that the Ford greenbelt ad, mentioned earlier, so aptly touched upon the fears and hopes of a generation.

Arthur Lower was perceptive in pointing to the 'great god CAR.' The great age of subdivisions could not have come about without the parallel great age of automobiles. The suburb and the car have always had a symbiotic relationship. Car-ownership figures were highest in the suburbs, and it was in these regions on the edge of the city that the car, first singly, and then in twos, became a common feature of the family home. The car untethered the homeowner from any central point, and the postwar suburban tracts thus spread across the landscape according to developers' access to land rather than to a transportation locus. The car also meant that suburban housing could become even lower density than in the past. The 3,000 square feet of the earlier streetcar-suburb lot grew to 5,000–7,000 square feet in the postwar automobile suburb.[68]

The automobile also reshaped the house. The dominance of the bungalow and ranch house was possible only because of the lower-density housing the automobile provided. And, of course, the automobile made its own demands on architectural style. Unlike the horse, the car did not smell (at least when turned off), and ease of access as well as pride of ownership dictated that it be placed adjacent to the house. Postwar suburban architecture increasingly incorporated carports or garages into the design and selling features of the new suburban homes. The car and its residence became a part of suburban-house design until, over time, larger and larger garages often meant the façade of the home was dominated by car-storage space. This notion of home and car as one reached its peak in a 1958 *House and Garden* article that predicted the emergence of 'living garages,' combination garages and family-rooms. All of the family's most precious possessions could then be together.[69] This new god of the 1950s was thus a powerful one, determining the way in which people lived and communities evolved.

As the baby-boomers approached their teenage years, they too would succumb to serious bouts of automania. As children in the 1950s, however, their relationship to the automobile was different from that of their parents in one important respect: Theirs was the first generation for which automobiles were unexceptional. Most of them were probably taken home from the hospital in the family car, and the car was just a part of existence, like the house. The very familiarity of the car meant that they did not sense, as their parents did, how much their lives were affected by it. Everything from shopping to family leisure, to dating and perhaps the very concept of distance and community itself, was transformed by the automobile. The car is as much a part of suburban life as the detached house and backyard barbecue.

MOVING TO THE SUBURBS WAS AN ADVENTURE that belied the later image of blandness and conformity. Most Canadians did not have any experience with this type of life: isolation from earlier friends, a community of strangers, a new house on the straggling edge of the city, dependence on the automobile. Often the countryside was, literally, just beyond your backyard. That was another reason why 'the frontier' was such a favoured metaphor. Settling the frontier, suburbanites were 'pioneers' (another favoured metaphor), laying the foundation of civilization – lawns, streets, and schools – for others to follow. And like the frontier trail-blazers of history, suburban adventurers loved to chronicle their story, always emphasizing, in time-honoured fashion, the hardships faced and the resilience and heroism settling demanded.

The road was a 'gluey quagmire,' but after much effort the furniture van made it through to the new suburban house. The van unloaded and the young couple 'staggered through the chaos to bed.' The next morning they arose only to discover there was no water. 'It's nothing,' said the husband. 'They often turn off the water in North York.' Actually it turned out to be an uncovered water main that had frozen in the harsh climate of this northern frontier. Pioneer ingenuity came to the fore, however, and the couple burned straw around the uncovered pipe to unfreeze it. 'Mud and chaos and frozen water pipes ushered the Mondoux family into some of the mysteries of suburban living,' concluded the adventure story. Like their pioneer ancestors, however, there were compensations in the shared spirit. 'The night we moved in ... I was tired to the point of tears,' the housewife reminisced. 'Our next-door neighbour came in with some sandwiches and coffee, and a beer for Ron. Nobody ever did that for us in the city.' A captioned photograph underlined the point: 'There's room to relax with friends, children and wide-open spaces.'[70]

Moving from the creation of surburbia to the suburbs themselves, two themes stand out – modernization and standardization. The vast tracts of new housing and the affluence of these years transformed the Canadian house, just as it had the urban landscape. The mass-development techniques and the ubiquity of the suburban ideal decreased regional and class variations. Of course, housing continued to vary by income, region, and taste, although the differences were narrower.

It is easy to underestimate just how much housing changed during the boom of the 1950s and 1960s, in part because many of the devices we take for granted were available by the early twentieth century. Central heating (albeit by coal), hot and cold water, flush toilets, and baths or showers provided comfort and hygiene. In the inter-war years, mechanical refrigeration and electric ovens were widely available. There was a catch, however: These were still luxury goods, to be owned by the more affluent urban resident. As late as 1941 four out of five Canadians had iceboxes, and the vast majority, nine out of ten, used coal or wood as a heating source. The majority did not have central heating at all. A bare majority (six out of ten) had piped water in their house, but fewer than half had a bath or shower. Even the flush toilet was far from universal, with just over half of Canadian dwellings possessing one. Only the very rich had more than one.[71]

For decades, therefore, average Canadians had seen many of these conveniences as things that, though technologically feasible, were for someone else. After the war, for the first time, that perception changed. What the critics of modern tract housing did not understand was that the houses may have been small, and unimaginative, even tacky, but they also made modern technology available to the average Canadian. By 1961 the vast majority of houses were centrally heated, and seven out of ten used oil, natural gas, or electricity, thus removing the labour from heating. In all but the poorest or most remote rural areas, piped running water, mechanical refrigeration, and flush toilets had become effectively universal.[72] Already new time-savers were appearing. Automatic clothes-washers and -dryers became available by the end of the 1950s and were, within a few years, a common aspect of middle-class life. Even dishwashers, though far from common, were increasingly seen in homes by the early 1960s.[73]

This revolution marked, not only the adoption of new technologies, but the broadening of a standardized North American middle-class lifestyle. The years of prosperity and nearly full employment, as well as determination on the part of baby-boomers' parents, meant that a higher percentage of boomers lived in houses than any previous generation in Canada – some 75 per cent by 1966.[74] They also tended to buy their houses earlier and to upgrade house size, appliances, and automobiles through a continuous twenty-year period. The modern house with indoor plumbing and central heating, the car, the fridge and stove acquired by the parents of the baby boom made their adult years seem truly affluent, standing in sharp contrast to their earlier experiences.

Modernization helped bring about standardization. That was both the promise and the price of mass suburbia. In order to assess the degree of standardization, I looked at seven Canadian suburbs in some detail as they were in 1961, by which time the baby-boomers ranged from preschool to early teenage years.[75] These widely separated suburbs were all postwar communities that depended on commuting to a nearby urban centre. Except for Burnaby, where an older core of homes existed, more than 80 per cent of the households in the areas had been built after the war. Moreover, family salaries indicate that these were the houses of the broad Canadian middle class.

The similarities are striking. True, a few superficial regional variations remained. In the West, houses were covered with stucco or wood, and in Ontario were more likely brick. Likewise, on the West Coast, furnaces were not yet completely universal. On the prairies, garages were tucked away in back alleys. These exceptions aside, suburban households in Canada were pretty much the same. The average number of persons per household grouped closely around the national average of 3.9, varying from a low of 3.5 in Burnaby to 4.0 in Dartmouth.[76] This finding may be attributable, in part, to the fact that house size was so tightly circumscribed, varying between five and six rooms in all cases. There was also an 80 per cent chance the house was a bungalow.[77]

Suburbia was a land of modern conveniences, wherever you went. The already mentioned flush toilets, refrigerators, and central heating were effectively universal. Also nearly universal was the automobile, with at least eight out of ten, and in most cases nine out of ten, households possessing a car. Only in St Laurent, the one francophone suburb examined, where automobile-ownership was less and multiple housing more common, was there significant variation. Otherwise, the home of the Canadian suburbanite varied little across the country.

Then there was the decor. In 1952 *Chatelaine* ran a series of tips on home decoration. To make the point, it began with a 'typical' livingroom of the inter-war period. Pleasant and slightly cluttered, the room had a good deal of wood, a brick fireplace, and an overall air that could be described as art deco with a touch of Victorian. *Chatelaine*'s decorators then transformed the room to meet postwar taste. The walls were painted sunlight yellow, and the neutral tan rug was dyed a bright green. The brick fireplace was painted as well. The various vases and knick-knacks were removed and hidden on built-in shelves. The chairs and chesterfield were covered in chintz. The old had been made new, and though, as *Chatelaine* duly noted, this wasn't as good as having a brand-new house, it did demonstrate what a few changes could accomplish.[78] These changes violate many current canons of taste and, as do many other decorating schemes, reveal that in many ways the 1950s was a very different age aesthetically. The twenty years immediately after the war showed three predominant traits: an irreverence for tradition and classical design, a belief in the possibility of synthetic materials, and a tendency towards mass production of relatively cheap goods. The result was an age typified by a mixture of innovation and shoddy materials, newness and tackiness, modernity and rapid obsolescence.

Underlying these themes was a self-conscious modernism. Designers, tracing their own ideas back to the 1920s, had for some time been evolving new ideas that stressed functionalism (form must follow purpose), curved lines, and a rejection of excessive ornamentation and frills in favour of lightness. During the Second World War, this design tendency had merged with a growing emphasis on mass manufacturing and what, for lack of a better word, might be termed 'engineered design.' The use of synthetics and of manufacturing techniques as a part of the designing process became not only accepted but touted as part of modernist functionalism.[79] The moulded-plywood chair of American designer Arthur Eames is always cited as the perfect example of the new principles of modernism. It is light in scale, manufactured from new materials, and aesthetically pleasing. The fact that it wasn't comfortable was beside the point.

Modernism in furniture design and interior decoration suited the postwar age. As one 1956 book of design noted, both the new tract houses and their owners seemed well fitted for the advent of mass modernism. 'Even the poorest designed of these millions of new houses provides a good background for modern furnishing' and, more important, 'their owners, usually young married people, have an open minded awareness of all things modern, be it motor car, refrigerator or day bed. They are interested in the future and mold their living patterns in that direction.' Also, manufactured modern design was easily tailored, as the book admitted, 'to a budget minded market.'[80]

The last point is perhaps the most important. Yes, small houses and light, even spindly, furniture went together. Yes, the population wanted new things, but the modernist designs that prevailed after the Second World War were particularly adaptable, as the design book put it, to a 'budget market.' Mass-production items, using relatively cheap materials, enabled the young family on a limited budget to have the latest in fashion cheaply. This notion of a mass market had been part of the original conception of the Bauhaus school some thirty years before. What Bauhaus hadn't anticipated perhaps was that, along the way, much of the art was lost in crude replication or bad manufacturing. That didn't seem to matter to the consumer, for whom furniture and decor weren't art but possessions, and like cars, became something to replace every few years.

Design possibilities were limited by the size and nature of the house. The floor plans the owners had to work with were fairly standard. An average house size of 1,000–1,200 square feet did not allow for grand entrance halls or multiple rooms in which to display one's taste. Instead the watchword of the age, for floor plan as well as for interior decoration, was, once again, 'functionalism.'[81] Interior finishes and decor were dictated by the presence of children as well as by modernist sensibilities. In a small house, the children ruled. It was practically impossible to maintain distinct 'formal' living areas that were off-limits to the kids. Besides, in this child-centred age, imprecations to keep off the furniture or out of the living-room carried only so much weight. Easy-to-clean surfaces became the alternative. As early as 1946, for example, *Chatelaine* presented a recommended house design in which the central feature was a 'big room' (that is, combination living- and dining-room) which had tile floors and plywood walls, and which, as the magazine said, 'you could clean with a hose if you had to.'[82]

Houses were being made easier to clean as well as cheaper to build through new technologies. This was the age of brand names – Arborite, Formica, Congoleum, Marboleum, and a dozen others. There was 'Congowall' to replace old-fashioned (and more expensive) ceramic tile on bathroom walls, and vinyl sofas that carried the notion of modern technology over to furniture. All were 'miracle' synthetic products that promised the cachet of the modern, and the practicality of easy maintenance and durability. Advertisers also tried to convince consumers that these were not cold, sterile products but exciting vibrant ones that deserved to overrun the entire house. 'Not just in the kitchen,' intoned one linoleum ad, 'though there of course too – but in the dining room, the hall, the master bedroom, the children's bedrooms, the bathrooms.' After all, it concluded, 'you can build with linoleum for no more than you would pay for hardwood.'[83] There was even stick-on modernity. A postwar ad promised 'breathless excitement as you work out your own decorating ideas with Decal transfers.'[84]

Furniture design was equally self-conscious and modern. Modern easy-to-clean synthetics, butterfly chairs, reclining chairs with built-in footstools, and, with the appearance of television by the middle of the decade, stacking TV trays provide but a few examples of modernism in furniture design. Rooms tended to be sparsely furnished and, as mentioned, relatively devoid of knick-knacks. In the average house paintings were almost hidden in frames designed to match the coffee table, and the art ranged from innocuous to bad. All of this was probably both a reaction against earlier styles and a practical response to the havoc caused by small children.[85]

Functionalism and modernism nevertheless still allowed for clutter, although postwar suburbanites wouldn't have called it that. They decried clutter as a remnant of the older, fussier decor of their parents and grandparents. Idealized home settings always showed living-rooms with an occasional vase, and an unprepossessing painting was all that one might expect in terms of formal 'art.' The clutter was a different kind. In an age when everyone seemed to smoke, ashtrays were an obligatory part of house decor. The designs were often extreme, occasionally outrageous, and they seemed to occupy every level surface. There was also the clutter of consumerism. In the kitchen ever more appliances appeared as the decade went on. Pop-up toasters, electric kettles, electric frying-pans, electric waffle-makers, and 'Mixmasters' were increasingly common. There were even electric swizzle sticks. There were also, of course, an increasing number of 'hi-fi sets' and televisions. Clutter had moved from art to technology – another manifestation of the sensibilities of the age.

Nowhere did the emphasis on modernity show more than in the favourite colours of the era. Earth tones were out, and brightness in. Decorator hints with titles like 'Don't Be a Color Coward,' 'Give Your House a Splash of Colour,' and 'The Colourful House' announced to the style-conscious the need to be imaginative, or perhaps outrageous in colour schemes.[86] This was the age of pink, aquamarine, and turquoise. Green kitchen cupboards, dark red counter tops, and a black-and-white tiled floor were perfectly acceptable. For the living-room, home decorators could suggest watermelon-pink chairs, Chinese-red shelves, and a sun-yellow lamp. By the early 1950s the lady of the house could 'feminize' her refrigerator by choosing differently coloured door handles. Within a couple of years, coloured handles were no longer sufficient. One refrigerator company suggested a 'decorator fridge,' made by covering your refrigerator in the fabric of your choice. Finally, by the middle of the decade, the logic reached its natural conclusion with the introduction of coloured kitchen appliances, first seen, appropriately for the age, in bright yellow.[87] A paint ad, perhaps pushing the limits a bit, showed a house with one wall in bright green; another in yellow; and curtains of yellow, red, and green. An astonished visitor is depicted as saying 'It's beautiful. Tell us your paint-matching secret.'[88] When decorating expert Catherine Fraser gave a course on the subject, she suggested the kitchen should have grey-green walls and matching venetian blinds. The ceiling should be painted tartan, in dark green, grey, coral, and yellow. The kitchen stools would then round it off, in coral, white, and yellow.[89]

By the time the interior was all put together, it could be quite overwhelming. Picture, for example, a living-room with a linoleum floor in yellow and green. The walls are aquamarine and blue. There is a reclining chair and a sofa in a turquoise-and-brown pattern. The sofa is flanked by two undersized end-tables on which sit two oversized lamps with yellow–green shades. A small coral coffee-table, on which sits an incongruous pink seashell ashtray, completes the scene.[90]

Such combinations were distinctive to the age. Design in these years saw two simultaneous events. First, there was the already mentioned self-conscious modernism. This implied a fascination with the new and indifference to classical fashions or materials. It also meant that manufactured designs and synthetic materials were not only acceptable but desirable. Second, in what has aptly been termed the 'populuxe' syndrome, design was mass-produced in order to convert 'high style' into consumer goods. The originators of the design might sneer at the result, but for the public the differences were lost amid mass advertising. Populuxe was also an attitude, a way 'of referring to a moment when America found a way of turning out fantasy on an assembly line.'[91] In the 1960s the loud patterns of the baby boom were often interpreted as a rebellion of the suburban blandness in which they had grown up. Perhaps so, but this raises two questions: First, were their parents also rebelling, seeking a distinctive mark in an age of conformity? Second, is the fact that the baby-boomers' first memories were of the bright multicoloured hues of the 1950s related to their own multicoloured taste in adolescence?

ANY MUSING ON COLOUR AND SUBSEQUENT taste is as fanciful as some of the more extreme notions of child-theorists in the 1950s. The fanciful, however, does raise a serious point: What was the larger impact of suburban lifestyle on a baby-boomers? Their parents, after all, moved to the suburbs in adulthood, and the majority of baby-boomers were born there. Their upbringing was thus physically different from the urban or small-town upbringing of their parents, and different again from the likely rural experience of their grandparents.

The question is also a loaded one. The suburbs have had a controversial history. Magazine articles probed the psyche of suburban life, trying to decide what made suburbanites tick and what made their society different. At first their criticisms were countered by the powerful desire to have society house itself. By the mid-1950s, however, the housing crisis was over, and suburbia's image began to deteriorate. Two 1956 books – William Whyte's *Organization Man* and John Keats's *Crack in the Picture Window* – mark the turning-point. Thereafter, the intellectual's stereotype of suburbia became fixed around the notion that, in Lewis Mumford's colourful turn of phrase, the suburbs were 'an asylum for the preservation of illusion.'[92] The 1960s then brought the anti-suburban stereotype home to the adolescents who were just themselves rebelling against their own suburban background. Their own critique, based on close personal knowledge and adolescent rebellion, broadened and maintained the stereotype of conformity, blandness, and distasteful Babbittry.

The issue here, though, is more restricted than any overall judgment of suburban culture. What distinctive suburban features affected the outlook of the baby-boom children? First, there was the classless or, more accurately, the single-class environment. The physical homogeneity of the subdivisions has already been discussed. These were similar houses designed for similar incomes. As S.D. Clark put it in his 1966 study, 'it was the people able to afford an $11,000 to $20,000 house who were the creators of the Toronto [and, one might add, the Canadian] suburban community.'[93] Wildwood, in Winnipeg, for example, was a successful suburb but offered a choice of only five housing designs, all within a restricted price range.[94] Thus the children grew up in a world in which social class was very much circumscribed. You might live in an upscale suburb like Don Mills, or a more basic, even working-class one, but your friends were likely from families who could, within a narrow range, afford more or less what your family could afford. This created paradoxical attitudes towards wealth. First, those very much poorer, or richer, were remote. As a child you had little or no contact with them. On the other hand, as Whyte noted at the time, equality creates very fine distinctions. 'To live without class you must be socially skillful – consciously and continuously.'[95] It was very important to have the same toys as your friends, and that your parents conformed with the social canons of neighbourhood life, in dress, behaviour, and possessions.

The geographical link between money and class is striking but hardly new. The postwar suburban experience, however, goes far beyond that. Earlier suburbs were developed gradually. Westdale, in Hamilton, for example, was begun in the 1920s and not filled up until the end of the Second World War.[96] The creation of a community was thus gradual. As the suburb developed, new families, usually with young children, would join the older residents, with grown-up children. To at least a limited degree, therefore, such a subdivision would mirror the age profile of the population as a whole.

The subdivisions of the postwar years were different. With land purchase, municipal permits, construction, and sales taking place within a year or two, the whole community could be new. This had tremendous implications. Such suburbs were made up of adults of child-bearing age and their children, usually initially quite young. The old, and to a large extent even the adolescent, did not exist. When Regency Acres opened in Aurora, Ontario, in 1961, for example, 96 per cent of home buyers were between the ages of twenty and forty-four. Only one buyer was over the age of sixty. That was unusual, not because he was alone, but because he was there at all. In Edge Park, in Scarborough, and Beverly Acres, in Richmond Hill, not one first-time buyer was sixty or over.[97]

Of course, this profile changed over time as new buyers came in and as people aged. Nevertheless, it remained skewed. In every subdivision surveyed across Canada, the average age of most 'heads' of the household was between twenty-five and forty-four. In contrast, the presence of seniors, or even near-seniors, was minimal. Thus, in 1961, in Calgary SW, for example, 39 per cent of the population was between twenty-five and forty-four. Only 3 per cent were over fifty-five. In Ottawa West, the comparable figures were 25 and 5 per cent. Even in Scarborough, where some subdivisions were now more than a decade old, the figures were 35 and 9 per cent. The suburbs were a world without old people.[98]

Indeed, there were only two age groups, and they were sharply defined. The one group was the large percentage of parents of child-bearing age. The other, overwhelming even the numbers of home-owners, were the children themselves. In every one of the subdivisions surveyed, children 0–14 years outnumbered the prime adult age group of those 25 to 44. More than one-third, and sometimes nearly half, of the suburban population was made up of children 14 or under in 1961! In every case but one, the 0–14 population was considerably larger than the adolescent and early-adult population category of 15–24.[99]

The baby-boom suburbanites thus lived in a very peculiar world. 'Here they are surrounded by others like themselves,' wrote William Whyte of their parents in 1956. 'Too young to have failed ... No crazy drunkards, no embittered spinster, there is rarely even death in the new surburbia – and though there are those whose hopes are already blighted, it is without the terrible finality that one can see elsewhere.'[100] It was a world restricted by class and income, and that usually meant by ethnicity as well. Perhaps even more important, the continuity of generations was broken. There were no old people, and even the adolescents, no doubt admired and perhaps a little feared, were actually small in numbers compared with the two great suburban generations – parents and children. From the beginning, the baby-boom generation lived in a world where generational distinctiveness was a part of daily life.

The sense of generation was reinforced by family structure. The extended family in which grandparents, aunts and uncles, cousins, and others were part of daily life had been in decline in Western industrial society for some time. The suburbs accentuated this situation. This was not the family neighbourhood, but a new community in which there were no ancestral roots or close relatives outside the immediate family. 'What emerged here,' concluded Clark, was not the 'solitary individual' but the 'solitary family.' Sidonie Gruenberg complained that 'the child sees no elderly people, no teen-agers.'[101] Old people, such as grandparents, always lived someplace else. In central Canada and British Columbia, that place was possibly an established urban area, whether city or town. In the West and the Maritimes, it was more likely the farm or a small town. Wherever it was, however, it wasn't the suburbs. Special occasions like Christmas, weddings, and funerals brought the extended family together, but day-to-day life comprised parents and children in the nuclear family, far removed from the neighbourhoods of other relatives.

Many have argued that the social circle was, indeed, not even as large as the nuclear family. Commuting times, it has been argued, removed the father from much of the family's daily life.[102] There is some truth in this, for until the modern 'technoburb' evolved, most fathers did work 'downtown.' The suburbs in the daytime were populated only by women and children. Statistical correctness notwithstanding, it is dangerous to jump to quick assumptions about what this means. Fathers had been going off to work as long as there had been offices and factories. Recent work has also indicated that the lives of mothers were not quite so straightforward as has been thought.[103] Moreover, in the case of both parents, the strong domestic ideal of the age, not to mention its particular child-centredness, imposed familial demands.

What is most important is that the baby-boomers lived in a world of children. I mean this not just in the sense that children have their own perspective on the world, but in the sense that the social environment was geared to them.[104] The experience of their parents had reinforced domestic ideals, and social workers and child-experts warned that children should not be stifled or hampered in their growth lest dire consequences ensue. Their parents had moved to the suburbs in large part for the sake of the kids. There, as the baby-boomers moved from the toddler years to childhood, they discovered a vast peer group. The absence of generational continuity only sharpened the sense of this child-centred universe.

It was in this childhood world of the 1950s that the baby boom would begin the process of learning and socializing. Given the prevalence of psychological theory, this was a crucial step in the minds of experts and parents. Mistakes could have disastrous consequences. Given the numbers of baby-boomers, the direction such socialization (by both peers and adults) took was bound to have a tremendous impact on society. It happened step-by-step, though. Children grew beyond the toddler years, made friendships, and discovered the neighbourhood. It is time, therefore, to move beyond the household and the infant, to the world of play and learning.

4

Consuming Leisure: Play in an Era of Affluence, 1950–1965

How are you tackling the serious business of play? For it is a serious business – nothing could be more mistaken than the notion that there is anything trivial in a child's preoccupation with its toys. That's why modern science has applied itself so seriously to the formulation of a constructive, intelligent, and progressive program of play.

Maclean's, 1953[1]

Children have always played. None the less, the leisure world of the baby-boom generation is unique. The prevailing image of domesticity and of the nuclear family included a world in which children and parents are not just kin but companions and playmates. The opportunities for play increased in the child-centred suburbs, where so many baby-boomers lived. The variety of playthings available was unprecedented as manufacturers produced vast ranges of goods to tempt the children of the postwar era. Television provided a brand-new form of entertainment which quickly became a part of the family routine. The size of the generation also made the world of leisure in the baby-boom era distinct. The world of play, theoretically anchored in family domesticity, actually had a different impact: The peer group was so large and so economically powerful that even in childhood it competed with the family's hold upon the values and sensibilities of the child.

PLAY WAS GIVEN CONSIDERABLE PROMINENCE by child-theorists during the 1950s and 1960s. This was part of a longer-term trend, closely related to overall changes in child-rearing theory. As children had come to be seen as distinct beings around the end of the nineteenth century, so, too, had children's activities come to be seen as distinct. Once that premise was accepted, adults asserted two beliefs about childhood play. First, they accepted that the leisure world of children would be different from theirs and was a part of growing up. In other words, children were special. At the same time they feared that children were 'morally fragile ... always on the verge of yielding to temptation.' Children, in other words, lacked judgment. The leisure activity of children thus had to be directed by adults and aimed at such constructive activities as religious study, crafts, or educational pursuits.[2]

In the twentieth century the idea that children were special but lacked judgment remained. However, the definition of appropriate leisure activity changed considerably. The educational theories of John Dewey and others emphasized the way in which play was an integral part of learning, both about the world and about social relationships. By the 1950s experts dictated that play was not only natural in a child, but central to growth and learning. The idea that 'play is child's work' was a theme that echoed through works on educational theory, family manuals, and magazine articles.[3]

The 'serious business of play' thus became a central part of postwar family duties. The dream of domesticity led directly to the promise of, and commitment to, happy hours of leisure together. This was, after all, the primary duty of the family now that technology had reduced household chores. As one book put it, recreation was now a more important family function than the daily wash.[4] Moreover, if play was the child's basic means of learning, the family's leisure time became, not just companionable, but vital to the nurturing of the children. The well-adjusted family would provide their child with the means to play lest psychological adjustment be stunted. To underline the point, Dr W. Bauer recounted in *Maclean's* the story of little Charlie, who was building wooden models. His father, however, was indifferent. 'It isn't long after that, that Charlie gets caught with a group of small boys – the newspaper calls it a gang – which has been stealing from the dime store.'[5]

Family structure was also increasingly geared to providing for the leisure of the children. The anti-authoritarian views of family life and the accentuation of the sexual division of labour meant that children could expect a full-time camp counsellor, leisure coordinator, and chauffeur in Mother. Father was present only in the evening and on weekends, but he was much softened when compared with the foreboding figure of Victorian times. Fathers too were supposed to be pals, to take an active part in the world of children and leisure.[6] Thousands of part-time hockey and baseball coaches around the nation testified to the power of this social role.

Finally, there was good health, without which play and leisure would have been impossible. The postwar generation was, on average, freer from malnourishment and better clothed than any previous generation in history. They were also relatively safe from serious childhood disease. One by one, through the first half of the twentieth century, diseases like diphtheria, measles, and typhoid had been eradicated or made less life-threatening. Tuberculosis remained a stubborn problem, especially in Native and remote communities, and whooping cough remained a danger for the very young. Overall, however, the mortality rate for children between age one and fourteen was cut in half between the late 1920s and the late 1940s. By 1950 fewer than one child in a thousand died between the ages of five and fourteen.[7]

At mid-century there was still one serious child-killing disease. Poliomyelitis, or 'polio' as it was commonly known, was much feared, and with good reason.[8] Unlike such infant-killers as whooping cough, polio had two frightening aspects. First, it was not primarily an infant's disease. Children of five, seven, or even twelve were as susceptible to its ravages as were infants. Second, even if not fatal it could have devastating and permanent effects. Polio was a virus that attacked the spinal system, causing uneven growth and twisting which often crippled the victim.[9] Further, nobody was sure what caused it, and thus parents were at a loss as to how to protect their children against it. As late as 1952 one doctor theorized that polio was caused by sunlight and recommended parents keep their children out of the summer light. However, it was not sunshine but human contact that spread polio. The disease was extremely contagious, and epidemics recurred frequently. In 1950, for example, there were only 41 deaths from polio in all of the country. In 1952, and again in 1953, however, the virus raged, especially on the prairies. Some 792 people died over those two years, primarily between the ages of five and nineteen.[10] Newspaper headlines talked gloomily of panic among parents. Swimming pools were closed, and schools delayed opening in an attempt to limit the disease's spread.[11] The oldest of baby-boomers most likely had a friend or acquaintance who was affected by the epidemic.

The 1952–3 epidemic was the last one. In the United States considerable effort had been directed against polio from the beginning of the

March of Dimes crusade in the late 1930s. The postwar epidemics increased funding for research and hastened results. In the spring of 1953, Doctor Jonas Salk announced that he had discovered a vaccine, and that initial testing had been successful. Unlike the United States, where controversy slowed down mass vaccination, Canada moved quickly. Some 860,000 Canadian children were vaccinated in that year.[12] By the later 1950s vaccination of Canadian children was carried on through the school system. This had a rapid impact, and polio fatalities dropped to thirty-six by 1955, and twenty-eight by 1958. Occasionally over the next few years, the figures went up, but polio had ceased to be a childhood disease and was now more likely to kill the uninoculated adult than the child. By 1965 the great killer, though not eradicated, had become so rare that not one child died from poliomyelitis.[13]

Affluence, a healthy population, and a social ethic which encouraged family togetherness and children's play mean that the baby-boomers were more favoured in their leisure time than any preceding generation in history. Yet, for all this, the image of family and play in these years is mixed. Popular imagery at the time and since emphasized a world of fun-loving domesticity. Television, popular fiction, and magazine articles depicted a society in which children had great fun within loving and caring families. Yet the real theme of the 1950s and early 1960s may be the degree to which non-family forces shaped the childhood world. The marketplace affected children as never before. Organized extra-family activities – from sports to Guides – enrolled more children than in any previous generation, and the vast peer group provided an alternative point of reference that became increasingly important as the children grew older.

THE MOST IMPORTANT NEW INSTRUMENT of leisure was undoubtedly the television set. In the 1950s, when television arrived, it was one of the most significant technological innovations of the twentieth century. Only the automobile clearly outranked it, and television became pervasive much faster. Most important, television transformed leisure habits. It brought families together but did so in a peculiar way: Increasing amounts of family time were spent in a semi-darkened room staring at flickering black-and-white images on a screen. If television brought the family members together, it also ensured they didn't talk too much. Television transformed an individual's relationship both to the immediate-family circle and to the outside world.

Television was first commercialized in the United States. It was a logical extension of radio, for the transmission of pictures by wave was similar to the transmission of sound, at least in principle. By 1925 experimental pictures actually had been transmitted, both in Britain and in the United States, and by the later 1920s business confidently predicted that television was just around the corner. The Depression and a series of patent and legal battles delayed things somewhat, but by the time of the New York World's Fair in 1939, RCA had a working, if limited, system of transmission and reception. By the Second World War, there were twenty-three limited-range television stations broadcasting in the United States. Even though most Americans had yet to see a television, the technology was available, and RCA and CBS had moved beyond the experimental stage in broadcasting.[14]

By war's end all the circumstances were finally right for television. 'Electronic assembly lines, freed from production of electronic war materiel, were ready to turn out picture tubes and television sets. Consumers, long confronted by wartime shortages and rationing, had accumulated savings and were ready to buy. Manufacturers of many kinds, ready to switch from war materials back to consumer goods, were eager to advertise.'[15] As early as 1948 there were about 100 television stations in the United States. In 1953 alone more than 7 million television sets were sold. By the very early 1950s, then, television was a mass-entertainment medium south of the border.

In contrast, television came relatively late to Canada.[16] While Americans were being swept up in the television craze, Canadians speculated about what television meant, argued about how it should be controlled, and continued to listen to their radios.[17] In the United States television began as a commercial medium, pure and simple. In Canada issues of nationalism, cultural control, and the position of the government radio network, the Canadian Broadcasting Corporation (CBC), occupied considerable time and ink.[18] In 1951 there were still no Canadian television stations, and only a handful of Canadians close to the border owned television sets. Finally, in fall 1952, the first Canadian television stations arrived, when CBC outlets opened in Montreal and Toronto. The next two years brought CBC television to Halifax, Ottawa, Winnipeg, and Vancouver, while private stations began to appear in smaller centres.[19] By 1960 there were some fifty-nine television stations in Canada capable of reaching more than 90 per cent of the population.[20] In the meantime television was becoming more affordable. In 1952 the average television set cost over $400, or almost 20 per cent of an average annual income. As is the case for most new technologies, though, prices soon fell. By 1956 the aspiring family in Vancouver, for example, could buy a Marconi TV with 21-inch screen and swivel base for $189.95. A basic Sylvania TV, with, presumably, no swivel base, could be purchased for under $170.[21]

And people bought. The decentralized medium of television perfectly matched the growing suburban patterns of Canadians. Its ability to reach into the home also served the needs of families with young children. Province by province, television fever caught hold. In southern Ontario and southwestern Quebec, the early creation of stations and, even more important, access to fuzzy signals from Buffalo or Rochester, made for some choice at an early date. Three, four, or even five channels were available to viewers, depending on the state of their antenna, the weather, and their location. This, as well as the relative affluence of the region, meant that as early as 1955 the majority of Ontario households had television sets. In contrast, the prairies were more isolated from American signals, and the CBC expanded channels to that region more slowly. It was towards the end of the decade before most people in all three Prairie provinces became television owners.[22] Even then most were utterly dependent on the CBC. Only as private stations developed, and, ultimately, with the arrival of cable technology, would coverage even out across the country. Despite the unevenness the overall pace of adoption was remarkable. Within a decade of the first Canadian signal, more Canadians owned televisions than telephones.[23]

From the beginning, writers, psychologists, and others speculated on the impact of television upon children.[24] Forty years of discussion since has created considerable theory and controversy but has not resolved the debate. Throughout the years optimists have seen the television as a liberating experience, exposing people to the wider world, scattering parochialism. True, it was not all it could be, but it was still a revolutionary force for expanding knowledge. The pessimists concluded early on that passive entertainment and the rise of commercialism would reshape the public into mindless consumers. Canadian academic Marshall McLuhan took a different tack and made himself an international star by arguing that the medium rather than the message was what really mattered, and that children of the baby boom and after would perceive reality differently because they were the children of the television age. If so, one of the things the baby-boomers seem to perceive differently is McLuhan, for lately his theories have fallen into disfavour.[25]

Amid all the theory and counter-theory, it is best to start with the obvious. The arrival of television was an event. Across the nation one of the most common childhood memories for older baby-boomers is the arrival of the first television set. The installation of the antenna and the adjustment of the still sensitive technology could take the TV technician (himself likely new to the technology) what seemed an endlessly long time. Finally the set would be hooked up, and children and parents could settle in to watch their favourite programs. Television shows would now become landmarks of one's life. Adults and older children grew up with such long-running shows as *Gunsmoke* (1955–75), *Bonanza* (1959–73) and *Ed Sullivan* (1948–71). Young children met the outside world through *The Friendly Giant* or *Howdy Doody.*[26]

Television was also a regulator of time, especially in an era of series loyalty and few channels. People often timed their lives around shows. Sunday-evening church services found that they could not compete with *Ed Sullivan* and gradually disappeared.[27] Everybody knew that *Hockey Night in Canada* was Saturday. The timing was equally specific for children. Unless you lived close to the American border, there were no morning cartoons; in the early years there was no morning television at all in Canada.[28] Instead prime time for children came in the late afternoon and into the early evening. The adult's afternoon matinee would shut off at 4:00 P.M. and Mother would presumably head off to make dinner while the children rushed home from school to watch as much television as they could. Tuesday might bring *Patti Page Presents, Science All Around Us,* and *Sky King,* while Friday would bring *Howdy Doody, Mighty Mouse,* and *Leave It to Beaver.*[29] Above all there was *Walt Disney.* It, not *Ed Sullivan,* is the longest-running show in the history of television and it, not *Ed Sullivan,* was the weekend highlight of television for children (and probably many adults).

A detailed assessment of the content of shows would take a volume of its own. Certain themes do stand out, however. First, as a mass medium, television usually mirrors middle-class social values. The 1950s were a conservative age, and it is not surprising that most shows in these early years celebrated the status quo. Children's shows were especially cautious lest parents object to incorrect or antisocial values being transmitted to their children. Certainly, the radicalism of the 1960s was not prefigured in the television programs of the 1950s. Ethnically this was a white, Anglo-Saxon medium. Indians were bad guys, though there could be good Indians as well. On American shows the favourite ethnic character was probably Spanish. On Canadian shows French Canadians were sometimes heroes, as in the cheaply made *Radisson and Groseilliers.* Just as often they were the evil villains, as, for example, on *Sergeant Preston of the Yukon.* As for stars, the stretch of ethnic diversity seemed to be reached with the thoroughly Americanized Annette Funicello of *The Mickey Mouse Club.*

Absence of ethnic diversity was matched by absence of moral complexity. The good guys were always good and always triumphed. Their personality conflicts were well resolved. One never saw angst beneath the mask of the Lone Ranger or on the face of Robin Hood. This was the era of the Cold War, and Canadian television extended the black-and-white world of good and bad to lessons on 'our way of life.' True, Canadian television was more muted in its message than that south of the border, where the Cold War fostered such paranoid programs as *I Led Three Lives* (1953–6), the story of an FBI agent who risked all sorts of things by posing as a Communist. Many of the programs for children were, however, imports from the United States, and, besides, the Canadian shows were essentially similar. From *Captain Video* in the early 1950s, through *Sergeant Preston of the Yukon* and *Superman* (1951–7), to *Rin Tin Tin* (1954–9), the messages were clear: Good and evil were both straightforward and unambiguous.

Nowhere was the moral code of television clearer than in its promulgation of the postwar myth of the family. Some of the most famous and successful shows of the first decade of Canadian television were what have accurately been termed 'comedies of reassurance.'[30] 'Typical' families were portrayed conducting their day-to-day activities, and in their actions and dialogue they reinforced the ideals of postwar American life. The most famous of all was the Anderson family of *Father Knows Best.* The show ran from 1954 to 1962, and the activities of the wise and kind parents, as well as Princess, Bud, and Kitten – the three children – came to symbolize the 1950s ideal of the family. Other shows as well, including *Leave It to Beaver* (1957–63), *My Three Sons* (1960–72), *The Donna Reed Show* (1958–66), and the longest-running of them all, *Ozzie and Harriet* (1952–64), had an essential role in shaping middle-class expectations as to what families should be.

The image of the family presented by TV was unambiguous. It was not poor, of course, or ethnic.[31] It was Protestant, but not ostentatiously so. It was middle of the road, middle class, and tolerant. Only in its perfection was it extreme. Life, according to this ideal, was not confined within the family but was centred there. Children were not perfect, but they were always learning and improving. Fathers were understanding, and mothers were saints, if fairly modern ones. Most of all the family was fun. The very fact that comedy was the vehicle emphasized the moral that life in any healthy, wholesome democratic family was both constructive and enjoyable. As has been aptly noted, 'the essential problem of family life' in these shows 'was not how to make ends meet but how to raise children effectively.'[32] In that sense, however idealized, the families of the 1950s did reflect the preoccupation of the age.

The list of shows and the Cold War themes point to another impact of television: Like radio before it, and mass magazines before that, television extended the cultural influence of the United States. Little children might watch the Canadian *Friendly Giant* or the Canadianized version of *Howdy Doody,* but they also watched *Roy Rogers, Lassie,* and *Wyatt Earp.* Towering above them all were the Disney productions. Weekdays brought *The Mickey Mouse Club,* and the weekends brought *Walt Disney.*[33]

The CBC did make efforts to counter the American juggernaut, but they were hampered by inadequate funds and technical backwardness. Stories abounded of cardboard sets that fell over, of seventeenth-century characters wearing wrist-watches, and of electric transmission lines showing up in the background of adventure programs about early explorers. Even if the stories aren't true, it doesn't matter – Canadian production facilities were far too limited to fill the hours of programming needed. From the beginning, television – even the CBC – was a continental medium. Canadian children of the 1950s grew up more exposed to American culture than were any previous generation. As they grew older, this experience would have a profound impact upon their perspective on Canadian nationalism and American society.

Television also had an impact as a medium, quite aside from the content of the programs. Even if the esoteric theories of McLuhan or Jacques Ellul seem problematic, there is no doubt that television was a new kind of entertainment. It was a home activity that was, at the same time, a communal one. This meant that once television was available across the nation – by 1960 – it was a powerful force for a generational sense of identity. In thousands of homes across the nation, children watched more or less the same shows and developed the same heroes. The games they played also depended on TV heroes and TV products. They also watched the same ads and learned at an early age how to consume in the great new marketplace they had created. In a way that radio never could, television gave a generation a common perspective on the world and their place in it.

TELEVISION WAS A COMMERCIAL MEDIUM, and children's programming, just like that for adults, depended on sponsors. The real message of television for the 1950s may, therefore, not be the content of the programs but the commercials. The very fact that adult sponsors saw children as important consumers is revealing of the fact that, even as children, the baby-boomers exerted their power. Moreover, from an early age, the ability to consume in a manner approved by one's peer group became a central part of baby-boom existence. Consumption of common products, in turn, shaped the childhood world of leisure and reinforced peer identity.

Television was not the only force shaping childhood consumption, of course. Parents who had grown up in the hard times of the 1930s and the spartan times of the Second World War might reproach their children for being spoiled by an overabundance of possessions, but it was the lack of gratitude their children exhibited that parents lamented. For parents were the ones who provided the money and who set the tone. They were determined that their children should have the things and comforts they had not known. Doctor Spock and the others assured them that such indulgence, so long as it was for the right reasons, would not spoil the child. On the contrary, the child knew best. 'When children show a universal craving for something, whether the comics or candy or jazz, we've got to assume it has a positive, constructive value for them.'[34] Over the next years children would exhibit numerous mass cravings and would, within their parents' means, generally have those cravings met.

On the other side of the equation was the manufacturer, for whom a rising standard of living, concerned and perhaps indulgent parents, and vast numbers of children created unprecedented opportunities. As ever larger numbers of babies were born in the late 1940s, businesses took notice. Long before the children themselves had any say in the matter, retailers were emphasizing to parents the necessity of buying their particular product. Producers of baby foods and patent medicines were the first to respond. Castoria, a foul-tasting laxative, was omnipresent in the magazines of the day. Specialty infants foods expanded in range and variety and their products assured parents that they were vital to a child's well-being. Typical was a Heinz ad that depicted a friendly doctor checking a smiling and obviously healthy baby. The title, 'Hands Your Baby Can Count On,' led into a text that praised the overworked doctor who was so busy these days with babies, and then concluded that 'Heinz is another ... you can count on.' Strained vegetables and orange-custard dessert would, apparently, ensure your child a happy, healthy future.[35]

Infant food may seem a digression from the world of leisure, but the point is that, from the beginning, the vast numbers of babies born after the war were big business. By the late 1940s more than 30 million pounds of infant foods were being sold in Canada. A decade later that figure would increase to more than 70 million pounds.[36] The same possibility of profit applied across the range of infant and child goods. From the 'Fur-Trimmed Chinchilla Bag' at $4.98 to the 'snap-leg gabardine overalls' for $1.89, or the omnipresent hooded snowsuits with names like 'Little Lamb', 'Starbright,' or 'Skating Star,' parents were encouraged to buy 'for the Well-Being of a Precious Little Baby.'[37]

By the 1950s advertisers and retailers were fully aware of the new importance of the children's market. As one business publication concluded, 'young Canada knows what it wants. It's a wise and successful adult who can pick the trends.'[38] Store catalogues devoted more space to children. Special Christmas catalogues were put out, and pre-Christmas toy inserts began to appear in magazines like *Maclean's*. Children could feed their imaginations on hopes that Santa would bring a 'Man Sized' Bronco revolver or a Patsy Palitoy doll that 'weeps real tears – blows bubbles – wets her nappie.' The doll carriages seemed to hint at the populuxe style as they promised 'plenty of chrome.'[39]

This tremendous economic power, exhibited by parents on behalf of their infant offspring, foreshadowed an impending revolution in the marketplace. From the time of the Industrial Revolution, but especially from the turn of the twentieth century, mass advertising and increasingly effective business techniques extended the world of commerce and consumption ever more completely to all corners of society. Indeed, as we have seen, one of the great concerns was that the complete dependence on outside goods eliminated many of the family's traditional purposes.

Of course, the penetration of the marketplace occurred unevenly. The urban and the affluent organized their lives around consumption earlier than did the rural and the poor. Adults, as the controllers of the funds, were more readily targeted by retailers and advertisers than were youth or children. As the twentieth century went along, however, the penetration of market forces broadened and deepened. Mail-order catalogues helped overcome the problems of isolation and lack of variety in small towns or rural society. Increasing affluence (the 1930s excepted) allowed a broader range of social groups to consume actively, and thus be drawn into the commercial networks. Improved marketing and distribution allowed national and international firms to overwhelm local ones and thereby encouraged the standardization of goods.

Typical of the changing world of consumption was the creation of a specialized market aimed at adolescents and young adults in the 1920s. For the first time in history, there was a distinctive set of national fads and fashions aimed exclusively at youth. Yellow rain slickers, open galoshes ('flappers'), multicoloured bandanas, and oxford stockings swept across the style-conscious elements of North America through the decade.[40] Retailers, for their part, both promoted fads and sought to catch up with the ever-fickle tastes of youth. Two elements were crucial to the emergence of this national and rapidly moving youth market. The first was the ability of business and the media to turn a local craze into a national marketing event. 'Fads depended on the same conditions – rapid communications, cheap mass-production techniques, large scale distribution of goods, and national advertising – that also created the natural phenomenon of youth.'[41] Such fads also depended on the insecurity of youth and the resultant desire to emulate their peer group.

The famous fads and fashions of the 1920s did not really touch children. There were no toy fads, and the children's market was not susceptible to rapid change. Their access to funds was too conditional and subject to parental guidance. The retailers and the media did not target them as potential converts to the latest national fads or crazes. Toys were important, of course, but the volatility of the fad, and the nationwide drive to emulation that created it, were missing.

This situation changed with the baby boom. The great youth fads of the 1920s were paralleled by the great childhood enthusiasms of the 1950s and early 1960s. Television played a crucial role, permitting children instant awareness of whatever fads or trends were emerging. It also reinforced identification with the peer group at the expense of parents. The media now aimed advertising at the child, showing children playing happily with the product. Possessing the latest fad distinguished you as a member of the neighbourhood and the national world of childhood trendiness, and separated you, not just from parents, but from those older or younger children who were not participating in the current craze. Thus the marketplace ever more finely divided the consumer base, and the young customer responded with enthusiasm and a sense of being special.

Three great fads, spread evenly through the decade, illustrate the great power of the baby-boomer as childhood consumer. The first is the Davy Crockett craze of 1955. The second is the rapid rise and equally rapid decline of the Hula Hoop in 1958. The third is the 1959 creation and instant triumph of the most successful doll in all history – Barbie. All of them caught on quickly through media attention and mass advertising, found their way into millions of homes, and were toys aimed at a specific age. The demand for all but Barbie faded almost as quickly as it had arisen. Both the volatility of the demand and the speed with which these fads developed marked a new era in toy manufacturing.

The arrival of the new era is symbolized by the Davy Crockett mania. It was sparked by a combination of the powerful entertainment body – Disney Studios – and the newly important medium of television. Disney Studios had, in 1954, decided to enter the television field with its program *Disneyland*.[42] The show was a success, but from the beginning the Disney people understood that new productions would have to supplement old cartoons. As a result the studio produced a series of programs on American folk heroes. The first of these was a three-part study of semi-legendary frontiersman Davy Crockett. On 5 December 1954, 'Davy Crockett, Indian Fighter' was aired, to be followed over the next weeks by 'Davy Crockett Goes to Congress' and 'Davy Crockett at the Alamo.' Simultaneously a theme song, 'The Ballad of Davy Crockett,' was released, sung by the star of the series, Fess Parker.[43]

The mythologized Davy Crockett had tremendous appeal for children. He was tough (he could grin a bear down), brave, and adventurous. The response was immediate. Crockett was so popular that Disney Studios, with some misgivings, packaged the three-part television series as one and released it as a movie entitled *Davy Crockett, King of the Wild Frontier*. This retread of the television show played in theatres across Canada and the United States. Insatiable fans lined up to see Davy one more time, and the movie grossed $25 million. The Billboard music chart for 1955 had no fewer than three versions of 'The Ballad of Davy Crockett' in its overall Top 40 for the year.[44] Most dramatic perhaps were the merchandising by-products of the craze.

Plastic flintlock rifles, posters, and even the unlikely Davy Crockett snow-sled appeared in stores and homes throughout North America over the next few months. Above all there was the coonskin cap. More than 10 million Davy Crockett hats made their way into children's hands, and the fad was so powerful that the price of raccoon skins in the United States increased tenfold.

The border proved no barrier, in spite of complaints that children should have Canadian heroes. The Crockett series, first broadcast over the winter of 1954–55, and rebroadcast the next year, coincided with television's arrival in Canada's major urban centres.[45] The awe for the new medium enhanced the impact of the series. Thus, Disney and television succeeded together, and the first great hero of the Canadian baby boom was an American, born in a log cabin in Tennessee and killed at the Alamo. By July 1955 more than 300,000 records of 'The Ballad of Davy Crockett' had been sold in Canada, and more than 250,000 hats. As a business magazine commented, the demand created some interesting variations on raccoon skin. There were 'hats made of plastic and cardboard with nylon tails, hats printed on fabric, hats that shed fur at the slightest touch, hats made of old fur of dubious origin and uncertain sanitation – and hats made of every possible substitute from wool to rabbit to skunk fur.' The original raccoon hats, licensed by Disney, cost $2.98, but cheap substitutes could be had for as low as $0.29.[46] The Davy Crockett craze had taught manufacturers a lesson they would not forget: If you could entice the baby boom, the potential for profits was immense.

The Davy Crockett craze was created by a powerful movie studio. The Hula Hoop, on the other hand, was a true fad. It came from nowhere, caught on, made some people rich, and then faded away. The Hula Hoop was a simple round plastic tube that most children (but few adults) could keep spinning by moving their hips and, if inventive, their shoulders, legs, or even necks. It had first appeared in Australia, and by 1958 reached North America. Once again, television advertising was essential to the spread of this newest toy. Within a few months some 20 million Hula Hoops were manufactured for the North American market.[47] Stores had trouble keeping them in stock, and the Canadian plastics industry found its capacity stretched by the demand.[48] Before long it seemed as if every child on the street had one. Then the fad died, as it was bound to (after all, who needed multiple Hula Hoops), and the kids moved on to other interests.

The final great craze was the Barbie doll, born in 1959. Barbie, however, is different, for this doll was not a passing fad but an enduring toy that captured the imaginations of successive baby-boom girls and their post-boom successors. Aimed at the preteen market, Barbie; her boyfriend, Ken; and her assorted friends, gadgets, and trappings are perhaps the ultimate 1950s toy. Outrageous in configuration, flashy (and even trashy) in style, Barbie was 'the symbolic queen of populuxe.' Purchasing a Barbie was also a bit like joining a book club, for it committed you to indefinite ongoing expenditures. 'She had party dresses, and gowns for the prom, and a wedding ensemble, casual clothes, outdoor clothes and outfits for many occasions.'[49] There were also the ever-present boyfriend, Ken, and the assorted friends, depending on her fame for their own livelihood. It was lucrative to be associated with Barbie, after all: In the first thirty years, some 500 million Barbies and friends were sold, along with more than a billion sets of clothes.[50]

Barbie, Davy Crockett, and the Hula Hoop were only the most dramatic among dozens of lesser trends and fads. Before Davy Crockett there had been Hopalong Cassidy holster sets and Roy Rogers cowboy hats. Zorro masks and plastic swords would follow. Barbie was preceded by Chatty Cathy dolls and assorted brand-name 'Brides Dolls.' Later, baby-boomers could add G.I. Joe (1965) to the list. The specific toys aren't as important as the pattern. Producer and consumer had discovered each other. The largest generation ever born, with access to unprecedented amounts of cash and exposed to powerful new media techniques, became a tremendously lucrative market for business. Toys were just the most obvious goods that pandered to childhood tastes. One might equally refer to food – cereals like Sugar Frosted Flakes (29 per cent sugar) introduced in 1951 or Sugar Smacks (56 per cent sugar) introduced in 1953. There were dozens of television programs, of course, and new children's magazines like *Humpty Dumpty's* (founded 1952) joined the newly expanded circulation of long-standing ones such as *Jack and Jill*. What children wanted or could be made to want, they got. The years between Davy Crockett and G.I. Joe brought home to the postwar world just how powerful this vast young segment of society could be.

The vast marketplace of children's goods also accentuated the special nature of childhood in these years. A distinctive market pursued children from the time they were old enough to insist upon Sugar Pops until they were ready to enter the vast, and even more lucrative teenage market. A good part of the appeal of a Barbie or Davy Crockett hat was the sense of common participation in a peer-sanctioned act of consumption. Toys were thus more than sets of individual choices. They were membership in a society, a society of preschoolers, children, or preteens in which values and actions were approved or disapproved of directly by immediate friends and neighbours, and sanctioned indirectly by the mainstream of the vast market of North American youth. Owning such toys meant you belonged. In 1954 historian David Potter, observing the wealth of postwar American society, concluded that such abundance emphasized the 'separateness' of the American child. What was not fully clear at the time, of course, was that the separateness from adult society was to a large degree offset by a growing identification with the generation who grew up in such abundance.[51]

LEISURE ALSO TAKES ORGANIZED FORMS. These formal organizations are distinctive, with written rules, funding, and by-laws. When they involve children, they are usually parentally supported, through both finances and volunteer activities. Finally, as this parental support implies, formal activities for children often reflect adult goals. Indeed, such activities link the peer world of youth and the more structured world of parents. They transmit approved parental values in forms likely (or hopefully) acceptable to children. They link the private world of family and the public world of education through a series of intermediate voluntary activities. These links are so crucial that the success or failure of such organized activities provide important signposts concerning the preparations of one generation for the coming of age of the next.

Youth organizations in Canada can be traced back intellectually to Victorian notions of 'useful leisure.'[52] Idle time was a waste of human potential and a dangerous temptation. Such notions arose from many sources. Christian evangelism worried about human moral weakness. Social Darwinism emphasized the need for physical and moral effort, while urban society seemed threatening to physical and moral well-being.[53] The growth of an urban middle class, which seemed especially prone to such organizations, resulted in a flourishing of service clubs, religious auxiliaries, ritualistic secret societies, and political debating forums. There were Empire Clubs and Canadian Clubs, theosophy societies, and nativist organizations.

The Depression and war years weakened many of these bodies. Money was scarce, and voluntary activities suffered accordingly. The 1950s, however, brought a revival. Depending on locale, class, and ethnicity, the parents of the baby boom joined the Lions, the Rotary Club, the Knights of Columbus, the Kinsmen, the Imperial Order Daughters of the Empire (IODE), and local community groups. Part of this urge to join was undoubtedly an extension of the communitarian spirit brought about by the war. Certainly prosperity helped as well. Part of this middle-class organizational tendency, no doubt, derived from the desire to be seen as a respectable and upstanding member of one's profession, community, or ethnic group. These postwar years were, in popular parlance, after all, the time of the 'organization man,' an outlook characterized by 'belongingness as the ultimate end of the individual.'[54]

As it was with the parents, so it was with the children. A young family involved in adult organizations would naturally seek parallel activities for their children. Here was the opportunity to ensure that your children belonged, while learning new skills and values. Here was useful leisure to prepare the new generation for the world that they would inherit. Children's groups were myriad as well. Some, like the YMCA and YWCA, seemed less active or relevant than in previous generations.[55] Other church groups like the Canadian Girls in Training, of the United Church, or the Junior Auxiliary, of the Anglicans, flourished. So, too, did the Canadian Amateur Hockey Association and, for that matter, almost any amateur sport involving children. Whatever the organization, two themes stand out. First, the notions of betterment and socialization were present throughout. Second, the combination of prosperity and sheer numbers allowed individual organizations to expand to an unprecedented degree.

Of all the formal organizations, none so obviously represented the desire to pass traditional values on to children as the Scouting movement. Lord Baden-Powell, the movement's founder, was almost a caricature of the obsessions of the turn of the century. A soldier, adventurer, Imperialist, and outdoorsman, Baden-Powell saw character and toughness as the key to national strength. Only a rugged program that instilled outdoor skills and traditional values could, he felt, save future generations from decline. 'The same causes which brought about the downfall of the Roman Empire are working today in Great Britain,' he warned. The 'decline of good citizenship' opened the door to all sorts of chaos and strife in the near future.

In the meantime Canadian-born naturalist Ernest Thompson Seton had founded a nature-oriented youth group known as the Woodcraft Indians. Baden-Powell, who had been thinking along similar lines, took inspiration from the movement's book, *The Birch-Bark Roll of the Woodcraft Indians,* and founded the Boy Scouts in 1907. This was a movement that would teach the quite long list of attributes apparently needed to revive good citizenship: 'observation and deduction, chivalry, patriotism, self-sacrifice, personal hygiene, saving life, self-reliance etc. etc.'[56] Girl Guides, initially envisaged by him as just a branch of Scouts, emerged as a separate organization a couple of years later. Both stressed obedience to society, parents, and leaders in order to ensure that the supposedly dissipate youth learned discipline. The movement was avowedly religious, and its religious code, in turn, reinforced the traditional values of honesty, loyalty, and manliness for Scouts, and femininity for Guides.[57]

Little had changed by the 1950s. The Scout and Guide movement were perhaps the most respectable of all youth-oriented organizations. The governor general was the patron of the movement, and both federal and provincial governments provided encouragement and recognition. Indeed, many of the concerns of the turn of the century were revisited in the 1950s. From the Canadian Youth Commission forward, the society of the postwar years was especially concerned about the 'youth problem.' Juvenile delinquency, as we will see in chapter 6, was an obsession in the 1950s. Likewise, parents, though themselves thoroughly domesticated, feared that the soft urban or suburban life of television, automobiles, and central heating was spoiling the younger generation.[58] Scouts and Guides seemed the perfect antidote.

Scouts and Guides were organized on clear hierarchical principles. The two organizations were divided into several separate bodies determined by age, and within each body a sense of achievement and of purpose is reinforced through the use of merit badges and other recognition of success. At the same time there was strict division both by age and by sex. At the junior levels there are Brownies for girls, and Cubs for boys ages six to ten (eleven before 1964). For the older children, there were Guides for girls and Scouts for boys, to age sixteen. From the youngest to the oldest, these organizations were sexually separate, with considerably more distinction between the male and female branches than Baden-Powell would have liked. The skills had become ever more 'appropriate' to gender, reinforcing gender roles as perceived in this gender-conscious age, and thereby avoiding sexual complications.

For all this gender sensitivity, the basic philosophy underlying the two groups was the same. They were designed to instil self-reliance and a degree of self-denial in an urban generation, to instil Christianity in a secular age, to foster obedience in an age obsessed with youthful rebellion. The ideal Brownie pack, according to the 1960 *Guide Commissioner's Handbook*, would contain Brownies who were 'alert, clean, tidy and punctual. Their uniform should be correct.' Guides should show 'quick, happy obedience to commands, and whistle and hand signals. Captain should be addressed as Captain and not by the first name.'[59] As the Brownie law said, 'A Brownie gives in to older folk. A Brownie does not give in to herself.'[60]

As with so much else in Canadian life, the Scout and Guide movement had been hurt by the Depression. Financially strapped provincial organizations often barely functioned, and membership declined throughout most of Canada. The vast numbers of the baby boom and the organizational tendencies of the baby boom's parents changed all that. Through the 1950s the number of Brownies and Cubs increased rapidly. Hundreds of new packs were formed, and Cub membership doubled between 1951 and 1958. (Brownie numbers doubled by 1957, albeit from a smaller base.) By the end of the decade every week brought a quarter of a million children to schools, church basements, and community halls to learn the mystery of Mogli or the Toadstool.[61]

Such fantastic membership increases would seem to demonstrate two things. The first is the sheer power of the baby-boom to transform everything, from the children's entertainment industry to organizations likes Scouts and Guides. The second is the impact of organized bodies like Scouts upon the baby-boomers. The first point is incontrovertible, but the second is uncertain. The millions of children who passed through Brownies and Cubs in the 1950s and early 1960s imply success for the movement. Likewise, as the first baby-boomers passed beyond Cubs and Brownies to Scouts and Guides, those organizations also grew. In each of 1954 and 1955, for example, the number of Scouts increased by more than 10 per cent.[62] Likewise, studies of the Alberta records of the organizations indicate that the structure of both movements was transformed by the infusion of people and money. Better organization and information, and a proper headquarters, were all now possible.[63] At the national level a new headquarters building and a similar improvement in support staff and publications testify to the changes the growth of the decade had brought.

Yet there were problems. Enthusiastic Cubs and Brownies did not grow into equally enthusiastic Scouts and Guides. As the 1960 *Guide Commissioner's Handbook* warned, 'The Guide age presents a real challenge, and if the Commissioner understands this, she will realize the magnitude of the Guider's job and the necessity of giving her support and encouragement.'[64] Guides were so concerned with the loss of membership that they lowered the age for entry in the early 1960s. The committee writing the report had to admit that there 'was a distinct lack of interest in our programme at certain ages,' and that the age revision was an attempt to meet this problem. There were other changes, including modernization of the program and attempts to maintain relevance for the current generation.[65]

The problem was that the Scout and Guide movement increasingly failed to retain their members as children moved from Brownies and Cubs upward. In the early 1950s Guides had accounted for 47 per cent of total Brownie/Guide membership. By 1964 Guides were under 41 per cent of the total. In the early 1960s the Scout and Guide numbers first stopped growing, and then began to decline. Scouts reached a peak membership of just under 96,000 in 1962, and thereafter began an erratic decline. Guides, by lowering the age requirements, were able to recover modestly after 1964. By the later 1960s, though, they too were in decline. In contrast the Brownie and Cub movements just kept on growing.[66]

This levelling-off was not attributable to demographics. Ever larger numbers of youth of appropriate age were available to Guides and Scouts until the 1970s. The difficulty was that these movements attracted ever smaller percentages of youth. Through the later 1950s and early 1960s, approximately 10–12 per cent of boys of Scouting age in Canada actually belonged to the movement. By 1967 the figure was 8 per cent. The baby boom was amenable enough to being steered as young children into Cubs or Brownies. But, as they got older they found that the formality, hierarchy, and authoritarianism of the movement had little appeal to them.

As instruments for the transmission of values, though, Scouts and Guides were minor compared with religion. When one looks back at the 1950s, religion stands as one of the great gulfs separating that age from the present. Canada was still avowedly a Christian nation in the 1950s. There was no state church and no disabling laws for non-Christians, but neither was there any notion that other beliefs deserved equal status. Lord's Day acts, though somewhat relaxed from earlier decades, ensured that God's day was observed. Laws prohibited the consumption of alcohol, shopping, and, in many jurisdictions, sports or movies, on Sunday. Politicians routinely gave speeches which talked of Christian principles, as Louis St Laurent did in the 1947 Gray lectures on foreign policy.[67] The Canadian Broadcasting Corporation formally supported Christian principles as part of its mandate. The census-taker did not even have a category for those who wished to declare themselves as having no religion. The educational system of every province except British Columbia allowed for religious instruction in the public school system. Indeed, in Ontario a 1950 royal commission specifically called for a retention of Christian values in school courses. This was done, and a half-hour per week was set aside for religious instruction. Even in British Columbia a non-denominational prayer opened the school day.[68] Overall, as the Anglican Church concluded, even in these modern, supposedly secular times, Canada was a Christian country.[69]

Such policies reflected public opinion. At war's end some 95 per cent of Canadians avowed that they believed in God.[70] In spite of considerable secularization in past decades, religious observance was a normal part of community experience. 'Back on that spring 1946 Sunday morning in Edmonton it seemed the natural thing to do,' writes Reginald Bibby. 'My father and mother bundled the three of us preschoolers into the 1938 Chev, setting out for the first Nazerene [*sic*] Church. They waved to the Jamiesons to the east, who were leaving to attend Mass at the nearby Roman Catholic church. Down the street the Proctors and the Fieldings, adorned in their "Sunday best," could be seen strolling towards their respective United and Anglican church services.'[71] 'It seemed the natural thing to do' because it was: In the postwar years, on any given Sunday the majority of Canadians went to church. A great majority belonged to a church, contributed to church coffers, and saw themselves as religious people, albeit not as religious as they felt they should be.[72]

Still, had you asked clergymen in 1945 what they saw as the trend for the future, they would likely have expressed concern. For, though the majority of Canadians still went to church, religion was less influential than it had been a generation before. Decades of urbanization and modernization had had their influence. Secular élites of intellectuals, politicians, and reformers now rivalled the church in social authority. Atheism was still not very respectable, except in radical circles, but religious indifference was common. Moreover, the Depression had been as hard on the churches as on other institutions. Finances were not good, and contributions were down. In 1945 Canada may have been a Christian country but, except for French Catholicism, religion seemed a declining force. The apparent materialism and secularism of the wartime generation didn't indicate that this would change, except perhaps for the worse.

Then something surprising happened. Membership in all the mainline denominations increased, both in absolute terms and as a percentage of the adult Canadian population.[73] United Church membership, for example, went from three-quarters of a million at war's end to more than a million by 1960. The Anglicans, Presbyterians, and Lutherans saw similar increases. The Roman Catholic Church, buoyed by significant numbers of postwar Italian immigrants, saw its rolls increase at an even faster rate. In these prosperous years finances improved even more than membership. From 1947 to 1957 the United Church built four times as many new churches as it had in the previous twenty years.[74]

Most surprisingly, perhaps, the majority of new recruits were those same young married suburbanites who people thought were completely caught up in the world of consumption. Once again the frontier metaphor could not be avoided. 'Religiously speaking, the frontiers of 1952 are out where farmers' fields are being turned into communities of bungalows with breeze-ways and picture-windows.'[75] Suburban explosion and religious expansion often went together. Typical was Wexford, north of Toronto. In 1954 it was still largely rural, and there was no United Church congregation in the area. By 1957 the suburbs had arrived, and five new United churches had opened, with a combined membership of close to 2,000.[76]

At first, observers were cautious about the revival. The Presbyterians, for example, noted in 1953 that there appeared to be 'quickening interest' in the church.[77] Before long, however, the phenomenon was too obvious to deny. Compared with the ongoing marginalization of religion elsewhere in the world, said one church historian, it was a 'source of wonder.'[78] By the later 1950s the Anglican bishop of New Westminster talked of 'a rising tide of enthusiasm and a new unity of purpose.'[79] Non-religious magazines soon picked up the theme and speculated on the causes and nature of the revival. Before long the issue of religious revival became one of the minor journalistic curiosities of the decade.[80]

Yet this was a most curious revival. As writers probed beneath the surface, they found little in the way of greater religious belief. Regular attendance at church was decreasing.[81] Ministers commented upon the 'obvious lack of knowledge' of many of the new church members.[82] The Anglican magazine lamented the irreverence of the congregation: 'They come early to get a good seat and to have a pleasant visit with their friends, carrying on a continual chatter about every subject under the sun little of which has any relationship to the Church's worship or work.'[83] The United Church complained in 1956 of irregular attendance and that the bulk of its membership seemed to have only a limited commitment to religion.[84]

Religious literature often takes a pessimistic view of the commitment of the flock. These laments were, nevertheless, on to something. The religious revival of the 1950s had more to do with the baby boom and middle-class sensibilities than with religious commitment. People attended church because it was another stabilizing force within a community that sought security. As one writer complained, 'they are neither intellectually convinced nor do they truly "believe." They merely accept, with one eye on the promised rewards of inner peace and life eternal.'[85] Another critic was more cynical, concluding that the revival was part of a collective 'failure of nerve,' and part of 'this generation's strange desire for conformity.'[86]

Much of the revival had to do specifically with children. To these parents, religion was the ultimate formal organization by which societal values could be transmitted to a new generation. That was how they had been raised. They were searching not so much for faith as for ethics for their children. Sunday schools were the real centre of many churches. Indeed, as it did other movements, the baby boom revitalized the Sunday school. United Church Sunday-school membership increased from about a half million in the late 1940s to more than three-quarters of a million by the beginning of the 1960s. The Presbyterian Church, which kept very precise records, saw Sunday-school attendance increase by more than 30 per cent in ten years (see figure 4.1). Anglican and Lutheran patterns were similar.

Whatever the reasons for the revival, church was the norm for children in the 1950s. Among mainstream denominations, however, religion for children was not basically a theological matter but a strand in the web of socialization. Church magazines and religious sermons became extensions of the family values seen in secular magazines and child-care books. The United Church *Observer* had a regular 'Family Page,' dispensing thoughts on bringing up children. The Anglican *Canadian Churchman* warned that parents who don't spend enough time with their children 'are gambling their own future and the future of their children.' Revealingly, that gamble was not lost souls but failed

FIGURE 4.1
Protestant Sunday-School Enrolment: The Big Three (1952 = 100)

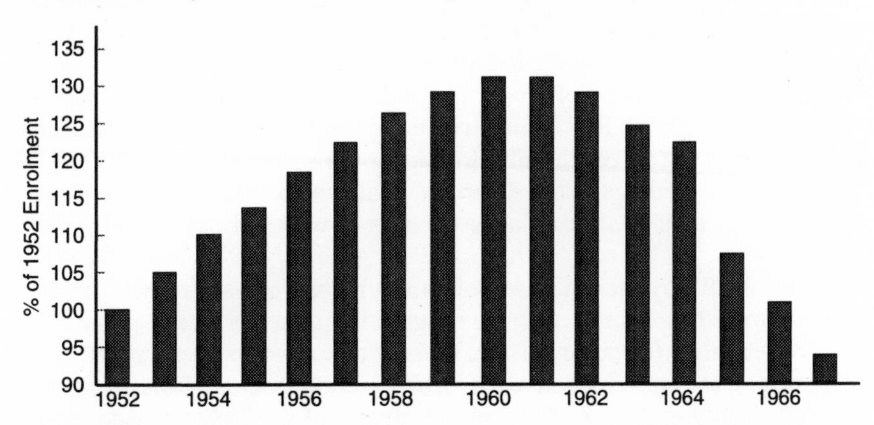

Source: Derived from *The Yearbook of the Anglican Church*; *Acts and Proceedings of the Presbyterian Church of Canada*; and *The United Church of Canada Year Books* for relevant years

socialization. 'They may hear from their own child the words of a young man which came over television the other night. When confronted by the authorities for a serious offence he promptly replied, "I know my father is a prominent man; he is a famous lawyer, but he spends all his time searching his law volumes and has paid not attention to his sons."'[87] Another article was even more explicit, asking 'Why are Boys and Girls who attend Sunday school seldom in Juvenile court?' Once again, the answer blended the religious and secular. Juvenile delinquents were full of hate and needed to learn love from the teachings of religion. 'I feel very sorry for juvenile delinquents. Often their parents do not believe in God and so the children do not go to Sunday School.'[88] In St Catharines, Ontario, another minister cited F.B.I. director J. Edgar Hoover: 'Out of 8000 delinquent children called to his attention, only 42 attended Sunday school regularly.'[89]

Sunday school dispensed religion, of course. No doubt many parents joined church primarily out of faith. Overall, however, those pessimistic about the revival were right: it occurred, as one writer put it, for non-religious reasons. The church taught children how to behave and reinforced family values. Religion was another avenue – like Benjamin Spock, like the suburban community, like Guides or Scouts – used by a child-centred generation to help bring up children. Mainstream religion, both Catholic and Protestant, mirrored the domesticity of the age. 'In the home, children must be taught to be tolerant with each other and be willing to share with the other members of the family. The family should have fun in the home as they work, share, and play together.'[90] Family, psychology, and religion blended into one when educational expert S.R. Laycock wrote that Scouts, schools, and church were all fulfilling an essentially similar function. These are the 'character building agencies,' said Laycock. 'Failure to provide wholesome recreational facilities for all ages for girls as well as boys is asking for trouble.'[91]

Reginald Bibby, in his study of modern religion, argues that most Canadians still see a function for religion but also feel free to consume bits of it, as they feel appropriate. Rites of passage – baptism, marriage, funerals – are interspaced with broad periods of religious indifference.[92] Clergy and other religious observers of the 1950s sensed even then that this was the emergent trend of the churchgoer. Canadians went more regularly to church than they would later, but they, too, were consuming religion. In this slightly more religious and much more conservative era, however, the socialization of children was another rite of passage, if a somewhat drawn-out one. This explains why it was a common habit for parents to send their children off to Sunday school while one or both of them remained at home: They already knew the rules.

Such obvious superficiality meant trouble in the long term for the church. As growth turned into stagnation, several sensationalist books, such as Pierre Berton's *Comfortable Pew*, published in 1965, lashed out at the smugness of the church and its lack of relevance to modern issues. Churchmen joined Berton in anguished debate about how to make mainstream religion more challenging or more relevant to the poor.[93] Sentiments of social outreach were revived, and efforts made to take the church back into the inner cities. All of this was irrelevant. The problem was that the church, like the Scouts and Guides, could not maintain its hold upon the baby boom. Older baby-boomers, brought up in the religious revival of the 1950s, often remained in Sunday school until their teens. It was the normal thing to do. Few remained in the church thereafter, however. For younger baby-boomers, Sunday school attendance was even shorter-lived as parents and peer group became more secular. As figure 4.1 indicates, the great surge of Sunday school growth had turned into decline, and then collapse, through the 1960s. United Church Sunday-school enrolment decreased every year in the 1960s and was, by the end of the decade, half what it had been.[94] Without children flowing into the system, the adult membership of all churches declined as well. Religion had become marginalized, even as social convention.

The baby-boomers were at the end of a long era. As a generation they were the last to be brought up in a society that presumed religious training and belief was part of day-to-day life. Yet because it was the end of an era, that belief was, for many of them, really more an extension of modern concerns about socialization rather than faith and doctrine. Then, as they moved into adulthood, they became the first of the truly secular generations, rejecting as a body the pretense of their parents that religion was central to their society. The question that remains, though, is whether some of the lessons taught in Sunday school were taken to heart. Was the idealism of the 1960s at all dependent upon the teachings of the 1950s, albeit in a form that would have shocked many Sunday-school teachers?

THE WORLD OF LEISURE FOR THE BABY BOOM was actually many worlds. Informal games with friends, the organized activities of Scouts and Guides, the formal and serious social activity of religion – all were part of it. Through all of these activities, though, certain threads link the experience of a generation. Previous generations of children had also had their favourite toys, and toy companies were always trying to guess what they wanted. Unlike previous generations, however, media such as television ensured that toy fads would be national, or international, rather than local. Television continued a process of homogenization that had begun with mail-order catalogues, modern advertising, and the rise of radio.[95] Television was a much more powerful force, however, especially when combined with unprecedented numbers and unprecedented affluence of the juvenile market. Consumer taste was a crucial part of peer identity.

This generational sense of identity does not imply a sense of opposition or resentment towards the previous generation. Indeed, the generational sense of the world of play was linked to the parental generation by existing and still powerful formal organizations. The nature and power of the linkage was mixed, however. The baby boom did bring revival to Scouts and Sunday school, but the revival did not last. Adult control of the world of childhood leisure was slipping in the face of a strong sense of peer group. Brownies and Cubs appealed to smaller children, but Scouts and Guides much less so to older ones.

Religion simply collapsed as a mass social institution, and the ability of the older generation to socialize this powerful new one was weakened accordingly.

Generational historians and demographers have argued that, throughout history, one of the main tasks of the adult generation is to tame the young barbarians of the next generation by introducing them to the rituals and values of the society.[96] If so, the baby boom's experience was ambiguous. Youth certainly very quickly learned the nature of consumption trends and easily assimilated the whole apparatus of the material culture. They were also so powerful and so identified as a generation, however, that the transmission of values always had to compete with the peer group's sense of propriety. The rapid decline of religion and the weakening of activities like Scouts and Guides reveal that the barbarians were not fully under the control of the adults.

5

School Days, 1952–1965

In September 1952, a revolution began. It was led by five- and six-year-old children, dressed in their best outfits and heading off to the adventure of Grade One[1] – the first wave of the baby boom, some 370,000 strong, was entering the school system in Canada. Not only were there more children than before, but their parents had higher expectations. Mass education moved upward from the elementary schools in the 1950s to the high schools in the early 1960s, and then to the universities. Governments, educators, and parents scrambled to expand a system pushed to the edge of chaos. Curriculum changed, philosophies were hotly debated, and unprecedented amounts of money were spent. By the time this revolution was over, provincial education spending was more than twenty-five times what it had been in the early 1950s.[2] The baby boom wasn't the sole cause of all the changes, but it was the catalyst, and it was also a participant, pushed along and shaped by the currents that swept an educational system in revolution.

The revolution was caused, in part, by the changing place of the school in modern society. In 1900 the grandparents of the baby boom could be expected to complete only about six years of formal education, and that education was not exactly central to their lives. The average Canadian child was absent almost 40 per cent of the time.[3] As urbanization and industrialization progressed, the pressure to obtain a better education increased. By the time the parents of the baby boom went to school, attendance was more regular, and the majority of children could be expected to complete Grade Eight. High school, however, was still for an élite. As one senior educator of the 1950s concluded, until recently 'a grade seven or eight education was considered adequate for the rank and file of citizens.'[4] Less than a third of those who began school between the wars completed Grade Ten. Less than one in ten actually finished high school. As late as 1951 the majority of fourteen- to seventeen-year-olds were not enrolled in school.[5]

Even without the baby boom, the educational system would have changed dramatically after the war. Canada emerged from the war a more urban, more technological, and more prosperous society than when it entered. As was true of housing, schools had suffered physically during the Depression and war. A spate of school construction in the 1920s had led to a glut by the end of the decade. Then, in the 1930s, school construction ground to a halt.[6] By the later 1940s, existing schools were both too few and increasingly run-down. The desperate situation of education was not lost upon governments, and across the country a series of royal commissions, parliamentary investigations, and other studies marked the transition from war to peace.[7] Ambitious plans were discussed for curriculum review, new capital expenditure, and improved teacher training. Education, the planners recognized, was no longer a peripheral experience either to the child or to society. As the 1940 Rowell–Sirois Commission concluded, 'if full advantage is to be taken of modern productive facilities, more intensive and longer periods of general education are required, more subjects must be taught, more equipment and more trained specialists are needed.'[8]

Yet, for several reasons, educators were woefully unprepared for the baby boom. Initially, demographers saw the postwar surge in births as temporary. Educators saw no reason to think differently. Even after the initial baby-boomers were born and growing inexorably towards their first days in school, the various educational systems persistently underestimated future enrolment growth. A 1949 Ontario report, for example, was almost 50 per cent under when it projected expansion in elementary-school enrolment for the next decade.[9] Second, political systems are not very good at inducing expenditure and taxation for anything beyond immediate needs. Even the more conservative projections should have warned governments that a large number of additional classrooms would be needed in the next ten to fifteen years. Governments, however, were faced with tremendous immediate demands, especially for new roads. The number of cars was, after all, growing almost as fast as the number of babies, and the road system was already under strain. The babies were still years away from school.

As well, the educational system was distracted by another issue. By the beginning of the Second World War, there were approximately three times as many students in secondary schools as there had been at the turn of the century.[10] After the war, the secondary enrolments increased at an even faster pace. By 1954 a majority, and by 1960 some two-thirds, of fourteen- to seventeen-year-olds were in school.[11] These changes meant that, in the later 1940s and early 1950s, the nature of secondary school became the centre of educational concern. Annual Reports from every province mentioned the issue. Commissions, such as Ontario's 1950 Royal Commission on Education (the Hope Commission), focused on the problem.[12] Ministers of education and parents of adolescents worried that the rapidly expanding high-school system would not be able to cope with the changes. 'In the last few years,' reported the Manitoba Department of Education in 1956, 'we have had many significant enrolment figures but the one which must attract our present attention is the increase in high school enrolment.'[13] The hyperbole could not be contained. It was, said one educator, the most significant social advance of the twentieth century.[14] High-school construction became a priority in practically every jurisdiction.

A mass secondary system also had significant implications for curriculum. High-school programs had been academic in focus and, at least in theory, demanding in character. They were geared for the middle class or above, and presumed a student body that was destined for the white-collar world. Suddenly educators were faced with, in the words of the director of education for Ontario, creating a system 'for all students of ordinary ability.'[15] The Hope Commission echoed the message in somewhat more diplomatic language: 'The pronounced trend toward universal education at the secondary school level has made necessary a curriculum designed not exclusively for university entrance, but to meet a great variety of needs.'[16] This changing role led to considerable discussion and curriculum reform through the 1940s and 1950s. Vocational and 'composite' schools were developed. Commercial programs and academic programs were revised, and then re-revised. The secondary-school crisis thus absorbed the energies of the school system in the immediate postwar years.

For all these reasons the response of educational planners to the approaching baby boom was inadequate. Then, each year from 1952 through the mid-1960s, the baby boom pushed enrolment to record levels. In the four years after the first baby-boomers went to school, enrolment increased by 668,000. By 1961 it was 1,200,000 above 1950–51 levels! Each year the wave pushed upward. A crisis of classroom space in Grade One in 1952 and again in 1953 became a crisis in Grade Nine a few years later. Grade Nine enrolment went up 13 per cent in 1960, and

FIGURE 5.1
School Enrolment by Province, 1965 as a Ratio of 1951 (1951 = 1)

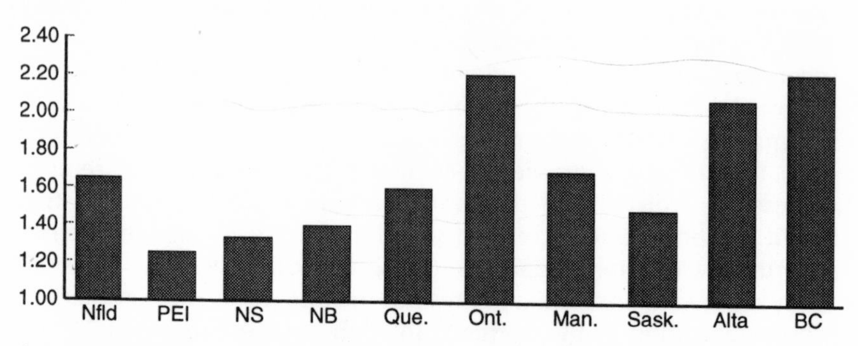

Source: Derived from Wolfgang Illing and Zoltan Zsigmond, *Enrolment in Schools and Universites, 1951–2 to 1975–6* (Ottawa 1967), Economic Council of Canada Study no. 20, Appendix

another 11.5 per cent in 1961.[17] By 1966 there were almost 5 million people in school in Canada, double what the figure had been only fourteen years earlier.[18]

Nor were these increases spread evenly. Though the marriage and birth rates were high in all provinces, the Canadian population was mobile, in search of better income or a more secure future. Thus, as figure 5.1 illustrates, the impact of the baby boom upon individual school systems varied tremendously. Saskatchewan's school enrolment actually decreased in 1952–3 before beginning a slow upward trend. It took Manitoba several years of baby-boomers before overall enrolment reached the province's 1931 peak.[19] Prince Edward Island never really felt the impact of the baby boom, and in the later 1950s the school system there remained much as it had been ten years earlier.[20]

On the other hand, the rapidly growing provinces saw student populations surge. Alberta's education expenditures nearly quintupled in the decade from 1946 to 1956, and it was not the fastest-growing of all the provinces. That distinction, and burden, belonged to British Columbia. In fifteen years that province saw enrolment go from just over 200,000 to more than 475,000.[21] At the local level, especially in the new suburbs, district reports took on a tone of desperation. 'The increase of 868 pupils and twenty-six teachers has every indication of becoming an annual problem,' wrote the inspector of schools for Burnaby in 1953. 'The number of new houses being constructed and occupied each month ensure a constantly increasing school population. Despite the fact that eighteen new classrooms and six portable units were brought into use during the year, June saw this accommodation immediately occupied.'[22]

The baby boom went to school in years of educational crisis. Their presence guaranteed that. However, the influence ran both ways. Postwar affluence, long-term tendencies towards increased education, and more regular school attendance meant that the baby boom was more affected by the Canadian school system than any previous generation had been. School encompassed not just childhood but adolescence and, as discussed later, often the young adult years as well. Parents saw school as vital to the success of their children and put tremendous demands upon it. As an Alberta royal commission put it in 1959, there has been 'unprecedented publicity given to the matter of public education.'[23] This is hardly surprising. Unprecedented numbers of tax dollars were being spent on education. An unprecedented number of families had children in school.

The public was also adopting a very broad definition of the school's role. Ontario superintendent of education J.G. Althouse complained in 1956 that 'educators are somewhat shocked to find the school blamed for delinquency, indolence, malingering, lack of moral fibre, materialism, and any other weaknesses which may be discovered in young people today.'[24] This view was disingenuous. Althouse was well aware that schools had assumed the central role in the modern socialization process. He was also probably well aware of the expectations of these child-oriented parents who formed Home and School associations in record numbers. His point nevertheless is an important one. This domestic generation was aware that yet another family function was increasingly being removed from the home, at least in part. This made the role of schools all the more crucial in the minds of the parents, and heightened their demands. Yet, at the same time, the school system was scrambling to deal with unprecedented growth. These were not circumstances conducive to orderly change.

THE BIGGEST PROBLEM WAS THE MOST BASIC: Where would the children go and who would teach them? The educational system simply wasn't large enough to accommodate all of these new arrivals. Much of the story of the 1950s and early 1960s was one of simply 'keeping up.' Buildings had to be built and teachers trained, first at the elementary, then at the secondary, and, eventually, at the university level. All of this created a sense that, in the words of one commentator, there 'have been few, if any, crises in Canada's educational history comparable to the one we are struggling through at present.'[25]

The greatest of all the crises was teacher shortage. What made this so difficult and intractable was that teaching had become an unattractive profession at the time Canadians most needed teachers. The Depression had starved the public educational system, and teacher's salaries had fallen. The boom of the war and the postwar years had provided a series of attractive career alternatives to teaching. In the meantime, governments, both local and provincial, were reluctant to increase school levies and, as a result, teachers' salaries languished relative to those in other areas of endeavour. By 1951 the average annual salary of a teacher in Alberta, for example, was 10 per cent lower than the average manufacturing wage in Canada; in Nova Scotia, 40 per cent lower.[26]

Low salaries were connected to the fact that, as of 1951, more than 70 per cent of all teachers were women.[27] The 'nurturing' character of the profession meant that teaching had long been seen as appropriate for women. Low pay had made it difficult to recruit sufficient numbers of men. The predominance of women, however, also shaped the nature of the profession. As has been noted, society looked askance at married women working, especially if they had children. This created a contradiction that reinforced problems of teacher supply. Women were encouraged to choose teaching as a profitable career. Yet all the messages of society told married women that they should not have a career outside the home. Many school boards reinforced social custom with specific rules discouraging, or even prohibiting, married teachers. For many female teachers, then, their 'career' was one of limited horizons, and there was a consistently high turnover of female teachers who left the profession soon after getting married. This meant that a disproportionate number of teachers were young, unmarried women or ageing 'spinsters.' This trend reinforced both the stuffy image of schoolteaching and the community belief that a teacher's behaviour should be regulated.

Low wages, low status, and improved alternatives during and after the war created a teacher shortage. As early as 1944 signs pointed to a 'crisis in teacher supply,' and a good many of the educational studies at the time focused attention on the problem. The themes were similar. Education was a vital necessity for the postwar world. The teaching profession therefore had to be given serious attention, its salaries improved and qualifications upgraded.[28] The postwar years only saw the problem escalate. Indeed, postwar enthusiasm for reform in education may have made matters worse. Several provinces moved to implement higher qualifications for teachers. Taxpayers did not like the idea of paying more, however, and teachers' salaries remained low. This was hardly a remedy designed to bring hordes of new recruits to the profession. Practically every jurisdiction began to lament the difficulty of finding enough teachers to keep up with student enrolment. Between 1945 and 1955, the pupil–teacher ratio in Ontario, for example, rose from 24:1 to 31:1.[29]

For all these reasons the schools were having trouble coping even before the baby-boomers appeared at the schoolyard gate. When they did arrive, something like panic set in: 'The supply of an adequate number of qualified teachers continues to engage the attention of all senior officials and, in fact, of all people in the free world.'[30] As early as 1949 the Hope Commission was sufficiently concerned that it issued a special interim report on the 'Teacher shortage.' The message was that, if it was bad now, it was going to get worse. The number of babies born since the war implied a 'startling' increase in elementary enrolment through the 1950s. Where, the commission asked, were the teachers for all these new pupils?[31] The answer, it soon became apparent, was: wherever they could be found.

Through the 1950s provinces stepped up efforts to increase the supply of teachers. Several set up 'recruitment committees' to visit high schools and encourage students to consider teaching as a career.[32] By 1954, British Columbia was providing an interest-free loan to any student entering Teacher's College.[33] It also sent one of its retired school inspectors off to the United Kingdom to recruit teachers. In Alberta, individual counties and municipalities offered to pay the expenses of students going into teaching in return for a guarantee of a period of service in the area. Ontario waived previous requirements that out-of-province teachers write an examination before being qualified for Ontario schools.[34]

The greatest source of qualified teachers was one previously shunned. As the superintendent of education in Quebec noted with a certain regret, several school districts in 1952 'have had to call on the services of married women.'[35] Other jurisdictions did the same. Suddenly the imperatives of family values and societal pressure seemed less urgent. Married women were crucial to the system's survival. Manitoba, for example, noted that, by the mid-1950s, married women made up 20 to 30 per cent of the teaching staff.[36] In Ontario, schools in some parts of the province would have had to close except for the return of married teachers.[37] There was an irony in this reversal of attitudes, of course. The situation is even more ironic when one considers the lament of Ontario in 1954 that nearly a third of teachers who left the profession did so in order to get married.[38] Having exalted the virtues of domesticity and family, society had to live with the consequences.

Recruitment committees helped. So, too, did the return of married teachers. But neither measure was enough. The only way to obtain sufficient teachers was to make it easier and faster to enter the classroom. To fill classrooms, the standards came tumbling down. There was no choice: If teachers were not found, there would be 'unstaffed classrooms and untaught children.'[39] Before the crisis, a prospective elementary teacher had probably finished high school and one to two years of teacher training. The baby boom made all of this impossible. Provinces instituted summer teaching programs and often reduced the number of high-school subjects required to be eligible to take the program. By the mid-1950s it was common for eighteen-year-old high-school students to head off to a six-week summer-school course and, by fall, find themselves teaching a class of their own.[40] Even then the supply was inadequate for several years. Rural areas found themselves in the position of hiring what the departments of education bluntly admitted were 'unqualified teachers.' Each year through the 1950s, any decline in the number of unqualified teachers in the system was taken as a point of congratulation.

The experience in Alberta was fairly typical. Teacher training in the province had previously been delegated to the University of Alberta. By the beginning of the war, an elementary teacher required credit in a number of Grade Twelve subjects plus one year at university in the teacher-training program. After the war the province planned to improve teacher training. In 1950 two years at university became the standard.[41] It was a wildly optimistic step to take, given the shortage of teachers and the impending arrival of the baby boom. Almost immediately, exceptions had to be made for rural schools. As time went on, things got worse. Enrolments in the provincial system increased by more than 35,000 students, or just under 20 per cent, in the next three years. The 1954 Speech from the Throne made special reference to the shortage of teachers as 'a matter of widespread concern.'[42] A few weeks later the government brought in the Emergency Teacher Training Act.

TABLE 5.1
British Columbia: Enrolment and Expenditure on Education, 1946–1961

Year	Number of teachers	Aggregate enrolment	Total expenditure ($millions)
1945–6	4,512	130,605	14.8
1946–7	4,833	137,827	20.1
1947–8	5,116	146,708	25.8
1948–9	5,496	155,515	35.5
1949–50	5,873	164,212	47.7
1950–1	6,272	173,354	54.2
1951–2	6,598	183,112	57.9
1952–3	7,105	195,290	58.4
1953–4	7,574	210,174	70.8
1954–5	8,185	223,840	80.8
1955–6	8,690	240,674	69.3
1956–7	9,474	260,069	77.7
1957–8	10,171	277,070	90.5
1958–9	10,839	291,223	101.3
1959–60	11,513	305,837	115.9
1960–1	12,137	321,760	133.4

Source: Province of British Columbia, *Public Schools of British Columbia: Annual Report for 1960–1, 214*

This allowed teachers to begin teaching after a summer course. Their training would be completed in the future.[43] As a provincial royal commission later commented, 'Alberta's teaching requirements had fallen from the highest in Canada ... to among the lowest.'[44]

Getting the teachers was one battle; finding the classrooms to put them in was another. In the late 1940s and early 1950s, several provinces and communities recognized the need for a large-scale school-construction program. Budgets increased dramatically in these years. In Ontario, for example, capital expenditures increased from $5.7 million in 1946 to $42.7 million by 1951. Other growing provinces, such as British Columbia (see table 5.1), Alberta, and Quebec, showed a similar pattern. With the arrival of the baby boom, even this rapid rate of construction became woefully inadequate. In 1952 Ontario reported that, for the first time, construction had fallen behind increases in enrolment.[45] By 1954 capital outlay had increased another 50 per cent, and still the demand could not be met. School boards, provinces, and citizens, caught between rising tax bills and a desire for adequate school facilities, poured increasing amounts of money into new construction. By the mid-1950s the national expenditure on school construction was consuming nearly $200 million a year. To put this in perspective, even a relatively small province like Nova Scotia was opening a new school every five days. Quebec was opening schools at the rate of one a day.[46] Even this might be only the beginning. *Canadian Business* estimated in 1955 that 'expenditure on school construction every year for the next ten years should be at least 85% higher than 1955's all-time high.'[47]

Not surprisingly, the pace of construction was most frenetic in the suburbs. As the Ontario minister of education reported in 1955, 'new communities have sprung up on land which one or two years before had been farming or fruit growing land ... The growth has been rapid rather than gradual. The new school accommodation required has not been additions to existing buildings, but new schools where no schools existed before.'[48] In Manitoba, for example, a vastly expanded school construction program more or less caught up with demand in rural and small town areas by 1956. In the Winnipeg suburbs, however, the race went on, absorbing half of the province's total construction budget. That same year Edmonton reported six elementary schools under way, 'all for the subdivisions.'[49]

The massive construction meant that, between 1952 and the mid-1960s, most pupils spent at least a part of their elementary years in a new building. If they did, they were, according to contemporary opinion, a fortunate generation. 'The school has ceased to be a massive, forbidding structure. New schools are beautiful, simple and uniform.' Another source commented on the 'better lighting, better ventilation' and increased fire safety of the modern schoolhouse.[50] Such enthusiasm was, like the designs of the schools themselves, part of the self-conscious modernism of the age. The same generation of architects who designed the subdivisions, after all, designed the schools. The same aesthetic that led to the linoleum-filled bungalow also shaped the school. For anyone who was in elementary school in the 1950s or 1960s in Canada, the physical image of the building, inside and out, is instantly recognizable. Like houses, elementary schools became almost exclusively one-storey affairs. Brick or concrete-block construction predominated, and the roofs were flat. Inside, classrooms were 700 to 900 square feet in size, and desks, anchored to the floor for previous generations, loosed themselves from their restraints. Like the modern bungalow, 'the modern classroom is finished in light colours, pastel with a dull gloss paint.' There were even more 'built-ins' and, for the better schools, modern linoleum was the floor covering of choice.[51] Ideally the good school was, said one architect, 'interesting, even exciting' in design![52]

That was if you could get into a classroom. In spite of all the construction, shortages continued until the end of the decade. A common experience of the 1950s, especially around the larger cities, was make-shift accommodation or split shifts. An examination of the reports of British Columbia's district inspector for 1954–5 reveals why split grades have become a part of the folklore of the 1950s. In North Vancouver, split shifts were needed because school building projects were not yet complete. In Victoria, students in five elementary schools went on split shifts. Richmond reported that shifts had to be implemented in several schools. The story was the same in Prince George, Langley, and Revelstoke. In Salmon Arm, they had pressed the lunch-room and basement of local schools into service, but to no avail – it, too, was implementing a split-shift system. Other places were luckier, but only relatively. Vancouver City congratulated itself on ending the split-shift system in a number of schools. In Okanagan and Hope, temporary classrooms made it possible to avoid the shift system Generally, however, the picture across the province was a bleak one. The inspector for Kamloops summed it all up: 'The school enrolment continued to exceed provision of new class-rooms, resulting in utilization of temporary accommodation, over-large classes, and classes on shift.'[53]

There were some things that eased the generally negative impact of the shortages and overcrowding. First, and perhaps most important, the 1950s was an affluent decade. Tax revenues were rising, and debt load at both the municipal and the provincial level was much lower than it had been twenty years earlier or would be twenty years later. The baby-boomers and years of neglect strained the system, but at least the governments could pour resources into education. Municipal expenditures on education increased from $118 million in 1946 to $440 million by 1956, and $1.2 billion by 1966.[54] Such increases were possible only because of the prosperous economy and low debt loads of the postwar years.

Recent administrative changes also helped. The Canadian school system in most provinces had evolved to serve a rural nation in an era when transportation was difficult. This meant that school districts had to be small. Outside of the cities a turn-of-the-century school district usually included one school and no more than two or three teachers. At the peak, for example, Alberta had 5,000 school districts, serving a population of just half a million people.[55] Such small districts presented real problems. The one-room school predominated, and pupils in the class often ranged in age from six to fifteen years old. There were few, if any, library resources, and what the students learned was often dependent on an underpaid, underqualified schoolteacher who stayed only as long as was absolutely necessary. It was also inefficient, as school financial resources were squandered in hundreds of individual buildings across the provinces. A survey taken at the beginning of the Second World War discovered that, of some 20,610 administrative units in Canada, an amazing 14,692 employed only one teacher, and another 1,430 only two.[56]

Improvements in transportation, the progressive impulse for reform, and, later, the financial crisis wrought by the 1930s led to changes. Several jurisdictions began a program of centralization. The emphasis varied between two goals, depending upon the province and the year. The first was administrative and had as its purpose the amalgamation of decision making and financing into larger units. The second was aimed at the schools themselves. Small rural schools were brought together to enhance efficiency, reduce costs, and improve teaching. In Quebec, for example, the Protestant School Board began a consolidated-school movement as early as 1905.[57] Ontario began soon after.[58]

The changes proceeded unevenly over subsequent decades. In the 1920s and 1930s, the educational reformers in both the United Farmers of Alberta and Social Credit parties pushed the idea. By 1935 the move towards larger administrative units and consolidated schools was well under way in Alberta.[59] British Columbia, Nova Scotia, and New Brunswick were not far behind.[60] Local sensitivities slowed consolidation down in Saskatchewan, but by the late 1940s the Department of Education talked optimistically of 'excellent progress' in consolidation.[61] The general trend was irreversible, however. The school bus made it possible to transport children greater distances. Rural depopulation made the notion of purely local schools increasingly impossible in many parts of the country. The one-room rural school still existed. In Prince Edward Island, for example, three-quarters of schools were still one-room buildings in the mid-1950s.[62] By the time the baby-boomers were in school, however, more and more children were being bussed from the farms or small villages into district centres, where they attended new one-storey brick schools designed according to standardized plans that could be applied in city, suburb, or small town.

School consolidation had an effect parallel to that of suburbanization. It homogenized the experience of the baby-boomers to a degree unknown among previous generations. Increasingly, in small towns teachers taught individual grades rather than three or four years at once. Finances were more evenly distributed, in part as a result of the provincial consolidations, and hence the quality of education – though not entirely uniform – was closer along the urban–rural continuum than had previously been the case. The growth of large-scale government bureaucracies to meet the new demands being made on education also ensured greater standardization of curriculum planning and textbook approval. The schoolhouse more than ever became a purveyor of, not just a common curriculum, but a common experience. The modern flat-roofed, large-windowed school with four to six classrooms was as much a part of Meaford, Ontario, or Vulcan, Alberta, as it was of Scarborough or Burnaby.

Of course, a child's perspective is different from that of a harassed educator or concerned parent. For the child, school is a day-to-day experience in which friends (or enemies) and teacher are the reality. The students noticed the changes, of course. It was exciting to start in a brand-new school. The blackboards weren't black at all, but green! The room was lighter and more colourful than those in the old school. The desks were new, light-coloured, Formica-topped, and unblemished by decades of predecessors' minor acts of vandalism. It was fun to have a playground filled with the latest in slides or swings. If the playground wasn't ready and was still largely mud, that was fun too. Even split shifts were generally taken in stride, and no doubt caused much more anxiety to parents than to children. They were a widespread experience, but they were also usually short-lived. A term later, a new school was available, and the classroom pace returned to normal.

One of the changes probably accepted as normal by the child was extremely significant nevertheless. Never had age been so important in school. In earlier generations the predominance of the small school meant that the 'child' in the row next to you might be three grades ahead and three or four years older. As schools exploded in size, and as consolidation took hold, that changed. The grade system, finely dividing children by age, reinforced and further refined the identity of one's peer group. A seven-year-old in Grade Two was divided surely and certainly from the nine-year-old in Grade Four. Teachers said so, parents said so, and the older child said so. School thus reinforced preschool experience and daily suburban life. Moreover, the school experience was now more universal, attendance more regular, and education more prolonged than for earlier generations. Taken together, these things meant that, for the baby-boomer, the sense of peer group was accentuated, and daily contact with those of differing ages and experiences postponed.

THE FIRST YEARS OF SCHOOL HAVE SEVERAL purposes. The basics of reading, writing, and arithmetic – the famous 'three Rs' – are always important. School is more than that, however. It is a means by which a culture, religion, language, or values can be preserved or eradicated for the next generation.[63] This is why education has so often become a terrible political battle-ground. Issues that echo through Canadian history, like the Manitoba School Question of the 1890s; the Ontario Schools Question of the early twentieth century; more modern debates on ethnicity, language, and religion – all testify to society's recognition of the cultural significance of the school.

While the vital cultural importance of schooling is readily accepted, it is difficult to demonstrate just what values were being taught at any time and what impact those teachings had upon any group. Specifically, what role did the curriculum of the 1950s have in distinguishing the baby boom as a generation from those which preceded and succeeded it? Was there any connection, for example, between the educational system of the first fifteen or twenty years after the war and the restiveness of the late 1960s? Did the school transmit the same messages to children as they were receiving at home? Was the child-centredness of the suburb re-created in the school?

This is a complex issue at the best of times. It was further complicated after the war by an intense debate on the philosophy of education. The issue was the hold of 'progressivism' upon the schools, and its impact. Progressivism had first been developed by American educator and philosopher John Dewey around the turn of the century.[64] Dewey and his followers argued that all children had a natural desire to learn, and that the role of the teacher was to tap into that ability. Education was to be 'child-centred.' Subject-matter had to be interesting to the child. The classroom was to become a much more dynamic place, recognizing the need to get children involved as active participants. The teacher should seek to develop a friendly partnership rather than an adversarial relationship with students. Curriculum, rather than being a fixed series of absolute stages, became much more of a process. The child progressed along that line, and it was the process of learning, rather than the absolute benchmarks, that the teacher had to encourage.

By the inter-war years, Dewey's ideas had spread to Canadian education. As a general rule of thumb, the Western provinces were more reform-oriented than the Eastern ones; the public or Protestant school system more affected than the Catholic. In Alberta and British Columbia, where the movement gained the greatest acceptance, both governments adopted such hallmarks of progressive education as the use of educational 'units,' a broader curriculum, and the 'enterprise system.'[65] Curricular guides talked of a series of projects of study which ignored traditional disciplinary lines. Even though other provinces were not as swept up as those in the West, progressive educational theory had made advances practically everywhere by the post-1945 period. Only the Catholic system of Quebec remained steadfast, condemning the 'laziness, the instability and the misconduct of young people' fostered by progressive education.[66] In contrast, by 1940 one Alberta educator could boast that the province was 'second to very few in America in so-called progressiveness.'[67]

Deweyite theory reflected the predilections of a democratic society. Its belief about the negative effects of authoritarian teaching matched mid-century concerns that, as we have seen, democracy was a fragile institution, ready to be challenged by insidious tyranny from Left or Right. The child-centredness of Dewey's theories also reinforced the filiocentric notions of family that existed in the postwar years. Then, in an age of modernism, 'new' educational theories were on the rise, and old issues of tradition, order, and discipline in decline. Finally, in an age of mass education, Dewey promised something for every child. Yet, for all these reasons, Dewey also became a lightning-rod. The discussion of whether Dewey was good or bad for the child was, in many ways, a discussion of whether the education system was doing its job. Throughout the decade a running battle was waged in newspapers and magazines, on radio and television, and in home and school associations about the worth of the 'new education.'[68]

To critics, Deweyite thinking was a blight. In 1953 Saskatchewan professor Hilda Neatby launched a stinging critique of the new education in her book *So Little for the Mind.* It did not pull any punches, arguing that those who professed Deweyite education were responsible for a serious erosion in the scholarship of Canadian youth. A sarcastic pen and an ability to turn Dewey's own words against him made the book a best-seller in Canada, going through four printings in the first six months.[69] Other prestigious figures waded in. Neatby was supported by Classics professor W.G. Hardy in a series of newspaper and magazines articles through 1954. Eugene Forsey argued that the modern curriculum was mush and that 'children need something they can get their teeth into, something solid, something to build mental bone and muscle.'[70]

The critics had a conservative view of human nature. You could not assume that any given child aspired to anything. The classroom should not, therefore, be dominated by the child (the learner) but by the teacher (from whom material could be learned). This was put most explicitly by the superintendent of education in Quebec: 'Certain schools of education, with strong naturalistic and materialistic tendencies, go so far as to free the child from all restraint, on the pretext of leaving him his entire liberty. This is a curious attitude when one considers that the child carries with him the seeds of both good and evil from his human nature tainted by original sin.'[71] Neatby would not have seen it in such theological terms, but she made essentially the same point: 'Somehow educators for all their talk of the world of today are still dreaming the simple philosophic dreams of the eighteenth century, that men are all naturally intelligent, reasonable and moral, needing only the opportunity for a free and full development of their faculties.'[72] The absence of direction in the child-centred environment was, according to its critics, a recipe for self-indulgence and mediocrity.

Those defending the 'new education' held two contrary assumptions. First, their view of humanity was much more optimistic, revolving around the notion that 'every child wants to learn.' Second, their defence of John Dewey's dictum that education must serve the whole child often really meant that it must serve all the children. They had no choice. Schools had to deal with masses of students who were captive by law until they reached age sixteen. The educational system was demanding and receiving unprecedented amounts of taxpayer and government support. Educators, warned J.G. Althouse, 'must seek to give to all our young something that will be of specific use to each.'[73] For the director of the Canadian Education Association, the changes were an essential part of democracy. 'Public education,' he concluded, 'must serve a society which is becoming more democratic and egalitarian.' He then went on to argue that 'scholarship is inappropriate as the major objective and incentive of general education for all.'[74] Instead, as British Columbia's superintendent of education said, schools 'must train all young people to their maximum with courses designed to meet the needs and capacities of all.' If that meant shop or remedial reading, or even driver education, so be it. These courses were all part of education's main objective, to 'make all our young people into worthy citizens.'[75]

The goal of citizenship made the process as important as the content. For the process was a lesson about the nature of society. 'Democratic citizens are never produced in an autocratic school environment.'[76] R.J. Love, head of the Department of Education at the University of New Brunswick, echoed this theme, arguing that 'the adoption of authoritarian principles would undermine and destroy our democratic ideals.'[77] Such rhetoric flowed naturally in these years. It was an item of faith in the wake of the Second World War and during the Cold War that a healthy people would always struggle to be free. Stalin and Hitler succeeded only because something in their societies led the public to abdicate their proper role as citizens. An authoritarian school system seemed a natural target for the blame.

'Over-teaching,' warned Althouse in a 1950 speech, 'has been the greatest menace to the successful formation of the habit of making one's own decisions and taking the responsibility which accompanies free choice.'[78] At another point he warned dramatically that schools with overly strict rules create 'admirable raw material for the labour gangs and legions of the totalitarian state.'[79] As the Hope Commission put it, 'two world wars within one generation, with the consequent social upheaval, have focussed attention upon the need for an adequate preparation of our young people for the responsibilities of citizenship. In no form of society are these responsibilities so great and so difficult to define as in a democracy.'[80] Democracy was under threat, and recent history demonstrated how easily freedom could slip away. For these reasons 'education for democratic living' became a much more pervasive art of school policy in postwar years.[81] The defenders had raised the stakes. Deweyite teaching was more than just a methodology, apparently; it was the first line of freedom.

This put Neatby, Forsey, and other critics on the wrong side of history. For all their erudition and for all the nerves they touched with accusations of a shoddy educational system, they were conservative élitists in an age of mass democracy. The Canadian education system never adopted all of Deweyite thought, not even in the Western provinces. Yet it is also true that the basic principles of child-centredness, anti-authoritarian teaching, and belief in the social importance of education did take hold through the 1950s and into the 1960s. Non-traditional subjects intruded to ever greater degrees in the classroom. There was more Art, more Health, more Music than a generation before. The goal of creating a free and unbowed citizenry ran parallel with the teaching of fundamental skills. This meant two things for the experience of the children. First, obedience to authority (a natural part of any child's upbringing) was always tempered by the doctrine that too much authority was dangerous. Second, the curriculum and the teachers (to a degree) reinforced the physical evidence given by the new schools, the large peer group, and the home. The children were central. In this case one educator of the 1950s was surely right when he said 'school reflects the aims, ideals and aspirations of the society that supports it.'[82]

The critics feared that society no longer supported anything, which was why they considered the educational system so bankrupt. That was not true. The democracy of the 1950s was one based on consensus, even conformity, and in that sense the schools did reflect society. To cite the Hope Commission again, the teaching of values implies 'the existence of standards of behaviour generally agreed upon by all, to which the standard of the individual could be referred.'[83] From the beginning of their school day, children found themselves affected by the notions of citizenship, democracy, and agreed-upon standards of behaviour that defined the school system. In practically all jurisdictions, the day opened with the Lord's Prayer and the singing of 'God Save the Queen.' The Red Ensign or Union Jack stood at the head of the classroom. In some classrooms the practice of reciting a pledge of allegiance to the flag existed, though some jurisdictions thought this too American.

To move from rituals of consensus to the actual values imparted in the texts is difficult. No full study has yet been done of Canadian school curriculum in the postwar years and, given the numerous courses, the ten provincial jurisdictions, and the myriad textbooks authorized for schools, a full study here is impossible. I was curious, none the less, to see something of the values which the texts conveyed.

All subjects develop values. The science texts of the era, for example, enthused about progress and worried little, if at all, about pollution.[84] An Alberta high-school English guide talked of infusing democratic ideals in the course, while the presence of books like *Animal Farm* and *Lord of the Flies* on another course guide is also a comment on values.[85] Given the vast quantities of material, however, it seemed best to concentrate on courses in which values are an explicit part of the curriculum. An examination of mainly textbooks used in two or more provinces made it clear that the values of the age emerge most obviously in that range of courses known variously as 'Health,' 'Family Living,' or 'Personal Growth.'[86]

Taught initially under such titles as 'Mental and Physical Hygiene,' Health courses have always attempted to mix common-sense teachings about cleanliness, nutrition, and disease with the more controversial subjects of ethics, family values, sexuality, and related moral issues. In an age which paid so much attention to social functioning, mental health, and the agonies of psychological upset, Health courses seemed absolutely necessary. 'The concept of good health to-day,' concluded the Hope Commission, 'connotes not only physical well-being but also mental poise and nervous balance, and professional aid should be available to this end.'[87]

The student reaction to such lofty ideals is less certain. Health courses always seemed to want you to be out of touch with the realities of your peer group. The students shown in the textbook pictures were always hideously out of date (which meant about two years). The ideals held up in the texts were always too good to be true, and sanctimonious behaviour kept creeping into the lessons. In one 1960 book designed for Grade Nine, the students get involved in dancing. They learn the waltz because 'there are some lovely waltz's on the hit parade right now.'[88] In an elementary-school book, the children were told a story with the moral, 'good posture wins friends.'[89] Then there was a test-case in which students were supposed to decide which character had a better attitude towards life:

> Bill and Ted were good friends and saw each other often as they were in the same classes. Their friends thought Bill was 'stuffy' because he often refused to go on dates or to hang around the corner drugstore with the gang. He said he had to do his homework. Ted was always ready for any kind of fun, but he had little time left for study. To prepare for exams, he copied answers from his text-books on small pieces of paper which he slipped inside his sleeve. Most of all, he depended on copying from Bill's paper. Bill knew this, but since Ted was a pal, he was caught, with serious consequences to both boys.[90]

This was hardly subtle. At least some of the young readers were likely to mock the sanctimonious Ted. Even given these failings, Health courses reveal much about the values of the age. 'The family' was 'the basic unit of the people,' and the family, of course, was to be run upon democratic principles. Home was, in the words of one high-school curriculum guide, 'a democratic institution.'[91] Family councils, joint decision making, and other such themes were as present in school textbooks as in marriage-counselling books and popular magazine articles. Within the family such traits as reliability, consideration, and good manners were stressed. Radiating outward from the family was the peer group, the school, and the wider society. Here the emphasis tended to be on similar traits, such as reliability, good manners, and the avoidance of conflict. What emerges strongly, especially in the books pitched at junior high and above, is the all-round sport or, in William Whyte's phrase, a junior version of the 'organization man.' That organization was, for lack of a better phrase, a 'domestic democracy.'

Nowhere was domestic democracy treated more clearly than in discussions about women. On the one side, there was the message of modernity. In a marriage, teenagers were warned, 'never decide who will be the boss. Your marriage is a partnership, with each of you thinking more about giving than receiving.'[92] Older notions of inherent male superiority were deliberately undermined as Health books sought to give women increased self-esteem. Likewise, practically all the books recognized that many women did indeed go out to work. There was discussion about career selection, and it was emphasized that the notion of male superiority was obsolete, formed in an era when brute strength mattered much more. Now, however, 'the jobs reserved for men are becoming fewer because muscles have a new role in modern life. People take for granted that women's muscles are equal to men's in a mechanized world.'[93]

Females might be 'equal,' but their roles were not to be the same. While texts talked about women having a career, they also suggested choosing one that would help to prepare for the real job – homemaking. Thus the same book that talked about the lessened role of muscle power then suggested the class 'make a blackboard list of jobs which provide valuable experience for future homemakers.'[94] Another book talked glibly of the excitement of 'dual careers' for women – working in a job and then coming home to maintain the house.[95]

Then there were anecdotes that purported to emphasize female equality while simultaneously establishing the difference between men and women. In one junior-high text, for example, Lucy has stereotyped and critical ideas about what a 'real lady' is like. Cartoons illustrate prissy girls doing needle-point and lounging while men play sports. Such Victorian images are obviously not part of the modern world, and Lucy goes with her family to hear a lecture by a woman who was well known because she had spent years in the jungle 'helping her husband' capture wild animals. Lucy is sure the woman will look ugly, 'huge with man's clothes, rough skin and no charm.' Lucy's father chuckles, and the text then stops. A cartoon at the bottom of the page, though, reveals the punch-line. A well-dressed, coiffured, and very pretty woman is being introduced to the audience, while Lucy's mouth hangs open.[96]

The messages in this and other textbooks probably appear more ambivalent and contradictory to us than they did to their intended audience, at least to the parents of that audience. The texts were really trying to accomplish two things. First, stereotypes of women as weak and frail creatures still existed. Educators believed that these ideas had to be put to rest and, in doing so, they saw themselves as fully in tune with the modernity of the age. As has been discussed in earlier chapters, however, this age was also overwhelmingly domestic in its orientation, and a part of that domesticity included strict separation of career roles. Women were the guardians of the family and, as such, their family roles were still viewed as most appropriate and as paramount. As an Alberta junior-high curriculum guide put it in 1961, a girl should be encouraged to believe 'that homemaking will enrich her life.'[97] Women were capable of having outside careers; it was just not natural to put such careers ahead of motherhood. In this the schools once again mirrored society. A 1960 Gallup poll revealed that only 4 per cent of men and 5 per cent of women believed that a woman should work outside the home if she had young children.[98]

From a later perspective the 1950s seem old-fashioned, reactionary, or distant, to the degree that issues of domesticity, gender roles, and conformity are emphasized. That is not the whole story, however, for it brings into relief only those values which later decades have forsaken. Yet much of the modern value system was being formed in the postwar years. The role of women is a case in point. For alongside domesticity was the notion of family equality. Alongside the belief that women should want to raise their children was the acknowledgment that they were capable of much else. The girls who took the lessons were subject to Dewey's notions of self-esteem as well. Later, as they grew older, they would apply some of the lessons in the ways that few of the educators would have dreamed possible or thought desirable.

The same mixture of traditionalism and change can be seen in the postwar treatment of issues of race and ethnicity. Before the Second World War, Canada prided itself on being open to all peoples, while most Canadians probably accepted the prevalent notion that there was a hierarchy, both of races and of cultures. Few would have been all that shocked to know that the prime minister, William Lyon Mackenzie King, dabbled in anti-Semitic theory.[99] Most Canadians, after all, held prejudices about one group or another. Such attitudes were both normal and respectable.

The war shook old assumptions. Auschwitz, Buchenwald, and the other 'camps' brought home the horrific potential of racial differentiation. This, in turn, shifted official attitudes about how race should be regarded. The process of change would be a long one and would not become a high priority until the 1960s. Nevertheless, the educational systems in Canada picked up on the shift in values, and from 1945 on, textbooks increasingly carried the message that democracy was not only anti-authoritarian, but also tolerant.

Sometimes, as in the elementary-school Health book, *The Girl Next Door* (1946), the issues of exclusion and inclusion were developed in non-controversial areas. In this case it was a girl with a serious disease, which, though never specified, was probably polio. The children of the neighbourhood befriend her, assist her in her struggles to recover, and accept her limitations.[100] In other cases the tone is more direct. Max Braithwaite's Grade Four text, *We Live in Ontario* (1957), attempted to deal with the influx of new immigrants which the province was experiencing. There was an emphasis on 'respect for others' and the positive things that immigrants could teach Canadians.[101] At times the rhetoric even tended towards a multicultural perspective, though the term had not yet been coined. 'The emphasis in this unit is to be on the cultural contribution of Canadians of various historical backgrounds. The term "melting pot" has become obsolete since it is obvious to us today that people with much different historical backgrounds have retained some of their culture in the new land.'[102]

Most striking, perhaps, was the way in which texts identified democracy with tolerance and inclusiveness. 'All human beings have absolute worth regardless of race, religion, or material possessions.' Democracy must accept the fact that 'human beings are equal by virtue of the fact they are human.'[103] A curriculum guide from the late 1950s warned that 'we must be tolerant towards the thought and way of life of others – these are needed by people everywhere and at all times. These outcomes of education, not primarily academic, must become functional in every child if we are really producing "education in a democracy."'[104] If followed to their full conclusion, these were quite radical ideals indeed.

Any argument that domesticity and modernism, even radicalism, mingled in the schools of the 1950s must be qualified. Racial prejudice still existed and was perhaps still the norm. Indeed, fostering tolerance was not precisely the same goal as eliminating racial prejudice. Second, the particular currents of education varied from province to province. In English Canada, however, it is reasonable to say that, by the later 1950s, if not before, the ideas discussed above predominated. The Catholic systems were more conservative, but even there the general currents of postwar thought were present, though cloaked in the context of the continuing absolutes of faith and original sin. Most texts were the same as in the Protestant systems, and the postwar years saw lay teachers, trained by the same methods as the public teachers, begin to replace priests and nuns.

The one real exception was in French Catholic Quebec. There the leaders of the educational system waged a concerted war against modernist influences. 'The task of our educational facilities is immense, never accomplished, and they must constantly be on the alert against the false ideologies which abound in this present troubled period of history,' wrote the superintendant of education in the early 1950s.[105] This conservatism showed up in every area of the schools, from religious instruction through discipline. As one illustration, there was absolutely none of the ambivalence about the role of women that existed in the English systems. The 'traditional family' was exalted, and the school board actually had a 'family propaganda team' that travelled throughout the province to argue 'in favour of the restoration of family life.' Most striking, however, was the Home Economics curriculum. This was not just a course but a whole program designed for girls at the junior-high level which prepared 'the soul and the hands for the virtues and tasks of home.'[106] The goal was straightforward. The average Québécois woman was presumed to have a limited interest in higher education. By Grade Ten or so she would drop out and marry. This course was preparation for that desired event.

This was the last gasp of an old world, however. In 1960 Quebec embarked on the famous Quiet Revolution, and in a few short years it transformed the values of the educational system. By 1965 the new government department of education called for 'the true democratization of teaching and education' and advocated the 'activist,' child-centred approach to learning. The government, for its part, poured millions of additional dollars into the system to assist in the transformation.[107] The argument, therefore, that the postwar educational system was a mixture of modernist enthusiasms and more cautious traditions must be modified for French Quebec only in the matter of timing. There the line was much sharper, and the experience of the students who went through the system much more divided. If anything, the transformation reaffirmed peer ties among Quebec baby-boomers.[108]

THE REPUTATION OF THE 1950S IS CONSERVATIVE, and historians have rightly noted that many educators were more cautious by the mid-1950s than they had been a decade or so earlier. The domestic ethic emphasized stability and security, and those values inevitably became a part of the educational system. All of this implied a decade in which education was a conservative experience. Ultimately, however, this was not the case. Too many of the values being taught in the classroom were dynamic in nature, and even destabilizing in their implications.

Of course, it is a long way from the theoretical statements of educators to an overcrowded classroom with a brand-new nineteen-year-old teacher. For this teacher, facing thirty-five 'exuberant' ten- or eleven-year-old children, traditional discipline was sometimes too tempting to resist. The entire system, after all, was under such pressure that, even more than usual, ideals had to give way to the mundane reality. Yet the ideal always set the agenda. The very fact that there were so many new teachers in the system accentuated the impact of the postwar sensibilities. The ideas did filter down. The approved textbooks, the curriculum guides that so emphasized democracy, and the teachers themselves, having experienced the Second World War, all had an effect.

And if fatigued teachers lost some of the idealism, the children could reinsert it, often in ways unintended by schools. The children absorbed the lessons unencumbered by history or past tradition. Democracy was absolute and could not coexist with racism or vast inequalities. Women were encumbered by no physical or mental handicap. The obvious differences in the roles of men and women were thus socially defined and, however deeply believed at the moment, susceptible to change. Moreover, not just content but process had a radical edge. Democracy in the schools implied that the children would follow a path because they believed it to be right not because they were told to do so. Questioning was encouraged, and the tradition of acceptance of authority considerably modified.

Reinforcing this perspective, the educational system was designed to affirm self-esteem. Every pupil was to be given the opportunity to show that his or her personal experience was worthwhile. As a 1959 teacher's manual for a Grade Three reader put it: 'See that each child has a chance to taste success in some area – whether it be in reading, singing, drawing, pantomiming, playing games, caring for a classroom pet or cleaning the chalkboard.'[109] Also, the school system was supposed, in the ideal, to serve as a client of the child. Activities were to conform increasingly to the child's way of doing things rather than forcing the child to conform to the ways of the adult world. 'Learning in school is facilitated, and incidentally made much more interesting and enjoyable, when instructional activities are based upon the routines normally followed by children.'[110]

It may be, therefore, that the stereotype of a materialist decade fostering a conservative educational tradition is misplaced. Education after the war had its conservative elements, but it also possessed dynamism and idealism. Charles Phillips, director of the Canadian Education Association, expressed this view in a series of 1956 lectures. 'The modern emphasis in general education is almost wholly immaterial, almost wholly spiritual.' Of course, there were practical courses. What dominated, though, was the emphasis on 'better citizens,' 'democracy,' and the improvement of society. As well, as Dewey taught, children learned better by working things out for themselves: 'More people believe that truth is mighty enough to prevail in experience. That experience is the best teacher.'[111]

The emphasis on experience, on self-worth, and on anti-authoritarian education would influence the 1960s. Most significant of all, however, was the real message of 1950s education: Child-centredness to an unparalleled degree. This reinforced every other experience of the young baby-boomers. Child-experts like Spock had said it from the day they were born. The child-centred families said it. The toy makers said it, and the child-dominated suburbs made it explicit. The sheer numbers of children confirmed it: This society is designed for you.

6

The Fifties and the Cult of the Teenager

In 1960 the first of the baby-boomers turned thirteen – the new decade and a new stage of life thus coinciding. This synchronicity is symbolically appropriate, for 'the sixties' became one of the great mythological eras of modern times and that mythology in turn created the mythology of the baby boom. It was in 'the sixties' (a period that actually extends, in historical terms, through the early seventies) that the baby boom became conscious of itself as generational force and began to think of itself as special, not for the economic affluence it had been given, but for the moral and personal attributes it possessed. The generation and the decade, with all the images it connotes, thus became inseparably linked.

The popular imagery of the 1960s is so powerful in part because of the contrast with the 1950s. The family decade was trashed by the youth revolution. The technocratic age of the organization man ran headlong into a romantic reaction. Feeling and personal fulfilment took pride of place over logical debate and quiet compromise. Conformity was assaulted by deliberately outrageous clothes, behaviour, and language. An age of timidity was supplanted by civil disobedience. Patriotism was smashed by cynicism. Most of all, the search for security and stability was mocked by those who sought emotional release and inner growth.

For several reasons such popular imagery, much of it generated by those who were active participants, is simplistic. First, as many others have noted, the 1950s were just as exceptional a decade as the 1960s.[1] The devotion of the 1950s to family and security, demonstrated in the high marriage rates, low divorce rates, and increased fertility rates, contradicted trends present since the nineteenth century. That such an emphasis upon domesticity did not last through the 1960s should hardly be surprising. Second, as many scholars of the 'beat' generation, and early civil-rights movements have noted, the 1950s was not devoid of protest.[2] Further, the two decades are linked in another and important way: The youth cult of the 1960s had its basis in the 1950s. Thus, when the baby-boomers arrived at adolescence, they did so not only as a group of children who had always been treated as important, but in a society that gave youth culture a distinct and important position. The uniqueness of the generation was thus reinforced and enhanced in the transition from childhood to adolescence, from the fifties to the sixties.

THE BABY-BOOMERS WERE NOT THE first people to discover the special qualities of being young, though occasionally they seemed to think so. Different cultures have defined youth in different ways, and with greater or lesser clarity. The only common link has been the idea of a period between childhood and full adulthood that belonged fully to neither. In many instances formal religious customs, such as communion or the bar mitzvah, gave sacred overtones to the entry into this intermediate world. At the other end, different events were used as markers, depending on time and place. In some societies marriage brought full adult status. Other cultures, especially rural ones, made inheritance of family lands the key event. In yet others, the intermediate phase had no sharp beginning or end; rather, it emerged gradually out of childhood and drifted slowly towards adult respectability. In practically all societies, though, considerations of status, law, and custom have distinguished an intermediate period between childhood, on the one hand, and full membership in the adult community, on the other.[3]

The arrival of urbanization and industrialization in Western society initiated long-term and fundamental changes to the concept of youth. There has been a general tendency, for example, from the eighteenth century to the present, to refine the distinctions between various ages. Thus, to give one example, when the average length of schooling increased by five to six years, as it did in Britain between the seventeenth and nineteenth centuries, it lengthened that intermediate period between childhood, pure and simple, and adulthood. To give another example, the general improvement of diet in the Western world over the past centuries has led to a constant lowering of the age of puberty. The length of time between sexual awakening and emotional and economic maturity has thus tended to increase, further emphasizing the existence of a special intermediate phase.

Yet the social and historical role of youth has not changed in a purely linear fashion. At various times there are relatively abrupt shifts which can be explained less by long-term trends than by short-term disturbances. This leads to the other major force shaping the role of youth historically. In the shorter term, 'episodic' forces enhance or diminish the role of youth in the wider society.[4] The turbulent world of early nineteenth-century Europe, for example, brought forward a youthful intellectual movement which was self-consciously distinct from the Enlightenment rationalists of the old order. These youthful romantics exerted tremendous influence on both thought and the direction of politics through to the revolutions of 1848. Thereafter, for many years, youth's hold upon the culture and mind of Europe faded.

The impact of the 1960s can be explained, at least in part, by the confluence of such an episodic shift in the role of youth with the longer-term trends brought about by modern urban-democratic society. The result was an upheaval by youth and the assertion of a generational identity such as that experienced by post-Napoleonic Europe. After 1945 long-term tendencies that emphasized the distinctiveness of youth were accelerated, while short-term cyclical forces shoved youth to the fore. Political and social change provided youth with a cause and an opportunity to assert itself upon the world stage, at least briefly. The baby-boomers grew up amid a cult of family and childhood, and they would themselves shift the emphasis towards a cult of youth as they reached adolescence. There was no reason understandable to the minds of youth why they should wait until adult 'judgment' seasoned their thinking. Indeed, adult judgment was mistrusted in a world that looked ever more to the spontaneity of youth.

The very demand for spontaneity denied the forces of the past. Yet, more than the baby-boomers realized, the youth culture of the 1960s was the product of previous generations. Much of their identity as a group originated in currents of thought dating back to at least the turn of the century. In those years the new social sciences, supported by medical theorists, asserted that adolescence was a special and unalterable phase in human growth. Its beginning was determined not by educational experience or the workplace, but by the onset of puberty and its end, for lack of a better definition, by the successful transition into the adult world. A stage of life that had previously been understood in educational and economic terms and more or less reserved to the middle class now became a scientific 'fact.' Indeed, educational and work experiences were no longer relevant to the definition, and adolescence was thereby extended to all elements of society.

The definition of adolescence in scientific terms developed simultaneously in many Western countries and was tied to Freudian theories of sexual development.[5] In North America the scientific certification of adolescence emanated from the man who first brought Freud to visit America, the president of Clark University, G. Stanley Hall.[6] In 1911, Hall published his grandiosely titled two-volume work on adolescence: *Adolescence and Its Psychology and Its Relations to Physiology, Anthropology, Sociology, Sex, Crime, Religion and Education.*[7] Audacious though such a title might be, Hall's work was a tremendous success. He was able to synthesize emerging scientific notions on adolescence in a way that became the standard for others in the field.

Hall was a psychologist but, as with many others of his generation, he had migrated to the discipline from a background in the humanities and theology.[8] In a kind of parallel journey, Hall was determined to remove the discussions of adolescence from the religious–moral realm to that of the sciences in general, and psychology in particular. Influenced by Charles Darwin and 'recapitulation' theory, Hall believed that growth from childhood to adulthood re-created the stages of human development from the primitive to the modern.[9] Biological change thus determined, or largely determined, psychological outlook. For physiological and psychological reasons, Hall asserted over and over again, the adolescent was a creature in a state of emotional stress. The 'profound effect of adolescence in producing disturbances of the nervous system and of the mind is recognized in many a custom of the savages.' There was good reason for this, he argued, for 'psychoses and neuroses abound in early adolescent years more than at any other period of life.' Drawing upon the recent work of Freud and others, Hall painted a picture familiar to postwar eyes. The traumas of growth and sexual development created a crucial and dangerous time of transition. Hysteria, insanity, melancholy, and moral collapse were all possible. Immoral or, more appropriately, socially maladjusted actions were almost to be expected.[10]

Other social scientists added to Hall's theories over the next decades, but the essential elements remained. As Kenneth Kenniston noted, Hall's description of adolescence as a time of '*sturm und drang,* turbulence, ambivalence, dangers and possibilities' remained central to practically all psychological discussions.[11] Such theory migrated into literature and movies, and, as Freud's ascendancy increased, became a popular public characterization.[12] The adolescent had gone from 'trouble-maker to troubled,' in the words of one historian.[13] More precisely perhaps, they were troublemakers because they were naturally troubled.[14]

Such attitudes remained durable because social and economic trends reinforced the idea of adolescence as a distinct experience. The average amount of time spent in school continued to increase with each decade. This is crucial to the notion of adolescence, for as long as most children left school at age twelve or fourteen, the concept of a distinct 'intermediate' stage between childhood and adulthood remained limited in application – too large a percentage of children worked on a day-to-day basis in an adult world. In 1921, for example, more than 40 per cent of all Canadian ten- to nineteen-year-olds were not in school.[15] For these 'adolescents' distinctiveness from the adult world meant only lower wages and limited independence. Their day-to-day life was an adult one – as apprentice, domestic, employee, or whatever. The truly special world of the youthful adolescent in the first decades of the twentieth century thus remained confined to two groups – the educated middle class and the young criminal.

After 1945 this situation changed. The earlier expansion of compulsory school-attendance laws had extended the world of adolescence upwards to the age of sixteen. Through the 1950s, adolescence in Canada was extended both in age range and in class as more and more teenagers remained for more and more high school. By 1954 the majority of fourteen- to seventeen-year-olds were in school; by the early 1960s, three out of four. Adolescence increasingly had its own particular institution – the high school – with all the social and educational implications that entailed.

Embedded in these long-term changes were short-term episodic forces. Youth culture in Canada has yet to be studied for most periods, but work on the United States indicates that, in the early part of the century, the 1920s marked the high-water mark of youth culture. Fads in fashion, food, and language swept the nation, and the image of the flapper became mythologized.[16] Canada was a somewhat tamer society, but the basic forces that unleashed the flapper era on American campuses were present in Canada: growing urban populations, a large youth population, relative affluence, and greater autonomy within the family.[17] Moreover, Canadian society was very much open to influences from south of the border – including movies out of Hollywood, American periodicals, and the new cultural medium of radio.

For almost a quarter-century thereafter, events diminished the importance of youth culture. That culture had depended upon affluence, but the Depression subordinated youthful frivolity to the grim reality of preparing for a difficult adult world. Adolescents and young adults stayed at home longer, and thus remained under the shadow of their parents. While the war changed much, it did not alter the low profile of the adolescent. The problem now was that the adult world was so accessible. The armed forces and the war factories absorbed hundreds of thousands of people still in their teens. The very notion of an adolescent subculture was temporarily subsumed within the larger and more imprecise term 'youth.' It was no accident that the Canadian Youth Commission ignored adolescence as a category and opted instead to look at fifteen- to twenty-four-year-olds.[18]

Immediately after the war, the deciding factor was numbers. The low birth rates of the 1930s skewed the population so that, by the later 1940s, the percentage of teenagers was at an all-time low in twentieth-century Canada. Nor did the immediate future for teenage culture look all that promising. The percentage of ten- to fourteen-year-olds, who would soon enter adolescence, was even lower – some 9 per cent of total population by 1951, and only 7 per cent in Ontario and British Columbia. This meant that, in the late 1940s and early 1950s, adolescents were unable to exert much of a cultural presence. Their numbers, their consuming powers, the interests – all were overshadowed by the young adults born in the 1920s who were buying houses, having babies, and contributing to postwar prosperity. So weak was the adolescent presence that a study by Canadian sociologists even challenged the notion that there was a distinct adolescent culture.[19]

Teenage cult figures of these years were a particularly moody and withdrawn lot. Typical was Holden Caulfield, the sixteen-year-old hero of J.D. Salinger's *Catcher in the Rye* or the less well-known Natalie Waite of Shirley Jackson's *Hangsaman* (both 1951). James Dean, in *East of Eden* or *Rebel without a Cause*, and Marlon Brando, in the *The Wild One*, brought the same dark edge to the screen. The moodiness no doubt captured some of the natural 'angst' of adolescence that the psychologists and sociologists were always talking about. It also reflected the obsession of the age with psychology. It may also have had a particular poignancy for this generation of teenagers. Powerlessness and purposelessness in an adult-dominated world is a theme that runs through these and many other works of the decade.[20] They could not change the world but they could resist its pull. In contrast, the baby boom never accepted such limits.

When adolescents are powerless to assert their own image, adults will. This is what happened in the decade immediately after the war. In the late 1940s and early 1950s, adult discussion about youth almost invariably focused on a particularly adult concern – juvenile delinquency.[21] The prevalent stereotype of adolescent culture included a leather jacket, jeans, and dangling cigarette. Such imagery stood as an antithesis and undercurrent in an age dominated by dreams of suburbs and children. It frightened and titillated the adults who found so much evidence of wayward youth. It also provided the basis through which a youthful identity reasserted itself.

By the end of the Second World War, the idea of the 'juvenile delinquent' was well established both in the public mind and in the law. The notion dated back to mid-Victorian England, where changing social and economic conditions, as well as Victorian evangelism, led to the belief that 'young criminals' should be treated differently from their adult counterparts. As early as 1854 the United Kingdom's Youthful Offenders Act allowed young criminals to be treated separately from adults.[22] Across the Atlantic, the Canadian colonies followed suit. [23]

The development of a distinct concept of the juvenile delinquent in law soon reorganized the very concept of youth. Juvenile delinquency acts provided for offenders from the ages of ten or twelve (depending on place and time) to sixteen or eighteen. Those under the minimum age were seen as children and not legally responsible. Those above that age were treated as adults. This division was reinforced by the 1890s crusade of J.J. Kelso to create Children's Aid Societies in Ontario. By 1894 the federal government extended the principle across the country. Children's Aid automatically intervened for offenders under the age of twelve. The final major step came in 1908, when the federal government passed the Juvenile Delinquents Act for offenders under sixteen.[24] Though there were later refinements, the basic concepts of this act were still in place at the end of the Second World War.

The emergence of juvenile delinquency as a cultural and legal concept in Canada had many implications. Delinquency became a catch-all concept. Those under sixteen were further distinguished from adult society. A whole new bureaucracy of 'child savers' developed as auxiliaries to the juvenile court system. Perhaps most important, the concept of delinquency blurred the line between criminal and non-criminal behaviour. The merger of Children's Aid services with the criminal justice system, the softening of that system for adolescents, and the emergence of special adolescent 'crimes' such as truancy meant that 'troublesome' youth could more easily fall under the umbrella of 'delinquency' in the eyes of society, social workers, and even the law itself. Delinquency legislation over a century had clearly distinguished between the youthful offender and the adult. It had paid a price, however, in that, at the other end, it had blurred the line between assistance for the troubled and coercion for the criminal.[25] Juvenile delinquency could mean anything from murder to skipping school or just being uncooperative with officials. Both the state of 'juvenile delinquency' and the definition of the 'juvenile delinquent' were thus especially susceptible to societal neuroses.

Two main forces made the issue of the juvenile delinquent important in the 1940s and 1950s. The first was the Second World War. The absence of fathers in the military and the absence of mothers in the factory forced families to adopt makeshift arrangements for child care.[26] This set of abnormal arrangements gave adolescents a degree of autonomy greater than normal, and there were some social consequences. Illegitimate births increased, as did the number of juveniles charged with various vagrancy and small-property offences.[27] These changes were reinforced by general anxiety about the postwar world. Juvenile delinquency was, said one 1946 article, 'one of the most serious and pressing issues facing Canada now that the war is over.'[28] A Quebec Catholic group, reporting to the Canadian Youth Commission, warned that three-quarters of all juvenile delinquents came from the homes of working mothers.[29] The juvenile-delinquency problem was thus incorporated into the general desire to reassert the 'normal' structures after 1945 discussed in chapter 1.

The second force underlying the obsession with youth crime is a little less obvious. After the war the image of the 'jd' problem persisted, and even strengthened. Sensationalist articles played up the problem of the juvenile delinquent. 'For fun, these young gangsters brawled. For thrills they stole and got drunk. What makes them tick? A reporter and a social worker find out.'[30] Yet all available evidence indicates that juvenile delinquency in the late 1940s and early 1950s was not a problem. The number of juvenile cases before the courts dropped to the lowest levels in more than twenty years, while high levels of employment ensured that youth moved relatively quickly from school to the workforce.[31] The contradiction between image and reality indicates that youthful crime reflected the anxieties of the age. The rebellious adolescent was the antithesis of the healthy family. The existence of surly boys, promiscuous girls, alienation, and even, on occasion, crime, challenged the myth of the perfect suburban society (and hence fascinated). There was also a warning, however. Public opinion, drawing upon the psychological fads of the age, blamed parents for a teenager's waywardness.[32] Thus juvenile delinquents reminded parents of their duties and responsibilities. Here is what will happen to your children if you are not good parents!

Canadian concerns were magnified by American obsessions. Dozens of articles on juvenile delinquency were published annually in major American periodicals. From the late 1940s, both the American Justice Department and the Senate became almost as active in rooting out juvenile delinquents as they were in chasing Communists.[33] It was Hollywood, however, that really convinced the American public of the dangers of juvenile delinquency. Through the late 1940s and the 1950s, at least sixty movies portrayed youth as alternately alienated and depraved, or both.[34] Hollywood produced dozens of juvenile-delinquent films in the decade after the war, including such forgettable cinematic events as *City Across the River* (1949), *Running Wild* (1955), *Teenage Crime Wave* (1955), and *Teenage Wolfpack* (1956). Two movies, however, defined the genre and made teenage rebellion both a popular myth and an art form. *The Wild One* (1954) starred a young Marlon Brando as an angst-ridden motorcycle-gang leader. A year later, James Dean glorified drag-racing and more teenage angst in *Rebel without a Cause* (1955). Dean's own death in a car accident only intensified the cult that already existed around him. Not only were both movies interesting in their own right, but their anti-heroes perversely confirmed the deepest values of the age. Both were rebels because their families had failed them. Both expressed their anguish in terms familiar to anybody who had read Freud or understood the popular notions of adolescence as a troubled age! Both thus reaffirmed the age even as they rebelled against it.

By the early 1950s the obsession with the juvenile delinquent was at an all-time high. Yet something else was happening. The very obsession with youth culture and with the tremendous popularity of Dean and Brando hinted that the episodic forces that had so worked against the cohesion and influence of a youthful culture were now reversing themselves. The forces that were to explode onto the scene in the 1960s were beginning to build.

BY THE MID-1950S THE WARTIME BABIES were entering adolescence. From this point until well into the 1970s, episodic forces accentuated the role of the adolescent in society. Between 1951 and 1961, the ten-to-nineteen age group in Canada increased by more than a million people. Each year more and more of the Canadian population were interested in adolescent fashions, issues, and identity. In the United States the adolescent population rose just as quickly and, on both sides of the border, the preteeners of the baby boom moved ever closer to adolescence. As well, high-school participation rates were having an effect. In 1954 the proportion of fourteen- to seventeen-year-olds still in school went over 50 per cent for the first time in Canadian history. Within six years, two-thirds of the age group were still students.[35] Not only were there more adolescents, but their activities were increasingly defined by an age-specific institution – the high school. The final ingredient was market power. The continually rising standard of living in Canada made the adolescent market increasingly important.[36] In turn, the very existence of a special youth market reinforced the sense that youth were distinct from both children and adults.

Out of it all, sometime in the 1950s, the cult of the teenager was born. In many ways 'teenager' was just a more age-specific term for adolescence, but in others it was a special word because, unlike 'adolescence,' it implied a whole culture rather than merely a state of hormonal transition. Teenagers were an American invention, but television, magazines, and the general pervasiveness of American culture quickly carried it north of the border. As well, as others have noted, it was not the baby boom that invented modern youth culture, though they transformed it.[37] Instead, the institutions, cultural forms, and economic power of the teenager were all in place by the end of the 1950s. Most important of all, so, too, was the conscious sense that youth had its own unique culture, not congenial to adults and therefore all the more special. By the time the baby boom reached adolescence, the distinct world of the North American teenager was well entrenched.

Once the world decided that teenage culture existed, it was not hard to find. Special magazines like *16 Magazine* (founded in 1954), *Teen* (1957), and the original *Seventeen* (1944) catered to a teenage, usually female, audience. These were hardly rebellious underground magazines. Controlled by adults, they taught adults' values.[38] None the less, they focused on what was distinctive about teenage culture. Movie reviews, profiles of stars, music, and, above all, fashion dominated. Collectively they told their audience what a teenager was like and what teenagers liked. Television also discovered the teenager. Practically all of the family sit-coms of 1950s and early 1960s had an adolescent character. Some, such as Ricky Nelson on *Ozzie and Harriet,* became major teen heroes. Advertisers weren't far behind. Soft drinks, chewing gum, and skin-care products, among others, created ads aimed specifically at the teen audience.

By the later 1950s the teenage culture was clearly defined.[39] It was also schizophrenic. In part it was based upon the images of alienation and disturbance that adults had decided was the nature of teenagers. The troubled figures of Holden Caulfield, James Dean, and Marlon Brando remained teenage idols through the decade.[40] The greased-back duck-tail haircut and leather jacket remained teen symbols, as the Elvis phenomenon testified. The market played to these images as well. The mail-order rebel could order a genuine black motorcycle jacket from Eaton's for $18.98. The more ambivalent rebel could buy a tamed-down 'simulated leather windbreaker' for only $14.98. The economy-minded rebel could buy a vinyl version for only $13.95.[41]

The rebellious teenager provides an important subtheme running through the decade. It also provides a subculture that, along with the Beats, serves as a precursor to the much larger-scale rebellion of the 1960s. Yet, in many ways, this was a very limited rebellion. Thousands of middle-class teenagers might vicariously thrill to Brando or Dean, but few of the males dared wear a leather jacket. After all, few of the females would have dated a leather-jacketed 'hood.' Hollywood heroes aside, the imagery of jeans and leather was associated with just the sort of poor, broken family environments that the whole middle-class suburban lifestyle was constructed to avoid. Instead, much of teen culture was designed both to emulate the adult world and to provide a ritualistic means of preparing for entry into that world.

The most obvious example of teen as pre-adult comes in the sex roles assumed by teenagers. Boys and girls emulated the particular postwar combination of 'modernist' (i.e., consciously anti-Victorian) freedom and strictly defined gender roles. The macho leather-jacketed image and the all-pervasive car-craziness of boys reflected a world that both took pride in manliness and feared for its future. Girls were supposed to retain their virtue and collect their silverware in anticipation of the big day. When the two sexes interacted, the role-playing became especially complex. The evolution of sexual mores is discussed in detail in chapter 10. It is worth mentioning here, however, that the 1950s may be the high point of the dating culture, reaching a peak in ritual and cultural function just before it began to fray in the 1960s.[42]

Adult sex roles were rehearsed in reserving to the boy the initiative in dating and the cost of providing for the girl's expenses. All dating etiquette talked in terms of the boy as 'manly' (opening doors, assisting the 'weaker' sex). The girl, even if she knew she wasn't weaker, deferred to this ritual. When one girl wrote to a teen magazine that she had many boys who were friends but none of them dates, the editor replied that she was exuding too much competence. 'In a dating situation it's a boy who likes to feel stronger. And can you blame him – when the world will expect him to act in this strong and protective way later on, as husband and breadwinner? So, if you are the strong and superior one, where is he then? Or, rather, where are you?'[43] One of the first things girls learned was to protect the fragile ego of their dates.

Going steady was condemned by adults, but it, too, was a logical preparation for the adult world.[44] Adults feared, of course, that this was indeed the case, particularly in terms of sexual activity. Even if sexual activity was not a problem, adults could not fathom why fifteen-year-olds would tie themselves down when there was obviously so much more searching to be done for a suitable partner. Yet going steady had a clear purpose in a dating culture. First, it was a form of insurance. Dates were an essential element of being a part of teenage culture – attending dances, parties, movies, and so on depended on having a date. Going steady was a means of ensuring a date's availability. Most important of all, though, going steady was a direct mimicry of an adult world that valued marriage so highly and expected it to come so early.[45]

The world of the teenager, therefore, was a peculiar combination of adult emulation and peer-group distinctiveness. Nowhere is this clearer than in the world of consumption. Teenage purchases and fads ranged from the tame to the outrageous. By purchasing in the teen market, however, the teenager was learning a valuable lesson for the adult world – how to consume according to the tastes that mattered: those of your peer group. The appropriate badges of membership in the peer group were displayed in thousands of variations across the country, depending on what was considered cool at any given moment and by any given group. Those too poor, too awkward, or physically or ethnically different often had a tough time of it, for the teenage world, like the adult world, demanded conformity. On the positive side, the activities and totems of peer-group membership provided both a form of security and a path for learning how to interact with the culture around them.

Consumption, peer pressure, and emulation met most closely in the world of fashion. To employ Tom Wolfe's phrase, fashion is not the mere 'embroidery of history.' Rather, it reveals much about the social conventions, values, and assumptions of the age.[46] The rise of the teenager was matched by a conscious effort on the part of designers and retailers to play to the youth market. There was a new consciousness of 'young style' influencing designers and department store buyers. Many of the fashion designs that would become common in the 1960s had their roots in the works of young designers like Mary Quant in the later 1950s.[47] In other words, the pendulum of fashion was swinging towards the young. Within a few years middle-aged men in tight pants and middle-aged women in mini-skirts would demonstrate just how tyrannical the fashion of youth had become.

In 1959 the swing was just beginning, and a teenager's wardrobe mixed parental imitation and youthful fad. The typical middle-class Canadian boy's wardrobe would include corduroy pants, some dressier 'automatic-machine washable' slacks, and an assortment of tartan and plain-coloured shirts. Sweaters were very popular – mainly in V-neck and cardigan styles. Sports-jackets and suits had gone from baggy to trim, and teenagers were, for obvious reasons, faster to adopt this style were their fathers. Ties were also narrow and increasingly sedate. Fedoras, common attire for any dress outfit a decade earlier, were now out of fashion for youth.

The middle-class girl had a more complicated and slightly more formal wardrobe. Party dresses were still quite fancy and involved crinolines, and sometimes even a hoop skirt, a tremendously impractical fashion. Nearly all of her day-to-day outfits would have a more relaxed look: casual dresses, or skirts and blouses; pleated styles were very popular, so too were jumpers. White blouses with frilly collars were common, but the 'sweater look' remained dominant. Cardigans over blouses, pullovers, and 'twin sets' of matching pullover and cardigan were a crucial part of any girl's wardrobe. Slacks were also now common – usually in tartan. They were worn only on very casual occasions, however, and blue jeans, though infiltrating wardrobes, still had a 'tough image' in middle-class urban and suburban circles. Both sexes wore 'car coats,' three-quarter length in corduroy or check. Girls would also likely own a longer dress coat. Saddle shoes, loafers, and, by the early 1960s, 'desert boots' provided footwear. In addition girls had dress shoes in various heel heights, and boys owned some hideous and unloved pair of black lace-up shoes for dressy occasions.

Though parents grumbled, the dress standards of the late 1950s were hardly outrageous. They were evolving, however. Both sexes had quickly absorbed the growing informality of the postwar years, and now wore casual clothes in situations where a decade earlier such dress would have been thought inappropriate.[48] Girls were still more restricted in this direction, but slacks were appearing more and more in public, much to the dismay of conservative elements. Neither sex thought anything of wearing casual clothes in mixed company. Most important, however, was the simple rhythm of teen styles. The national and international peer group held sway to the degree that budget and parents and awareness allowed. White socks might be in or out, wide ties might be replaced by narrow ones, poodle skirts might triumph one year and fade the next, but the ritual went on. The fashion-conscious teenager knew that being distinctive required a keen sense of peer tastes.

A second area of consumption profoundly affected by the teenager was the movie theatre. The changing nature of the movie industry and movie audience both reflected and reinforced the growing interest in the teenager. This had not always been the case. In the 1940s movies were a truly mass entertainment. Neighbourhood cinemas provided relatively easy access for people without cars. Downtown theatres, featuring the first-run 'blockbusters,' were major attractions, drawing people to the city. For the average Canadian couple, a 'night on the town' did not consist of cocktails and dancing, but of a fairly straightforward dinner and a visit to one of the big movie theatres. This made the movies big business. In 1950, for example, Winnipeg had 43 movie theatres, and Toronto 124. Overall there were more than 1,800 movie theatres in Canada, and there were more than 23 million paid admissions, nearly 2 for every man, woman, and child in Canada.[49] More than a quarter of the average family's recreation expenditures went on theatre tickets. 'Going to the movies' on a regular basis was a part of the rhythm of life of the families of postwar Canada.

Children, adolescents, young adults, the middle-aged, seniors – all had to be attracted to these moviehouses if an industry of this size was to make money. Both society and the industry acted on the assumption that movies were for everybody. On the production side, the so-called Production Code clamped strong controls over sexual innuendo and language in movies. At the distribution level, provincial censorship boards snipped out anything they found offensive. Movies of the late 1940s were more restrained in language and depiction than much modern-day prime-time television.[50] Producers grumbled about restrictions on their freedom, but they went along, at least in part because it was good for business. Not every movie was suitable for all ages, of course, but the overall image of the industry was kept, if not wholesome, at least acceptable to the average family. By the late 1940s the formula seemed to have been found. Family-oriented movies, peace, new-found prosperity, and a pervasive network of movie theatres boded well for the postwar industry.

Of course, everybody knows the punchline – television. Television privatized family entertainment in a way radio never could. In the United States, the problem for movies was apparent by 1950. In Canada, where television arrived later, movies thrived through the early 1950s. Between 1950 and 1952 paid admissions increased by 1.5 million. Then, as television spread across the country, the collapse began. In two years movie attendance dropped to 1945 levels, and in just six years (1953–9) movies lost half their audience. More than 450 theatres closed across the country, and family spending on movies fell from more than a quarter to just over a tenth of all recreational expenditure![51] As television became pervasive, movies ceased to be a normal part of family life. Many did not go to movies at all any more, and those who did went rarely.

The movie industry tried all sorts of responses. These were the days of Cinerama, 3D, CinemaScope. There was even Smel-O-Vision: 'First, they moved – 1893. Then they talked – 1927. Now, they smell – 1959!' Most of all it was the era of the spectacular, big-budget epic. The idea was to give a range of colour and spectacle that demanded a large screen. The favourite themes were biblical. *Samson and Delilah* (1949), *The Robe* (1953), *The Ten Commandments* (1956), and *Ben Hur* (1959) allowed producers to mix violence, sexual temptation, and innuendo in a spectacular setting, and with a moral message acceptable to censors.[52] All of these movies were indeed spectacular, and some were even good. They were also horribly expensive. What the movie industry needed was not one expensive spectacle every other year but a means of attracting steady customers to cheaply and quickly made productions.

The solution came in the teenager. Through the 1950s a growing percentage of movie production was aimed at the adolescent.[53] Such memorable titles as *I Was a Teenage Werewolf* (1957), and *I Was a*

Teenage Frankenstein (1957), *Bop Girl Goes Calypso*, and *Teenagers from Outer Space* (1959) provided the newly identified teenage market with a special, segmented form of entertainment. Certain characteristics linked these movies. First, four genres dominated; juvenile delinquency (*Crime in the Streets, Hot Rod Rumble*), science fiction–horror (*Attack of the Fifty-Foot Woman, The Blob*), music (*The Girl Can't Help It, Love Me Tender*), and clean teen (*Gidget, Tammy and the Bachelor*). Many sank without a trace after a brief run. Others became famous or infamous and were influential in the formation of a teen identity. Many, such as *The Blackboard Jungle* (1955), combined genres to double the appeal to the teenage audience.[54]

There are no precise statistics on movie goers in Canada in the 1950s. Every indicator, though, is that the shift towards the teenage audience was substantial. In the United States marketing surveys indicated that, by the later 1950s, a majority of those who attended shows once a week were between the ages of ten and nineteen. In contrast, 40 per cent of those fifty-five and over went to shows only once a year.[55] In Canada, as in the United States, the size of the teenage market was growing, while each year more and more children and adults over thirty stayed home, glued to the tube. Teens, however, had every incentive to get out of the house. It was a part of growing up, and the movies were both an entertainment and a chance to be on your own. Their attachment to their peer group encouraged them to go. The dating culture ritualized the movie. The movie companies catered to the audience. It was a match that transformed the nature of movies within a few short years.

Nowhere was the changing nature of the movie market clearer than at the drive-in. The drive-in movie was a natural offshoot of the automobile culture and had first emerged in the United States before the war. In Canada, fewer cars per capita, a thinly spread population, and cold winters meant that, in 1947, there were still only seven drive-ins in all of the country, accounting for a mere one-third of 1 per cent of theatre attendance. Ten years later there were 229 drive-ins in Canada, attracting 7 per cent of all moviegoers. Most important, attendance at drive-ins held its own in spite of the spread of television.[56]

Despite its image as a 'passion pit,' initially the drive-in theatre catered to the family. In the immediate postwar years, traditional theatre attendance hit all-time highs as dating couples or young marrieds combined companionship with the latest Hollywood entertainment. Then the baby boom began, and all of those couples found themselves with small children and an entertainment dilemma. Baby-sitters were expensive, if available at all. Yet to take preschool children to a theatre invited chaos from the children and annoyed looks from the audience. The exploding ownership of automobiles brought a new possibility, however. The family could pack itself into the car and head off to the drive-in, where peanuts, popcorn, and toys could keep the kids amused. 'Bring the Children ... Come as You Are' was the way one drive-in chain enticed families in 1953.[57] Double features often catered to families by showing a children's movie first; when that was finished, the kids would, parents hoped, drift off to sleep in the back seat. The adults could then settle in to watch the spectaculars on the large screen in relative peace. Many baby-boomers have fragmented memories of curling up in the back seat while Charlton Heston performed one or another great deed in living colour on the big screen.

This market was extremely vulnerable to the lures of television, however. Kids could be entertained at home for free and put to bed at a reasonable time. By the mid-1950s, attendance at drive-ins in Canada began to slip.[58] However, the combination of the car, the dating culture, and the teenage orientation of movies provided a new source of income for drive-ins. Double horror features – triple features, dusk-to-dawn features all wooed the teenager. They could be a more troublesome audience than adults, but they had an endless and uncritical appetite for both the movies and the concessions. By the end of the decade, the image of the drive-in had gone from family outing to teenage passion-pit. It had, however, survived the onslaught of television by playing to the new market power of teenage culture.

AS A SYMBOL OF TEENAGE CULTURE, clothes and movies were insignificant compared with the great innovation of the decade – rock and roll. More than any other form of teenage expression, music distinguished the generations. More than any other teenage expression, the new music met antagonism from parents and the voices of authority in society.[59] Of course, such antagonism helped make rock and roll special and helped music to become the emblem of youth, an emblem that became even more powerful and all-pervasive in the next decade. The significance cannot be overstated. The period from the later 1950s to the early 1970s was unique in the history of music. In these years 'teenage music,' or 'young people's music,' emerged as totally separate from adult music. Its distinctiveness was not just a matter of proclivity towards a specific song, singer, or dance fad, but a matter of genre. The very medium of music had a different significance and had a different role for old and young.

In 1950 there was no teenage music – period. Individual artists like Frank Sinatra could and did attract an adolescent audience, but Sinatra's crooning did not distinguish him in form or content from artists appealing to adults. The big hits of the year included Guy Lombardo's 'The Third Man,' Patti Page's 'The Tennessee Waltz,' and The Weavers' 'Good-Night Irene.' None of these songs was distinctively 'young.' Indeed, the barely begun baby boom had more of an impact upon the market than adolescents. Gene Autry's 'Rudolph the Red-Nosed Reindeer' was a Number 1 record for several weeks.[60] The same patterns held true throughout the early 1950s.

There were technological as well as demographic and cultural reasons for this. Until the 1950s music was just as family based an activity as the movies – perhaps, more so. The vast majority of families at war's end had only one radio and it was centrally located, usually in the living-room. Even as late as 1953, when statistics began to be kept on such things, fewer than a quarter of Canadian households had more than one radio.[61] Even fewer had a phonograph, which at the time was clumsy in design, relatively expensive, and restricted to the 78-rpm record format that was both vulnerable to scratches and limited in appeal. In a very real sense, therefore, access to music was a matter of family taste and adult arbitration. So long as that was the case, radio stations played music oriented towards a broad audience. The record producers saw their market in similar terms.

Recorded music was becoming more accessible year by year, however. Growing affluence increased the number of radios in the home. By 1959 the number of multiple-radio homes had increased by a few percentage points. More important, though, were two other developments. First, as television arrived in the home, it replaced the radio as the family's entertainment centre. Adolescent access to radio – indeed, adolescent control of at least one radio – became increasingly common. Second, radios moved outside the home. As automobiles spread, so, too, did car radios. In 1953 such devices were still a luxury, but, by the end of the decade, more than half of Canadian cars had radios.[62] In fact, radios did not even have to be attached to cars. The new teenage market helped propel the transistor radio into a mass-market item. The turning-point came in 1957, when a newly renamed Japanese company, Sony, brought a cheap and serviceable radio to the North American market. 'Rock music had created millions of teenage consumers eager for these tiny, tinny sets.'[63]

The revolution in radios was matched by that in record-players. Through the decade, growing market demand helped create new technologies. Stereo appeared as early as 1957, though it wouldn't be common until the 1960s. By the end of the decade, 78s had been replaced by the much smaller and less breakable 45s and the 33.3 rpm 'LP.' The record-player, or 'hi-fi,' as it had become known, changed character between the early 1950s and early 1960s. Like the radio, the record-player had migrated from the living-room to the rumpus-room or bedroom. Big cabinet-style productions were fading away as an important market item to be repalced by light, portable, and cheap systems – in other words, systems designed for the teenage market. The result was dramatic. In 1955, 89,000 record-players were shipped from Canadian factories. By 1957, the number was more than 270,000.[64] The teenage market was obviously both a powerful force and a powerful incentive to those who could innovate to meet its demands.

On the creative side, all sorts of activity was taking place. In the United States, a powerful mix was occurring as white artists experimented with the musical ideas coming out of black-based blues and so-called hillbilly music. As well, black artists, though still mainly popular with other blacks, were gaining more and more access to recording studios and beginning to influence whites as well. This was especially true in the South, where several songs that we would later know as rock and roll were being played regionally. Music was a competitive business, and several Northern U.S. promoters, radio managers, and record companies were well aware of the distinct, energetic, and raunchy music. Some began experimenting with it, and by the 1953 and 1954 the mix of the cult of the teenager, the emergent music, and the increased access to sound was beginning to come together south of the border.[65]

Canada was hardly at the forefront of all this. The black and Southern music which provided the drive and energy for the emergence of rock and roll was not part of our culture. Canadian radio stations were staid in comparison with their avant-garde American counterparts. Nevertheless, Canada too was laying the groundwork for the rise of new musical forms. The teenager was having an influence even before 'rock and roll' became a common term. As early as 1954 the Canadian pop-harmony group The Crew-Cuts hit Number 1 in the United States with their song 'Sh-Boom.'[66] Coiffed in stylish (what else?) crew-cuts and decked out in casual but ever so neat attire, the group had obviously set out to appeal to teenagers.

The rise of rock and roll from a regional phenomenon to an international music form is a long and complex story that cannot be covered here in any detail. The key years are 1954 to 1957, precisely the same ones that saw the teenager come to the fore demographically and culturally. In 1954 Elvis Presley recorded his first record, and 'DJ' Alan Freed began work at a New York radio station and set out to promote rock and roll as 'the' new musical form. Bill Haley and His Comets reached the Top 10 with 'Shake, Rattle and Roll.' In 1955 the teenage juvenile-delinquent movie, *The Blackboard Jungle* used Haley's 'Rock Around the Clock' and sent both the movie and the song to best-selling status. (In a symbolic scene in the movie, the juvenile-delinquent teenagers trash their teacher's jazz records.)[67] Through 1954 and 1955 rock and roll got increasing air play in the United States. Rock concerts began to be held. The crossover between black and country music and the white middle class was well under way, with teenagers as the medium.

Another medium, television, was crucial to rock and roll's takeover of teenage music. Elvis Presley's appearance in 1956 on *The Milton Berle Show* and then, more important, on *Ed Sullivan* created the first rock and roll superstar.[68] The next year a Philadelphia-based show, *American Bandstand*, changed its format and went national on ABC. It became a weekly showcase for new stars and a source to which both Canadian and American teenagers could turn to ensure that they were up to date with the latest music, fashions, and dance tips. Teenage dance and deejay shows were extremely cheap to produce, and imitations of *American Bandstand* began to appear in Canada, from Halifax to Vancouver. To the cruel observer, however, they often demonstrated only that these local teenagers had not properly learned their lessons about peer dance and dress. The rise of rock, specifically, and the teenage market, generally, also reshaped existing shows. CBC's *Cross-Canada Hit-Parade* (1955–9) was, of course, respectable, but it was a showcase for the pop songs of the week. As the teenage hold over music increased, so too did the program's orientation towards that audience.[69]

Thus Canadian youth was quickly integrated into the North American rock-and-roll culture. By 1956 Canadian teenagers were as aware of rock and roll as were their American counterparts. Elvis Presley's record 'Hound Dog' sold more than 200,000 copies in Canada that year. His first movie, *Love Me Tender,* was a hit across the country. Canada even had its own teenage star when, in 1957, 'Diana' became a hit in both Canada and the United States for Ottawa's Paul Anka.[70]

Rock and roll had thus overwhelmed national boundaries. Until the so-called British invasion of 1963–4, it was an American-based phenomenon with an international reach, Paul Anka or Britain's Cliff Richard notwithstanding. What is important about rock and roll for the purposes of this book, however, is that it erected generational differences in the same way that it ignored national ones. Sexual overtones, black origins, juvenile-delinquent imagery, and payola scandals didn't help the image of rock and roll with adults. A few well-publicized concert disturbances at Alan Freed rock shows completed the picture. Adult authority condemned the new music. One American psychiatrist labelled it 'a communicable disease with music appealing to adolescent insecurity and driving teenagers to do outlandish things ... it's cannibalistic and ritualistic.'[71] A Canadian evangelist warned that 'It works on man's emotions like the music of the heathen in Africa.' Frank Tumpane, a popular columnist with the Toronto *Telegram,* started an Elvis Suppresley Fan Club.[72]

What such opposition did, of course, was to make teenagers identify with the music as a particular possession of their generation. Adult diatribes made rock and roll more enticing. Rock not only survived the onslaught but became an institution. By the early 1960s, when the baby-boomers began to enter their teenage years, rock and roll was neither a fad nor an issue. It was just what young people listened to.

ALL OF THESE CHANGES SINCE THE WAR meant that, by the time the baby-boomers turned thirteen, they were well aware that being a teenager was something special. What few fully understood was just how important teenage culture had become. The Western world had fixated on youth. By the early 1960s, the power and distinctiveness of teenagers as a group were unmistakable. For better or worse, teenage culture was now a major force in most Western nations.[73] The music and movie industries depended upon it, and other goods producers catered to it. The idea of high-school life and of the teenager had become a firmly implanted part of Western folk-lore. To be young was often confusing, but it was also an age now doted upon by society. Continuing affluence only reinforced this tendency. To be young was to be the future.

Compared with what was to follow, the relationship between this newly powerful cult of youth and adult society seemed tame. Indeed, an accommodation seems to have been reached. Teenage society was given a special and semi-autonomous role within society, and in return teenagers demonstrated that such a society would be respectable. It is striking how, both in Canada and in the United States, the image of youth improved around the turn of the decade. The fear of juvenile delinquency receded, though crime statistics showed it was actually on the increase. Much, though not all, of the earlier antagonism to rock and roll had ebbed, in part because a whole host of 'clean teen' singers like Pat Boone had sanitized the genre.[74] Even Elvis Presley was becoming, if not respectable, at least acceptable. He had shown his character, after all, when he had not complained about his conscription into the army in March 1958. His next album, 'GI Blues,' showed a respectable, uniformed Elvis on the cover.[75] In Washington a new youthful president, John F. Kennedy, provided new political inspiration to American youth. Their Canadian equivalents could only look south of the border with envy at initiatives like the Peace Corps.

Yet there were cracks all over the place. The undercurrent of teenage (or more broadly, youth) rebellion had not disappeared. On the margins of young society, elements of disaffection, or outright hostility, towards adult culture persisted. The outlaw motorcycle gangs had become a standard element in both Canadian and American cities. The infamous Hell's Angels were still only a California phenomenon, but in Canada such gangs as the Satan's Choice, Black Diamond Riders, and others maintained the tough, anti-establishment theme of the early 1950s.

Another movement had different social origins and expression, but it too was a challenge to the conservative, corporate, and suburban values that so dominated the decade. The so-called Beat movement towards the end of the decade challenged the whole ethos of the society that spawned the organization man.[76] Writers like American Paul Goodman warned that, as the memory of the Depression faded, mere material success wasn't going to hold society together. It was the adolescent, moreover, who was the first to recognize this fact. 'Our abundant society,' Goodman warned in 1960, 'is at present simply deficient in many of the most elementary objective opportunities and worthwhile goals that could make growing up worth-while.'[77] For him the problem of wayward youth was not just a reflection upon individual families failing to do their duty to their children. Now society itself was under indictment. The social malaise that created the suburbs, not the family who failed to live by suburban ideals, was the basis of youth problems. This theme, if it moved in from the social margins where it existed in 1960, had the potential to reshape completely the image of the youthful rebel. From a social misfit, albeit one not wholly to blame, the youthful rebel would, under these new terms, become the perceptive person in a maladjusted world.

The baby-boomers, learning the newest dances and refashioning their wardrobes to deal with newly found interest in the opposite sex, didn't know it but they were entering a youth culture that was both powerful and fragile. Powerful because youth culture could no longer be denied. Fragile because the equipoise between this culture and its adult counterpart was under stress. That stress was about to rupture the checks and balances that had shaped postwar society.

7

The Arrival of the Sixties

The sixties have assumed mythical proportions. The Kennedys, student protest, Vietnam, drugs, flower power, free love, and militancy mix together in a way that seems surreal by the staid standards of later years. It is also an age with a contentious reputation. Some look back on it as a time of hope and idealism. Others condemn it as the 'decade that would not die, the decade whose long half-life continues to contaminate our own.'[1] Whatever the assessment, most would agree that it was an era of agitation and excitement, leadership lost authority. Ideological debate reasserted itself after the calm of the 1950s. Most of all, perhaps, it was the age of the 'generation gap,' for the story of the sixties is inseparable from that of the baby boom. The youth rebellion was central to much of the fractiousness and dismay, much of the idealism and hope. It was the moment in history that forever defined the baby boom as a distinct generation.[2]

This notion is important. One of the problems for people trying to ascribe historical meaning to a 'generation' is that the term is so elusive. People, after all, are born continuously. How does one decide where one generation ends and another begins? For those who theorize about such things, one answer comes from the idea of a 'social moment.' As one historian has said, generations are essentially 'an age group shaped by history.'[3] If so, there is no doubt that the social moment for the baby-boom generation was 'the sixties.'

To understand the relationship between the generation and the decade, however, requires some disentanglement of historical fact and myth. For, however much the baby boom was a force within the decade, so too were events of the decade crucial in shaping the history of the baby boom. Economic circumstances, and social and political tensions coincided with the arrival of the baby boom at adolescence and early adulthood. It was this coincidence that gave the decade its character, and the baby boom its moment in the sun. The question, then, is: What created the sixties? What was the stage upon which the baby boom entered as it widened its horizons beyond the world of childhood?

First, some definitions are necessary, including the very term 'the sixties.' It does not refer to the decade running from 1960 to 1969. If a ten-year period has to be chosen, it would be the one extending from approximately 1963 to 1972.[4] More useful, however, is a definition that stretches the sixties from its forewarnings in 1959 or 1960; through the heady (no pun intended) years of radical dissent and counter-cultural efflorescence (1965–8); through polarization, repression, and decline (1969–72). Through these years causes came and went, musical and clothing styles shifted towards the ever more experimental and outrageous, and, as in other great social upheavals, the energy and enthusiasm that underpinned the movement gradually yielded ground.

The notion of 'revolutionary youth' also requires clarification. This was not a generation in revolution. Not all baby-boomers were students at university, much less students on a picket line. Moreover, many of the best-known radical leaders of the decade were pre-boomers. François Ricard described the baby boom in Quebec as a choir or a chorus in a play. The baby-boomers, he argues, provided the support and received the benefits, but were not, in the initial phase, the key actors.[5] Moreover, a good many baby-boomer students never did join the chorus. Large percentages of 1960s youth remained apolitical or opposed to the radicalism that was so associated with their generation. It is accurate, however, to say that, though the generation was not revolutionary, it had a revolutionary impact. It is also relevant that, compared with the eras of the generation before and the generation after, this was an age in which the rhetoric of political activism and the influence of radical ideas were pronounced. Why this was the case and why a small percentage of committed radicals came to appropriate the voice of a generation is, of course, one of the major questions that must be answered.

Even with these caveats, the fact remains that 'the sixties' were different. Not everybody was a radical, but the era was inflamed by the rhetoric, and occasionally the acts of radicals. Only a few were true 'hippies,' but the counter-culture shaped the sensibilities and created temptations for masses of youth. It is too simple to talk of a 'generation gap,' though there was one, but it is reasonable to talk of this as an age of fragmentation. Intergenerational struggles paralleled intragenerational, interclass, gender, and other contests. A society that a decade before had talked about the end of ideology now seemed to have endless ideologies. Through it all, the baby-boomers began to come of age. Their future politics, social values, and personal lives were all very much the product of this complex decade.

THE TURMOIL OF THE 1960S AND EARLY 1970S had at its roots a crisis of authority in Western social and political institutions. The patriotic pulls of the war years, Cold War jitters, the cult of domesticity, and the strong economy of the postwar years produced relative quiet on the political front through the later 1940s and 1950s. The populists of the Depression era were either tamed or tossed from office. Louis St Laurent's Liberals ran a cautious, technocratic sort of government. The Left censored itself, marginalizing radical movements and seeking approval within the framework of the Cold War.[6] Canadians were never as obsessed with Communists as were their southern neighbours; none the less, the Cold War had an important psychological effect, even in Canada. In a war, even a cold one, a loyal citizen does not challenge in any fundamental way the beneficence of his or her allies. As a result, it is not too much to say that, from the beginning of the Second World War until the rise of dissent in the 1960s, the West was a relatively closed ideological system. This had an effect on domestic as well as international politics. The black and white imagery of East versus West and the creation of what might be termed a 'garrison mentality' deterred a critical assessment of internal conditions. It is striking that none of the major domestic themes of the 1960s – Quebec separatism, Natives' rights, the poor – were politically important issues in the 1950s. People knew that democracy was not perfect, but they believed it was well intentioned. No alternative form of government was even comparable. Whatever its faults, the Western world was a bulwark of freedom in a world beset by tyranny.

The 1960s brought the death throes of this black-and-white world. A series of events undermined the credibility of the Western allies, especially the United States. From the late 1950s through the early 1970s, a cleavage opened between American policy makers and the populace of much of the Western world. With only minor modifications, the administrations of Eisenhower, Kennedy, and Johnson pursued traditional Cold War diplomacy. Richard Nixon, elected in 1968, was a transition point, but much of his regime was dedicated to the same underlying principles as those of previous presidents.

The theories of these Cold Warriors were fairly straightforward. Communism was monolithic, expansionist, and evil. The current international tensions were the result of Joseph Stalin's paranoia and tyrannical designs on Eastern Europe after the Second World War. Moreover, with Eastern Europe reduced to satellite status, communism aimed outward at the third world, where poverty and ignorance created a fertile breeding-ground for revolution. From 1948 onward, containment of communism became the fundamental feature of American foreign policy. Aid to friendly democracies was best. Aid to friendly dictators was acceptable. Destabilization of unfriendly pro-Communist regimes was tolerable, and war, if necessary, was fought in the name of ending tyranny. The most interesting thing about the Cold War, perhaps, was its impact upon the psyche of those involved. This was not an international diplomatic struggle for a superior position in world affairs, but a moral crusade: evil against virtue, Christ against anti-Christ or, more accurately, a re-creation of the struggle between democracy and tyranny that predated the Second World War. 'The Communist sweep over the world since the World War 2,' warned American secretary of state John Foster Dulles in 1952, 'has been much faster and much more relentless than the 1930s sweep of the dictators.'[7]

Early postwar events, from the forced establishment of Communist regimes in Eastern European countries through the North Korean invasion of South Korea, gave the West a firm basis upon which to construct a moral crusade. To those in the West, the Soviet Union was behaving as an imperial power, enslaving nations for its own purposes. The Berlin Wall, constructed in August 1961, became the perfect symbol of the failure of communism to hold the support of its own people. John F. Kennedy recognized this when, in the wake of the Bay of Pigs, he turned his attention to the Berlin issue.[8] His 1963 'Ich bin ein Berliner' speech restated the traditional Cold War themes of good versus evil in the strongest possible setting. This was a Cold War Canadians understood and to which they contributed through NATO.

Even before Kennedy's speech, however, the Cold War was moving onto bumpier moral ground.[9] In 1960 American pilot Francis Gary Powers was captured by the Soviets after his U2 spy plane was shot down. In an embarrassing comedy of errors, the Americans first said he was a lost weather pilot, and then admitted and tried to justify the spy flights. In a world that believed in good versus evil, it was a profound shock to find that the good guys were indulging in behaviour that, since the famous Gouzenko affair in Ottawa, had been thought to be a vice peculiar to the Russians. Worse yet, they had then lied to their own people about it. At the same time, under Nikita Khrushchev, the Soviet Union was, though still a dictatorship, moving away from the terrorist tactics of the Stalin regime. A new emphasis on consumer goods and a quieter style of international rhetoric took away some of the edge of the great Soviet Empire.

Then, the same year, Fidel Castro overthrew the corrupt American satellite government in Cuba and installed a revolutionary regime that quickly moved towards communism. The place of Cuba in the unravelling of the Cold War is complex. There is no doubt that it frightened many Americans to have a Communist power just ninety miles from Florida. It was also a source of great triumph and great embarrassment for the United States. The triumph came when, in 1962, American brinkmanship on Soviet missiles forced Khrushchev to back down. On the other hand, the Bay of Pigs fiasco the previous year was a tremendous blow to American prestige.[10] So, too, was the simple fact that the United States could no longer control what, since the late nineteenth century, had been a semi-colonial state. In Latin America, Castro's Cuba served as a beacon for (and funder of) various pro-Communist insurgencies.

Most important of all, however, Cuba symbolized the movement of the Cold War to new territory. Through the 1950s and early 1960s, a worldwide process of decolonization was going on. Many of the new post-colonial regimes had no reason to love their former colonial masters. Democracy, moreover, is a particularly tricky form of government, and many regimes found the advantages of Communist, or radical-socialist, regimes irresistible. They also found that the Soviet Union would help fund the transition to left-wing nationhood with generous foreign aid.

The dilemma for the West was that third-world communism often had genuine popular support. The populace in large parts of Africa, Asia, and Latin America were frequently suspicious of and occasionally hostile towards the United States. In 1958, for example, something of the antipathy towards American foreign policy in Latin America was revealed when a riot broke out in Venezuela to protest the visit of Vice-President Richard Nixon. Nixon's car was surrounded and spat upon by hundreds of angry demonstrators – an incident captured in the pages of *Life* magazine.[11] In Africa and Asia newly decolonized nations often aligned themselves with the Soviet bloc, obtaining military and financial support in return. The link between communism and 'wars of national liberation' was not yet fully established. That would take Vietnam. The failure of Western diplomacy to deal with issues of decolonization, however, meant that the Western anti-Communist rhetoric had to compete with Soviet and Chinese rhetoric about colonialism.

Canada, though still firmly within the American alliance, felt these changes. In the postwar years, Canadian foreign-policy makers sought to establish a special rapport with recently decolonized nations.[12] Canada's history, as Canadians like to remind people, included a period as a colony. Sometimes the desire to be the helpful middle power clashed with Cold War imperatives. Canadians, for example, were uncomfortable with the hawkish American position on Castro and continued to trade with Cuba in spite of the American embargo. Such trade was both an irritant to the Kennedy administration and a source of tension between the two countries. Likewise, the Cuban missile crisis was viewed ambivalently by Canadians. They welcomed the victory of the Americans, but the brinkmanship involved seemed once again to point to the dangers of a superpower out of control.[13] Through the 1960s going to Cuba became a political statement. As a 1966 Canadian Union of Students memo put it, those who went there saw 'for themselves the nature of the Cuban revolution.'[14] They also distinguished themselves from their American counterparts, who were not allowed to visit the country.

By the early 1960s a minority of Canadians were beginning to question the nature of the Cold War alliance that had developed since 1945. Some wanted Canada to become a sort of Sweden of the new world, existing outside the framework of the Western alliance. Those charged with responsibility were well aware that the Western alliance was dictated by geography, economic self-interest, and the sheer power of the United States. Even in government circles, however, individuals were beginning to question the degree to which Canada had linked itself to its giant southern partner. It is revealing that every administration from the late 1950s to the early 1970s had strong nationalist voices calling for a more autonomous position for Canada in both economic and political matters.

The continental alliance became a major issue during the 1963 election. John Diefenbaker's Conservatives were seriously disaffected towards the Kennedy administration. Kennedy reciprocated.[15] Moreover, the Diefenbaker government had refused to take nuclear weapons under a 'joint key' system for BOMARC air defence. The result was a bitter election. The old Co-operative Commonwealth Federation (CCF), now the New Democratic Party (NDP), moved more definitely into a position hostile to the presumptions of both the nuclear-arms race and the Cold War. Diefenbaker tried to rally a confused and tired administration around the issue. He lost, but in the process explicit anti-Americanism re-entered mainstream Canadian politics for the first time in at least a generation.[16] The ability of the Communist spectre to hold the allies in line was less and less certain.

Doubts about the Cold War in turn encouraged doubts about the vast military arsenal that had been assembled in the name of anti-communism. In the United States, the late 1950s saw the rise of anti–nuclear war movements like the Committee for a Sane Nuclear Policy (SANE). By the later 1950s protests against the once-feared House on Un-American Activities Committee (HUAC) were becoming more common. In one memorable riot in May 1960, the police had to use firehoses and tear gas to break up an anti-HUAC demonstration by students in San Francisco.[17] It was an important incident, for it symbolized a turning in the American political landscape. No longer was anti-communism inviolable as a national creed.

In Canada there were mirror movements. The Combined Universities Campaign for Nuclear Disarmament (CUCND), founded in November 1959, was inspired by both American and British anti-nuclear bodies. Modest in style and membership, it nevertheless raised serious questions about the Cold War and, as we shall see, provided a nucleus for later radical organizations.[18] On the right occasion it could tap growing concerns about the nuclear-arms race. In 1961, in combination with the Voice of Women, it was able get 142,000 signatures on an anti-nuclear petition.[19] The same year the newly formed NDP referred in its founding manifesto to the 'absurdity of relying on military strength' in a nuclear age and essentially adopted the position of the anti-nuclear movement.[20]

Internationally and at home, therefore, a disjunction was developing between the policy makers and military officials, who still essentially viewed the Cold War in old terms, and a dissenting segment of the public that challenged the moral certainties that had been part of Cold War rhetoric to that time. It was against this legacy that Vietnam unfolded. The rhetoric of the Cold War looked increasingly hollow in a dragged-out contest that was increasingly related to third-world liberation and to the national aspirations of former colonies. The Vietnam War forced the growing doubts about the moral certainties of the West to a critical stage. By the time Vietnam began to come to Western attention, however, there was much greater dissent and doubt than there had been even five years earlier.

THE COLD WAR WAS PLAYED OUT ACROSS the globe and involved most of the nations of the world in one way or another. Yet one domestic American event was just as important in shaping the 1960s. In the postwar years, blacks had pushed with increasing effectiveness against Southern segregation. Some of the steps had been legal ones, as in the 1954 Supreme Court decision which challenged educational segregation. Others had been personal crusades, as in the efforts of Montgomery blacks to end segregation on buses in that Alabama city in 1955.[21] These movements received their due share of attention and comment in the broader national community and in Canada. Initially, however, the confrontation remained regional, as Southern segregationists and the National Association for the Advancement of Colored People (NAACP) battled in the courts and legislatures. Towards the end of the decade, things changed. Civil rights moved increasingly from a subject for the courts to one that galvanized mass protest. The lessons of the Montgomery boycott had been well learned, and the adoption of union sit-in tactics raised the level of confrontation, and hence the newsworthiness of the event.[22]

Segregationist governments in the South reacted viciously to the protests. The image of the South that took shape after 1960 was unprecedented in the lifetime of the baby boom. Here was an element of Western democracy using the forces of the state to deny rights to its own people. Moreover, as civil-rights protest mounted, that state force became increasingly violent. Every new civil-rights effort brought pictures of police dogs attacking protesters, of fire hoses trained on demonstrators, and of the courage of peaceful protest in the face of thuggery. Television was bringing something new into the homes of North Americans.

The public reacted, both in the northern United States and in Canada. For one thing, the street scenes from Montgomery, Selma, and elsewhere were moral theatre: good against evil, armed violence against passive resistance, the establishment against the poor. The issues were stark, and the Southern 'system' seemed a straightforward case of humanity against inhumanity. In a post–Second World War climate, such *formalized* racial prejudice flew in the face of prevailing notions about democracy and freedom. Part of postwar education had been an ongoing rhetoric about the need to accept people as people. There must be 'respect of the individual, regardless of colour or creed,' as one later 1950s Alberta teacher's guide put it.[23] At the same time this was a comfortable issue, both for northern Americans and for Canadians. Surely such corruption of democracy was peculiar to the southern United States.[24] People could demand change in Alabama or Mississippi while assuming that their own lives, in Boston, Toronto, Winnipeg, or elsewhere, would be unaffected. Only later, as civil-rights issues moved north and as Canada discovered its own pockets of discrimination, did the issues become more complex.

In the meantime, the civil-rights movement made an indelible mark on the postwar generation. Issues of race and racism moved to centre stage and have shaped the outlook of baby-boomers to the present day. This generation had already been conditioned to look upon racism as an issue by the memories of the Nazi horror transmitted by educators and parents. What the civil-rights movement did was to take the abstract and make it real and current. This was the first generation in history to assert that a belief in racial inequality was so unacceptable as to not be a subject for serious intellectual discussion.[25] The term 'racist' became, with 'fascist,' the ultimate epithet in the 1960s, replacing the increasingly ineffectual term 'communist.'

Perhaps the most important impact of the civil-rights movement was the way it legitimized resistance to governmental authority. For the parents of the baby boom, the Second World War and the Cold War had imposed deep traditions of loyalty to the state. The civil-rights movement broke the hold of these obligations and brought issues of personal morality versus the law to Western democracies in a way the end-of-war Nuremberg trials could not. It taught, further, that if the state was recalcitrant, dissent was insufficient. Drawing upon notions of Christian witness and Gandhi's non-violent civil disobedience, the movement demonstrated the effectiveness of mass protest and legitimized the approach in the mind of the media and the public.[26] Much of the tolerance for student protest, disruption, and disobedience derived from this earlier resistance to authority.

The closest thing Canada had in the 1960s to such a grand and idealistic cause was the Quiet Revolution in Quebec. This movement, which captured national attention after the defeat of the Union Nationale in 1960, initially embodied a spirit of reformism and idealism. Here was a people throwing off the shackles of ignorance, rejecting the 'great darkness' of the Duplessis era, and seeking to modernize its institutions almost overnight. Here, at last, was a rejection of the conservative structure which had always been at odds with the postwar faith in modernism, social science, and technology.

Quebec's Quiet Revolution was thus a dream in tune with the optimistic reformism of the early 1960s. As it progressed, however, it took on a harder and more radical edge. Terrorist groups arose, most notoriously the Front de Libération du Québec, which mimicked third-world liberation rhetoric and commitment to revolution. The Quebec student movement soon progressed beyond modernism to separatism, adopting along the way romantic notions such as student syndicalism. These more radical elements, as one observer noted, 'would not be anthologized in English-Canada as the bright new sound from Quebec.'[27]

Quebec gave Canadians a local cause. Here was an internal matter that raised issues of justice similar to those in the American South. Separatist Pierre Vallières took this to its logical conclusion when he aligned French Canadians with the blacks of the American south. The Québécois, he said, were the 'White Niggers of America.'[28] Vallières's provocative title had less to do with oppression than with authenticity. The idea of authenticity was everywhere in the 1960s, from music to politics, to relationships. One's actions, emotions, and experience had to be linked. It was a notion that fit well with the psychological enthusiasms of the previous decade, and which reflected as well the search of youth for a means of breaking through the superficial materialism of the suburban cultural mainstream. A claim to authenticity, therefore, went a long way in asserting one's person or politics in this decade.

There was a clear hierarchy of authenticity in North American radical circles in the 1960s. The black movement had gained pride of place, both through its long oppression and through the action it had taken to challenge it – whether in Selma or later in urban ghetto riots. Black was beautiful, as the phrase went, and black fashion, black slang, and black heroes were an essential part of 'the sixties.' Indeed, the reluctance to criticize anything black led to amazing quiescence on the part of white radicals towards such violent and hostile groups as the Black Panthers. As one American radical accurately noted, 'nothing made the idea of the revolution more vivid to the white left than the Black Panther Party.' In the face of such authenticity, a great deal of doubt could remain buried. 'If they were menacing, well, that's the style of the street, and anyway, how else could the oppressed get justice? If they were authoritarian, didn't a movement of street brothers reared in hellish circumstances require discipline ... But mostly the Panthers' claims weren't challenged at all.'[29] Tom Wolfe parodied the whole tendency of what he termed 'radical chic.' The idea of the Black Panthers amidst the liberal literati of New York, said Wolfe, 'runs through Leny's [Leonard Bernstein's] house like a rogue hormone.'[30]

What Vallières was claiming, therefore, was the sort of 'moral title' that had been acquired by the black movement in the United States.[31] That he was able to pull it off, at least among those sympathetic to Quebec, is attributable to the fact that, in Canada, the Quebec cause had become became the greatest single reform question of the 1960s. In that limited sense, Quebec was indeed parallel to the American civil-rights movement. For English-Canadian reformers, Quebecers had an authenticity that they, white Anglo-suburban kids, could never match. This led to two tendencies. The first was the honest desire to comprehend and accommodate Quebec aspirations in the hope of reconciling the two peoples. Second, and often parallel with the first, was the belief that, if you linked your cause to the Quebec crisis, it would have greater legitimacy: 'Those who desire socialism and independence for Canada have often been baffled and mystified by the problem of internal divisions within Canada ... So long as the federal government refuses to protect the country from American cultural and economic domination, English Canada is bound to appear to French Canadians simply as part of the United States.'[32]

As in the United States, however, the links between majority and minority weren't easily maintained. Quebec nationalism was not all that attuned to accommodation with English Canadians. Efforts at partnership were often rebuffed by the Québécois, especially among youth organizations. What was most ominous was that such rejection often came in the face of tremendous sympathy and goodwill. As Stewart Goodings of the Canadian Union of Students noted in 1964, 'the whole structure of the organization was changed to meet the demands of French Canadian members.'[33] Yet, as we will see, the next year the francophone universities broke away to form their own body, the Union Générale des Étudiants du Québec (UGEQ).

Finally, the analogy between the civil-rights movement and the Quiet Revolution reflects the way in which Quebec was becoming Canada's particular obsession. Through the 1960s much of English Canada accepted the premise that French Canadians had been treated unjustly and that correcting these injustices was a prerequisite to the survival of Canada. More radical circles often seemed to celebrate the belief that Quebec might separate and, among students, Quebec's 'right to self-determination' became a means of supporting Quebec's demands.

There were exceptions. The farther west one went, the less sympathy for or interest in Quebec there was. As late as 1965 the student newspaper at the University of British Columbia dismissed the interim studies of the federal government's Royal Commission on Bilingualism and Biculturalism as 'Frogwash.'[34] The more radical Simon Fraser University paper was no more sympathetic to Quebec claims. Though the rhetoric of Quebec separatism did move westward later in the decade as a part of the general ambiance of the era, there is little evidence that student movements in the West ever really took the concerns of Quebec to heart. Nevertheless, even with its regional dimensions, the Quiet Revolution has to take pride of place among reform movements in the 1960s. It energized a whole generation of Quebecers, French and English. It had the political power and clout to capture the attention of the federal government and national media.

The moral authority and unity of purpose in Quebec circles could not be matched in English Canada. Yet English-Canadian dissenters also had a claim to moral authority: They were not American. In the 1950s and early 1960s, of course, not to be American was to be missing something. Canadian baby-boomers had grown up in the shadow of everything from the thoroughly American Barbie to the World Series. Most of all, they had grown up knowing that American kids belonged to the most powerful, richest nation on earth. Yet anti-Americanism has always been a visceral part of the Canadian psyche.[35] Quiescent though it had been through the Second World War and postwar years, it waited to reappear. A quick succession of events propelled it forward: the 1963 Canadian election (April), Kennedy's assassination (November 1963), the escalation in Vietnam (beginning in August 1964), invasion of the Dominican Republic (April 1965), and the Watts ghetto riots in Los Angeles (August 1965). Just as dissent had grown over the Cold War, so too were some Canadians wondering about the character of the leading nation of the Western world.

This is not to say that there was a sudden revolution in Canadian consciousness. Even the New Left, it must be remembered, remained closely linked with their American counterparts. As one Student Union for Peace Action (SUPA) member commented on the Canadian and American movements: 'I don't think there is a difference.'[36] That was in 1965, however, and as the decade went on the image of the United States continued to deteriorate. This led increasing numbers of young dissenters to distinguish between the two North American nations. Independence was both desirable for socialist goals and a means by which the socialist appeal could be enhanced. 'In order to proceed toward a socialist society, Canada will have to be freed from control of the Americans. Conversely, a free independent Canada is possible only through a socialist economy in Canada.'[37] Also important for the claim of moral authority was the growing belief that Canada was one of the victims of that imperialism, a view that was increasingly part of Canadian radical sentiment as the 1960s went on. Canada as a country and Canadians as citizens thus laid some claim to identification with their third-world cousins. Canada, as the cliché went, was just a richer version of a third-world colony of the United States.[38]

Other issues arose as the 1960s went on: Natives, inner-city poverty, student power, and, most revolutionary of all, the role of women. In the early 1960s, however, doubts about the Cold War, the civil-rights issue in the United States, and the Quiet Revolution in Canada were the points of dissonance that eroded the quietist foundation created in the 1950s. These were the primary issues that raised questions about the beneficence of the existing system. They created powerful centres of dissent within society and had the ability to appeal, when the conditions were right, to the conscience of the nation as a whole. By the time the baby-boomers were in their mid-teens, these themes were already a natural part of the political landscape.

A CRISIS OF AUTHORITY AND THE RISE of great movements of dissent provide the historical discord for which the decade is so well known. The way in which such discord evolved, however, and the way in which the baby-boomers evolved with that discord, were linked to another prominent phenomenon of these years. The 1960s were prosperous. After the 'Diefenrecession' early in the decade, the economy rebounded nicely. From 1962 to 1972 annual growth rates never went below 4 per cent and were, in the better years, running at more than 6 per cent. Unemployment declined steadily from the early 1960s, and Canada achieved something close to full employment by mid-decade. Inflation remained low, for the most part. In other words, the 1960s saw the return to the strong economic growth that had characterized the post-war years.

It has been a popular assumption that the affluence of these years was crucial to the unfolding of 'the sixties.' Critics of the decade's counter-culture and radicalism have interpreted events as stemming from the same 'we can have it all' mentality that the baby-boomers first acquired as children in the 1950s. Even those more sympathetic still see a causal relationship between affluence and the recklessness of the decade. Youth were able to turn their attention to issues of social justice and personality because the economy removed the immediate worries about food on the table and a job. As one Canadian sociologist put it, these were the 'part of a generation that did not have to worry about the basic wants; they were nourished in the lap of relative luxury.'[39]

There is considerable truth in such a hypothesis, but there is more to the relationship between affluence and the 1960s than that. Remember, society continued to adjust itself to the moving wave of the baby boom. By the middle of the decade, the front edge of that wave were in their late teens. Those baby-boomers born in the 1940s were finishing high school and were ready to move on. A growing percentage, of course, went on to university, and, as we will see, the students were the ones who garnered the attention of the media and eventually defined much of the mythology of the baby boom. Yet, in purely numerical terms, university was still a minority experience. The majority of baby-boomers and their wartime predecessors moved from high school into the workforce. In 1965 176,000 youth completed Grade Twelve. Only about one in six of these went on to further education. For the rest the immediate goal was to get a job.

For a large part of the baby boom, therefore, the protected world of youth was coming to an end. Yet the affluence of the economy shaped their lives as well. It meant that, unlike their parents and unlike their children, their experience of the shift from school to work was relatively painless. By 1965 unemployment was under 4 per cent.[40] Between 1964 and 1967, the economy created nearly 145,000 new jobs for Canadians under the age of twenty-five.[41] Table 6.1 shows something of where the jobs were by the time the leading edge of the baby boom was in its mid-twenties. They took jobs as clerks and in sales, joined the construction trades, or worked on farms. Many more of them worked for government than did their parents, and many of them found work as teachers or nurses, bringing along the younger elements of their own generation. Many women still remained outside the paid labour force to be housewives and raise children, though there were fewer children than a decade earlier. As they left school they also began

TABLE 6.1
Chief Occupations, Ages Fifteen to Twenty-Four, 1971 Census

Occupation	No. of people employed	Percentage of total	Rank
Clerical and related	117,915	11.17	1
Construction trades	96,250	9.11	2
Sales	81,175	7.69	3
Farm occupations*	52,865	5.01	4
Transport operations	51,215	4.85	5
Protective services	39,275	3.72	6
Total of Selected Occ.	438,695	41.55	

*Not including farm ownership
Source: Derived from *Census of Canada, 1971*, table 8, 'Labour Force 15 Years and Over by Detailed Occupation'

to merge into the adult world. They were still influenced by the youth culture of North America, bought rock albums, and followed clothing trends. Their world of work or family, though, was somewhat different from that of their contemporaries who attended post-secondary institutions.

The absorption of so many baby-boomers into the job market raises an intriguing question: What might have happened if this huge group arrived on the job market in a time of recession? Had the economy been weak, baby-boomer unrest might not have been on campuses but among the unemployed. Given the high expectations of the 1950s, it is unlikely that these high-school students would have passively accepted unemployment. As it was, however, the strong economy absorbed the majority of the school-leavers without great difficulty, and the political focus of the decade turned towards those who stayed in school.

As well, affluence may have influenced the decade in another way. Recently, economic theorists have revived the notion that underlying all the shorter-term business cycles are 'long wave' cycles of fifty or sixty years' duration.[42] For various reasons having to do with innovation, these underlying cycles are very powerful. On the upswing, booms can expect to be sustained and vigorous. Recessions will be short-lived and weak. Certainly such a model would fit the pattern of the 1950s and 1960s, just as patterns characteristic of a downward cycle would fit the 1990s. Such theories might remain left to the world of economic theorists except for one thing: Long waves may affect, not only prosperity, but social attitudes. In the upswing, the argument goes, the society becomes 'more liberal and progressive.' Social reforms are popular and ideas that urge equality and inclusion of left-out groups gain attention.[43]

All of this makes sense. Certainly the early 1960s were an optimistic period. People thought things could be accomplished, as poll after poll confirmed. In 1960 more than 70 per cent of Canadians thought the human race was getting better, 52 per cent (as against 15 per cent) thought Canada would be even better by 1970, and 75 per cent thought Canadians were becoming more intelligent. Moreover, Canadians appear to have been even bouncier than citizens in other countries. An amazing 95 per cent of Canadians said they were happy with their lot in life, the highest among the countries polled. As the Gallup pollsters themselves summed it up, Canadians were 'staunchly optimistic' in their views.[44]

The 'long wave,' optimism, and the youth movement are inseparable. Youth could be radical in part because age was receptive to reform. By the early 1960s the 'establishment,' whether political, intellectual, or media, had an increasingly reformist tendency. The churches were certainly ready. Pierre Berton's *Comfortable Pew* was greeted less with cries of outrage than with cries for reform. In Ottawa circles, new social reformism led to such major initiatives as equalization (1962), reduction in the age of eligibility for old-age pensions to sixty-five (1965), and Medicare (1966). In Quebec, the Quiet Revolution was initiated as a top-down event, with the government instituting the massive reforms. South of the border, John F. Kennedy's 'Camelot' gave the impression of a new idealism and new social reforms. Attitudes on divorce, birth control, premarital sex, and other key 'moral' issues were becoming more liberal by the beginning of the 1960s, several years before the 'youth revolution,' Vietnam, or other causes came to the fore.[45]

The link between any 'long wave' and a more liberal society is hypothetical. The more immediate relationship between prosperity and 'the sixties' is undeniable. As we will see, prosperity sustained and extended the power of youth culture. It also created an optimism and enthusiasm for experimentation with alternative lifestyles, free of the hang-ups of materialism, that could make sense only to a generation that took material comfort as given. As various writers have noted, the boomers had never experienced the disruptions that had made suburbia a parental quest. They didn't 'feel that they were particularly privileged or fortunate to live in such a comfortable environment.'[46] This difference in perception was, perhaps, the most basic generation gap of all. From it many others would flow.

THE MOST PRIVILEGED OF THIS PRIVILEGED generation were those who went on to university. Though still a minority, they did so in larger numbers than ever before. The story of the 1950s' high school now repeated itself at the post-secondary level. Provinces poured vast sums into the expansion of the system and still could not keep up with demand. Students entered this expanding, and thus unstable, system with high expectations and a strong sense of peer affiliation. These characteristics, and the mood of the times, proved a volatile combination. Perhaps nothing captures the mythology of the 1960s more than the image of campus protest. For it was within the protected walls of the university that the high-school world of teenagers could be extended into something more complex and more sophisticated – the youth world of those largely free of parental constraint but not yet part of the adult world.

Universities have always been centres of controversy. This is not surprising, for universities shape fundamental values and train the élite of the next generation. Those within university take ideas seriously and often express them vociferously. Those watching from outside want to ensure that their own values are not, somehow, being undermined for the next generation. Governments find that their role as financial provider clashes with the university's insistence upon autonomy. In other words, forces outside the system have a stake in what goes on. The faculty and the students traditionally resist interference. They then often battle among themselves and with administration, to see whose voice will be the most powerful.

While controversy is a part of Canadian university history, however, so is a certain institutional stability, and even stodginess. Campuses in Canada had been used to long periods of institutional calm interrupted by infrequent changes of direction. Indeed, by the mid-1950s, the Canadian university system had experienced only two truly fundamental shifts of direction. The first came from the mid-1830s to the end of the 1860s, with the founding of the first colonial colleges. Small, operating on a shoe-string budget, and often subject to interruption, institutions like Queen's, Dalhousie, and the various colleges of the University of Toronto were created in large part as theological bodies.

They were tied to individual denominations and had the specific purpose of training the clergy. At the same time, they provided other degrees and courses to a secular audience, always through the filter of a Christian education. Once these colonial universities were in place, there was little change and few new institutions for a generation.

Early in the twentieth century, two contemporary events reshaped the system. First, between 1900 and the First World War, the rapidly developing Western provinces established the Universities of Saskatchewan (1907), Alberta (1908), and British Columbia (1908). At about the same time, the university system in English Canada was secularized. This involved a shift of allegiance from church to state and, within the system, a reconstruction of curriculum along secular lines. Of course, any respectable university president of, say, 1920 would have extolled the Christian nature of his institution. Neither the institution nor the president, however, operated through the rules and finances of any particular denomination. Religious colleges still existed, but they were no longer the basis of the system.

Then the universities again settled into the sort of institutional quiet that suited them. The Depression and war meant that no major new institutions were established, and the basic codes of conduct, rules of governance, and social customs of faculty and student altered little between the early 1920s and the 1950s. True, the influx of veterans after the Second World War brought new life and considerable chaos. The veterans passed on, however, and university enrolment actually declined in the early 1950s, as did the number of people obtaining degrees.[47] The institutions sank back into the sort of stasis that had become standard over the previous thirty or forty years. The professoriat was dominated by the Oxbridge tradition, though American Ivy League schools also had their representatives. The universities as a whole were small. Between 1945 and 1955, total Canadian undergraduate enrolment increased by fewer than 10,000 students, and the number of professors by fewer than 1,500.[48]

Stability in size was reinforced by a relatively hierarchical system of governance. Even moderately successful presidents could expect to serve until retirement, and deans, department heads, and other administrators also remained for the long term. Longevity concentrated power and policy in a few stable hands. This worked all the way through the system, so that curriculum, admissions policy, and other matters changed only slowly, if at all. Legislation reinforced this sense of glacial change. The governing system of the University of Toronto was, in the early 1960s, still based upon an act dating back to 1906.[49] The curriculum mirrored the system of governance and was 'uniform and unchanging.'[50]

There was also considerable agreement as to the purpose of university. In part, of course, universities were there to provide skills for the job market. Of course, this not usually portrayed in such crass terms. Rather, administrators and faculty argued, the university stood for the discovery and pursuit of truth. That truth would be achieved, moreover, by the triumph of reason over emotion, superstition, and ignorance. Claude Bissell, president of the University of Toronto from 1958 to 1971, looked to the doctrine of the famous political economist Harold Innis to sum it up: 'The university should be disinterested, objective, keeping a wary distance from government and business, dreading subservience to established power, preserving itself as an immaculate source of criticism.' It was, Bissell, concluded, 'an ivory tower, but with spartan furnishings and many observation posts.'[51]

Such attitudes had deep intellectual roots, with precedents ranging from ancient Greece to the eighteenth-century Enlightenment. Most recently, however, it had been a means of redefining the role of the university during the process of secularization. The human mind had to be free to enquire without limits, to follow the evidence without qualms or prejudice. This was the finest development of what American intellectual Jacques Barzun in 1959 described as 'the house of intellect,' and the university was the finest flower of that intellectual endeavour.[52] Passion should yield to reason; prejudice to facts. In the ideal, at least, consensus was possible once the best arguments had been made and the best evidence marshalled. The university's dogma was to pit itself against unreason. The university was there 'to humanize and civilize,' as one mid-century article in *The Dalhousie Review* put it.[53]

The relationship between the institution and the student was also the product of tradition. In earlier centuries, in Britain, Europe, and the United States, their privileged social position and personal proclivities had given students considerable autonomy within the system. If the colleges tried to crack down, or if civil authorities tried to interfere in the students' privileges, civil disobedience and outright riot were often the response.[54] By the twentieth century, such traditions had been modified considerably.[55] Riot and protest had been ritualized into hazing and frat rushing. The students retained their sense of élitism, and the university, in turn, recognized a primary role as the transmission of 'Christian or middle-class values to the leaders of the next generation.'[56]

This transmission of values by the university went beyond the classroom. Much more than today, post-secondary education was the province of the young. You left high school at age eighteen, went to university for three or four years (more if in medicine or law), and left, never to return. Yet science had defined these as the troubled years of adolescence. The law defined the age of majority as twenty-one. Thus most students were neither adults in legal terms nor thought of as fully responsible by adult society. Parents sending their children to university expected the institution to take responsibility for more than the education of their children. *In loco parentis*, the universities attempted to regulate the personal as well as academic conduct of students. Such rules encompassed sexual relations, alcohol, swearing, and occasionally even smoking.

As late as 1959 the University of Saskatchewan considered it a reform to allow 'well-supervised social evenings with dancing on Sundays on a trial basis.' The last initiative was conditional that it 'not interfere with church attendance.'[57] In the mid-1960s, women at the University of Alberta residences faced myriad rules, with 11:30 P.M. curfews every night but Saturday, and a specific number of passes to extend the curfew on special occasions. 'No restrictions were placed upon the hours kept by male students.'[58] Students, of course, spent much time and effort subverting any and all rules, but few, if any, challenged the basic assumptions underlying their existence.

One of the reasons for this reticence is that student culture seemed to accept and, indeed, revel in the notion of extended adolescence. Popular imagery of the 1950s campus portrays it as an extension, slightly more sophisticated, of high-school culture. A full-scale study of student life after the war has yet to be done, but the popular image seems to be essentially correct. The ritual of dances and dating, going steady and its more serious analogue, getting engaged, mimicked the adult orientation towards marriage, stability, and defined gender roles. Fraternities and the traditional rivalries between freshmen and sophomores created a sense of both belonging and hierarchy.[59]

By the mid-1950s, however, clear warnings existed that universities were about to undergo another major convulsion. The rising school enrolments, both elementary and secondary, hinted of the future. In 1955 a report commissioned by the National Conference of Canadian Universities (NCCU), the Sheffield report, linked public-school enrolments to the future of higher education, warning that enrolment in Canada could double in the next decade. The NCCU reacted swiftly, sending the report to every daily newspaper in Canada.[60] The next year it sponsored a conference which, having taken the report to heart, talked of the 'crisis' in Canadian higher education, predicting post-secondary enrolments could reach as high as 133,000 by 1965. As it would turn out, even that alarmist figure was far too low. In Ontario, universities reported to the Department of Education under none other than J.G. Althouse, who, as we have seen, already had experience with the implications of the baby boom. He also took the Sheffield numbers seriously and warned the government that the days of stability and quiet neglect were about to end. 'Can the universities and Provincial Government defy public opinion and deny to 10,000 to 20,000 young persons who could pass today's tests the right to higher education?'[61]

Compounding the demographics were changing attitudes towards higher education. In 1951, only one in twenty eighteen-year-olds went on to university. As late as 1954, 68 per cent of Canadians believed that boys should leave school at age sixteen.[62] By the later 1950s, however, various pressures emphasized the importance of advanced education. Best known of these is the crisis of confidence that the 1957 launch of the Soviet sputnik created in educational and political circles of the Western world.[63] Reports issued through the later 1950s invariably talked about the desperate need for advanced research in engineering and science.

Yet the sputnik scare may be less relevant than another trend. From the 1950s through the 1970s, there was a tremendous expansion of white-collar positions in administration, finance, and the public sector. Society needed teachers (as we have seen), civil servants, nurses, doctors, and bankers. For example, the number of government workers increased from 318,000 in 1951 to 710,000 twenty years later; the number of teachers from 153,000 in 1951 to more than a quarter of a million by 1971. The list could go on, but the point is that, for those coming of age in the later 1950s and through the 1960s, high levels of education were needed to take advantage of the growth in the white-collar sector. Moreover, in absolute terms, the bulk of new jobs were not for specialists but for those with a general education in arts or science. There were thus very practical reasons why the middle class, for the first time, began to see post-secondary education as essential for the success of its offspring, and not just in engineering or science. Society, for its part, saw the production of increased numbers of sociologists, economists, and even historians as necessary to meet the tremendous demands of the robust white-collar sector.[64]

Such pressures for expansion challenged the basic values of the conservative Canadian university. Already, the largest American institutions seemed to have mutated into something quite different from Bissell's ivory tower with observation posts. In a 1963 essay, President Clark Kerr of the University of California captured the implications of growth in a single word, the 'multiversity.' Looking at his own system, with a budget of half a billion dollars, he noted that the postwar university had become so large and diverse that there was no 'single vision' to guide it.[65] 'The intellectual world has become fractionalized as interests have become more diverse.' Even more alarmingly, the bigger the university became, the more utilitarian it had to be. Compromises had to be made between competing interests. Funding agencies had to be satisfied. Thus, it was that the 'location of power has generally moved from inside to outside the original community of masters and students.'[66]

Among radicals of the 1960s, Kerr's multiversity would become a symbol of all that was corrupt about the modern university. Ironically, though, many staid university administrators at the beginning of the decade were just as unenthusiastic about such a vision. The university was for an élite, and the university was more than the handmaiden of society. Sometimes this was a matter of mere snobbery. The president of McMaster University complained in the 1950s about students 'where taste is not severely disciplined and where education is looked upon chiefly as a means of upgrading in the economic sense.'[67] More substantively, however, universities agonized over the relationship between mass culture and education, as the high schools had a decade before. To cite Jacques Barzun again, the notion that a college education is possible for all, or nearly all, was considered 'wasteful, dangerous and unjust.'[68] Hilda Neatby's critique of the secondary schools was, after all, from the perspective of a university professor who feared that her incoming students would decline in quality. At the very least, such views held, the overexpansion of the system would distort the traditional 'community of scholars.' Thus, throughout the 1950s, university presidents argued that expansion should occur only within the abilities of the traditional system of curriculum and culture to absorb the new students.[69]

The pressures only got worse, however. By the mid-1960s, university enrolments of eighteen-year-olds rose to one in ten, and by the early

1970s to one in six.[70] After receding in the early 1950s, university enrolment climbed at an increasing rate. By 1961–2, when the baby-boomers were, at most, in early adolescence, university enrolment figures had doubled from a decade before. J.A. Corry of Queen's University could look back somewhat fondly on what he termed 'the indifference of the public' to the university system.[71] The fact was, however, that Queen's and all the other institutions turned, their pockets full of newly enlarged government grants, to respond to the rising tide. Sheffield's dire predictions had proved too cautious. As Sheffield himself bluntly commented, looking back on his earlier estimates, 'the pace of expansion must be greatly accelerated.' John Deutsch, a vice-principal of Queen's, put the issue of such growth in more expressive language when he termed it a 'problem almost too horrible to contemplate.'[72]

By the mid-1960s the pace of expansion was frenetic. In the five years between 1963 and 1968, Canadian university enrolment increased as much as it had in the previous fifty! Across the country governments scrambled to open new universities – Trent, Brock, York, Lethbridge, Simon Fraser – or to upgrade church institutions, minor colleges, and branch campuses into independent, fully functioning universities – Calgary, Regina, Sir George Williams, Waterloo. Existing universities exploded in size. The University of Alberta (including its Calgary campus) increased from just over 8,700 students in 1962 to nearly 22,000 on what were now the Universities of Alberta and Calgary, just seven years later.[73] In 1962, York University didn't exist. By 1969 it had more than 7,000 students, and there was no end to its growth in sight.[74] Capital expenditure of $100 million in 1955 rose to $1.5 billion by the end of the 1960s.[75] The continued dominance of 1960s buildings on most Canadian campuses offers mute testimony to the physical transformation wrought by the decade and a half of expansion.

These new buildings had to be filled by professors. In 1961 the Dominion Bureau of Statistics warned that Canadian universities would have to double the number of faculty in the next decade.[76] In fact, the number would nearly triple.[77] This meant that there was a continuing shortage of qualified staff. Graduate schools expanded frantically in order to produce more PhDs. Salaries increased at a rate well above inflation.[78] Yet the problem continued. By the time the baby boom hit the universities in the mid-1960s, administrators were becoming more and more aggressive in their searches. The Association of Universities and Colleges of Canada (AUCC) launched 'Operation Retrieval,' which scoured U.S. graduate schools for Canadians studying abroad.[79] More common, however, was the recruitment of non-Canadians. In some of the newer universities, the majority of the professoriat was new to the country.

The nature of university life had remained more or less constant for two generations, and parents fortunate enough to attend could expect, when they sent their children off, that administrations, professoriat, and campus life would resemble their own experiences. Then, from the late 1950s through the beginning of the 1970s, everything exploded. The small and clubby university was replaced by the 'multiversity.' New systems of governance had to be designed to handle an expanding faculty and student body. Old paternalistic traditions broke down under the sheer weight of numbers. Growth itself, in other words, subjected the entire system to severe stress.

The precise relationship between this destabilization and the upheavals of the 1960s is complex. Many argued, then and since, that students were disappointed by the new factory-like university. This was recognized as a problem at the time, as several academics and administrators warned that universities were turning into mere job-apprenticeship centres. As Claude Bissell warned in 1961, administrators 'have talked about universities as essential preparatory grounds for society, where the executive brains are nurtured, the research talents sharpened, and the professional skills developed.' This, he went on, 'is a dangerous argument, and it backfires upon those who use it, for it presents universities as training schools and glorified apprentice shops for business.'[80] That was not what the university was supposed to be and, in an affluent age, when jobs were plentiful, students expected more.[81]

Yet students are less conditioned by traditions and memories than, say, the professoriat. As significant as the 'factory syndrome' is the simple fact that old traditions and mythologies which stabilized the system were overwhelmed – by a new professoriat not tied to the old Oxbridge traditions of Corry's contemplative thought; by hordes of pre-boomers and boomers who, as children of the electronic age and products of their own youth culture, disdained the rituals and formalism of a college culture with its roots in the 1920s.

The other stabilizing notion that weakened with each passing year was that of privilege. The modern university had never hidden the fact that the élite it served was more than merely an intellectual one. As universities shed their Bible School origins, they also condoned or actively supported practices that emphasized, not just learning, but social poise and well-rounded personality. The 'collegiate man' (or, less often, woman) was supposed to exemplify the best elements of modern society. That, after all, was the element of society that the graduate was going to enter.[82] The rituals of privilege were a natural part of a social élite's preparation for adulthood, but they also helped foster an almost mystic identity with the institution that represented that privilege. By the 1960s, however, privilege was just another tradition to be overwhelmed. For the students of the 1960s, the real power and privilege derived, not from being a 'Queen's' or 'Vic' man – every year there were more and more of those – but, as they had learned from childhood, from their youth. University was their right, not their privilege, and they would, if they so determined, reshape old traditions to fit new sensibilities.

THE POSTWAR WORLD HAD BEEN SHAPED by many things: the drive for security, the cult of domesticity, the morality of the Cold War, and a certain faith in the future. By the early 1960s, the postwar era was ending. The Cold War was becoming more complex. Vietnam would soon challenge some of its most basic assumptions. Affluence, now taken as a normal condition, meant that the previous generation's memories of depression and war had less hold. This affected both the earlier emphasis on security and stability and the cult of domesticity itself. Gallup polls confirmed that the mood of the nation was becoming more liberal. As for domesticity, the birth rate peaked in 1958 and, by 1962, the baby boom was over, long before the Pill had any meaningful effect.

In other words, much of the glue that had shaped society in the previous fifteen years no longer bonded quite so firmly. Yet, as with any time of rapid change, the future was neither clear nor without controversy. The political landscape verified this. In the south, change had been signalled by the election of the nation's youngest president, John F. Kennedy. Yet that election had been only by the tiniest of margins, and only with the help of some corrupt machine politics in Chicago. In Canada, the Conservative populist Diefenbaker lost office to the Liberal reformer Pearson in 1963 but, once again, the people seemed indecisive. Pearson was unable to gain a majority from a begrudging electorate. This was a harbinger of a lack of political authority that would soon extend across the Western world. Social and cultural change thus took shape in the midst of a crisis of authority and, indeed, hastened that crisis.

In precisely these years, another quite independent phenomenon was occurring. A vast generation, unprecedented in its affluence, reared on lessons of fulfilment and post-Holocaust notions of democracy, tied by a sense of peer affinity, made the transition from adolescence to young adulthood. A larger percentage of the young than ever before in history made this transition in a world of higher education that both reinforced their sense of identity and encouraged them to challenge received wisdom.

8

'Hope I Die Before I Get Old': The Rise of the Counter-Culture, 1963–1968

'Consider the contradictions of being a 30 billion dollar market and a drop-out.'

Statement made at a Student Union for Peace Action Conference, *c.* 1964[1]

'The trouble with freedom is that somebody has to put the garbage out.'

Maclean's on Rochdale, 1969[2]

In September 1964 the Beatles came to Canada. Several thousand young people crowded the streets around Maple Leaf Gardens in Toronto. Rumours sent people rushing from one entrance to the other in hopes of a glimpse of the 'Fab Four.' Police on horseback tried vainly to keep the streets clear, and excited fans had to be restrained by overworked officers. The mood was festive, however, rather than threatening. People sang their favourite songs, called the name of their most-loved Beatle, and waited excitedly to get inside. On dozens of transistor radios, the people listened to the latest hit songs. At one point, when Manfred Mann's new hit 'Do Wah Diddy Diddy' came on, hundreds of people joined spontaneously, belting out the lyrics they knew by heart. The British invasion had come to Canada.[3]

Two miles away and eight years later, almost to the week, Rochdale College was in the final phase of collapse. The idealistic experiment in alternative living and education on Bloor Street had descended, in Douglas Fetherling's words, into 'a kind of tower of urban decay and chaos' and was theoretically under the control of Clarkson, Gordon and Company.[4] The chartered accountants hired a private security firm, but it wasn't easy to assume control of the building. When the force first appeared in Rochdale's lobby, it was met by a jeering crowd. Some of the residents stripped. Others urinated on the trousers of the 'rent-a-cops.' The security guards had to retreat, and Rochdale subsequently declared itself 'a self-governing community,' denying access to any external security force that had not been granted permission.[5] It would be three more years before Rochdale was finally emptied. The dream had died long before that, however. 'There's so much I want to bury,' wrote one resident, 'drugs, politics, astrology, perhaps a certain kind of irresponsibility ... I have already moved out, in spirit.' There was also irony in the message defiantly scrawled across one of the walls – 'We shall return' – for Rochdale was being converted into a senior citizens' residence.[6]

These two scenes represent the alternative images of the counterculture of the 1960s. On one side is the Woodstock image of youth harmoniously joined together, free of the hang-ups of adults and enjoying the friendship, the music, and the freedom. On the other side is Altamont, where violence, drug addiction, and absence of purpose signified the lost innocence of a generation. In a few short years, the great youthful experiment in redefining culture in its own image began, expanded, and fragmented. In between, however, an international youth community adopted a generational style distinct from that of adults, flouted respectable society, and asserted that theirs was a special generation, different from that of those only a few years older –'Never trust anyone over thirty.'[7]

This was naïve, but the naïvety existed on both sides. Adults treated the 'hippie' phenomenon as something akin to an invasion from another planet. Dozens of books appeared on 'hippie' culture. Self-proclaimed 'hip' professors headed off to experience and observe this new 'subculture.'[8] At the height of fascination, busloads of the curious glided through the streets of Haight-Ashbury in San Francisco while the tour guide passed on bits of hippie slang to passengers. In Toronto, thousands of suburbanites drove in to cruise Yorkville Avenue and see for themselves what these 'hippies' were all about.

Why was so much fear and fascination vested in youth culture in the 1960s? Rebellion against adult taste has been a recurring element of modern teenage style. Zoot-suits, bobby-soxers, and so on had come and gone. Adolescent rebellion had always been balanced by the influence and power of adult society to control and direct youth. The fear or the hope of the sixties, depending on the vantage point, was that this time it was different. The postwar generation, large in numbers and economically powerful, threatened to eclipse the adult world. In music, dress, and attitudes, the younger generation seemed increasingly unwilling to accept adult values. Indeed, one of the most dramatic assertions of the counter-culture was that eventual integration into adult society was optional, and probably not desirable. 'The system is designed to turn you off. The system has already turned the teachers off, and they, in their turn, perpetuate the system. The system lives off itself. The system eats your mind.'[9] The power of adult society to 'tame the barbarians,' as Landon Jones put it, had never seemed weaker.

ONE OF THE MOST STRIKING THINGS ABOUT the rise of sixties culture is how quickly things evolved. The rise, flowering, and decay of the whole movement took less than a decade. In the early 1960s, as the baby-boomers moved into their teenage years, youth culture seemed unusually tame. The sneering subcult typified by James Dean and Marlon Brando was fading, and adult-controlled and adult-marketed stars dominated youth entertainment. 'Gidget' movies, starring the perky Sandra Dee, were hits on the drive-in circuits, as was Cliff Richard's musical, *Summer Holiday.* True, the adults had lost the battle to eliminate rock and roll. Even there, however, the music was pretty docile. *Rolling Stone*'s history of rock and roll describes the early 1960s as 'the dark ages.'[10] Many of the 'stars' were manufactured by the record studios (Fabian comes to mind) or were pleasant non-entities. Dick Clark still held sway on *American Bandstand* and brought the latest '45s' to the international audience. If there was a fad, it was for new dances. How to do The Monkey, The Jerk, The Monster Mash, The Watusi, The Pony, and The Mashed Potato was vital knowledge to the 'in' teenager in the early part of the decade.

Typifying the state of pop music was the greatest dance fad of all, The Twist. Ernest Evans was a chicken plucker who was picked up by Cameo-Parkway records. His name was changed (à la Fats Domino) to Chubby Checker and, after a minor song or two, he recorded a new dance song, 'The Twist.' The dance was easy to do and fit the teenage desire for outrageous action. By the end of 1961, Checker's record had been at the top of the charts for twenty-three weeks, longer than any other record that year. Follow-up Twist records appeared, and there was even a movie. Not until 1963 did the dance begin to fade, pushed aside by hits like Leslie Gore's, 'It's My Party' and the Four Seasons' 'Walk Like a Man.' In the meantime Evans sought in vain for a new dance craze but, by 1965, he was off the hit parade and on the night-club circuit.[11] Nothing in this was threatening. None of it pointed to what was about to happen.

Yet the dance-craze era was grist for a later turn of the mill. The Twist and other crazes of the early sixties demonstrated how ideas could reach out and galvanize youth. Fad after fad, dance after dance, swept across the continent, transmitted by Dick Clark and by hundreds of radio shows to parties and high-school gyms. Dances invented in Philadelphia or Los Angeles in July would be well known in Toronto or Edmonton by September. By then, of course, a new dance was surfacing in California. Finally, by the early 1960s, rock and roll had overcome all resistance. Only the most die-hard of parents now tried to prevent their teenagers from listening to rock. This victory of teenage culture over adult resistance demonstrated something only dimly understood at the time: If the youth culture of North America wanted something, it would be very hard to resist. The infrastructure of the youth rebellion was in place long before the youth knew they wanted to rebel.

The notion of rebellion against adult mores did exist. At the turn of the decade, it came from currents running just under the surface of what appeared to be a stable culture. In the United States the 'Beat' movement had attracted considerable notoriety. The success of Jack Kerouac's *On the Road* (1958) drew attention to the whole concept of a youth culture that scorned the mainstream. Images of bearded poets and, more titillating, free love drew the scornful attention of newspaper columnists around the country. Old-time radical Paul Goodman portrayed the Beats in more sympathetic terms. To him these rebels were the natural reaction to a society that lacked 'the opportunity to be useful.' The problem, he said, is not to get youth like the Beats to 'belong to society, for they a priori belong by virtue of being the next generation. The burden of proof and performance is quite the other way: for the system of society to accommodate itself to all its constituent members.'[12] By the beginning of the 1960s places like Greenwich Village had become well known to the general public as the site of an alternative and vaguely threatening culture.

The Beats themselves weren't very important in Canada in the 1950s. Indeed, they hardly existed except in the imagination of journalists.[13] The American Beat influence was a part of the background to the counter-culture, however. It provided an alternative model for youth – especially older youth – who wanted to assert their distinctiveness both from the adult world and from the mass teenage culture of Fabian and Pat Boone. In the early 1960s, it must be remembered, rock and roll was still seen primarily as a juvenile music form. The older, more intellectual youth looked instead to other more 'sophisticated' music.

Folk music provided the perfect alternative. Here was an adult music form, but one with a pedigree of protest and integrity. Singers like Pete Seeger and Woody Guthrie looked back to the lively politics of the 1930s. Then, in the early 1960s, the civil-rights movement revitalized the tradition of folk protest and created a bridge between old and new causes.[14] Folk had also been popularized by this time. Groups like the Limeliters, the Kingston Trio, and Peter, Paul, and Mary packaged folk traditions in slick and appealing ways for a mass audience. Such popularization even meant that Pete Seeger got to act as host of a television folk show, *Let's Sing Out*, in the late 1950s and early 1960s. It provided a showcase for most of the élite of folk. More 'mixed' musical shows like Mitch Miller's *Sing Along with Mitch* also routinely had folk as part of their repertoire. By 1963 the power of folk had been recognized in such sanitized groups as the New Christy Minstrels and ABC's *Hootenanny*.[15]

Canada had a much smaller musical community, and practically no opportunity for aspiring artists to record. None the less, by the early 1960s folk music was also having an impact here. The background tradition in Canada was not so much protest as it was country music. Singers like Ian and Sylvia, and Gordon Lightfoot, were active by the early part of the decade.[16] Ian and Sylvia recorded their first album in 1962, and both Canadian and American folk-singers were very much in demand for university concerts. By the early 1960s folk was sufficiently established that there was an annual festival in Ontario, named after Stephen Leacock's fictional town of Mariposa. As folk continued to grow in importance, the festival became a musical highlight of the year, attracting artists from across Canada and the United States.

The folk culture was even beginning to create small semi-bohemian 'artistic' or 'beat' communities in Canada's largest cities. By the early 1960s, an area of St Catherine Street in Montreal was known as an eclectic community of young musicians and artists. As early as 1964, Toronto's Yorkville Village was well established as a centre of folk activity. Coffeehouses like The Inn on the Parking Lot, The Mynah

Bird, and The Purple Onion drew considerable crowds of young people and helped encourage young transients and drop-outs to move into the surrounding old houses.[17] In Vancouver the warm climate acted, as it always had, to draw the restless from across the West. In this case, Granville Street became the centre of activity, then Gastown. Kitsilano was quickly developing as a 'youth' neighbourhood.

Two distinct centres of youth activity thus existed by the early 1960s. The first was the mass culture of rock and roll. The second was the more intellectual world of folk. Unlike rock, folk had a political focus. It also acted as the music of a subcommunity of older youth that existed on the fringes of society in the larger cities. There were few true beatniks, but folk was, like rock, a part of the infrastructure of youth. Even the completely 'straight' middle-class teenager knew the Kingston Trio and was likely to be tempted to visit the new youth-oriented coffeehouses. Though less of a mass-market phenomenon, folk provided a conduit whereby the languages and traditions of protest could be passed from the generation of the 1930s to that of the 1960s.

At this point several things happened. Between early 1964 and the end of 1966, the youth subcultures merged and became politicized. The political sensibilities of folk merged with the mass market of rock. The 'beats' became the 'hippies,' and the distrust of adult values and styles moved from the fringe of youth culture to its identifying characteristic. 'The fifties' became 'the sixties.'

AS ONE CULTURAL HISTORIAN HAS SAID, 'rock was the culture of the sixties in a unique and special way.'[18] It became the mass medium that, much more than television, was the centre of youth entertainment in the 1960s. Thousands of transistor, car, and regular radios, stereo sets, and live concerts acted, in effect, as 'a medium of propaganda, identifying the young as a distinct force in society.'[19] Rock, therefore, may be the best place to begin in trying to understand the changes that occurred in mid-decade.

In 1964 and 1965 rock began its golden era. Until then rock and roll was an American medium, and it was thus a surprise that the source of this revival was Great Britain. Aside from the minor successes of Cliff Richard and the Shadows, British bands were virtually unknown in North America. Numerous histories of the 'British invasion' have shown, however, that by the late 1950s several British groups had become fascinated with American music, both rock and roll and the imaginative and powerful black music that lay behind it. In various clubs and circuits in Britain and on the Continent, groups like the Beatles absorbed the lessons of black music and blues.[20] By the early 1960s songs like 'Love Me Do' (recorded in 1962) demonstrated that the lessons had been taken to heart.

The story of the Beatles' rise to fame, their packaging by manager Brian Epstein, and the transmission of Beatlemania to North America has been well chronicled elsewhere.[21] By the time they arrived for their heralded appearance on *Ed Sullivan*, it was a major event right across North America. The 9 February 1964 airing was watched by more than 73 million Americans.[22] Thereafter every record company scrambled to bring a seemingly endless list of British groups to North America: Gerry and the Pacemakers, the Dave Clark Five, Herman's Hermits, the Rolling Stones, Freddie and the Dreamers. Some became legends in their own right and others have been mercifully forgotten, but in 1964 they all gathered media attention, lucrative North American record contracts, and screaming teenagers.

The British groups were joined by a new wave of energetic American rock groups like the Jefferson Airplane and the Grateful Dead, and by singers like Jimi Hendrix and Janis Joplin. At the same time 'black music' such as soul and the 'Motown' sound continued to increase its appeal to the mainstream. In Canada, the music was just as energetic if, as yet, more local. The Guess Who, formed in Winnipeg in 1963, and singers like Neil Young, then playing in an obscure group called the Mynah Birds, would go on to international fame as the decade went on. Whatever revisionist thoughts or criticism may be levelled against the 1960s, it is hard to deny the originality, creativity, and excitement of the music. It retained the unswerving loyalty of a generation at a time when many other gods were to fall from their pedestals.

The British invasion also redefined the image of rock, and in so doing prepared the way for rock as the medium of the counter-culture. Until the arrival of the Beatles, rock had two images, loosely divided along class lines. The tough, leather-jacketed image competed with the preppy, 'clean-teen' image of Pat Boone. The former had a certain vicarious appeal to most middle-class teenagers but was far too closely associated with the world of motorcycle gangs and far too unfashionable to appeal to the majority of suburbanites. Thus the majority of early 1960s teenagers adhered basically to parentally defined styles involving cleanliness, short hair, and respectable dress. Glance through the high school or university year books for the years 1960 to 1965, and row upon row of clean-cut students stare back at you, interrupted by only the occasional 'ducktail' among boys or excessive eyeliner on the part of a few girls.

Then, along with the British groups, came British definitions of style, definitions forged along the complex class and social lines of British society. In Britain, dress had become a major peer-group point of definition. On the one side were the 'rockers,' drawing upon the imagery of the motorcycle and leather jacket associated with 1950s rock and toughness. On the other side were the 'mods,' sporting trendy clothes and Beatles haircuts. Whereas the rocker image was toughness, the mod image was stylishness – being 'with it,' being a part of the modern wave of music and style that was sweeping Britain. Their role models came from the Beatles, the Edwardian imagery of the Kinks, and other trendy groups of the day. Style was soon a uniform and part of a battle for control of the peer group of youth. 'You've got to be either a mod or a rocker to mean anything,' as one young mod put it.[23] Pitched battles of mods and rockers occurred throughout 1964 and 1965 and were duly sensationalized and broadcast to North America by the press.

In North America there was never any contest. The baby boom in North America was much more resolutely middle class than its counterpart in Britain. It was also a generation that had learned to be stylish from a very early age. Before long the leather jacket ('greaser' image, as it was known in North America) was pushed even farther to the margins of society, a region populated by school drop-outs, motorcycle outlaws, and criminals.[24] What the mod image did was merge the fashion-consciousness and respectability of the middle class with a distinctive youth style that was not defined by or terribly acceptable to parents – long hair, short skirts, paisley shirts, and stylish boots.

Teenage fads come and go, and are often distinctive from those of adults. The recurring clash between adult and youth fashions took on new import in the sixties, however, for three reasons. First, the youth market was of extraordinary size and affluence. By 1965 half of the population of North America was under twenty-five years old. Second, the cult of the teenager, and especially of rock, had previously created an effective medium for transmitting the latest in peer-group values. In fan magazines, on album covers, and on television, rock idols transmitted continent-wide images on what being cool meant. Teenagers then modified these to fit budget and parental-tolerance levels, and incorporated them into their own wardrobe and sense of identity. The mainstream media, all agog with youth issues by this time, reinforced the image. 'Now it's chic for girls all over the world to come on skinny and wear long hair and wispy little mod dresses.'[25] For boys, of course, the main style statement was hair. Grease and duck tails disappeared and Beatle-inspired 'mops' took over. 'The girls love long hair,' enthused one boy with adolescent bravura. 'Can't resist the sight of it.'[26]

The third reason is perhaps the most important, however, for it transformed culture into politics. Throughout the 1950s, issues like 'respectability' or its negative counterpart, 'conformity,' had been a significant part of the social glue. It was this influence that allowed the adult world to subordinate James Dean to Pat Boone. The clean-teen image at the beginning of the 1960s implied that, whatever foibles teenagers might demonstrate, their ultimate goal was adult respectability. Then, during the 1960s, adult society itself became less respectable. Kennedy's death robbed that world of much of its magic. The senescent phase of the Cold War made traditional politics increasingly unattractive. This was especially true once the fatal Vietnam venture escalated in 1964 and 1965. Emulation of adults became less desirable, and what started as a fad soon began to take on political connotations. People who wore the uniform of mini-skirts, long hair, boots, and blue jeans were declaring themselves a part of the new youth sensibility. As William O'Neill has put it, 'aesthetics were exchanged for ethics' or, more appropriately perhaps, aesthetics became a statement of ethics.[27]

Once clothes assumed political significance, reactions increased proportionately. Indeed, in this post-sixties world, it is difficult to conceive of the hostility and fear created by the rise of the new sixties youth fashions. People with long hair were routinely threatened or harassed. In the United States students were sent to jail for 'disrupting the peace' – that is, for coming to class with long hair.[28] Families broke up over the length of a boy's hair or his decision to comb his bangs down 'like the Beatles.' Girls were suspended for wearing blue jeans to school (not sufficiently feminine) or wearing dresses that were above the knee (too feminine?).[29] The principal of Baron Byng High School in Montreal summed up the rationale of the age: 'These eccentric habits are meant to distract the attention of other students and that's exactly what we don't want.'[30]

Throughout the country, incidents testified to ongoing skirmishes between young and old based on appearance. A Vancouver restaurant owner threw a couple out of his establishment because the male had a beard and the girl had a 'beard-like attitude.'[31] In Edmonton a judge created controversy when, spotting two long-haired males in the audience, he interrupted court proceedings to insult and embarrass them. 'There are a couple of girls in this courtroom,' he announced loudly before ejecting them.[32] Sometimes the comments seemed confused. The Baptist minister E.M. Checkland argued in 1967 that, because hippies had 'adopted the flower as the symbol,' they had rejected the animal and machine side of human nature. 'They think of themselves as sheep.' Such reactions accentuated the generation gap. 'Youths who tried the fashion of long hair found themselves on the other side of the great cultural divide. Many of them elected to stay.'[33]

These daily controversies were significant in two ways. First, this was the 1950s at its most repressed. North American society did not tolerate difference with any equanimity. The search for security had led to intolerance of diversity. Conformity in dress, manners, and outlook was a badge of social respectability.[34] Second, the battle over fashion was a struggle between generations for control. Rejection of the outward symbols of respectability was threatening the tenuous balance that had been achieved among family, work, and social demands in the postwar years. This was particularly evident in the case, as always, of sexual identity. The increasingly androgynous styles of the 1960s directly assaulted the uncertainties about gender role, manliness, and Freudian sexual impulses which so obsessed the postwar generation. Old standards of gender behaviour clashed directly with new generationally directed styles. 'Get your hair cut. You look like a girl' was a potent insult to those who subscribed to 1950s standards of manliness. It meant nothing to an adolescent youth looking to a peer group for clues on behaviour and dress.

The conflict of values had special meaning when Father, imbued with thousands of Freudian notions on child rearing and the ever-present dangers of sexuality, watched his adolescents suddenly adopt 'non-manly' fashions. When John Lennon remarked flippantly that all he had to do to prove he was a man was have sex with a woman, he assaulted the sensibilities of a generation. For girls the analogous process was the increasingly open sexuality of the decade. As we will see in chapter 10, the fear was that, if boys were becoming girls, girls were ceasing to be ladies. As one teenage girl complained in 1966, the belief that morality was breaking down was wrong: 'that because two people engage in sex they are not moral if they are not married. I take very great exception to this. I don't feel this is true at all.'[35]

Adult hostility further ingrained youth culture as a political statement. This is perhaps most clearly demonstrated in the subculture of language. Throughout the 1960s, language, like clothes, had become been a means of distinguishing young from old. Drug slang separated 'straights' from 'freaks,' and drug words were converted into metaphors like 'trippy.' Other terms, like 'far out,' 'cool,' and 'groovy,' derived from the Beat culture. Obscenity, too, played an important part as a symbol of youth's absence of inhibition and for the shock value it conveyed. In the 1960s, obscenity went up-scale and became coeducational. Words that would have been reserved for the locker-room became a normal part of any university party or, in some cases, seminar. Inventive combinations of drugs and obscenity sometimes merged as in 'far fuckin' out' and, indeed, the much maligned word 'fuck' took on special significance. Females used it almost as freely as males, and at times it seemed to be exclamation, adjective, verb, and noun rolled into one. The only problem was that, as Peter Gzowski lamented, by the end of the decade 'the big F has lost its power as a dirty word.' 'Motherfucker' had to be invented so that the shock value could be regained.[36]

Underlying the intergenerational conflict over style and language was parental fear of failure. The permissiveness which in the 1950s had been thought necessary for proper child development now turned out to be the underlying cause of the decadence of youth. 'Today's parents are afraid of their children,' wrote BC journalist Simma Holt in 1967. 'The fear by parents to use their authority is seen by those involved in the lives of young people as one of the basic causes of the juvenile explosion.' Especially critical, she noted, was the 'abdication of father as head of the family.'[37] A McGill sociologist even transformed these assertions into science, arguing that the Beatles became effeminate father figures for 'sexually mixed-up girls looking for someone to love.' The 'feminine male' figure of the Beatles, or those who emulate them in style, provided a refuge from a hostile father figure.[38] Teenage culture had merged with the Freudian generation.

Rock conveyed energy, style, and, with the British invasion, fashion. The one thing rock wasn't used to conveying was an idea. That had been left to folk – 'serious' music. At festivals like Newport in the United States and the newly founded Mariposa in Ontario, folk musicians carried on the tradition of their genre, exposing social injustice and calling for reassessment of the world condition. The other great shift that occurred in the period from 1964 to 1966, therefore, was the acceptance by key folk artists of the importance of rock. Coming down off the intellectual heights on which they had been ensconced, folk musicians worked with rock sounds and technologies. Rock musicians, in turn, moved into the folk world of ideas. The barriers faded, and the music became all the more powerful.

They key moment in this transformation is usually taken to be Bob Dylan's use of an electric guitar and rock beat at the Newport Folk Festival in July 1965. 'It was a benediction of sorts: the folk movement, in the form of its biggest star, had wielded its influence decisively on rock and roll.'[39] It is as appropriate a moment as any, but, as with so much else in the 1960s, it was the result of much complex interchange. Dylan got the idea for electric rock when he heard the British group the Animals transform 'House of the Rising Sun' into a brilliant mix of rock and blues.[40] On the west coast, new San Francisco sounds were developing that had a soft-rock beat. Groups like the Mamas and the Papas, the Byrds, and others were developing a sound that would soon be known as folk-rock. By the beginning of 1966, rock (soon to add subgenres like acid rock and psychedelic rock) formed a continuum with folk-rock, and folk. From the one end flowed energy and the mass market. From the other end flowed the tradition of political comment. The result was a tremendous vitality and the transformation of an entertainment form into the voice of a generation.

'It's no small matter,' wrote American cultural historian Morris Dickstein, 'that the young of the sixties had a serious culture created by people not far from their own age, which could give expression to those universal post-adolescent longings, joys, and traumas that were once the province of fatally precocious poets.'[41] It is a crucial point, for, at some point, music, styles, and ideas began to merge to create what became known as 'the revolution.' Rock and folk grew closer together. 'Mods' triumphed over 'rockers.' Clothes were softer in style, androgynous, and bright rather than aggressive and tough. Yet the rocker sensibility triumphed in at least one sense. The sense of alienation from society and distrust of authority that was inherent in the leather jacket of James Dean or the blue jeans of Elvis Presley was incorporated into the modern sensibility of youth. By the mid-sixties, style was politicized and political entertainment was mass market.

IN EARLY 1965 THE HEAD OF THE VANCOUVER drug squad gave an interview to the student paper at the University of British Columbia. He admitted that, for the first time, drugs were becoming a problem, not just among the 'down-and-outers,' but among middle-class university students. Just a month earlier a UBC student had been sentenced to six months in jail for possession of marijuana. The drug-squad head warned students that they were playing with fire. 'I have never known a woman addict who was not a prostitute or at least promiscuous, or a man addict who was not a criminal.'[42] Perhaps, but he would soon.

Nothing divided official society from the emergent counter-culture more than drugs. In Canada, as in the United States, the legal system had evolved a stringent set of controls to deal with the abuse of drugs in the years around the turn of the century. Reformers had condemned the unscientific or destructive use of drugs in society. The really great battle was over the prohibition of alcohol, but along the way opium and related drugs were restricted. This was made easier as opium use was a habit confined largely to Asian immigrants. In 1908 its possession or sale was made illegal.

For the next twenty years, the issue continued to rouse reformers. In 1922 reformer and judge Emily Murphy wrote the sensationalist work *The Black Candle*. Not only did she attack opium and its derivatives, but she widened her net to cannabis. 'Persons using this narcotic smoke the dried leaves of the plant, which has the effect of driving them completely insane. The addict loses all sense of moral responsibility ... While in this condition they become raving maniacs and are liable to kill or indulge in any form of violence to other persons, using the most savage methods of cruelty without, as said before, any sense of responsibility.'[43] In 1923, and again in 1927, the Opium and Drug Control Act was made more stringent, and the number of drugs included was increased.[44] By then the reforming zeal had passed, and no changes were made to the law for more than thirty years. This didn't imply that the society had grown tolerant of drugs. Indeed, the drug user had not only been criminalized but given a particularly dark niche in Canadian society. 'The drug addict,' declared a 1952 RCMP publication, 'is a psychopathic individual possessing a prior tendency toward becoming a habitual criminal. From an early age he commits crimes or associates with those who do so.'[45]

For all this, illegal drugs in Canada were a relatively minor problem, confined – as the Vancouver policeman noted – to a marginal criminal class. The drug trade that did exist, however, was often hard core, based on heroin addiction. Trade in so-called softer drugs like marijuana simply did not exist. In 1955, for example, a House of Commons Committee concluded there was 'no problem' with marijuana in Canada. Only a few charges were laid each year, and most of these cases involved 'visitors from outside the country.'[46] All the illegal substances together led to only 300 to 500 charges a year through the late 1950s and early 1960s (see figure 8.1). As late as 1963 the *Annual Report* of the RCMP was confident that there was no real drug problem in Canada. The new Narcotic Act of 1960, the excellent work of the police, and severe court sentences had, the report concluded, actually reduced the already low level of drug usage in the country. As for cannabis, a grand total of fifteen ounces were seized during the year. The report could reasonably conclude that 'the situation with regard to this drug is not considered serious.'[47]

The police confidence was misplaced. After about late 1963, police began to notice an increased drug presence among the 'beatnik' communities.[48] About the same time a new drug appeared on the streets, lysergic acid diethylamide, or LSD.[49] All of this, in turn, aroused the interest of the media, who sent out reporters to investigate the appeal of drugs to youth. On campuses across the country, the issue of 'dope' began to receive attention. South of the border, open advocates of drug usage were beginning to appear.[50] Most ominously, as in the case of the unfortunate UBC student, the occasional arrest on campuses for marijuana possession indicated that drug usage was crossing into a whole new community.[51]

The associations of youthful middle-class individuals with drug usage was novel. So, too, were the drugs they employed. For the vast majority of youthful 'dopers' in the 1960s, the drug culture was founded on two basic substances. The first, and by the far the most common, was cannabis and its derivatives. In spite of the erroneous classification of it under 'opiates' in the 1960 Narcotics Act, cannabis was a relatively mild non-addictive drug that had been used for centuries in many Asian and Middle Eastern cultures. In North America it had maintained a low-key presence among Latin Americans in the United States, and had been used by entertainers before entering the beatnik community and, from there, the youth culture of the 1960s.[52]

Most who wrote or testified about cannabis usage celebrated two things. The first was a relatively mild 'feeling of well-being' that could lead to heightened awareness of friends, music, time, and surroundings. Little chance of a serious reaction existed, though 'anxiety' was sometimes the unwanted result of getting high. It was thus a relatively non-invasive drug. The only persistent physical reaction seemed to be a stimulated appetite. Indeed, when the Royal Commission on the Non-Medical Use of Drugs searched for evidence of casualties among marijuana users, the only instance it could find was a person who died of a distended bowel while on a post-high eating binge.[53]

The second aspect of pot was its ritualistic role. The cost of the drug, its illegality, and the belief that those who used it were privy to an experience not shared by the general public made a sense of ceremony crucial, especially in the early years. The door was locked, and a towel might be stuffed under it in the vain attempt to prevent the smells from escaping. Incense was often burned, both to mask smells and as part of the ritual. Water-pipes, 'roaches,' or glowing hash on the end of a cigarette was shared communally – another part of the ceremony. All was consumed. Even the butt ends of the roaches were eaten. 'The ritual is important, see? Deep drag, pass it on, suck in air, hold it in – hold it in! – then exhale. Man and it just wipes you out. So they say.'[54]

The second favoured drug of the sixties was LSD. First concocted in a laboratory in the late 1930s, LSD had already had a bizarre history by the time it became a part of sixties culture. In the 1940s and 1950s, two overlapping groups of people had experimented with this potent new drug. One was the medical profession, interested in the possibilities of LSD as a cure for mental disorders such as schizophrenia. Numerous medical experiments were conducted, including many in Canada. As early as 1953 the drug gained some public attention when a *Maclean's* journalist took a dosage and spent 'twelve hours as a madman.'[55] In the 1950s Abraham Hoffer and his laboratory in Saskatchewan became a centre for experimentation.[56] As well, the Central Intelligence Agency of the United States was exploring the use of LSD as a possible tool in espionage.[57]

In its early years, then, LSD was not illegal. Right from the beginning, though, this drug was somewhat different. Those involved with it could not resist its charms. Doctors engaged in early experimentation often dropped acid themselves, initially for experience and then simply for fun.[58] This was harmless enough, though it did strain their scientific objectivity. More sinister were the efforts of the CIA to investigate LSD as a disabling agent or brainwashing technique. Funding was provided to, among other places, the Allan Memorial Institute at McGill. There, unwitting patients were fed varying doses of LSD. In the United States similar experiments were being conducted and, even more bizarrely, CIA operatives began experimenting upon themselves, drugging each other's drinks, and at one point even planning to spike the organization's Christmas punch! By the later 1950s they were operating a house in San Francisco to which prostitutes brought men home and laced their drinks with the drug. The CIA watched the results through one-way mirrors.[59] The medical self-experimentation, the Christmas punch, and hundreds of personal experiments with the drug by government agents and medical officials indicated just how easily LSD could tempt those involved. By 1960 an amazing number of famous people, from Cary Grant to Clare Boothe Luce and Ethel Kennedy, had been turned on by scientists, sometimes as therapy and often out of curiosity.[60]

The real turning-point for the drug came from the Harvard experiments of Timothy Leary and Richard Alpert. Leary had been conducting studies with polyscibin, the active ingredient in the 'magic mushroom.' For both Leary and Alpert, this was something more than detached inquiry. They had become enthusiasts for the drug's potential as a mind expander after being turned on to LSD by a member of the British Cultural Exchange named Michael Hollingshead. The experience deepened Leary's faith in the potential of mind-expanding drugs. Before long he was preaching the wonders of LSD to all who would listen, much to the discomfort of his Harvard colleagues. In 1963 he and Alpert were both fired.[61] The United States restricted the use of LSD, and Canada made it illegal.

Timothy Leary and his Beat acquaintances like Allen Ginsberg were important in the popularizing of drugs among baby-boomers, but they were only a part of the link. Another connection came in the creative community, through the Beats to the pop star. By the mid-1960s, in both the United States and the United Kingdom, dope was beginning to become an integral part of the rock-music scene. Drugs were hardly new in artistic circles, of course, but it was different this time. Until the 1960s musicians and others had kept drug use a quiet secret within their own community. As was the case for communism or homosexuality, fear of public condemnation, as much as the legal penalties, kept deviant practices tightly guarded. When the life story of drummer Gene Krupa was made into a movie in 1959, it defensively emphasized that his conviction for marijuana possession was a frame-up. He had a reputation to defend, after all.[62]

The attitude of the 1960s was very different. When, in 1964, Bob Dylan introduced the Beatles to dope, a symbolic milestone had been reached. The 'clean-cut Fab Four' had, as it were, gone underground.[63] At about the same time, on the west coast, a new series of bands was on the rise who not only accepted drugs but saw them as an essential part of their artistry. Ken Kesey and his Merry Pranksters, along with bands like the Grateful Dead, were immortalized by Tom Wolfe's *Electric Kool-Aid Acid Test.*[64] By 1966 many of the major rock stars were not only doing dope but praising it as an essential part of their creative experience. In February 1967 Mick Jagger was arraigned on possession charges and gave television interviews on the young generation and adult hypocrisy about drugs. In the United States, songs like Dylan's 'Mr Tambourine Man' and the Jefferson Airplane's 'White Rabbit' (perhaps the best metaphor for the sixties ever performed) alluded to the use and benefit of drugs. Acid rock and the psychedelic age had begun.

Health authorities and police responded by stepping up their efforts to stop drug usage among middle-class youth. In Canada arrests under the Narcotics Act tripled between 1966 and 1968.[65] Officials repeatedly warned of the dangers of drugs. Campuses, now seen as the most vulnerable point for the spread of drugs,[66] were especially targeted. Professors gave talks on their dangers.[67] Police stepped up surveillance and infiltration of student ghettoes. The medical health officer of Vancouver purchased a large advertisement in the student newspaper, the *Ubyssey,* warning that 'no one should allow [LSD] to enter his or her body.'[68] It was a losing battle. In a test of credibility, with the police, medical authorities, and politicians on one side and the rock stars on the other, the establishment was bound to lose. As the Royal Commission on the Non-Medical Use of Drugs (LeDain Commission) later commented, the scare tactics of adults on drugs have 'backfired.'[69] As early as 1966 the RCMP complained that all the police received for their efforts was 'abuse, accusations of police brutality and sensational TV coverage.'[70]

The battle over drugs was one of the misfortunes of the decade. On the one side, the failure of the law to differentiate 'soft' drugs like cannabis from 'hard' drugs like heroin put thousands of occasional users at risk. Until late in the decade, many police officers and judges seemed unwilling to distinguish between types of drugs or, for that matter, between casually selling a joint to a friend and being a major dealer. The law was also capricious. In many jurisdictions, possession of marijuana was routinely subject only to a small fine. In others, six-month jail sentences were meted out. British Columbia seems to have been the harshest of all, and the infamous Les Bewley the harshest of the BC judges. Teenagers were often given the maximum six months in jail for first-offence possession. As a judge of the Provincial Court of Appeal bluntly put it in one such 1968 case, 'the deterrent aspect, as I said, is the important one. The rehabilitation of the offender is secondary.'[71]

Health warnings paralleled the legal apparatus. Ad campaigns did not discuss differences between drugs, lest they be seen as condoning any of them. This was counter-productive. From the beginning, much of the press was sceptical about the dangers of marijuana. *Maclean's*, for example, ran an article as early as 1964 that raised the possibility that it was a 'harmless drug.'[72] Scare tactics on marijuana were quickly discredited. Soon movies like *Reefer Madness*, an old paranoid FBI film, were playing on college campuses as satire on the anti-drug message. Ads that talked of marijuana as a 'Killer Drug' were gleefully reprinted by student or underground papers.[73] LSD was a more potent drug, but the case against it, too, in the early campaigns was overstated. As soon as it appeared, the press began to write sensational stories about crazed hippies jumping out of windows, murdering their parents, and so on. At the medical level a widespread story tied LSD to chromosome damage.[74] Later research found no evidence at all of such a link.

The discrediting of the establishment meant two things of some importance to the culture of the sixties. First, in dismissing the absurd scare tactics about pot, youth culture tended to dismiss the very real dangers of the drug world. In the absence of trusted information, people took to very dangerous drugs. Heroin always remained on the fringes, but speed freaks (amphetamine users) became a significant subgroup within the counter-culture.[75] New and untried chemicals were riding the coat-tails of LSD, often with disastrous effects. Further, the celebration of the drug life understated the psychological impact of drugs on immature or disturbed personalities.[76] Lives were ruined in the 1960s by drugs and by criminal prosecution. The souring of the drug culture would be one of the key forces bringing down the decade.

For the moment, however, another impact is more relevant. The rising popularity of drugs accelerated the development of a counter-culture. This was not, as the police liked to argue, because 'druggies' became dirty, uninterested, and criminal. Rather it was because skirmishes over drugs were like the battles about hair, except in the much more serious arena of criminal law. They confirmed the divide between generations and implied that the establishment was out to repress youth and self-expression. As one underground paper argued, psychedelic drugs were good because 'people who take them are no longer obedient slaves of the state. They perceive that living is pleasurable and that pleasure is good.' This was why 'the state has mounted

FIGURE 8.1
Drug Charges Laid in the 1960s

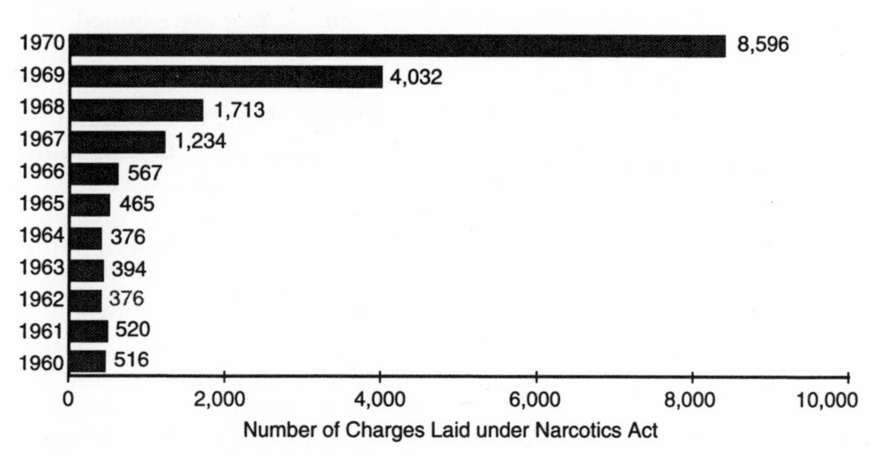

Source: *Canada Year Book*, 1963–73

an intensive campaign to eliminate psychedelic drugs and their use.'[77] Such campaigns failed. Indeed, they backfired. As one young Montrealer put it, 'the fact that kids who don't consider themselves criminals are breaking the law all the time can only lessen their respect for all laws in Canada.'[78] By the end of the decade, 30 to 50 per cent of university students had used drugs, and perhaps 20 to 25 per cent of high-school seniors. At the University of Alberta, students in residence who admitted to drug use grew from 19 per cent in 1966 to 26 per cent just five years later.[79] Surveys south of the border also indicated that even those who did not take drugs condoned the use of the softer drugs like marijuana.[80] Thus youth allied themselves against the values of the older generation.[81] The police were charging more than 8,000 people a year by the end of the decade, and there was no sign the arrests were having any effect on drug usage (see figure 8.1).

AT WHAT POINT DID THESE FASHIONS AND FADS – from music to drugs – become a 'culture' or, rather, 'a counter-culture'? One answer, of course, is that the counter-culture already existed, under the Beats, but it got bigger. More meaningful, however, is the concept of a small, artistically based movement exploding into a mass movement. The power of the counter-culture came, not from the few hippies who withdrew to communes, or from the artistic communities, or even from the 'free colleges' such as Rochdale. Rather, its power derived from the fact that the preoccupations of a great mass of youth – rock, dope, sex, and clothes – had been politicized. This did two things. First, it confused the adult, who were never sure where style ended and political revolution began. Second, it gave non-political, non-activist students the sense they were part of the generational struggle against adult authority. This was the real force behind the sixties revolution – the attachment, however sporadic and conditional, of a mass of youth to concepts of alienation and social resistance demonstrated among their more radical counterparts.[82]

The other answer is that fashion and fads became a counter-culture when they were accepted as an integral intellectual and ethical movement. By, say, 1967, the counter-culture was a political movement expressed through non-political means – music, style, language, drugs. Further, for all the exaggerated claims made by the counter-culture's proponents, this was a movement that really did run 'counter' to many of the prevalent cultural trends of the day. That was why it became political. This was why people could see smoking dope, long hair, flower power, or love beads as revolutionary. It is possible, said one optimistic political activist, 'that Allen Ginsberg and Abbie Hoffman and Paul Krassner are the Rousseau, and the Diderot and the Voltaire, of the new American revolution.'[83]

Ginsberg and Hoffman were hardly Enlightenment figures. Indeed, for a historian the interesting thing about the revolution is that it was so classical in shape and direction. In the late Enlightenment rationalist discussion, Cartesian logic and the products of the earlier scientific revolution had sought to banish the mysteries and superstitions of the Middle Ages. Then, through the fires of the French Revolution and Napoleonic Wars, the rationalist age was converted into the romantic sensibility of the early nineteenth century. Particularly among youth, logic and science were no longer sufficient. Emotion, the search for meaning, passion, and experience became necessary.[84] Similarly, in North America, science and technology had assumed an ever more dominant position during the first half of the twentieth century.[85] Religious influence was assaulted by critical enquiry. The force of tradition was challenged in the home by experts on marriage and family. In government, new classes of 'experts' managed the economy, the society, and the Cold War. Science thereby intruded far beyond the purely mechanical, redefining the very nature of discussion about human society along the way. Everywhere its reach was extended it carried with it the 'drive for order, control and system.'[86]

The counter-culture of the 1960s was, like the youth movement of the early nineteenth century, a romantic revolution, resisting the pre-eminence of the rational and scientific world.[87] The profusion of new goods seemed to its proponents marginal, or maybe even hostile to real happiness. It was not that the 1960s were anti-technological, as such. Many reformers of the decade saw technology as the means to freedom. 'In 20 years, if we worked on it,' concluded a leader of a free school in Vancouver, 'we could get rid of all the jobs the people are doing because they're useless ... We can program machines to do the other things they [workers] are doing without destroying human initiative.'[88] Others saw that freedom or slavery to technology depended on the approach. 'We need to turn the economy away from plastic nonsense,' warned Toronto writer Bill King. 'If junk consumption decreases and artificial job creation ceases, the work week will someday average ten hours.'[89] Material comfort and security had less meaning to a generation raised in affluence than to one raised in depression. Much of the vaunted pride of ownership of the 1950s seemed increasingly shallow. Other, more personal values were what mattered.

There was also a growing fear that, in the words of C. Wright Mills, 'increased rationality may not make for increased freedom.'[90] This was true in both the personal and the political sense. Politically the technocrats were the ones pursuing the Vietnam War and producing planned obsolescence, a rational series of decisions that were 'totally irrational when viewed as a whole.'[91] Personally, the rationality of the age seemed to shut out the very possibilities of passion and experience.

The romanticism of the 1960s was reactionary, rejecting a society that had put tremendous emphasis upon science and technology. While always denying that materialism was an end in itself, twentieth-century society had described progress in material terms. The Depression, wartime victory, and the Cold War pushed these values to new levels of importance as a security-oriented generation sought refuge in material well-being. The claims, as Goodman and others had noted, however, had become extravagant and out of accord with personal experience.[92] The starting-point of the romanticism of the 1960s was the feeling that the promise of postwar society had not been met in a personal as well as a social sense. 'Work isn't everything, work isn't holy,' complained well-known Toronto hippie David DePoe.[93] On the contrary, the dominance of technology had a stunting effect on the human spirit. So few people find real love, argued one writer, because 'severely dehumanized societies like North America in the grip of a liberal or materialistic philosophy' destroy the ability to feel.[94] 'We are a generation of romantics – unable to really touch one another – only to dream about it.'[95]

Emotion had to be restored through experience. Without emotion both the individual and the society became a mechanism rather than a living organism. Indeed, the metaphors of life and death, of sexuality and sterility, abound in the literature of the decade: 'It is a matter of life or death, of sexuality, intelligence and humanity, or sterility, passive stupidity and a hideous Armageddon.'[96] An Easter Be-In in Vancouver celebrated life against 'the plastic and dead city of Vancouver.'[97] More apocalyptically, one writer termed the whole counter-cultural movement 'a war between the living and the dead.' If our thoughts are not connected to action, wrote one proponent of the counter-culture, 'they then are severed and dead.' You are 'dead,' screamed one student at another during a Canadian Union of Students (CUS) seminar, 'insensitive,' and 'motivated by a self-destructive death wish.'[98] The choice is simple, said *Guerilla*, an underground paper in Toronto: 'Life or death.'[99] The means to life was experience. 'The visionary poets, mystics and revolutionaries of history have pleaded with all mankind to seek the freedom beyond our limited perceptions. The people must crave the freedom to wave their bones and flesh in the emptiness. Or we shall get caught up in our own genitals and mechanical perversions, stifling before life.'[100]

The search for experience was very much tied to the prosperity of the decade. Free from immediate worries about the future, with more disposable income than previous generations, middle-class youth of the sixties could take the time to investigate the world. Technology also smoothed their way. Air fares were decreasing, and the automobile was now everywhere. When you were young, travel did not necessarily cost a great deal. Thousands hitchhiked across Canada or backpacked around Europe. When they did so, they were confident that they would find a members of their peer group along the way with whom they could share the rituals of youth, legal or illegal. Yet it is indicative of the decade that the travellers did not see themselves as mere tourists, but as individuals getting in touch with life. By being free, if only for a summer, they were escaping the domesticity of suburbia. They forgot, of course, that many of their parents had also headed across Canada in the 1930s or been to Europe in the early 1940s.

Even personal escape had a social dimension. When Leary called for people to 'tune-in, turn-on, drop-out,' he saw it as an act of social conscience which would, by the very act of abdication, help transform society. Later, in exile in Algeria, he wrote to the drug community that 'you are part of the death apparatus or you are part of the network of free life.'[101] 'The hippie alienation,' wrote one political activist, 'can be seen as a backlash, the dynamic produced by a contradiction in a technological society – possibly the contradiction between the demands of technology and those of humanity.'[102] For those who sought evidence of the impending revolution, therefore, every non-conforming act had revolutionary potential. The youth movement, said New Left activist Melody Killian, 'is saying No to tracking and channeling, No to killing and lying, No to hate and putting our heads in boxes, and chaining our bodies with codes that kill love. That no-saying is really a great big yes to love.'[103] When a BC legislator condemned LSD, the UBC student paper retorted that LSD 'implies a rejection of all the legislators hold dear – television, ranch-house, gestapo police, junior executive job, genocidal but still holy war, do-as-I-say-not-as-I-do.'[104]

Once this mood set in, people were easily able to find writers to support their concerns. By the 1960s several thinkers, including Jacques Ellul and Canada's own George P. Grant, had questioned the beneficence of technological society.[105] These writers provided an intellectual underpinning for emerging sensibilities. So, too, did the original romantics. German writers like Herman Hesse enjoyed a new vogue in the 1960s, with anguished tales of the search for morality and virtue. Likewise the French existentialists, Jean-Paul Sartre, Albert Camus, and Simone de Beauvoir, questioned the meaning of the modern world and elevated personal angst to philosophical canon. William Blake, the romantic English poet and mystic, became a favourite as well.[106] The Beats also provided more immediate antecedents, and the writings of Allen Ginsberg and Paul Goodman were often cited.

Still, for two reasons it would be a mistake to see any of these writers – even the Beats collectively – as the intellectual heroes of the counter-culture. The 1960s was not a particularly literary revolution, and not sufficiently unified to devote itself to systematic analysis or study. When Rochdale began a series of educational seminars, those involved quickly found the residents did not want to master books. That was 'alien to them ... Their orientation was toward sensual, bodily kinds of activities.'[107] As the New Left often despaired, the counter-culture was too individualist and personalist to adopt a consistent ideology.[108] The intellectuals provided a rationale, but the inspiration came from the sort of immediate and emotional experience that was praised as a necessary part of getting in touch with one's feelings.

It wasn't the philosophers who could provide such an experience, but the musicians. An American survey discovered that the musicians, with their ability to tap into emotion, were far more respected among youth than any activist leaders – including even Robert Kennedy.[109] Rock and the counter-culture evolved together. In 1964 the Beatles burst on the scene with 'I Want to Hold Your Hand' and 'She Loves Me,' typical adolescent love songs, totally unexceptional in lyrics and politics. They were matched in the United States by the upbeat songs of the Beach Boys ('I Get Around') and the Supremes ('Baby Love'). Then everything changed. In the summer of 1965, not only did Dylan go electric but the Rolling Stones' 'Satisfaction' reached Number one in both Canada and the United States. In September, Barry Maguire's very political song 'Eve of Destruction' reached Number one in the United States.[110] In San Francisco the new acid-rock sound was developing and would soon emerge into public view. Later that fall another British rock band, the Who, set the generation gap to music with 'My Generation.'

Rock had transformed itself from a teenage music form to the political-cultural medium of a generation. Over the next three years, the music was tremendously creative as it sought to keep pace with and express the power and flux of the youth movement. As the youth mood changed, so too would rock, reflecting the mood and ensuring that it was transmitted instantly to millions of young people. From the gentle flower-child folk-rock of the Mamas and the Papas' 'Monday, Monday' (1966), through the artistic triumph of the Beatles' psychedelic 'Sgt Pepper's Lonely Hearts Club Band' (1967), through the dark lyrics of Jim Morrison and the Doors – 'We want the world and we want it now' – a rock group or song could always be found to give voice to the mood of the period. 'I knew all the new music intimately,' Douglas Fetherling wrote of the period. It was 'as though some generational organ inside me had sucked it in from the atmosphere and drawn it through my pores.'[111]

Second, the emotionalism of the counter-culture made it impatient with intellectual canon, even sympathetic canon. Paul Goodman once lamented that he often had his own ideas thrown at him, 'part of the oral tradition two years old, author prehistoric.'[112] The emergent counter-culture, as with many youth cultures, felt exempt from history in a way that Grant and others could not. The revolution of feelings, of drugs, of sex, that seemed to be sweeping North America was the key to transforming society. Personal angst thus merged with social utopianism. Throughout the decade the notion that change was imminent and that it could spring from elements of the youth culture is a pervasive and recurring theme. LSD would bring the miracle, said Leary. If enough people turned on, the old ways would die amid the bright new colours of the psychedelic age. Many agreed with him and took the drug as a semi-religious experience. Flower-power, said a million buttons; slogans and pictures showed the power of love, as did lyrics like the Beatles' 'All You Need Is Love.'

The notion of transforming redemption has strong religious overtones, and it is thus not surprising that several observers at the time noted the religious aspects of the counter-culture – mysticism, personal conversion, and the search for an ultimate truth.[113] This was not a sweeping evangelical movement, however, but a fragmented offshoot of the general romantic rebellion. The idea was to dabble. The *I Ching*, black magic, astrology, or drugs might point the way to the truth. Timothy Leary in all seriousness adopted the *Tibetan Book of the Dead* as the pathway to the new universe of post-LSD understanding.[114] Others turned to religious offshoots from Asia. This too was often just experimentation, as with the thousands who got involved in meditation after the Beatles led the way in 1967. Sometimes the commitment was more serious, however. The India-based Hare Krishna movement came to the United States in 1965 and migrated north to Canada soon after. Its combination of anti-materialism, mysticism, and communalism involved a total rejection of the outside society. It also implied a total surrender of individual freedom to the organization.[115] This was soon to become a pattern as Process, the Moonies, Scientologists, and other, weirder and often dangerous, groups offered to provide answers to the quest for truth.

Those involved in religious cults were, as were the true hippies, only a small minority of youth in the sixties. Like the hippies, however, they illustrate the larger tendency of the counter-culture broadly defined. Having rejected the mundanity of modern society and having decided that something better was possible, one was left with the problem finding a direction. Having a belief – political, social, or religious – was the important thing, for it was the passion of belief that released the inner soul. The feeling became more important than the substance behind it. 'What are you trying to communicate, Ted, information, this intellectual game thing, or your commitment to it? ... You seem tense and hung up and want us to accept it ... What do you feel?'[116]

Such attitudes downgraded any hierarchy of values in favour of a hierarchy of experience. Drugs became equated with high mystical experience. *Rolling Stone* magazine could proclaim that 'music will set you free.' The hippies of Rochdale could mock Marxism with hedonism. 'For the past 6000 years civilization has been an excuse for an extended party ... Even in social structures the struggle between classes arises from the desire for a bigger and better party. The people who control governments, nations, and continents have legal access to a greater number of drinks than the oppressed masses.'[117] Once the quality of belief became the important issue, the object of the belief became demeaned. A letter to the *Georgia Straight* summed it up: 'Find a faith and keep the fucking thing.'[118] It didn't matter too much what faith. Perhaps that is because the real underlying belief of this generation was in itself. Through its own efforts it could transcend history and revolutionize society.

The amazing thing about the 1960s is the breadth of this belief. For it must be emphasized yet again that the real power of the counter-culture was not at the extremes but in the way in which middle-class youth empathized with the currents of the more alienated. Music provided a connection for practically all; drugs and clothes for many. Pollsters consistently found that a large percentage of kids from normal suburban homes 'looked up to hippies because they shared a common philosophy.'[119] This was, after all, 'the' generation, and the sense, of being involved in a vast peer-group revolution was very very powerful. Without that sense, the counter-culture would have had little more impact than the Beat movement of the 1950s. As it was, the youth movement took over the culture of the decade and threatened to absorb the civilization into the barbarian hordes rather than the other way around.

THE TWO GENERATIONS WASTED NO OPPORTUNITY to demonstrate just how politicized the issue of youth culture had become. Dozens of confrontations occurred around the country from the mid-1960s to the early 1970s. Any number of them could serve as an example of the generational clashes of the era. One particularly well-documented test of wills came, however, to Toronto in the summer of 1967. The ostensible issue was whether Yorkville Avenue should be closed to traffic. The Yorkville confrontation soon became much more. It was street theatre in which two cultures sought attention, employing all the social, stylistic, and rhetorical devices they could muster. Here was a metaphor, used by both sides, for the confrontation of the new against the old. Indeed, in a case of art imitating life, the Yorkville issue was literally turned into theatre. The National Film Board did a piece entitled *Flowers on a One-Way Street* that was part documentary and part celebration of the counter-culture.[120]

Yorkville's earlier reputation as an area of folk-music coffeehouses and cheap rooms had ensured that, as the counter-culture developed, so too did the reputation – good and bad – of this small area of downtown Toronto. The coffeehouses expanded, supported by the fast-growing student body nearby at the University of Toronto. A congenial peer community, easy access to drugs, and the music made the community a magnet for the young from across Ontario. Young 'hippies,' as they were increasingly known by 1966 or so, displaced the older population and filled the cheap apartments and rooming-houses of the area. [121] In 1968 the opening of Rochdale College, a drug dispensary of major proportions only a few blocks away, would add to the popularity of the area.

The area also attracted other kinds of attention.[122] Yorkville was becoming a magnet for tourists. On weekends thousands of middle-aged 'tourists' drove in from suburbia to gawk at the 'hippies.' By early 1967 Toronto newspapers ran regular reports about drug arrests and the 'long haired slatter[n]ly youths and their untidy girlfriends.' By April the Toronto *Telegram* was referring to Yorkville as a 'cancer that is spreading through Metro as more teenagers crowd in from around the nation.' It warned further that 'these kids live for pure lust. They've lost touch with Christianity and all of the meaningful values of life.'[123] In the legislature, Conservative MPP Syl Apps brought down the *Select Committee Report on Youth*, which condemned Yorkville, while Toronto controller Herb Orliffe urged work camps to deal with the problem of hippie kids.[124]

The person who took charge of this adult battle against Yorkville was Metro politician Allan Lamport. Sixty-five years old, balding, overweight, and with a tendency to dress in suits that were too small, Lamport had first been elected to civic politics in the late 1930s. Mayor of Toronto from 1952 to 1954, he was both an establishment figure and, even within that crowd, a representative of an older school of politics. He was, in many ways, almost a caricature of the older generation. A supporter of capital punishment and the Red Ensign, and an opponent of the merger of the armed forces, he was an unabashed defender of traditional values.[125]

In the face of such an experienced politician, the largely poor and disorganized youth of Yorkville might be thought to be at a disadvantage. The counter-culture had its own constituency, however, and, as Marshall McLuhan noted, this generation knew how to use the media. Indeed, in a community as loosely structured as Yorkville's, leadership depended upon the ability to attract and hold attention. The person who proved best at doing this was named David DePoe and, on the surface, he was everything Lamport was not. Young, thin, and bearded, DePoe was a resident of Yorkville and defender of the youth culture that emerged there. In 1967 he had been hired as a 'volunteer' by the Company of Young Canadians (CYC; discussed in chapter 9) to look into the problems faced by Yorkville youth. As the director of the CYC wrote to Prime Minister Lester Pearson, 'Mr. DePoe is working to develop from this base [Yorkville] a useful and meaningful participation by members of Yorkville community in society.'[126]

Yet in many ways DePoe and Lamport were alike. Both were fundamentally political animals.[127] DePoe understood what would appeal to his constituents, and he, like Lamport, was instinctive in his use of the dramatic gesture and hyperbole to raise the stakes in any discussion. The media therefore loved him. In early 1967 DePoe first came to public attention, and notoriety, by demonstrating against the Vietnam War while on the government payroll as a CYC member.[128] By September of that year, he had been transformed into 'the' symbol of the counter-culture in Toronto. The *Star Weekly Magazine* dubbed him 'Super Hippie' and put him on its cover: 'You may not like him but you ought to hear what he has to say.'[129] DePoe was in fact very good at using the media, perhaps not surprisingly as he was the son of a national CBC broadcaster, Norman DePoe. He had the social skills, education, and political savvy to take Lamport on.

In the late spring of 1967 Lamport began his campaign against Yorkville in earnest. In Council, he called on police to sweep the rooming-houses around Yorkville to 'ferret out rooms where boys and girls are living together.' Over the next few weeks, he got Council to pass a series of resolutions aimed at eradicating the disreputable elements of Yorkville. Building inspectors were instructed to enforce rooming-house by-laws. Coffeehouses were inspected and reinspected for any violations of health rules. Police stepped up foot patrols. Even the *Globe and Mail*, no great ally of Yorkville, was moved to complain about the apparent 'siege of Yorkville' by Metro Council.[130]

The youth community responded. By the summer of 1967 Yorkville residents, now conscious of their special 'counter-culture' status, sought to stop the hordes of 'tourists' who ventured in from the suburbs to look at the youth parade. Complaining of harassment and high noise levels, they asked that Yorkville Avenue be closed to traffic. That request was soon followed by sit-ins on the street itself and confrontations with police. Over the next two months, city authorities and the counter-culture skirmished frequently, both politically and physically. In mid-August fifty Yorkville residents and supporters were arrested during a street-closing demonstration, with complaints that the police had used gratuitous force to teach the unloved hippies a lesson. Further demonstrations, both in Yorkville and at City Hall, led to meetings, attempts at compromise, and a great deal of talk.[131]

Throughout the contest the rhetoric was hyperbolic, designed to appeal to respective constituencies. Along the way a by-law issue was turned into a theatre of virtue.[132] Rational discussion proved impossible. Indeed, rational discussion seems to have been far from the minds of both sides. They were enjoying the battle too much. Pragmatic issues that might have led to compromise were transformed into matters of high principle, extending far beyond Yorkville. In one incident, for example, a group of Yorkville residents met with City Council to try to find a way out of the impasse. Within seconds the meeting collapsed, undermined by the rhetoric on both sides. 'Why don't you get a job' was matched with obscure references to the threat of nuclear war.[133] Both sides had thus participated in a hijacking of the Yorkville community to symbolize, in one participant's words, the problem of the 'generation gap.'

The real contest was between youth and authority. Lamport knew this and directed his rhetoric at the whole counter-culture, offering at one point to help the hippies buy soap![134] He also toured Yorkville, with reporters in tow, commenting on the unhappiness of the residents, their poverty, and the need for some guidance for lost youth. That day he was the father figure, looking pityingly on wayward children. At other times he was fierce, condemning the hippies for their lack of respectability, hard work, and propriety. He was the figure of tradition. As one city councillor complained, 'I wonder what sort of speeches they were giving on Nazareth's Board of Control 2000 years ago?'[135] Lamport's very extremism, however, was part of his style. He was named 'the scourge of the hippies,' and was re-elected by grateful citizens in the fall municipal elections.[136]

For their part, DePoe and his supporters transformed the closing of the street from an issue of neighbourhood preservation into part of the revolution in human consciousness. This was symbolized in one exchange cited in the NFB documentary, where a young hippie confronts a crew-cut, straight American. The American is, of course, unsympathetic to the whole Yorkville culture. The Canadian youth replies that 'if the street is closed the people will communicate and learn to love.' What was at issue was a 'cause ... the understanding of other people.' This was the pattern throughout. Yorkville was a challenge to nuclear war, Vietnam, and the selfish materialism of the adult generation. It was also, as DePoe bluntly admitted, 'a race against authority.'[137] At one point demonstrators from Yorkville entered City Council and sat in the Council chairs. 'They were totally aghast,' DePoe amusedly commented. 'We were sitting in their chairs, *their chairs* ... they didn't have the slightest idea what to do with us. Lamport was having purple fits of course. "Anarchy!" Wow.'[138] Modern society is being held up 'against some sort of morality,' he comments at another point, and found 'wanting all over the place.'[139]

When it came to the politics as theatre, the adults could not touch the youth. When at one point the *Telegram* referred to DePoe as 'artfully dressed,' it said more than it knew. DePoe was striking, not only in his rhetoric, but also in visual presentation. He epitomized the new culture. He freely admitted to taking LSD and was, of course, up to date on current music. His goatee beard, stylish hair, and 'in' clothing were very much a part of his influence. The most striking scene in *Flowers on a One-Way Street* comes when DePoe, freshly out of jail, goes to a 'Little Help from My Friends' demonstration at Queen's Park. Arriving in brimmed hat, beard, and dark glasses, he is treated like a rock celebrity. Young women, many looking like high-school students down for the day, greet his arrival with a mixture of adoration and lust. The young men want to be associated with him. Everybody toked up, played relevant music, and made appropriate speeches. 'So we become frustrated,' DePoe told his supportive audience, 'and that thing this morning went down. Maybe more things like that will go down if we get more frustrated.'[140] He was, said the *Toronto Daily Star*, 'the young man who sums up, as far as any one person can sum up, everything that has been happening among so many young Canadians.'[141]

The *Toronto Daily Star* liked to equate events in Toronto with all of Canada. In fact, Yorkville is just one example – though better documented than many – of clashes between counter-culture and establishment in the later 1960s. The struggle between the 'scourge of the hippies' and 'super-hippie' therefore must be kept in context. Nevertheless, the Yorkville issue is instructive. By 1967 the counter-culture was not just fashion but a political battleground. Moreover, and key to understanding the 1960s, was the way in which the mass of ordinary youth identified with David DePoe and his hippies rather than Allan Lamport or the Toronto Police. One might not be a hippie, but in the struggle of street theatre, the image of the love generation, doing your own thing, and artful styles had it all over the blue uniforms of the police and the fuddy-duddy reactionary views of Lamport.

POLITICAL ACTIVISTS OF THE DECADE SPENT a great deal of energy debating the role of the counter-culture in the 'coming revolution.' Some despised it for living off the exploitation of the third world. Others saw it as a useful, if unwitting, ally. Neither of these interpretations seems exactly right. The real significance of the counter-culture was the politicization of the non-political. Style, language, drugs, and so on were forged together through the counter-culture and transformed by youth into a political and ethical statement. In this way normal adolescent rituals took on a new significance. In this way small fringe societies of artists and rebels grew and, even more important, gained empathy from large segments of youth. The average university student, the teenagers in high school, and the true hippies, as well as the political activists, were considerably different in terms of their priorities and their degree of estrangement from society. The real point is that they were all linked culturally – the symbols of music, of the romantic resistance to technocracy, of the desire to 'be free' reached across the various subgroups. Only a small minority of these young men and women were truly drop-outs or, for that matter, truly political. They could be mobilized, however, by the right issue and the right leadership, at least for short periods of time. Further, the shared symbols and rhetoric made the concept of generational revolution all the more real to an uncertain adult world. The numbers, certainty, and generational sense of identity, on the one side, versus the uncertainty and confusion, on the other, would be one of the primary forces in the revolutionary power of the New Left in the 1960s. That was the real significance of the counter-culture.

9

Youth Radicalism in the Sixties

First organizational Meeting of the Anarchy Club will take place Thursday noon in room 5407. Constitution will be ratified and officers elected.

The Simon Fraser Peak, 30 November 1966

We're totally repelled by the structure of the world. I think our objection to life on earth is probably total now.

UBC student Stan Persky, cited in *Star Weekly Magazine*, 13 January 1968

Just as youth style became politicized, so politics, at least radical politics, was appropriated by youth. Indeed, in the minds of many older Canadians, the hippies – with their long hair, beards, casual fashions, and lack of respect for authority – were indistinguishable from the political radicals – with their long hair, beards, and disrespect for authority. It was all a part of the generational rebellion. Dope smoking mixed with anti-Vietnam marches, university protests, and fiery rhetoric about the need to tear down the 'system.' It was all incomprehensible. Here was the most privileged generation in history, in one of the most affluent Canadian economies ever, out to destroy everything that earlier generations had built. Movements rose and fell, and protests erupted instantaneously. Campus life, which so many of the older generation had never had the opportunity to experience, seemed a tinder-box of radicalism. 'Everywhere,' said one 1966 memorandum, 'it seems, young people are protesting. In Toronto, against U.S. actions in Vietnam, in Quebec City against the provincial government, in Selma, against segregation, in numerous countries throughout the world, against authoritarian regimes.'[1]

This era of political activism is central to the mythology of the baby boom. Most obviously, it affected those who were the activists of the New Left. Bringing a new style of politics to bear, they did much to shake up assumptions about North American society. Abbie Hoffman, Jerry Rubin, and the Students for a Democratic Society (SDS) became household names in the United States. Canadian radicals tended to be less outrageous, and thus less able to grab the limelight. Nevertheless, figures like Stanley Gray, Peter Warrian, Martin Loney, Sharon Yandle, and others received considerable attention from university administrations, the media, and government: 'They're sober, they're serious, they're organized.'[2] As one cynical university president commented, 'Bliss was it in that dawn to be a student leader but to be on CBC was the very heaven.'[3] Whether famous or not, though, many of these student activists saw the events surrounding the movement as defining the decade.

Yet the radicalism of 1960s would not have been mythologized if it had been confined only to committed activists. For just as few youth were true hippies, only a very small minority of students were radicals. Yet the radicalism of these years touched much of the student population at one time or another. The idealism of the era meant that individual causes or concerns – Vietnam, Native poverty, campus politics, women's liberation – could gain the support of many who were far from being political activists. Second, the radicalism of the era was attractive to many because it was an expression of the power and purpose of the generation. The sense of generational identity was sufficiently forceful, given the mood of the decade, to challenge the credibility of the adult world. As American historian Edward Morgan put it: 'the psychological distance between activists and audience must be smaller than between audience and target.'[4] For a period of six to nine years, much of the youthful middle class saw the politics of protest and generational disaffection as closer to them than the institutions of society at large.

By oversimplifying the generation, the media reinforced the idea that to be a student in the 1960s was to be a radical. For the popular image was not only about a generation, but directed to it. The media and the peer group – two very powerful forces – gave adolescents clues as to expected behaviour. To be youthful was to be politically aware, politically critical. To be youthful was to be powerful. The political issues of the age swirled around the young, and postwar babies were at the centre of the demands for change. Only a small percentage of young people in the 1960s were political radicals, but a much greater number, especially in the universities, grew up in an age in which youth and radicalism were connected. New ideas swarmed over the generation. Though some of these ideas would fade, the radicalism of the sixties shaped the ethics of a generation and defined the political agenda for the next decades. This is not the place to write a full history of youthful radicalism in Canada, but it is crucial to understand something of the way in which the 'movement' of the sixties redefined politics and the way in which generation and ideology interacted.

WHOLE SCHOOLS OF HISTORY HAVE BEEN founded on the notion that supposed sharp breaks with the past hide continuities. For that reason the act of picking any event as the beginning of the 'radical 1960s' is more symbolic than real. Still, as a symbol of the new era, two events stand out. The first was a small march on Christmas Day 1959. In the cold of the Ottawa winter, eighty faculty and students went through the empty streets to place a wreath on the National War Memorial. They represented a group known as the Combined Universities Campaign for Nuclear Disarmament (CUCND) and were said to have been 'the first student [political] demonstration since 1945.'[5] The second incident came three years later, and it did not even take place in Canada. At Port Huron, Michigan, groups of American (and a few Canadian) students came together to restructure a moribund organization known as the Student League for Industrial Democracy. Rechristened 'Students for a Democratic Society' (SDS), the Port Huron activists would quickly become one of the most visible political forces on campuses across the United States.[6]

These two groups capture between them the most significant strands of the New Left of the 1960s. The CUCND has been described as a 'moralistic, protest, issue-oriented group.'[7] It has also been described as the cradle of the Canadian New Left.[8] Though its membership was never large, it is significant, representing a growing trend in the Western democracies to challenge the basic assumptions of the Cold War. Linked to groups like the Committee for Nuclear Disarmament (CND) in Britain and the Committee for a Sane Nuclear Policy (SANE) in the United States, the CUCND took on the entire notion of the arms race and what had become known as 'the nuclear deterrent.' Like later movements, the CUCND was university centred, believed in direct protest, and saw political parties as ineffectual. Its members also employed, at least in embryonic form, some of the attention-getting tactics that youth protest in the 1960s would take to new heights. Symbolic Christmas Day and Thanksgiving marches, picketing of the governor general's residence, and even a Massey Hall folk concert on behalf of peace were all part of the search for attention in the age of mass electronic media.[9]

Perhaps the CUCND's most important characteristic was its religious basis. One of the persistent themes of the sixties is the link between student activism and a religious sense of duty.[10] Such religiously based activism has been a marked feature of Canadian politics in the twentieth century, engaging individuals from Prime Minister William Lyon Mackenzie King through NDP leader Tommy Douglas.[11] The CUCND was thus a link between traditional strains of Canadian reformism and the emergent activism of the 1960s. It was a link not only historically but often personally as well. As several activists noted, the first stop on the road to campus activism was often in organizations like the Student Christian Movement. The belief in service, duty, and commitment brought them there, and the same beliefs often led them onward to new stops and new organizations.

The SDS represents the other side of student activism in the sixties. For though the Canadian New Left was not a mere replica of its American counterpart, events in the United States provided a major impetus to Canadian organizations. This is hardly surprising. The baby boom had grown up in the golden era of the American superpower. American television and American music had been and would remain essential to Canada's own youth culture. So, too, were American politics. Through the sixties the focus for many would shift from Kennedy's Camelot and *Time* magazine to SDS activist Mark Rudd and the radical New Left magazine *Ramparts*, but the American influence remained constant. Likewise, American issues were key to the early years of campus-based activism. The civil-rights movement, as was discussed in chapter 7, was important to the Canadian protest movement. Vietnam, a war in which Canada was only 'complicitous,' remained the most important rallying-point for protest throughout the decade, and campus issues often borrowed directly from inspiration south of the border. After the 1964 free-speech riots at the University of California, at Berkeley, the *Ubyssey* proclaimed its sense of generational solidarity: 'The boundaries of Berkeley campus now extend to the northern point of Point Grey.'[12]

Though many would later dismiss the Port Huron statement as a 'liberal' document, it was in fact a landmark in the history of the New Left. Its emphasis on participatory democracy, alienation, and the politics of prosperity linked critiques of postwar society by people like Whyte and Goodman with the emerging politics of the New Left. In its dismissal of anti-communism as paranoid and its emphasis on the third world and anti-colonialism, it set the stage for much of the rhetoric of the decade. Most of all, though, the SDS represents the final strand in the New Left–explicit generational politics. Like so many others, those at Port Huron had been inspired by the civil-rights movement.[13] It was at Port Huron, however, that the civil-rights support group adopted generational politics. Indeed, the final Port Huron statement opened with an avowal of generational distinctiveness: 'We are people of this generation, bred in at least modest comfort, housed now in universities, looking uncomfortably to the world we inherit.' Moreover, it focused youthful politics on the university: 'The new left must consist of younger people who matured in the post-war world, and partially be directed to the recruitment of younger people. The university is an obvious beginning point.'[14]

By 1962–3, the CUCND had a number of younger members, and they were often more influenced by the spirit of Port Huron than by the single-cause CUCND. The pacifist rhetoric and religious moralism came across as old-fashioned, even priggish. For this group the future lay with the exciting and turbulent events in the United States. Many newer members spent the summers working with their American counterparts, learning the techniques of civil disobedience and imbibing the ideas of the student Left in the United States.[15] Compared with issues like civil rights, Vietnam, and the need for a radical reformulation of politics, the CUCND's ban-the-bomb position looked hopelessly obsolete.

In 1964, the CUCND leadership abolished the organization in favour of a new, more broadly defined replacement – the Student Union for Peace Action. SUPA, as it was known, was explicitly a New Left organization, influenced by the SDS and firm in its belief in direct action, non-violence, and participatory democracy. Peace was still a goal, but the organization now argued that 'peace and social issues are interrelated.'[16] The single-issue organization, dominated by traditions of religious concern and moralism, had evolved into a youth-based, New Left umbrella organization. Along the way it had become generational, both in membership and in its view of politics.

From its beginning, SUPA was the single most important New Left organization in Canada. Toronto historian Ken McNaught said it continued in 'the tradition of J.S. Woodsworth and Henri Bourassa.' Its rival, the Company of Young Canadians (CYC), was tremendously influenced by it and recognized SUPA as the most important radical organization in the country.[17] By 1965, when it held its a national conference at St Calixte in Quebec, young journalist Peter Gzowski covered it for *Maclean's* and termed SUPA 'the heart of the new left.'[18] Based in Toronto and always Toronto-centred, it nevertheless had a significant presence on many campuses. It also inherited a well-produced journal, *Our Generation against Nuclear War*, which in 1966 reappeared with the abbreviated title *Our Generation* and a New Left focus.[19] Those involved in it – people like Art Pape, Peter Boothroyd, Dimitri Roussopoulus, John Conway, Danny Drache, Krista Maeots, Jim Harding, Clayton Ruby, Cathie Kneen, Charles Boylan, and others – included most of the leading advocates of student radicalism of the 1960s.[20]

SUPA was an eclectic organization and would be, over the next three years, involved in everything from student power to critiques of technological society. Three activities dominated, however. The first was a major 1964 effort to work with various disadvantaged communities in Canada. Drawing upon the theories of American Saul Alinsky on the importance of grass-roots political organization, SUPA organized community projects in Kingston, Montreal, and Halifax. These were followed by such activities as the educational–social centre for youth in Victoria under the direction of Lynn Curtis, and work with Saskatchewan Natives in the Neestow project. The latter was a major initiative of SUPA in 1965, and was one of the early indications of the importance of Native issues to the New Left.[21] The second focus was the anti–Vietnam War effort. SUPA came into being just as the war was becoming a major issue, and much of its energy went into teach-ins and demonstrations against the war. Vietnam was both an obsession in its own right with SUPA members and a tactic. Many realized that the war was one point where the radicals were increasingly close to the opinions of the masses of university students. By 1966 and 1967, anti-war politics was a cause of the majority of university youth rather than merely that of the New Left. SUPA was well aware of the potential of Vietnam as a means of radicalization.[22]

Whatever the focus at a given moment, SUPA believed that it had to concentrate on 'consciousness raising.' The organization held information sessions, and endless talks and demonstrations, and distributed pamphlets and buttons to try to show youth that the so-called generation gap was part of a much broader political issue. 'Building large organizations at the grass roots level,' wrote one SUPA paper, 'involved choosing an issue around which large numbers of people could be organized. It was hoped that the issue would not become an end in itself – the organizing and the organization was to "radicalize" people.'[23] SUPA members tried to create organizations on campuses across the country, and correspondence flowed back and forth as members communicated ideas (and frustrations) on the process of organizing youth in Canada. In Toronto the Research and Information Publications Project became the focus of activity by 1966.[24]

SUPA was always very well attuned to the importance of the media. In this it predicted the sort of *provocateur* tactics that would bring so much attention to the radical youth party, the Yippies, in the United States. Thus, to give one example, in the fall of 1966, two SUPA members burned a Canadian flag on Parliament Hill. Predictably, mainstream media and politicians were outraged. It was exactly the reaction SUPA wanted, for it provoked debate and, before long, Jim Russell of Carleton could report that 'our chance of organizing a solid SUPA group is very good now.'[25] By 1966, SUPA was well established, known nationally, and staffed by some of the most capable leaders of the New Left. By then a challenge had arisen, however – not from the Right, but within the Left.

The other truly national symbol of youth politics in these years was an unusual body known as the Company of Young Canadians. It was, of all things, a voice of dissident youth created and funded by government. In April 1965, a new umbrella group, the Canadian Christian Assembly of Youth Organizations (CCAYO), was holding a major conference in Ottawa. The CCAYO was one more manifestation of the growing youth consciousness that was abroad in the land. All sorts of youth-related issues were being debated in a mildly reformist tone by earnest young delegates. Then, out of the blue, some of the leading officials of the conference were invited to a dinner at the Château Laurier by none other than Tom Kent, senior adviser to Prime Minister Lester Pearson. Kent told the youth leaders that the government intended to create a youth organization 'something like the Peace Corps' in the United States.[26]

The suggestion seems to have been made with little thought. Nobody had done any work on precise purpose, organization, or structure of the new body. Later on, officials would say the hope was to 'provide a new instrument through which the idealism of Canadian youth' could be channelled.[27] That was probably true in a vague way. So, too, was the other side of the coin: the desire to channel that 'idealism' in non-radical, non-violent directions. Indeed, the initial image of the U.S. Peace Corps was tremendously appealing to government officials. It was popular with the public, clean-cut in its image, and it even got potentially disaffected youth out of the country! Certainly the government vision was far from radical. Minister of defence Paul Hellyer even investigated the possibility of a formal liaison between the CYC and the Officer Training Program of the armed forces.[28] As it turned out, things evolved along somewhat different lines.

Initially, the government presumed that, as a publicly financed youth organization, the CYC would remain under the control of sober adults, though youth would play a role in policy formation. To this end it appointed an organizing committee made up in part of youth leaders but including such respected figures as J.F. Leddy, the president of the University of Windsor.[29] The mood of the 1960s was different, however. The youthful activists hired by government moved quickly to establish an organization distinct from the traditional public service. First, they ensured that the operation worked 'without government control or interference.'[30] Second, they created an internal structure based on the 1960s antipathy to bureaucratic structure. The basis of the operation was a group of paid volunteers, who, it was intended, would elect the governing council. Central accounting and controls were vague, if not chaotic. Third, those involved in the early stages of the CYC never had any intention of moving overseas. Their aim was to transform society at home. Within a year the elder officials of the council had been pushed into subordinate roles by active young councillors and the paid staff. Government had, a bit to its surprise, not only put youth on the payroll but had given them control of the finances and direction of the organization.

In a 1966 memo, Stewart Goodings, the acting secretary of the CYC, wrote that the body would be 'thoroughly non-political.'[31] It might have been non-partisan, but it was certainly political. Once the organization threw out the old fogies, it quickly adopted Alinsky's concept of community organization. Volunteers would be sent out 'to bring to the attention of people in a community the kinds of resources which are available to them,' and to 'tackle some of the problems of poverty, injustice which exist in the communities and larger societies.'[32] From such a principle the conclusion to be drawn was clear. The CYC should be 'an institution of protest, a mechanism for dissent.'[33] It was the principle of participatory democracy at the community level.

If this sounds reminiscent of SUPA, that's because it was. The government officials who created the CYC may have wanted the organization to look like the American Peace Corps, but for the youth activists of the CYC the real inspiration was SUPA.[34] Initially, indeed, the CYC seems to have hoped that it could absorb much of SUPA into an organization which, with government funding, would have the resources that SUPA did not. Many SUPA activists were enticed to come over to the CYC, the most prominent being Art Pape, who was on the Provisional Council by the beginning of 1967. The CYC also supported SUPA by, for example, funding the national conference at St Calixte in the fall of 1965.

Such links were controversial. Many in SUPA believed that the CYC was a co-opted organization, controlled by government legislation and government money.[35] Many blamed the CYC's temptations for growing factionalism within SUPA itself. On the other side, the CYC's appropriation of radical politics was bound to create controversy among voters. CYC members displayed all the paraphernalia of the 'youth revolution,' from casual clothes to long hair. Given the politicization of style in the sixties, the older generation reacted as might have been expected. From the time of its first training session, at Antigonish in 1966, the CYC bore the brunt of a press and public attack for being a preserve of 'neurotics, hippies and show-offs' or 'adventure seeking beatniks.'[36] The next year was even more controversial, beginning with David DePoe's prominent role at an anti-Vietnam demonstration in Toronto. Later that same year, accusations of 'orgies' at training sessions, a controversial 'Know-place' school project in Vancouver, the Yorkville demonstrations, as well as several other incidents, made the CYC a regular target in the press. Even the premier of Newfoundland, Joey Smallwood, got into the act, writing to his fellow Liberal Lester Pearson: 'I was not aware that you had any grudge against this Province. I am surprised that you would send, or permit the sending, of bearded beatniks into any part of this province, to initiate agitation.'[37]

Throughout it all, the CYC was unapologetic. Its leadership believed that youth was alienated from society, that radical change was needed, and that government was part of the problem. Indeed, from the CYC perspective, the only respectable position was to be a critic of society or, as one young trainee reported to the prime minister, 'we were to be "shit disturbers"' and 'social change, not service was to be our role.'[38] Throughout the period 1966 to 1968, CYC leaders like Stewart Goodings, Doug Ward, and Alan Clarke were adamant in defending both the unconventional structures of the CYC and its political radicalism.[39] Clarke, for example, refused to apologize for the participation of DePoe and Curtis in anti-Vietnam demonstrations: 'We want the Company to mirror the whole generation, and a generation concerned with questions of democracy and justice at home is likely to have equal concern for the same problems abroad.'[40]

The government was naïve when it formed the CYC. Politicians sought to 'harness' the energy of youth in a service organization that would give meaning to young lives while preventing uncontrolled radicalism. The politicians really did not understand that, by 1966, it was already too late for that. Generational cultural baggage now implied distrust of the established order – cultural and political. The most active youth were also often the most critical and ideologically disinclined to accept what was scornfully known as 'co-option.' Instead of taming youth, the government ended up funding criticism. Instead of clean-cut Peace Corps workers they got 'dirty bearded hippies' and 'promiscuous women.' Instead of social service, they got social activism. For better or worse, therefore, the government of the day was a contributor to the infrastructure of dissent. In many ways by 1967 the CYC had succeeded SUPA as the umbrella organization of youth radicalism in Canada.

SUPA and the CYC were the pre-eminent national organizations propagating New Left ideals in the years between 1964 and 1968. However, the radicalism of the 1960s emanated from many directions. The Student Christian Movement, for example, remained influential on many issues and, in the mood of the sixties, translated the idea of Christian stewardship into a radical critique of contemporary society.[41] As the decade went on, dozens of other groups appeared. Some, like the anti–Vietnam War 'Days of Protest Committee' were single-issue groups, focused on a certain event. Others, like the Canadian branches of the Student Non-Violent Co-ordinating Committee (SNCC), the Canadian Liberation Movement, and the Students for a Democratic University (SDU), sought to direct the ferment of the time in particular directions. There were also the official student organizations, from the 'national' Canadian Union of Students (CUS) and francophone Union Générale des Étudiants du Québec (UGEQ), to the individual student governments on campuses. Because they were youth organizations and because, as is discussed later, campuses were at the centre of political activism, these bodies were very much drawn into debates about New Left ideology and activism.

CRITICS OF THE NEW LEFT HAVE occasionally characterized it as a conspiracy by a small number of agitators with a hidden agenda. The movement was too chaotic and prone to internal ideological strife for that. Those who romanticize it like to portray it as a sudden grass-roots upsurge of enthusiasm for reform. SUPA, the CYC, and the other bodies indicate that the leadership was too concentrated and the infrastructure too sophisticated for that. Instead, the New Left as a political movement was enthusiastic and inventive but backed by a relatively small number of left-wing, largely young reformers. The New Left, however, was also a mood. Pretty well anyone who went to university between 1965 and 1973, for example, would be familiar with the notion of 'the movement' and 'the revolution.' By the latter half of the 1960s, such terms had become as much a part of the rhetorical landscape as 'the generation gap' and 'the hippie.'

As the term 'New Left' implied, this radicalism saw itself as distinct from those causes that had gone before. The ideology and mindset of the 'Old Left' had developed against nearly a century of industrialization in Europe and North America. Class had been a central defining issue, and Marxism the basis of discussion. In practical terms, the major institution of the working class had been the union, though the pragmatism of the major North American internationals frustrated those who wanted a more politically activist outlook. Of course, there were exotic offshoots, from anarchists through syndicalists. In Canada the centre of the Old Left had focused on non-violent change. The majority of Leftists of the Depression and war years believed in the reality of the class struggle but looked to unionism and the CCF party (founded in 1932) as a means by which justice could be sought within the existing parliamentary framework. 'We aim to replace the present capitalist system,' said the party's founding manifesto, 'with its inherent injustice and inhumanity, by a social order from which the domination of one class by another will be eliminated.'[42]

The farther left one went, the more prominent the issue of class became.[43] Infused with a Marxist belief in the international nature of the working-class struggle, radical groups looked to the Soviet Revolution of 1917 as the harbinger of a new world order. Even such moderate socialists as CCF leader J.S. Woodsworth were tempted by the myth of the first 'worker state' in history. At the extremes this had led to acts of ridiculous contradiction, as in the Canadian Communist Party's twists and turns in the wake of Soviet policy changes. For the Left as a whole, the association with the Soviets had proved extremely difficult in the Cold War years, and a great deal of energy was spent by the CCF on ensuring that they dissociated themselves from communism.[44]

The New Left was different. First, it happily rejected the Soviet Union without any fear that it was betraying the first workers' state.[45] This freed it of a great deal of controversial baggage. More important, the heritage of the New Left was not the industrialization of Europe, Marx's proletariat, or even the class struggle. Sure, Marx was still read, and capitalism was still condemned. The sixties would see a revival of Marxist heroes and Marxist writing. Canadian scholars like Stanley Ryerson and C.B. Macpherson enjoyed a new vogue in classrooms and university discussion groups across the nation.[46] This was a revolution in an age of affluence, however, and like the counter-culture of which it was a part, the New Left lived as much in fear of technocratic bureaucracy as it did economic misery. It was, in other words, the classic example of what political scientists have taken to calling a 'post-materialist ideology.'[47]

This meant that class, in the traditional Marxist sense, though important, was no longer the key 'agent of social change.' The New Left often argued that other social groups, such as students, were now the central forces for change. This made the 'generation gap' a matter of tremendous political significance. Of all the forces confronting society, argued one Quebec writer, 'the intergenerational conflict seems to me to assume a fundamental importance.'[48] Another wrote that the roots of discontent were family rather than class: 'that all-important institution, foundation-stone of our society, primary cell of the church – primary place of fucking up of things, for our parents and hence for us.'[49] SUPA, said one of its most articulate ideologues, 'does not accept the Labour Party, class struggle thesis of social change. Instead SUPA has pushed forward the ideas of Student Syndicalism which suggests that student consciousness and social action can be linked with the problems of minorities, the unemployed youth.'[50] The president of the Ontario Union of Students argued in 1968 that student power was a vehicle to social reform in which students would 'bring about the kind of social change they want – both inside and outside the university.'[51] The New Left was thus, in the first instance, both a generational movement and one that, perhaps self-centredly, saw youth as the primary agents for the redemption of modern society.

The youthful radicals of the 1960s maintained an uncertain relationship with the traditional 'working class.' There were genuine efforts to understand and reach into a world which few of them knew directly. Sometimes the efforts succeeded, especially when New Left activists reinforced relatively weak strike efforts. Often, however, such initiatives met with hostility and rejection. The 'hard hat' image of some workers led some New Leftists to turn their back on the traditional 'worker,' arguing that the well-paid unionized steel worker or carpenter was more representative of the old order than of any bright future. The image of the reactionary – the 'beer bloated middle class proletarians' – competed with the traditional Marxist notion of the worker as the engine of progress.[52] Others argued that modern liberal democracy 'frustrated the potential for class politics.' Thus other avenues were necessary.[53]

Modern society was, in the emerging ideology of the New Left, divided into two camps: those with access to power and those without. The precise position of a group might depend on circumstances. Thus, for example, students were generally from a privileged social and economic group. In that sense they expected to assume a degree of power and influence. Yet, within the university system, they were powerless. In other instances, the worker might be, especially if there was no union to protect his or her interests. For the most part, though, the New Left focused upon those who seemed to have been excluded from the 'good life' of postwar affluence. Exclusion usually led to poverty, but it was the exclusion rather than the social class that now determined the real relations in society.[54] 'Discrimination' – against the black, the francophone, the Native, the woman – was the most powerful accusation levelled against a society that promised abundance and democracy for all. As one contemporary analyst of the New Left noted, the movement was interested in 'the "left-outs" rather than just the economic "have-nots."'[55]

These victims were the most obvious cast-offs from a modern technocratic juggernaut. 'The new left political philosophy,' concluded one SUPA discussion, 'comes from an analysis of the effects of technology creating a new lumpenproletariat.'[56] In a way, though, all were victims of a technocratic society that replaced emotion with efficiency.[57] The twin evils of bureaucracy and technocracy were the primary agents suppressing individuality, emotion, and humanity. The opposites were thus established – the cold, impersonal, exclusionist, and inhuman rationalism of the technocracy, and the humanity, satisfaction, and inclusiveness of a reformed society. 'We yearn for a world in which man is at the centre of his man-made universe.'[58]

In effect the New Left fused three strands of Western thought. Marx's concept of 'alienation' was tied to the romantic idealism of the 1960s and the postwar emphasis on psychology. Marx's concept of 'alienation', after all, fit well with the widespread idea of a generation searching for purpose or the counter-culture's reaction to technocracy and materialism. 'The feeling of being separate, isolated, and alone can be so frightening,' wrote one New Left activist. 'People are driven to orgiastic habits to overcome the pain. We drink. We take drugs. We cathart. We join groups that act as a reference group, and give us an identity.'[59] The statement of 'Aims and Principles' of the Company of Young Canadians spent more time on alienation and homogenization of modern society than it did on poverty or illiteracy: 'Most people tend to be rather insensitive to others and consequently relationships of trust and understanding are rare. There are a number of social forces, imposed through childhood and adolescence, which make it difficult for people to be honest with each other. We are not sure why this happens, although the increasing complexity of the modern world and its compartmentalization seem to be important factors.'[60] Another CYC document promised that the organization 'is placing more emphasis on human relationships than on economic or social growth.'[61]

The antidote to alienation was involvement. As an extra-parliamentary opposition, the New Left saw direct action as crucial, both as a tactic and as a personal statement. As a tactic it was a way to bring pressure to bear on authorities, to raise mass consciousness, and to put your body on the line, as the civil-rights workers did in the South. It separated real commitment from empty theorizing. As one student radical said, 'We have to overcome the temptation to segregate intellect from action, which can result only in stupid acts and impotent thought.'[62]

Direct involvement was also essential for the salvation of society as a whole. No phrase had more power or meaning in the 1960s than 'participatory democracy.' Much of the anger of the New Left was focused on 'a society that does not allow the people affected by decisions to participate in decision making.' It was a central theme of the Port Huron statement; underlay the principles of community action followed by both SUPA and the CYC; influenced student demands for involvement in their university; and stood as the antithesis of the structured, delegated power inherent in modern technocracy. It was the phrase that, with its rhetorical parallel, 'power to the people,' supplanted, or at least rivalled, class struggle. The real problem, after all, was not poverty but 'participation.' 'Affluence has not moved us toward a fully democratic society.'[63]

Marx, though far from displaced, was joined by a whole host of theoreticians who saw alienation in much broader terms than he ever did. As with the broader counter-culture of which the New Left was a part, the whole notion of existential angst was essential. One writer defined the ideology of the New Left as 'Gandhi-Camus existentialism.'[64] Psychologists like Sigmund Freud and Erik Erikson continued to be a powerful force in the thinking of the baby boom.[65] Equally important were the theoreticians of technocracy – Jacques Ellul, George P. Grant, and others. Herbert Marcuse, who had earlier published on Freud, turned his efforts to politics, and in 1964 published *One-Dimensional Man.* This influential, if unreadable, work condemned the functionalism of the 1950s and argued that the great alliance between affluence, technology, and rationalism was a subversion of democracy rather than its fulfilment. People were too caught up by the system even to realize they wanted change. 'The machine seems to instill some drugging rhythm.'[66] Principles of community organization were picked up from the previously mentioned Saul Alinsky. Later in the decade, the anarchism of the American radical group the Yippies reasserted the notion that the revolution was as much a trip as drugs. 'The Yippies are Marxists,' wrote Jerry Rubin. 'We follow in the revolutionary tradition of Groucho, Chico, Harpo and Karl.'[67]

As such a range of writers implies, the ideology of the New Left was extremely eclectic. The varied additions in psychology and philosophy forced a radical rethinking of Marx's emphasis on historical materialism. The New Left was an emotional reaction before it was an intellectual analysis.[68] Like the broader reaction of the youth culture, that of New Leftists posited that some way had to be found out of the mind-numbing jungle of rationalism and functionalism. Some way had to be found to integrate ideas, action, and emotion. 'I'm convinced that by using neo-freudian and neo-marxist ideas we can develop an inclusive model around which to understand North America,' wrote one SUPA member. He then added, though, that 'we must also analyze ourselves, and this demands something more than a neo-freudian, neo-marxian self analysis. I think existentialism is the key.'[69]

Individual well-being, including psychic well-being; individual resistance to authority, including leftist authority; the individual search for truth, including resistance to any specific dogma, made the New Left a singularly open movement in which personal inspiration (and emotional satisfaction) was as important as the theories of even the most exalted of writers. The SUPA minutes from St Calixte made a point of emphasizing that personalism was very much in the spirit of the meetings. 'Sometimes in the course of discussion a great deal of tension was built up – and then we all went to the pub, and danced in the street on the way home, and sang "Ain't gonna let no council turn me around."' As for the rules of procedure, they were simple: 'Gonna talk when the spirit says talk.'[70] In this, too, the New Left revealed its affinity with the broader romanticism of the age. 'I think everyone wants to be happy,' concluded one Victoria activist. 'I want to be happy. I want others to be happy. That's what we're trying to do. Is there something wrong with that?'[71] American Kenneth Kenniston noted at the time that activists he interviewed 'take for granted an intimate connection between inner life and social action.'[72] The central values of the New Left, wrote one of the leaders of SUPA, 'should be individual development and excellence of human relationships.'[73]

Such an emphasis on individual satisfaction ran counter to great deal of revolutionary theory. To achieve success, tradition had it, there had to be a committed 'vanguard,' a consistent policy and discipline. It was also elemental that the good of the cause took precedence over the individual. For those committed to such notions, the eclecticism of the New Left could be extremely frustrating. 'We are pursuing a "Golden Chalus" [*sic*] and our movement has become a haven for neurotics and fanatics, people unable to cope with and manipulate reality,' complained SUPA member John Conway as early as 1964.[74] Jim Harding later admitted that when 'I look back on my political past I recognize a definite adolescent change in my thinking. Quite clearly I needed to believe in an agent of historical change.'[75]

Such musings were more than theoretical asides. Ideological strain destroyed more than one New Left organization in the decade. The most significant casualty was SUPA. By 1967 the CYC had drawn off members and support. Growing radicalism threatened SUPA from the left. Several members, including Stanley Gray of McGill, launched an offensive against the eclecticism and dilettantism of the organization. Debate raged among the leaders of the movement, with enthusiasm and invective worthy of the great schisms of Lenin's day. SUPA was accused of failing the revolution. It was, said one memo, 'a mixed bag of political activists and alienated youth,' which meant that the organization had been as much a 'quasi-therapeutic community for alienated kids' as a political movement.[76] The cause was contaminated by the hedonism of the counter-culture. By the end of 1967, SUPA was no more.[77] It was succeeded by a body called the New Left Committee, which was both more ideologically rigorous and much less influential.

The ideologues who so criticized SUPA failed to understand the social movement that was taking place around them. Yes, SUPA was intermixed with counter-cultural values, but that was its strength rather than a weakness. The broad youth movement was the real force of the decade, and if political activists were to make headway, they would have to form links in that direction. 'Politics in the widest sense,' said one SUPA member, 'must be made as interesting as pot.' If the youth culture had become politicized, then the politics of youth must become cultural. The inspiration of protest, said one writer, must be 'the Provos of Amsterdam, Zoltan Sziol ... , Zenkgakuren, Anarchism, Dada and Surrealism, Pepsi, Tim Leary, panty raids, the students of the world, American civil-rights-folk-songs-turn-ons, Bob Dylan, rocknroll, Epoxy, Skatol.' The tactics must include 'chalk drawing on the sidewalk, Black Masses, public 15-minute semi-spontaneous orgies, a poet on every corner, the right of spontaneous spectacle – enthusiasm, participation, IMAGINATION AND BEAUTY: spontaneous solidarity and creativity.'[78]

The counter-culture and its deliberate anti-rationalist celebration of the spontaneous, the witty, and the merely silly also served as a leaven on the moral righteousness of the New Left. It is hard, in these more repressed times, to imagine the mixture of satire and seriousness inherent in the published announcement about 'two campaigns of solidarity at McMaster: an International Day of Solidarity with the Oppressed People of Manitoulin Island, and an International Day of Solidarity for [Those] Oppressed by Loquacious After Dinner Speakers.'[79] This was the genius of the Yippies, which combined New Left goals, considerable media savvy, and outrageous satire. 'Ideology,' wrote Yippie leader Jerry Rubin, 'is a brain disease.'[80]

At various times the political activists debated whether the 'hippies' were agents of the revolution or mere hedonists living off the pain of the exploited third world.[81] The reality would seem to be, though, that the political activists and the broad youth culture of the generation gap were symbiotic. Without the broad sense of youth alienation, the New

Left would have remained as marginal as many fringe movements in the past. Yet the New Left (except when the ideologues got too pure) wrote and thought in the same sort of personalist, eclectic, and romantic perspective that shaped the broader counter-culture. This meant that, given the right occasion, a small minority of activists could gain the support of a much broader spectrum of youth.

IN FALL 1971, STUDENTS PACKED a large auditorium at the University of Toronto. Radical leaders talked about the need to stop the power structure and, if need be, to close the campus down. Liberal professors appealed for calm and understanding. When the speeches ended, several students marched across to Simcoe Hall, where they occupied the wood-panelled senate chamber and refused to leave. For a few hours the curious and mildly supportive milled around, but as the evening wore on they drifted off, leaving a small core of protesters in this 'liberated zone.' That night the university gave up on talks and called in the police. A few students were hauled off to jail, at least temporarily. The issue was trivial – whether stack passes to the planned Robarts Library should be issued to the 'common' people of Toronto. Yet such was the climate of campuses by the end of the sixties that neither the cause nor the results were surprising. Such things had become a normal part of university life.

Six years earlier a different mood was caught by a student photographer. In a photo in the *Ubyssey*, on 20 October 1964, the president of university, John Macdonald, leads student politicans in a sing-along while Frosh president Kim Campbell and the Engineering Society president wear goofy hats and play the piano. In the meantime water balloons are thrown at student delegates by friends.[82]

The contrast symbolizes the rapidity of change on campus. For a short period of time – perhaps eight years – campuses were central to social activism. As late as 1963, long after universities had begun their rapid expansion, there was little to differentiate contemporary campus life from that of five, seven, or ten years earlier. Traditional curricula were still in place, if under strain. Student governments were, as the *Ubyssey* photo illustrates, tame. Nationally, the Canadian Union of Students (CUS) avoided taking positions that might offend any particular group of students. It did lobby on behalf of students, but usually in concert with the Association of Universities and Colleges of Canada.[83] Both sought to direct government attention to the needs of universities in the face of unprecedented growth. Besides, the bulk of CUS activities were in its role as a service organization, providing insurance, cheap travel, and so on, to its membership.

The one exception to this quietism was in Quebec. The Quiet Revolution had brought massive infusions of capital and, equally important, infusions of new reformist values into the educational system. Old classical virtues of piety, obedience, and tradition – long strained by modern Quebec urbanism – were unceremoniously tossed aside. Students were actively encouraged by governments and faculty to become involved in the planning of their education. Equally important, francophone students were overwhelmingly *nationaliste.* They wanted to establish their own structures, plans, and policies. Thus, in fall 1964, the new body Union Générales des Étudiants Québéçois (UGEQ) was formed. Between 1964 and 1966, every francophone university withdrew from the CUS to join the UGEQ.[84]

Quebec nationalism was the primary force behind the creation of the UGEQ. Ideological forces also played a part, however. In Quebec the notion of student 'syndicalism' arrived earlier and was more completely accepted than in English Canada. Behind this vague slogan lay two general themes. The first was that the student had a right, perhaps even a duty, to be a social activist. As Daniel Latouche, one of the UGEQ's first vice-presidents, wrote: 'They stepped down from their Ivory tower and their football games. They abandoned their red or their blue university jackets and decided to go to work to change profoundly the nature and functions of their traditional student structure.' The second theme was one that appears and reappears through the years of student protest. The student, it turns out, wasn't a privileged member of middle-class society but at one with the working class. The student was 'a young intellectual worker,' and thus working-class strategies, such as unions, were more appropriate than the old models of the student council or model parliament.[85]

The withdrawal of the francophone universities stung the CUS, especially since it had rewritten its entire constitution just a year earlier in a vain attempt to retain a national student structure.[86] As well, the sharp rebuke delivered by Quebec students must have stung potential activists within English Canada. 'They had a nation to build, and couldn't afford to lose time planning travel schemes, debating championships or Second Century Weeks.'[87] In response to this and to events south of the border, the CUS began to change. At its annual meeting in New Brunswick in 1965, the air was alive with the new currents of student protest. Speakers recounted events in Berkeley, and talk of travel arrangements took second place to the politics of liberation.[88]

The meeting marked a turning-point. By its 1966 meeting at Dalhousie, the CUS had adopted the idea of syndicalism and 'pushed political activism to the forefront.'[89] From then until its demise in 1970, the CUS adopted the position already held by the UGEQ and SUPA: Students should be agents of social change. Under such able activists as Richard Good (vice-president, 1965–6), Doug Ward (president, 1966–7), Hugh Armstrong (president, 1967–8), Peter Warrian (president, 1968–9), and Martin Loney (president, 1969–70), the CUS took a whole host of radical policy positions, including, as early as 1966, support for the 'moderate but progressive outlook' of the Vietnamese National Liberation Front.[90] The leadership of the CUS also forged close links with SUPA and the CYC. Indeed, the leadership of the various organizations overlapped as SUPA activists wrote papers for the CUS and Doug Ward joined the board of the CYC as a director. By 1967 the realignment of the CUS was complete. It had transformed itself from a service organization into an activist body, sympathetic to New Left ideas and programs. 'In the face of technological revolution, man has to guarantee his security and identity, to keep from becoming a slave-worshipper kneeling before the idol of the machine.'[91]

Activism led to controversy. Even before the organization became politicized, students occasionally complained about cost, services, and so on.[92] As the union moved to the left, the occasional rumblings became a persistent roar. Retaining membership in the CUS became a test issue as Left struggled against Right for control of student governments. At the University of Alberta, for example, the mildly New Left administration of Richard Price in 1965–6 led to a reaction by students, and the new student president, Branny Shepanovich, rejected both the New Left and the political activism of the CUS. Alberta withdrew from the CUS, while the CUS branded the university 'the home of student fascism in Canada.'[93] Other smaller universities followed. When tiny St Dunstan's in PEI left, there probably wasn't much of a shock wave, but the exit of the small but well-known Bishop's University in Quebec caused greater consternation. Most controversial of all was the on-again, off-again battle at McGill whether to belong to the CUS, the UGEQ, both, or neither.[94] Sometimes the CUS seemed to be spending more time fighting its internal battles than promoting political interests or student concerns.

The battles over the CUS were re-enacted in scores of individual contests around the country. Each campus had its own rhythms. Some campuses were generally quiet – Acadia, Bishop's, Queen's and Western, for example. Others were the scene of ongoing strife and controversy, such as McGill and the Université de Montréal. Even the tame ones, however, were caught up in a surge of student power that transformed the structure of university governance, curriculum, and the very nature of what it meant to be a student.

The first national student issue chronologically was tuition. Protests appeared more or less spontaneously as governments sought to cover the costs of an education, while an exuberant student body sought to protect its own interests. Initially the protests were sporadic and short-lived, such as the clash between students and the board of governors in 1964 at the University of Alberta or the brief walkout at the University of Manitoba in February 1965.[95] By the fall of that year, however, the issue became a nation-wide concern. Vincent Bladen, a well-respected economist, had prepared a report for the Association of Colleges and Universities of Canada (ACUC) on university finances. Bladen recommended many things, but he did not recommend the abolition of tuition fees.[96] Then, with the AUCC due to discuss the report at its annual meeting in Vancouver, some 3,500 UBC students marked the first National Student Day by marching on the AUCC conference. Both sides were polite, but the AUCC, though firm in its resolve to collect fees, was surprised at the size of the protest.[97]

The issue became more ideological when, in response to the Bladen report, the CUS did a study of just who went to university. It showed that the children of professionals and managers were overrepresented in the student population.[98] This was hardly surprising, but a growing number of student leaders believed that university should be available to those who were capable rather than wealthy. 'Accessibility' became a rallying cry of student reformers that would echo from that first march in Vancouver to the University of Toronto demands for open stacks. The question, said the editor of the University of Toronto *Varsity,* was whether 'education is to be a noble duty or a marketable commodity.' Another student paper concluded as early as 1965 that 'education should be considered a right rather than a privilege.'[99]

Another, even more wide-ranging bit of subversion was beginning to take hold by mid-decade. The postwar generation of boomers and immediate pre-boomers had grown up in an era of affluence. Moreover, they had always been told by the professional social experts, their teachers, and their pastors and priests that materialism was not in itself an end but a means to personal fulfilment. That was the aim of child rearing. That was the very function of the family. In the junior- and, to a lesser degree, secondary-school system, that had been the purpose of education (and the focus of Hilda Neatby's attacks). Presumably that should be the purpose of the university as well. An older generation would not have denied this, but, with memories of depression and unemployment, would also have stressed career training and overall economic efficiency. Such ideals were increasingly out of tune with the anti-technocratic, romantic mood of the 1960s. Education was idealized as a much more lofty pursuit. 'The only meaningful goal of the university,' concluded the student government of Glendon College, York University, was 'a process of enlightenment by which one shuns the constraint of tradition, prejudice and ignorance, in the search for a truly human existence.'[100]

This widely held view implied several things. First, it altered the relationship between professor and student. The professor ceased to be a certifier of specific skills but a guide or, as one paper phrased it, a 'resource person.' The student's personal journey of discovery, rather than mastery of any specific content, became central. The student became more of a consumer (something baby-boomers understood well) rather than an acolyte or apprentice (something they did not). Thus, when a Honours Political Science and Economics student at Toronto felt his degree didn't meet *his* standards, he dramatically tore it up in front of hundreds at convocation. The system, he said, should place less emphasis on facts and more 'on interpersonal relationships.'[101]

Education had to counter the technocratic machine. The word 'educere,' said former SUPA member and CUS representative Peter Boothroyd, means 'to lead out. The very origin of the word implies that education is a process whereby a person becomes more open, more broadly aware. It means being freed of the suspicions which have been inculcated in us by the socialization mechanisms of society.' Every term-paper deadline, examination, and so on 'is training for white collar jobs in the bureaucracies.' A few years earlier such a conclusion would have been both obvious and unexceptional.[102] In the 1960s such a notion was death, for it implied unwilling absorption into a hostile, mechanistic, and flawed society. Matt Cohen, a founder of a short-lived free school in Toronto, warned that students are 'in the process of becoming social cannon fodder.' 'The reality,' warned the *Georgia Straight,* 'is that University exists to serve the wealthy and powerful, to train students to serve their needs and to have faculty pursue truths that are useful to them.'[103] Radical campus activist Jim Harding warned that 'students are socialized to role, status, and motivational habits that complement a similar hierarchical social organization in society at large.' McGill radical Stanley Gray pointedly noted the university's real role was the creation of 'technically qualified and efficiently socialized robots.'[104]

Education could only take place, according to this critique, in a climate free from intimidation. The whole process of marking, concluded Boothroyd, 'is threatening' and 'prevents people from becoming free, from becoming educated.'[105] As for certification of doctors or engineers, that should be left to post-university certification bodies. In university they would be exposed instead to the spirit of the new educational freedom, and thereby carry the message into their careers. They would be 'agents of freedom rather than agents of control as they tend to be today.'[106]

Such perspectives assaulted the traditional view of the university as a privilege and opportunity. Instead the university began to look like an Orwellian dictatorship. At the extreme were such widely influential articles as American Jerry Farber's 'Student as Nigger.' Written in California in early 1967, Farber's article was widely reprinted across Canada and the United States. It was even read into *Hansard*.[107] Farber's success was attributable both to rhetorical overkill and to the fact that because he tied student politics to issues that resonated among youth. He compared the educational process to Auschwitz and Mississippi's seregationist Lowndes County. Students, he said, have been programmed, brutalized, and brainwashed through their entire education. 'What school amounts to, then, for white and black kids alike, is a 12 year course on how to be slaves.' They are pathetic in their eagerness to please. 'They write like they've been lobotomized. But Jesus can they follow orders!' Professors, for their part, were the same craven cowards they had always been or, in his more abbreviated phrase, 'teachers are so chickenshit.' They are dumped on by legislators, administrators, and chairmen. In class, though, they could get their revenge. 'What then can protect you from their ridicule and scorn? Respect for authority. That's what. It's the policeman's gun again. The white bwana's pith helmet. So you flaunt your authority ... You conceal your massive ignorance – and parade a splendor[ous] learning.'[108]

Farber's piece was outrageous; that was what made it so effective.

He carried the critical rhetoric about the university to an extreme. For, in the face of such terms, otherwise shocking rhetoric suddenly seemed reasonable. When History professor and television personality Laurier Lapierre could talk, apparently seriously, about 'the road to fascism' at McGill and get an audience of 1,500, it says a great deal about the popular image of the university by the latter half of the 1960s.[109]

Students entering a university are cast into a new social group. Choosing some subgroup within the large student body, they seek to adapt and adopt the ways of their new community. For students after about 1965 (the very year the baby-boomers first appeared on campuses in large numbers), the student scene was increasingly politicized. The rhetoric of radicalism, anti-Americanism, and student power was the rhetoric of young society. Not everybody agreed with it. Not everybody joined in, even in opposition, but peer society reflected the new political consciousness and spoke the rhetoric of revolution. It was the language of distrust and conspiracy, and any number of incidents could, with little warning, create major confrontations.

What, given this mood, were the forces that turned some campus incidents into mass protest? First, students were in some ways ideal as agents of agitation. As one SUPA member noted, 'students are, of course, conveniently concentrated on campuses, have flexible time schedules, and are free from adult responsibilities, all of which make it relatively easy to organize them to work for social causes. More importantly, students, who feel a tension between their past and present sheltered and supervised roles in home and school and their future roles in the world of adult responsibility, are rebellious; students are intellectual, students are idealists.' The need, therefore, was to educate. There were sufficient contradictions, problems, and obvious evils in modern society that, given enough pamphlets and talk, real life was the 'lever' to move students to action.[110]

Beyond an aware student body, the forces leading to mass protest seemed almost deterministic. John Searle, Berkeley professor and free-speech activist, argued in 1968 that a successful campus revolt had a certain structure. First, there had to be a committed number of activists. Second, there had to be an issue, but 'almost any old issue will do' so long as it could be linked to what he termed 'a sacred topic' (such as the war, academic freedom, race). Third, the administration had to resist, and thereby allow the specific issue to be converted into a broad attack on the structure of the university. Finally, the original issue gets buried as both sides escalate the confrontation into the rhetorical equivalent of nuclear war – 'he's a racist, he's a fascist' and so on.[111] The resistance of the university, the transformation of the issue from the specific to the general, and the escalating rhetoric served, according to Searle, to draw moderates to the side of the activists and make the protest campus-wide.

The Canadian experience generally supports Searle's analysis. A radical, activist presence was crucial to mobilizing student discontent. Nor was there any single issue that led to mass protest. Course requirements, tenure, officer training on campus, the unionization of food workers, the pay of maids in dormitories, the language of instruction, transfer credits, representation on committees – all became volatile issues at campuses in the latter half of the 1960s. The key was to strike a chord among the student body at large. Sometimes the issues were linked in a straightforward way to major political events. At Toronto, for example, protests against Dow Chemical reflected disgust at the Vietnam War. In other instances the issues were more local. A small Marxist group, the McMaster Student Movement (MSM), was able to create considerable support on the issue of the treatment of cafeteria workers. At Queen's the issue was political censorship as a socialist Engineering student named Chuck Edwards accused his faculty of discriminating against him for his politics.[112]

The Canadian experience also indicates some details that Searle omitted. Control of what might be termed 'the student power structure' was important. Activists on student councils, for example, raised questions about aspects of the university that otherwise might not have been noticed. Once the issues were raised, moderate student councillors often adopted at least part of the radical concern. Even more crucial than the outlook of the student government was control of the student paper. The paper provided the main source of campus news for students. If the paper was conservative, radical issues tended to be dismissed or downplayed. Through 1964–5, for example, the *Ubyssey* was consistently anti-radical. Typical was its dismissal of an anti-Vietnam protest as 'small and pink.'[113] Yet much more than those of regular newspapers, the editorial positions of student papers were volatile. The editor and much of the staff changed yearly, and so too could the whole perspective on the campus. By the 1966–7 academic year, to continue the example, the *Ubyssey* was a consistent supporter of anti-Vietnam protest, student power, and New Left candidates for student council. This is a world, said the paper, 'where half of Canada's population will be less than 25 years old in 1967. It is a world where youth must be heard.'[114]

The student Left and Right struggled throughout the decade to control the levers of power. Sometimes, as in the already mentioned battles over CUS membership at the University of Alberta, the council was the focus. Real invective, though, was reserved for struggles to control the student paper. McGill was an especially bloody battleground as left-wing editors repeatedly fought more conservative student governments or faced condemnation by subgovernments like the Engineering Society. Editors were fired, emergency meetings held, demonstrations planned, and the independence of the press reasserted several times.[115] McGill was not alone, however. At Loyola, Ryerson, Université de Montréal, and elsewhere, attempts, usually futile, were made to control the student press. At Simon Fraser, concerns about one 1966 issue of the *Peak* led to a faculty-imposed suspension of publication. The paper responded by going underground, publishing the *Free Peak* until the suspension was lifted.[116] Such skirmishes reflected not only the recognition by the authorities of the power of the student press, but served in their own right as a cause around which reformers could rally.

Indeed, the various attempts to control the student press point to the final key ingredient in the development of campus unrest. Searle is perhaps too kind when he argues that administrative resistance to demands was in itself a contributing factor. More often the simple fact was that the administration mishandled situations. They were both too tough and too soft. Universities had traditionally assumed a quasi-parental supervisory role in relation to their occasionally troublesome and all too often high-spirited students. Moreover, many of the administrative traditions of universities, including their treatment of 'error,' were descended from the church-based leadership which had dominated Canadian university administration until well into the inter-war years. The administrator and the senior faculty member thus assumed the role of a moral authority figure as well as official of the university. Universities saw themselves as being forced by circumstance and history to take on a role that comprised family pastor, teacher, and parent. Overall, the university's approach to students was a kind of benign authoritarianism.

In the first years of protest, administrations often moved in the traditional manner to assert authority. Demonstrations were banned, or students expelled. Campus security was called upon or, if necessary, the police. Such tactics backfired badly. The University of California at Berkeley, the great symbol of student power, exploded in 1964 when the administration sought to impose a series of arbitrary rules upon an unwilling student body. Attempts to force the issue only made things worse. Over the next years, the Berkeley combination of an adamant and even reactionary board and a radicalized student body ensured that the violence and unrest would continue.[117] Very quickly the lesson from Berkeley percolated through to Canadian campuses. Authoritarianism had no moral basis in the upbringing or earlier education of this generation of students. Very quickly most universities abandoned much of their *in loco parentis* role. Where they didn't do so voluntarily, protest soon forced a decision. Some also began to look seriously at rules of governance in order to increase the role for both faculty and students. Through the 1960s more and more student representatives appeared on senior university bodies. Refusal to give students a voice usually led to protest. Curriculum was also revised in a set of changes that cumulatively altered the nature and philosophy behind the degree, especially in Arts.[118]

Yet all of these concessions created another kind of confusion. Weakness in the face of student demands was, by 1967, as much a problem as arbitrariness in clinging to old rules. By the later 1960s, administrators feared students much more than students feared administrators. Yet these same administators had risen to power in an era in which their authority had been unquestioned. This created inconsistencies, between campuses and within them.[119] Indeed, weakness one day and arbitrariness the next was a common pattern on the most troubled of Canadian campuses. None of this is surprising. The university was exploding in size, changing in its role, and facing new aggressiveness on the part of students. Many administrators had nothing in their background or training that prepared them for the new militancy. It would require several years and increasingly nasty confrontations before the two sides began to understand the new groundrules of post-1965 university life.[120]

OF ALL THE UNIVERSITIES IN CANADA, none was so continually plagued by trouble and controversy as the new campus designed by Arthur Erikson for a mountaintop in Burnaby.[121] What happened there provides a classic case-study of the way in which disagreements over fundamental values in society and education, combined with flawed structures and strong personalities, could almost paralyse a campus.

Simon Fraser was a product of the affluence of the 1960s and of the enthusiasm for education. In 1963 British Columbia's Social Credit government passed an act to charter a new university. It was to be an 'instant university,' with land purchased, buildings constructed, staff hired, and university opened by the fall of 1965.[122] In order to accomplish this Herculean task, Premier W.A.C. Bennett turned to Gordon Schrum, an energetic and outspoken businessman. The hastiness of Bennett and Schrum dictated the governance of the university. Speed and efficiency rather than dialogue and collegiality was the need of the moment. The administration was centralized in the board of governors under Schrum, and in the office of the president. The intermediate levels of administration – deans being the prime example – effectively didn't exist when the university opened.

Yet the university was also billed as the epitome of progressive education. The architecture, set dramatically atop a mountain, was described as a mixture of the 'Acropolis and Inca ruins.' The trimester system provided continuous learning, while early calendars expounded in visionary terms a progressive approach to learning. 'Education does not end outside the classroom door' and 'freedom from organizational constraint [is] necessary if they are to develop the intellectual capabilities to the fullest extent.'[123] New, located on the trendy west coast, and billed as an alternative to staid UBC, Simon Fraser did two things that were to cause it endless trouble. First, it raised expectations that had little to do with the reality of a still-unfinished university trying to cope with overenrolment, unpaved parking lots, and other problems inherent in an 'instant university.' Second, its deliberate attempt to bill itself as 'different' attracted both students, especially at the graduate level, and staff who were strong critics of traditional education and all its works. SUPA activists like Jim Harding, already having been in trouble for activism at Regina; John Conway; and others appeared at SFU graduate school over the first years.

The combination was volatile. From the beginning Simon Fraser was a campus looking for an issue. Cafeteria space and the quality of the food, the absence of residence accommodation, the unpaved parking lots, and so on were a constant source of complaint.[124] Such complaint was, in a way, a form of group cohesion. In the absence of any campus traditions, in the face of an only semi-complete campus and unfulfilled idealism, the community – student and faculty – was casting around to find its identity. Part of that search for community involved questioning whether, as one newspaper editorial charged, the SFU dream 'is a blatant lie.'[125] Initially there was no focus for the growing disillusionment, and not even any certainty that disillusionment, was appropriate. It would not take much, however, to turn indiscriminate grumbling into protest.

The initial focus of discontent shows just how volatile the mood was. In 1965–6 Shell Canada was in negotiation with the board of governors to build a gas station on the campus, a reasonable necessity, given the isolated mountaintop location. In return for a monopoly on the campus gas trade, Shell would support construction of a student residence, something also sorely needed. In the parlance of recent years, this seemed a win–win situation for all. This was the 1960s, however, and before long the presence of a gas station became a major issue of student protest. 'The most beautiful view on the top of this mountain is being blotted out by a gas station,' lamented the *Peak*.[126]

It was not really the view. The gas station itself was much less of an intrusion on the view than were many campus buildings. Instead, the Shell station became a metaphor for every way in which the first year of Simon Fraser had generated discontent – the corporate ties of the board, the commercialism of society, the failure of this university to act any differently from any other. By June 1966, a series of protests against Shell began. Though Shell eventually got its station, the protests were important. They gave radicals on campus a common cause, linked activist students with staff, and raised doubts in many minds about the political perspective of the board. 'After all, money is the only real morality.'[127]

Shell was a symbol, and the protests surrounding it a skirmish, compared with the battles soon with be joined. At the centre of what became known as the 'troubles' was one of the most radical departments in a generally radical university – the Political Science, Sociology and Anthropology Department, or PSA, as it was known. This was a department that, by the nature of its disciplines, sought to resolve social issues. It was thus committed to the 'social experiment' that Simon Fraser was supposed to be, and it attracted bright, young, and quite radical staff and students. Harding and Conway were both in the department as graduate students. So, too, was a British activist and future president of the CUS named Martin Loney. The faculty were young – in their late twenties and early thirties, for the most part. The majority of them were from either the United States or Great Britain, and even among the Canadians the tendency was to have been educated outside the country. Twenty-one of twenty-three faculty took their most advanced degrees abroad.[128]

The political 'culture' of the PSA was activist, anti-war, and New Left. Professors like Louis Feldhammer was an advocate of 'black power' and bought fully into the new syndicalist vision of the students as a class or, as he termed it on one occasion, 'a privileged underclass ... They are exploited and babied at the same time.'[129] Throughout the academic year of 1966–7, the PSA faculty and students were immersed in campus politics. Within the department, professors and students instituted some of the most radical forms of governance in the Canadian academic community. Not only was there student participation, but participatory democracy was a reality, with each student having a vote equal to faculty's on most matters. A greater contrast is hard to find than between the extreme democracy of the PSA and the still centralized and essentially authoritarian structures of the board.

What catapulted the PSA into the centre of campus controversy, however, was an off-campus incident and subsequent action by the board of governors. In March 1967, five graduate students of the department headed off to support a local high-school student. He had been dismissed as editor of the school paper for satirical remarks made about high-school teaching staff. Demonstrations led to arrest, and the arrest led outraged board members to call for action. Since all the involved graduate students were teaching assistants, the easiest answer seemed to be to dismiss them from those posts. That decision turned out to be a big mistake. The campus exploded, and activists found themselves carried along by a wave of mass protest.

Over the next few days, a power struggle erupted, with the board on the one side and the mass of students and the faculty association on the other. Articulate radicals like Sharon Yandle, a former SUPA member, organized a strike committee that was, significantly, supported by moderate, and even conservative student leaders.[130] The board's actions galvanized the campus in opposition to this apparent assault on free speech. It was, as Yandle subsequently reported, 'one of the most successful incidences [*sic*] of student action in the history of the North American and especially the Canadian university.'[131] After days of protest, mass rallies, and condemnation of the board by students, faculty, and administrators, the board was forced to back down. The five teaching assistants were reinstated, and the board's power on campus had effectively been limited.[132]

The PSA incident politicized the campus. Over the next year the relatively conservative president of the student government was forced out, and student radicals were elected to the powerful senate. The student paper, though open to varying points of view, became more radical in its perspective. Its masthead gloried in the rhetoric of the youth revolution – 'We are the people our parents warned us against.' Well-known campus figures like Martin Loney openly preached the politics of confrontation under the slogan 'out of confrontation comes consciousness,' while continuing chaos in the PSA led to investigation by the Canadian Association of University Teachers. Crisis followed crisis. Open senate meetings, transfer credits and accessibility, student representation on the board, political intimidation in the PSA department, hiring and tenure decisions – all became issues of protest. Extra-parliamentary bodies like the SDU or the quasi-parliamentary bodies like the PSA Council now carried as much force as the elected student government, the senate, or the board of governors. Presidents came and went, routinely vilified by activists. Board and administration attempts to regain control were often ill-conceived, or outrageous in their own right.

By 1968 the governing system of SFU was on the verge of collapse. The Canadian Association of University Teachers (CAUT) censured the university in March, commenting on the 'serious malaise' affecting the faculty.[133] Martin Loney, as the new student-council president, urged on the politics of confrontation. The council issued 'minimum demands,' calling for abolition of the office of president and chancellor and their replacement with elected officials; the restructuring of the board to put it in the control of students and the public; as well as democratization of department structure. For good measure, the student government also censured the president of the university and demanded his resignation.[134] Anti–New Left students then censured the student council, which itself resigned. Just to make matters worse, the PSA department erupted again, this time with charges of political bias in matters of hiring and tenure.

During this period, the students had a greater sense of direction than the administration. Three acting presidents held office within the space of a few turbulent months. Given the relations with the community, one can see why. A student activist receiving an invitation to attend a reception honouring an outgoing president did not just decline – not in 1968! 'Oppressors like these must be denied the gratification of pleasantries with those they oppress. Oppressors must face the naked hate of their victims.'[135] On the other side, administrators had reached the end of the line. 'I have tried to make my views known in words of one syllable,' protested the acting vice-president academic. 'I believe it is high time we abandoned our present chaotic approach to governing ourselves. We must be critical in selecting those who will make decisions on our behalf and we must allow these people to get the job done.'[136]

The climax came in late 1968 and into 1969. In December 1968, police were used for the first time – to evict students occupying the president's office. In good 1960s fashion, they were watching *Alice in Wonderland* on TV as the police stormed in.[137] This was a signal. The board and administration were determined to reassert control, and the perpetually troubled PSA department seemed the best place to start. It was placed in trusteeship. In response several teaching assistants and faculty of the PSA went out on strike. In the interim the strikers offered 'free courses' with such titles as 'How Does Our Culture Fuck Us' and 'Studies in Guerrilla Warfare.'[138] Meetings of the senate degenerated into mass demonstrations and angry rhetoric. In September 1969, yet another occupation led to massive police response, with 114 students arrested.[139]

The controversy would go on for years. The university remained under CAUT censure, and student activists worked hard to keep the issue alive. The fact was, though, that the era of 'the troubles,' as SFU still refers to them, was passing. As early as October 1969, faculty activist John Leggett warned that the strike was futile and that radical activism was counter-productive.[140] He was right. The campus was worn out by the disruptions, and acquiescent in or positively supportive of administration's reassertion of control. The faculty members of the PSA remained fired, and the CAUT censure was ineffective. In 1976, when former NDP leader David Lewis lectured on campus, he was challenged by the student government for violating the CAUT censure. He responded by dismissing both the cause and the protest, referring to the tone of 'sheer vindictiveness' in defence of a cause that was long past.[141] The SFU 'troubles' had come to an end.

10

Sexual Revolutions and Revolutions of the Sexes, 1965–1973

Along the walls of a school gym in 1965, Grade Nine students gather in a fashion dictated by custom and fear. Boys are on one side; girls on the other. Shy laughter and envy greet the brave boy who crosses the floor to ask a girl to dance. Others follow, propelled by the fear of being odd-boy-out more than by the desire to dance. Girls wait just as nervously, afraid that the wrong boy will ask, and afraid even more that they will be passed over altogether. Gradually the floor fills with awkward teenagers doing awkward dances and making stilted conversation. In such ways classmates who easily joked and laughed together only a few hours earlier enter the world of adolescent sexual relations.

THESE TEENAGERS WERE, OF COURSE, bound to the fads of the moment – music, dance, and clothes – dictated by the teen culture. Yet, in another way, the rituals and assumptions they made in their clumsy early intersexual relations were profoundly important and based on deeply rooted social values. The dating customs of these 1965 teenagers were little different from those of teenagers of ten, twenty, even forty years earlier. Elaborate rituals had evolved, based on assumptions about the proper adult roles of men and women and, accordingly, their proper roles in preparing for adulthood. The mating dance, reflected imperfectly in that high-school gym, was, after all, a ritual designed with a purpose. It reflected, in a manner designed for adolescent consumption, the perceived social norms for the men and women of a few years hence.

These girls and boys approached sexual relations encumbered with a prodigious amount of cultural baggage. Consider the view of society likely held by a girl in that gym. Born about 1951 or 1952, she had been raised in a society that was one of the most domestic in Canadian history. All of the desires, longings, and fears discussed in chapter 1 had made the cult of marriage, family, and children central to Canadian values of the 1950s. She could not help but notice, for instance, that 'everybody' got married, and most did so at a young age – more than 40 per cent of women were married before the age of twenty-two.[1] Marriage also meant a number of corollary things. First, it was the only socially acceptable gateway to sexual activity. It was also a prelude to children, usually more or less immediately. Further, marriage lasted until death; divorce was rare and becoming rarer. All of these features were glorified by a popular culture that exalted the family (and hence, marriage) as the central institution of society and clearly differentiated the roles for men and women within that family.

The expectations were clear. Yet something was about to go awry. The clues were either read but not absorbed, or understood but rejected. The decade from 1965 to 1975 brought a dramatic reorientation of the sexual values that had been in place for at least forty years, and, in many ways, since the rise of the Industrial Revolution. Dating would wither away, perhaps to be replaced, as Beth Bailey has argued, by an interrelationship based on sexual activity.[2] The images and assumptions of domesticity would be replaced by a confusing clash of values concerning the rights of men and women in a new world. The teenagers of the 1965 dance didn't know it, but they were on the eve of the most profound of all the revolutions of the 1960s – the one between the sexes.

WHAT HAPPENED NEXT IS COMPLEX, but interpretation has focused on two issues. First, writings in the 1960s and early 1970s emphasized the so-called sexual revolution. This encompassed many changes in social and sexual behaviour but centred on the collapse of social authority surrounding premarital chastity for women. Subsequently the revolution led to the critique of other taboos, including, most significantly, those involving same-sex relationships. In 1960 most Western societies thought it was crucial to preserve and enhance monogamous, heterosexual in-marriage relationships. Law, custom, and middle-class norms condemned or, among the more liberal, pitied any deviation. In most circles this social consensus collapsed sometime between the early 1960s and later 1970s, just about the time the baby-boomers were entering adulthood. The collapse of old sexual mores is thus an important part of the history of the baby-boom generation.

Yet, like that of drugs, the significance of the sexual revolution became increasingly controversial in later years. The sexual revolution proved to have its costs, whether from a radical or conservative vantage point. Well-known feminists like Gloria Steinem have rejected the open sexuality of the 1960s as just one more means of exploiting women.[3] Conservatives have pointed to the weakening of marriage and the subsequent impact upon the family. All have noticed that the ravaging impact of AIDS makes the notion of 'free love' extremely problematic. Nor did the abolition of older notions of chastity usher in a new uncomplicated equality of men and women. Sexuality was not as simple and easy as the young baby-boomers would have it.

As attitudes towards the sexual revolution became ambiguous, the really important event of the 1960s came to be seen as the rise of the modern women's movement. Initially labelled in good 1960s fashion as 'women's liberation,' this upsurge of protest was both controversial and a logical outcome of postwar culture. It was so controversial because it upset many of the basic assumptions of postwar society and challenged thousands of implicit and explicit beliefs about the nature of the two sexes. When the report of the Royal Commission on the Status of Women appeared in 1970, the *Toronto Daily Star* termed its recommendations 'packed with more explosive potential than any device manufactured by terrorists.'[4] The relationships between men and women, and the assumptions that shaped them, are so crucial to social interaction that, if anything, the *Star* was guilty of understatement.

The women's liberation movement of the 1960s was initiated by preboomers. Yet the movement has been closely identified with the baby boom for two reasons. First, the women's movement was an extension of the mood and the logic of the 1960s. Aspects of the movement's rationale, and personnel, had roots within the New Left.[5] More generically, the mood of idealism, as well as the experience of the postwar female, eroded the underpinnings of the old order. The second major reason is simply a question of timing. Baby-boom women took up the cause and made it a mass movement. They were the generation that bridged the gap between the old and the new. The result was often an early life – and a domestic society – divided by 'a geologic fault' from adulthood and the new issues raised by the sexual revolution and women's movement.[6]

It is this geologic fault that connects changes and provides the link with the larger world of the baby boom. For both the sexual revolution and the assertion of equal rights by women were generationally based events: The children renounced the world of their parents. Female baby-boomers, in particular, did not accept the constraints placed upon them by 1950s assumptions of domesticity and sexual conduct. This is not to say that their parents were automatically opposed. Many older women were instrumental in bringing issues such as sexual equality to the fore. Likewise, undoubtedly, less formal clues were present in the lessons mothers, or fathers, taught to their daughters. Like other baby-boomers, they were told they were special and should accept no constraints. As a generation they took this to heart and, as in other areas, often extended the notion far beyond the expectations of parents.

The peculiar characteristics of the 1950s accentuated the generational differences. As was discussed in chapter 1, the postwar world was especially dedicated to differentiated gender roles. Older girls may have seen mothers go off to the factory to help the war effort. Older sons and daughters may have experienced their first years in a family where Father was away and Mother was responsible for everything from financial planning to breadwinning, to family discipline. Not so their postwar brothers and sisters, however. The postwar drive to re-establish the stable family had many implications for the role of women. As we have seen, female participation in the paid labour force decreased in the ten years after the war.[7]

Recently, some feminist writing has challenged the domestic image of the generation and emphasized the substantial number of women who did participate in the paid workforce. Such arguments make an important point. Large numbers of women continued to work in the labour force, even at the high point of the cult of domesticity. Even after the war had ended, approximately 25 per cent continued to participate in paid work from the late 1940s until the early 1960s, after which the figures increased. Expectations for women, though, created a pattern that was very different from that for men. As figure 10.1 indicates, the work patterns of women were geared to family responsibilities. A large number of young women were in the paid workforce but, whereas men remained there, women withdrew during their twenties.

There were exceptions, of course. Many women had to work out of necessity. Unmarried women were far more likely to work, and there were many, even among those with a middle-class husband and children, who challenged custom to create a lifelong career. For the most part, though, the image of gender differentiation was very specific. Married women with children were not supposed to work. This meant

FIGURE 10.1
Labour-Force Participation Rates, 1961

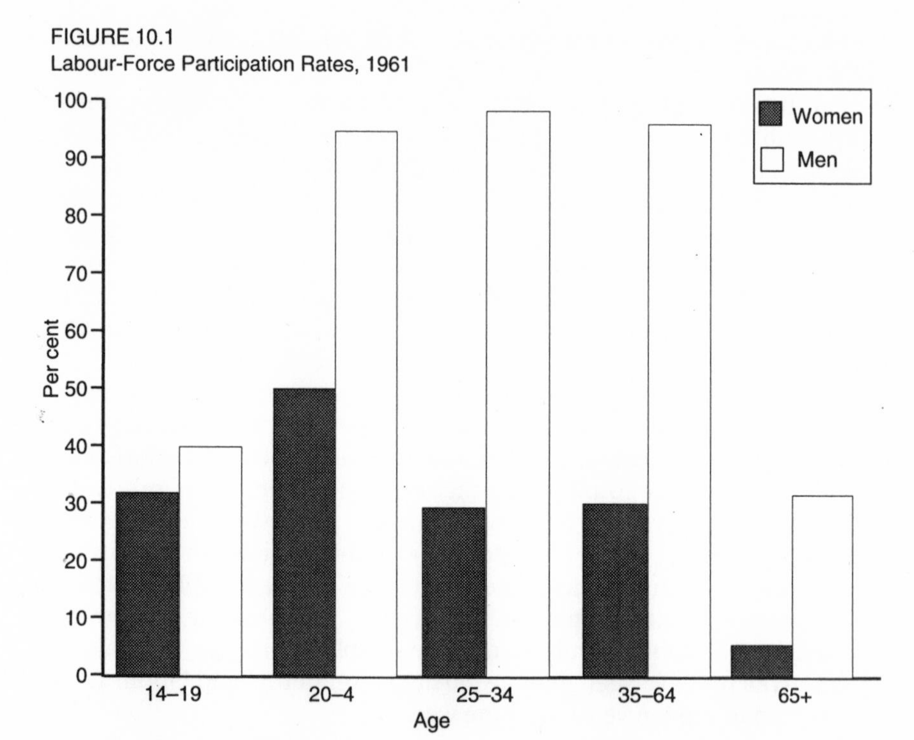

Source: F.H. Leacy, ed., *Historical Statistics of Canada*, 2d ed. (Ottawa 1983), tables D107–23

that, if anything, the child's perspective exaggerated the domesticity of the era. For one's mother and the mothers of friends were unlikely to be working, even if they had done so in the past and intended to do so in the future. One of the first things children learned is that men had careers, and women, whatever the exceptions, did not.[8] Mother stayed home. Father went to work.

The child also knew why Mother stayed home. Mothers were there to take care of you. Fathers could be pals (and indeed were taking on an ever greater role in the family), but the daily needs of the child were a mother's responsibility. At 7:30 or 8:00 A.M., Father left for the factory, the office, or other mysterious places known as 'work.'[9] So did the fathers of your friends. From then until 5 P.M. or so, the home became the preserve of the mother and the children. Contemporary writers condemned this tendency, but for the child it was both normal and proper.[10] It was also a reflection of deeply seated social values. A woman who put work ahead of children was suspect. Some argued she was selfish in her duty towards her children. Some believed her husband failed in his role as provider.[11] As one popular book of the 1950s said, 'In one sense, of course, a woman cannot be more than a wife and mother. She would not want to be.'[12] A survey by the Canadian Home and School Association in the late 1950s discovered a unanimous belief that women with younger children should not work outside the home unless financial necessity demanded it.[13] As late as 1960 only 5 per cent of women and 4 per cent of men thought a woman with younger children should take a job.[14] For those mothers who did work, there must have been considerable guilt. As one woman concluded after quitting a job, 'I couldn't escape the gnawing feeling that I was neglectful.'[15]

A well-adjusted woman would not want to sacrifice her children for a career. More meaningful work existed at home. As curriculum guide for a junior-high home economics textbook put it, the aim is 'to instill in each girl the belief that homemaking will enrich her life and the lives around her.'[16] The woman who rebelled against such a role was deviant, resisting what should be natural. As the president of the American Institute of Family Relations commented in one case, 'In fact Jan was afraid to be a woman.' Problems in relationships with her mother had caused psychological problems. 'The origin of her vehement dislike of housework and cooking was clear. Such tasks reminded Jan too painfully of her mother and of their common femininity, against which she was in futile but acute revolt.'[17]

The cult of domesticity was a cult of orthodoxy. There was little room for alternative approaches. Those women who did not fit into the proper role were either persecuted outright or banished to the edges of society. If working women were criticized, divorcees were subject to condemnation, and spinsters pitied. Lesbians didn't exist at all in the minds of the respectable middle class, except as the stuff of sensationalist fiction. For the children, none of these alternatives was even broached. For them the family was paramount, and few people could envisage a stable family without distinct gender roles. Therefore, in magazine articles, school textbooks, newspapers, and other media, the demand was not for change – at least not of the fundamental relationship between men and women – but enhancement. It was also an age that resisted any challenge to the traditional family.

For example, children needed two parents. From that it followed that unhappy marriages had to be endured, 'for the sake of the children.' Divorce was constrained by law and frowned upon socially.[18] It was also at odds with the expectations of most Canadians. Thus, like the calm before a storm, divorce in Canada actually decreased in the 1950s. Only about 6,000 couples dissolved their marriage annually, or fewer than 40 per hundred thousand of population.[19] In contrast, by the time the baby-boomers began to marry, the divorce rate was 200 per hundred thousand. It would be a rare child today who would not know somebody whose parents were divorced. It was a rare child in the 1950s who did.

Of course, people knew that not every family worked as well as the ones on television shows such as *Father Knows Best* and *Leave It to Beaver*. They were not that naïve. The point, though, is that every family was supposed to strive for some approximation of a well-defined ideal. Part of this orthodoxy was that normally a girl would get married, stay married for life, have children and be a full-time mother. Circumstances might force – even understandably so – deviation from this ideal. Some mothers might have to work out of economic necessity. Some women might not get married and thus work to support themselves. Some marriages might end in failure. These were second-best options, though. The family was supposed to take precedence. We must counter the individualism of the modern world, wrote a famous marriage expert in *Maclean's* in the year 1947. 'The nation must again become family oriented.'[20] It did.

All of these cultural mores transmitted a clear message to children in the 1950s. Life was not open-ended. Age and gender dictated what was appropriate. In Winnipeg, recounts Melinda McCracken, everything was set out for all children to see. 'Young boy meets young girl, they fall in love, become engaged, are married, lose their virginity together and eagerly await the first child.' With the child (or children) on the way, the family identity became central to social and personal values. They 'functioned socially as couples. They were known as the ... s (the Struthers, the Carsons, the Wrights, the Kayes, the McCrackens). The husband, working at his job or profession, was away all day at the office making money. The wife raised the children and maintained the home. That was what was expected of people; marriage was more important than individual fulfillment, and in fulfilling the central role people's lives were justified.'[21]

In earlier chapters I have emphasized the way in which the war generation saw themselves redefining the institution of marriage to adjust to modern democracy. Equality and companionship were emphasized over authority and discipline. Psychology and love, not finances and tradition, were to rule the modern household. Those things should not be forgotten. Yet, from a later perspective, there is a sense that the baby-boomers were born into the final years of an 'ancien regime.' Challenged by depression, war, and the psychological theories of chaos that surrounded them, the older generation set out to build security and achievement within the family. The result was a cult that deliberately sought to keep at bay the forces of disintegration which they had tasted and rejected. Given our knowledge of what came next, Judith Stacey's comment that the 1950s were a 'last gasp orgy of modern nuclear family domesticity,' seems appropriate.[22]

SEXUAL DIFFERENCES IN PLAY, DRESS, and behaviour were hardly confined to the postwar years. Indeed, in many ways, the 1950s were more relaxed about such matters than previous generations had been. The very informality of the postwar world, though, increased anxiety about the proper roles of boys and girls. With each passing decade, the old verities of life were being undermined. So much had changed, in fact, that the emphasis on sexual differentiation was almost defensive – an insistence that any further changes would threaten sexual identity. Both sexes, it seemed, stood on the edge of chaos.

Naturally, the children picked up the clues that were around them. Boys and girls began to assimilate appropriate roles as young children. The baby-boom boy, therefore, soon observed the postwar obsession with manliness and its counterpart, the fear of domestication or feminization. This was accentuated, of course, by the belief that sexual orientation was a matter more of psychology and proper ('manly') upbringing than of any genetic trait. Yet how did one bring up a boy in a domesticated world? 'Now that women are emancipated all over the place,' complained journalist Frank Tumpane in 1950, 'the situation is reaching the point of downright danger to the male sex.'[23] The result was an exaggeration of male toughness – from the Marlboro man to the leather-jacketed motorcyclist. Cowboys ruled both the movies and the television screen. Dale Evans aside, there were few cowgirls, and they always yielded to the men.

There is no doubt that much of the emphasis on virility grew from fears that male sexual identity was a fragile creature. Something about the generational experience threatened the male sense of sexuality. Some argued, as did the Canadian Youth Commission, that it was the loss of authority suffered by unemployed breadwinners during the Depression. Other statements indicate a reaction against the 'manly' competence displayed by working women in the war years. Still others blamed the insecurity on the traumatic shift from military life to backyard barbecuer and gardener. Perhaps it was a rigid sense of heterosexuality created by the military experience. Whatever the reasons given, much of the writing of the age seems obsessed with the 'demasculinization' of men.

This fear was clearly expressed in the most famous cult movie of the postwar years, *Rebel without a Cause* (1955), staring James Dean. The movie is far from subtle, explaining that much of Dean's adolescent restlessness is attributable to his father's failure as a man and his mother's dominance. 'Ah, she eats him alive and he takes it,' says a disillusioned Dean to a policeman at one point. 'It's a zoo. He's supposed to be my pal, you know, but how can I give him anything ... I don't want to hurt him ... If he had guts to knock Mom cold one time then maybe she'd be happy and stop picking on him. But they make mush out of him. Just mush! I'll tell you one thing, I don't ever wanna be like him.' At another point, just as Dean is undergoing his most intense personal anguish, his father comes wandering in to his room, wearing an apron and bumbling about in a kindly but ineffectual manner. The symbolism could not have been more obvious.[24]

Daughters were instilled with different fears from those visited upon their male siblings. Occasional rhetoric condemned tomboys, but the real anxiety was not loss of sexual identity but loss of sexual control. Society put the burden of sexual purity on the female. Boys were expected to initiate, and the girl was suppose to decide what was appropriate. The boys were supposed to prove they were men, and the girls had to prove they were respectable. 'It's up to the girl to stop it,' stated one teenager matter-of-factly to a magazine reporter.[25] 'The boy is expected to ask for as much as possible,' reported famous anthropologist Margaret Mead; 'the girl to yield as little as possible.'[26] This belief was the heart of the famous double standard. Boys, it was assumed, were biological aggressors. Girls, given charge of the future of the race, acted instinctively to protect their offspring by refusing sexual activity until they were certain the male would remain around to provide for their offspring. Less grandiosely, in a society where female financial security was centred on marriage, the social custom of withholding premarital sexual favours was also practical economics. Havelock Ellis, the controversial American expert on sex, was, in this case, frank rather than different in his advice. 'If you really want to be married,' he wrote in 1963, 'it is usually a good idea to keep all your sexual desire (and his) pin-pointed toward that marriage goal.'[27] Boys, in Melinda McCracken's colourful description, 'looked evil because sex was evil, and evil was sexy. Girls, on the other hand, were the fantasy objects; dressed up in strapless and semiformals, in piles of net, they looked like the fantasized fairy or angel cum bride – pure, innocent, virtuous and unattainable.'[28]

Behind this ritual of chase and resistance was the most fundamental of all the sexual mores of mid-century – the cult of virginity. Whatever liberal currents were stirring, society still condemned sexual activity outside of marriage.[29] The precise rules a couple faced varied, depending on circumstances, but one line was never supposed to be crossed. In the parlance of the time, 'going all the way' was not acceptable. As other sexual activities became more tolerated, society tried to maintain the distinction between marriage and premarriage by elevating the cult of virginity above all other deities. Girls were told that, if they lost their virginity, they also lost their value to boys. 'Few fellows want to get stuck with a tramp,' as one dating book bluntly put it.[30] Boys were convinced that it was somehow a loss of honour (and proprietary rights?) to marry a girl who had 'given herself' to someone else. In this way the double standard was institutionalized. Moreover, it was a durable standard. In 1959 an American poll indicated that the vast majority thought premarital sex was morally wrong. Even more striking is the fact that, for all the changes, the percentage that felt this way was precisely the same as it had been a generation before.

Given such conventions, the growing sexual freedom of the age only added to the stress, especially for girls. Everybody from Freud to Kinsey had been raising the stakes for women. The 'well-adjusted' woman enjoyed sex. The modern woman knew how to give pleasure. Hollywood and magazines emphasized sexual attractiveness to a degree unparalleled in history. Joseph Kinsey's two books, on male sexual behaviour (1948) and female sexual behaviour (1953), challenged the assumptions of the generation about how society behaved.[31] Sex was now sufficiently open and important in the public mind that society placed a premium upon successful sexual relations. Yet old taboos lingered, and contradictions abounded between marriage expectations, personal fears, and social restrictions.

The modern woman could not, in other words, deny sexuality without being cast aside socially and branded maladjusted. The omnipresent discussion of 'problems of frigidity' in everything from magazines to major novels says much about the obsessions of the age. As society had become more relaxed about sexual matters, it had accepted that growing up involved sexual experimentation. 'Petting,' as was discussed in chapter 1, was a common part of the lexicon as far back as the 1920s. By the 1950s only the most rigid families truly expected their sons, or even their daughters, to approach marriage without having had some sort of erotic sexual contact. 'Sex play is an important part of every steady relationship,' one journalist confidently asserted in 1959.[32] Even the churches (or the more liberal ones, at least) could argue that 'it is natural and good to behave erotically, irrespective of the need for procreation.'[33]

Yet the girl who took such cues too seriously found herself condemned. The other side of the coin of frigidity was nymphomania, another popular subject in trashy novels and magazines. The teenage girl of the years from 1950 to the mid-1960s was expected to follow a road that led, as it was supposed to, to sexual fulfilment. To go down the path too fast, or to resist its pull, however, was to risk social censure and personal guilt. 'The growing significance of sexuality in the youth culture,' notes Breneis, 'and the sexualization of popular culture unfolded amid prudish families and narrow, even cruel, sexual norms. Thus girls were encouraged to pursue the sexual cues that assailed them but were threatened with the loss of respectability (and acceptable futures) if they did so.'[34]

Illustrating the contrary pulls in sexual matters was the postwar debate over censorship. In the 1950s censorship in Canada remained powerful. In fact, the definition of 'obscenity' remained grounded upon a legal precedent established in 1883. Drawing upon this nineteenth-century definition, censorship boards assured that sex on screen was restricted to innuendo and implication. Not that there was much danger anyway. In the United States, the Legion of Decency had asserted its power over Hollywood by the 1930s.[35] Any movie that wanted access to the mainstream theatres had to abide by the Legion's rules. Caution took over among movie-makers and, by the postwar period, Hollywood had become very good at censoring itself. The Cold War and postwar cult of domesticity only accentuated the situation. Pornography, after all, 'serves to weaken the moral fibre of the future leaders of our country.'[36] The desire to re-establish security and stability in the wake of the war added to the power of the censors and the caution of movie-makers. As one Canadian censor commented in the mid-1950s, nobody in the past decade had called, written, or otherwise shown any interest in reducing censorship.[37]

Nobody may have phoned but, by the later 1950s, the pressure was building to relax social purity laws. A whole host of psychologists, writers, and educators argued that modern society should reject the narrow-minded puritanism of Victorian Canada. 'God created sex and there is nothing nasty, dirty or sinful about it. He created sex for the mutual comfort and consolation of man and woman. He gave it as a gift to be enjoyed.'[38] Sex was natural and enjoyable in its own right. This was, the experts said, a matter not just of personal choice but of deep human nature. Freud in particular had emphasized the deep-rooted power of sexual desire. Such power had to be accepted and channelled constructively. Denying sexuality was harmful not only to the individual but to the family. Frustrated desires, improperly handled sexual development, and denial of emotion could bring on the sort of pathological anti-family behaviour that was most dangerous to society. Remember, for example, that homosexuality was firmly believed to be a psychologically induced sexual deviation. The family was a means to fulfilling happiness, and sexuality was a natural and desirable part of married life.

The 1950s was, sexually, a society at war with itself. Amid the cult of domesticity, there was a persistent and significant trend towards the loosening of old strictures on sex. Look at the events of the decade. In 1953 the release of the second Kinsey report demonstrated that female sexuality was alive and well, at least south of the border.[39] The same year a new men's magazine, *Playboy,* brought mild photographic fantasy into a new glossy and pretentious format. In Canada, Robert Fulford noted sarcastically that the magazine's great achievement was to turn 'evidence of dirty-mindedness' into 'symbols of sophistication.'[40] He was right. *Playboy* was able to convert the decade's tendency towards pop philosophy and 'belongingness' to its own ends. The image of the 'playboy' was of the sort of upwardly mobile, popular, trendy, and well-adjusted individual that both belonged to the right crowd and dictated taste. The fantasies of the magazine's lifestyle undoubtedly appealed to many suburban males (not to mention suburban adolescents) who dreamed of a hip urban life. In fact, the values of *Playboy* were successful because they appealed precisely to the sort of things William Whyte's organization man understood, albeit in racier fashion – success, belonging, and approval.

The publication of *Playboy* indicates the changing attitudes towards sexual expression. By the later 1950s, the support for censorship was eroding rapidly. In Canada attempts by Quebec censors to ban a film critical of the Vatican provided impetus for an attack on the state's interference with freedom of expression.[41] In both Canada and the United States, the literary élite mounted attacks on censorship of novels like *Lolita, Ulysses, Catcher in the Rye,* and *Lady Chatterley's Lover.* One by one, administrative or court decisions extended the bounds of what was permissible.[42] In the United States, Hollywood film-makers increasingly challenged the production codes until, by the early 1960s the code was near collapse.[43] Canadian censors retreated in confusion, fighting an uneven rearguard action. By the time the first baby-boomers reached university, though, sexuality was freely depicted in both literature and movies in ways that would have been completely unacceptable only a decade earlier. With each passing year, adolescents grew into a world that shielded them less and less from the powerful and enticing world of sexuality.

Nor, by the beginning of the 1960s, was the once-powerful force of religion an effective restraining force. As we have seen, churches were in the midst of a crisis of values by the beginning of the 1960s. Certainly they were not able to enforce sanctions against a populace moving towards liberal sexual views. Indeed, many argued that, if the church was to maintain its adherents, it would have to adopt more modern values. Thus liberal theologians went out of their way to emphasize that the church did not condemn sex. 'The traditional morality tells me that sex belongs exclusively within monogamous marriage. Unfortunately, sex doesn't behave like that, and for many the discrepancy between morality and emotion is intolerable. I am not happy when someone tries to get me to say whether a given action in the sexual sphere is right or wrong ... I need to know whose action it is.'[44] Absolute morality was being replaced by relativistic and situational ethics in the area of sexual conduct.

When the church tried to hold the line, it was ignored. This was most dramatically demonstrated by the fate of the Roman Catholic Church in Quebec. In spite of the liberalizing currents sweeping the church under Vatican II (1962–5), the major prohibitions on sexual conduct continued. Most controversial of all, a 1967 Papal encyclical, *Humanae Vitae,* condemned the use of birth-control devices. A younger, urban, and well-educated generation, however, was simply not willing to accept such constraints upon the real religion of the age – personal fulfilment. In the years after 1960, Quebec secularized more rapidly than did any other part of Canada. As one history of modern Quebec nicely put it, 'the consternation with which [the church position on birth control] was greeted soon gave way to indifference.'[45]

Before the years of the so-called sexual revolution, therefore, there had already been a considerable evolution in the attitude towards sexuality. By the early 1960s, Canadians were inundated with three mutually reinforcing themes. First, sex was natural; more than that, sexual desire and its accommodation were essential for the well-adjusted human being. Second, large segments of the population increasingly criticized censorship as puritanical and repressive. Third, the long-term secularization of society had weakened the notions of sin and temptation even in the relatively staid Canadian context. Children born after the war grew up in a society where sex was more open than in any time in modern Canadian history.

As children, baby-boomers received contradictory messages. The 1950s and early 1960s were more liberal than previous decades, but the changes were partial rather than complete, limited to rhetoric and depiction rather than action, oriented more towards men than towards women. Most of all, old and new values sat uneasily juxtaposed. Everywhere the children coming into adolescence were more exposed to sexual display than their parents or grandparents had been. Yet the belief remained that sexual purity (redefined in slightly less onerous terms) was essential, especially for girls. And in an age when education assumed a larger proportion in the socialization of children, schools were of little help. True, sex education did appear on the curriculum of at least some school boards. Yet a survey of 'health' texts and curricula from the late 1950s and early 1960s implied that sex was about the least important of human activities. Clothing, manners, cleanliness, and hints on doing homework occupied much more space than did matters even partly related to sex. The fact was that schools, caught between untrained and awkward teachers and fickle and touchy parents, could do little. If they did, they faced attacks, such as the 1953 accusation in the BC Legislature warning that students were having their minds 'poisoned' by too much sex.[46] It was perhaps not surprising then that, as one curriculum guide of 1961 admonished, 'treatment should be general.'[47]

By the 1960s society's rules for sex had become unwieldy, if not impossibly contradictory. In 1959 a 'prominent' university professor even predicted that, in the future, adolescents might engage in a series of 'pre-marital marriages,' which was a delicate way of referring to premarital sex. 'Finally, when they are mature in their twenties, they will settle down with a single partner.'[48] There is no indication that the predictions raised any alarm. Professors, after all, are always making eccentric and frequently incorrect predictions.

OF COURSE THE UNNAMED ACADEMIC was correct. Within a few years, the sexual revolution was the topic of the day. Theologians worried about it. *Maclean's* magazine, not to mention such imports as *Newsweek* and *Time*, published regular articles about the changing morality of youth. It was both a controversial and a popular theme for television documentaries to agonize over.[49] Vancouver journalist and future MP Simma Holt wrote a book about it, in which she said: 'The problems young people face are intensified, the breakdown of morality is greater and there is little or no guilt about sexual freedom.'[50] Her image of society descending into amorality and chaos was precisely the sort of fear that had so animated much of the social control of the 1950s. It was also an image that was already becoming old-fashioned. The cult of youth would have its way, and the rest of society would ultimately have to accommodate it.

In fact, most media were sympathetic, if slightly sensationalist, in their approach to the issue. Typical of this approach was the 1969 Peter Peters television documentary *If I Don't Agree Must I Go Away?*[51] The central character of the film was not only a striking young woman 'living in sin' with her boyfriend, but a Quebec Catholic. The Quiet Revolution, the sexual revolution, and the youth revolution were thus tied neatly together. The story is about the struggle of this young Catholic to reconcile her current lifestyle with her religious upbringing. The theme is hardly startling, but the journey she takes during the course of the film is symbolic. First, she returns to her old priest, seeking absolution, or at least understanding. He is sympathetic but ultimately says that a Catholic cannot ignore the rules of the church. She must obey. This is not what she seeks, and she heads off to Carleton, where she enrolls in a sociology course. The professor is young and long-haired and has a patter reflecting all the slogans of the decade. 'All I want,' says one student, 'is the freedom to do my own thing.' Finally her mother provides absolution. 'Everything's going ahead, everything has to change.' Thus ultimately the new forces were not to be denied and the church wasn't necessary. Anguish had turned to indifference.

However sensationalist, the media's interest in the sexual revolution was not misplaced. The sexual revolution was real and had very specific effects upon the social moral code. In a decade premarital virginity was demoted from the centre of mainstream morality to the margins of conservative religious and ethnic groups. This snapped the fundamental link between sex, marriage, and procreation and brought other radical changes in its wake. If premarital sexual activity was neither a sin nor aimed at procreation, then neither abortion nor single motherhood could be judged in traditional terms. Neither could same-sex relationships, legalized in 1969. As with all revolutions, though, the main question is: What triggered the final collapse of the old regime? How is it that, even with the accumulated contradictions of the end of the 1950s, rules of sexual conduct that had existed for decades, if not centuries, were overturned so quickly?

Part of the answer is that sexual morality may have been the foremost example of modern situational ethics. Sexual activity, as such, was no longer what was condemned. Instead, society judged when sex was appropriate and when it was not. Such a shifting scale of conduct implied an external social constraint rather than an internal moral one. What was safe? What was acceptable? No one was asking now what was wrong (though terms of right and wrong were often invoked). By the 1960s, situational ethics among youth seems to have centred on three major concerns: fear of disease, fear of pregnancy, and fear of criticism. Anything that diminished these fears implied a redefinition of appropriate sexual morality. This is precisely what occurred through the 1960s.

Social disease was already failing as a restraint on sexual activity by the beginning of the 1960s. The fear of venereal disease was but a shadow of what it had been now that penicillin and other antibiotics promised painless remedies. Other complications existed, and public-health authorities dutifully warned about the ongoing dangers of socially transmitted diseases.[52] For most, however, social disease seemed a thing of the past, a relic of Victorian and Edwardian times. Modern science had conquered VD just as it had conquered polio, diphtheria, and other diseases. Of course, with the advantage of hindsight we now know that the baby boom came to sexual maturity at a particularly fortunate time in epidemiological terms. In just over a decade, AIDS would arrive, and mortal disease and sex would be linked once again. By then, of course, the sexual revolution had run its course and there was little possibility of returning the genie to its bottle.

In contrast, fear of pregnancy was still a potent force in 1960. True, birth-control measures were more available than they had been a generation earlier.[53] Yet both law and custom sought to keep such information away from the unmarried, especially adolescents. Indeed, increased access to information seemed to have little effect on illegitimate births, which remained more or less constant from the 1920s to the beginning of the 1960s.[54] Fear of pregnancy was the ultimate force underlying the moral preaching and muffled warnings about 'respectability.' Lest the dangers be forgotten, contemporary dating manuals provided reminders: 'The unmarried mother faced a terrifying set of problems. Where can she go? What will she do with her baby? How will she continue with educational and vocational plans? How can she safeguard her reputation? Will the father of her child marry her? She feels the wrath of her parents and often times feels guilty that she has brought disgrace upon her family.'[55] Nor was there an easy escape should the worst happen. Abortion was illegal and, when carried out, expensive and dangerous.

All of these difficulties were compounded by the tremendous social stigma attached to the unmarried pregnant woman. Pregnancy out of wedlock was overlaid with sexual prurience, challenged the convention of female propriety, and threatened the notion of the family-centred society. Society at large viewed the woman herself as a problem; family and many friends viewed her as an embarrassment; and the legal and educational system treated her as a pariah. High-school girls who became pregnant were usually forced to leave school. Friends who became pregnant just 'disappeared,' sent off to live with relatives or institutionalized in homes for unwed mothers until the baby came to term. Sylvia Fraser's succinct comment about a friend who got pregnant sums it up: 'Lulu is pregnant. Lulu is over. She is no more.'[56] A few bravely or naïvely chose to raise their children. Many more put theirs out for adoption or sent them away to relatives.[57] Fear of pregnancy and the social stigma attached to it were powerful forces maintaining the sexual social order.

Then a new and remarkable birth-control device appeared – the Pill. The spread of these small tablets, marketed under names like Ortho-Novum and Envodin, became almost as much a symbol of the changes of the 1960s as long hair or rock music. For a teenage girl or young woman to proclaim herself 'on the Pill' was a political statement to friends and lovers about a new and liberated attitude towards sexuality. Gaining access to the Pill in the face of parents and conservative medical practitioners was, in some communities, more difficult than buying LSD or grass. And, like other emblems of the decade, the Pill has a certain mythology. It was said to have been developed by accident, a by-product of the search for a fertility drug.

In fact the Pill was the product of a long, systematic search. As early as the 1920s the process of suppressing ovulation through the use of hormones was understood. Many obstacles lay between the theory and any practical application, however. Through the inter-war years, scientists made progress on means of extracting hormones at reasonable cost, on understanding the nature of progesterone, and on the manufacture of steroid chemicals.[58] The real push to develop the birth-control pill, however, belongs to the postwar years, and to a propitious junction of talent and money. The talent belonged to American scientist Gregory Pincus. Pincus had been doing work on ovulation since before the war. A man with a flare for bad publicity, he was once portrayed in the *New York Times* as the person who created life in a test tube.[59] At least in part as a reaction to this, Pincus had been released from Harvard and had managed on shoestring financing at Clark University into the postwar years.

Then the money appeared in the person of the intelligent and enthusiastic Katherine Dexter McCormick. From a well-to-do family and married into the very rich McCormicks of harvester fame, McCormick was a widow by 1950. She was also a long-standing supporter of Margaret Sanger's movement for birth control. McCormick heard of Pincus and became an eager supporter. Through the 1950s, she personally gave somewhere between $100,000 and $180,000 a year to his Worcester Foundation. Her money and enthusiasm for birth control both focused efforts and accelerated progress. As the historian of the movement commented, her support transformed the Worcester research into 'a crash program to develop an oral contraceptive.'[60] By 1956 the Pill had moved to the stage of clinical trials, ironically and disturbingly, among the poor Catholic population of Puerto Rico. By 1960 the Food and Drug Administration of the United States had approved the drug Enovid as an oral contraceptive. Without Katherine McCormick, the birth-control pill would still have been developed. Without her, however, it might very well have missed the 1960s.

The arrival of the Pill is not just a story of technology triumphant. It is also one of changing social values. In the United States, organizations like Planned Parenthood emphasized the miseries of third-world overpopulation and the notion that smaller families meant greater economic growth.[61] This gained wide acceptance in a postwar world that increasingly saw world overpopulation as a problem. As the Canadian magazine *Saturday Night* said rather melodramatically in 1962, 'in 2026 the population of the world will reach the point where there will not even be enough standing room for everyone on the surface of the globe.'[62] No doubt Planned Parenthood was sincere in its third-world concerns, but it is also true that was easier to promote birth control for the huddled masses overseas than to discuss the moral implications of promoting it for the daughters of traditional middle-class American families.

The intersection of morality and technology is even more apparent in Canada. Practically everyone seemed to realize the Pill's potential. In the understated reports of a study by the Canadian Medical Association, that potential was summarized in two sentences: 'No patient conceived. Side effects were not serious.'[63] This was a revolutionary form of birth control. From the beginning the association supported it. Also, the early record of American sales made both drug companies and stock markets aware of what the *Financial Post* termed the 'tremendous market potential' of this new pharmaceutical breakthrough.[64] Moreover, influenced by the same arguments as south of the border, a majority of the public favoured birth control.[65] In 1961 the Health Protection branch of Health and Welfare approved the birth-control pill for sale. All this implies that Canada was on track with both the United States and Great Britain, which approved the Pill about the same time. The story is more complicated than that, however. The course of the Pill's progress, from newly legalized drug to symbol of sexual freedom, provides at least a partial road-map of the changing moral values of a turbulent decade.

Canada was different because it was illegal under the Criminal Code to 'offer to sell, advertise, publish an advertisement of or [have] for sale or disposal any means of preventing conception.'[66] This law, dating from the nineteenth century, was increasingly under fire and largely unenforced. Nevertheless, it was an obstacle to the spread of birth-control information. Doctors worried about their legal liability should they dispense birth-control information, even to married women.[67] In 1961, the year the Pill was introduced into Canada, a Toronto man was convicted for selling contraceptives. That case, isolated though it was, both became a symbol of Canada's antiquated birth-control laws and inhibited physicians from volunteering information to patients. Through the decade, parliamentarians like Robert Prittie of Burnaby called for the repeal of the law. The efforts always failed, however, in the face of government timidity and the strong opposition of Catholic and more conservative MPs. We are now experiencing 'depravity, promiscuity and a rampant recklessness among the young,' noted one opposed MP.[68] Not until 1969 and the wide-sweeping reforms under Pierre Trudeau's government was dissemination of birth-control information finally made legal in Canada.

This legal issue determined the manner in which the Pill infiltrated the lives of the baby-boomers. In both Britain and the United States, birth control was much more openly discussed. The Canadian legal prohibition, archaic though it was, reflected a general conservatism here on such matters. A mid-decade survey of North American medical schools showed that, in the United States, the vast majority taught that birth-control advice should be given to patients when requested. In contrast, only two of seven among Canada's non-Catholic schools suggested giving advice on request. Even more surprising, and again in contrast to the United States, the majority of Canadian non-Catholic schools taught that the diaphragm was the most effective form of birth control. As for Canadian Catholic schools, all taught that only the rhythm method was acceptable. As the report laconically stated, Canadian medical schools 'appear more conservative' than their U.S. counterparts.[69] Likewise, when the Pill was first introduced, there was no doubt in the minds of politicians and authorities that birth-control advice, if it was given at all, was only for married women.

As a private matter, and because until 1969 birth-control information was entangled with the Criminal Code, the spread of the Pill from married to the unmarried is difficult to trace. The general patterns can be seen, however. First, the situation changed in a short period of time. Before about 1966 it was extremely difficult for the unmarried woman to find a doctor to prescribe the Pill.[70] By the early 1970s, adult women, whether married or not, had little difficulty obtaining birth-control information and prescriptions from doctors. In between, the adoption of the Pill was uneven. Not surprisingly, women in large urban centres found it easier to find an appropriately liberal doctor. Second, instrumental to this change was the fact that the medical profession had become strong advocates of family planning. Finally, women themselves were, as had been the case with earlier methods, often the most insistent that information about the new technology of the Pill be widely disseminated.

As with so much in this era, the university campus was especially important in the changing attitudes towards birth control. Both the high educational level of the women involved and the presence of a sympathetic peer group made it easier to learn about birth control generally. When the Pill appeared, the grapevine let it be known which doctors in the area were sympathetic and which ones would give you unwanted lectures on the virtues of chastity. The change also happened in more direct ways. At a time when so much was under attack, it is hardly surprising that student bodies disputed traditional morality. As the decade went on, students broke old taboos by making access to birth control an issue of campus politics.

As early a 1965 an unofficial student group at the University of British Columbia defied the law, the administration, and their own student government by offering information on birth control.[71] The next year, students at McGill were holding sessions on the issue.[72] Other campuses followed within the academic year. In the face of such grassroots demand, student governments soon took up the cause. In 1967 the Student Administrative Council at the University of Toronto distributed birth-control information on campus.[73] In 1968 student bodies at both McGill and Sir George Williams published handbooks on birth control, both of which quickly spread across the country. Typical of the changes that were taking place was the way in which detailed information on birth control arrived at the University of Alberta. Until the late 1960s, the undergraduate female Wauneita Society had been known for giving teas and tips on etiquette. In 1969 the contribution of this increasingly anachronistic organization was somewhat different – namely, 'an utterly candid book on birth control.'[74]

For the most part university administrations tolerated the movement. Unwanted pregnancies were hardly desirable, and besides, in the face of rising student radicalism, administrators weren't likely to offer much resistance to something relatively peripheral to scholarship. Indeed, the administrator's main concern was not with birth-control or student sexual habits but with governmental or parental wrath. For that reason there were few grand pronouncements. Instead university health services quietly began to dispense birth control prescriptions to students. In 1967, UBC was still careful to say, at least for public consumption, that only married women were prescribed the Pill.[75] On the other hand, it was reported that York, Western, Waterloo, and the University of Toronto were among those that had yielded to student demands.[76] Within a couple more years, such health-service policy was effectively universal on all but Roman Catholic campuses. Even there things were changing rapidly.[77] By the early 1970s, it was as unthinkable that a campus service would ask a woman about her marital status as it would have been a decade before for it to have dispensed birth-control information to an unmarried woman.[78] The McGill health service, said its director, 'does not try to discourage students from intercourse.'[79]

The Pill did not, by itself, bring about the sexual revolution. What it did was provide a means to eliminate the fear of pregnancy as a restraining factor. Also necessary for the sexual revolution to occur was the baby boom's rejection of the idea that premarital sexual intercourse was wrong. In 1960, fear of disapproval was an additional restraining force on sexual activity. That fear was not simply that one's parents might find out. Rather, the double standard meant that, at least for the girl, the fear was that censure might come from friends.[80] Boys might think of you as a tramp, even the boy you were with. Other girls, struggling to maintain their own sense of values in the midst of the contradictions of the age, might not be any more sympathetic. Indeed, if dating was competition for eligible marriage partners, then there were good reasons to ostracize those who would change the rules.

Then, in a short period of time, the shaky structure fell apart. The changes can be charted, at least in a general way, in a series of American surveys done by sociologist Robert Bell. In 1958 Bell confirmed a situation that seems to have been in place since the 1920s. The majority of college women remained virgins. The only significant exception to this rule was the approximately one-third of engaged females who had had sexual intercourse with their prospective spouse. 'Engagement,' he noted, was 'very often the prerequisite to a girl having premarital sexual intercourse.' A decade later, it had all changed. Not only were more college females engaging in sexual intercourse, but there was no longer any prerequisite other than what Bell termed 'the individual decision.' Unless ethnic tradition or religious sanction acted as a restraint, the decision of campus women was likely to be in favour of premarital sex. More than two-thirds of female students classified as 'Protestant' acknowledged having had sex.[81]

Tradition has it that Canada is a more conservative country, and therefore exact figures used in surveys south of the border must be transferred with caution. Yet journalistic and anecdotal evidence from the 1960s indicates that, on major urban campuses, the variation in sexual behaviour was, if anything, narrowing across North America. Various studies through the decade demonstrated that the most powerful force affecting sexual behaviour was the attitude of the peer group. A permissive peer group likely meant permissive behaviour.[82] And this was a generation that, from the time of Davy Crockett, Barbie, and Dick Clark, had seen their peer group as North American. All through their lives, the media, especially television, had transmitted clues on behaviour, fashion, and issues across the youth culture. The sexual revolution of the 1960s was the same. Every time the issue was discussed in magazines or on television, it reinforced the notion that the peer group had decided to go its own way.

The peer component of the 'sexual revolution' was an integral part of the much broader revolution involving clothes, hair, drugs, and music. The exaltation of sexual activity was, aside from normal adolescent behaviour, consistent with the romantic mood of the 1960s. In an age when experience and authenticity meant so much, it is hardly surprising that intimate human contact was highly valued. 'If,' said Myrna Kostash, the sexual revolution had an ideology, it was that, 'inasmuch as sexuality is inextricable from personality, a person has the inalienable right to sexual self-expression and self-creation. Furthermore: a person's sexuality belongs, not to society and its marriage brokers, but to that person.'[83] The youth culture of the decade thus celebrated and supported sexual expression as a central part of the new spirit.

The counter-culture, or, more accurately, the image of the counter-culture, was especially important in this regard. Those committed to the counter-culture extended notions of sexual freedom picked up from the Beat movement. Outside media trumpeted sexual promiscuity as perhaps the most sensational of the 'hippie' values.[84] In reality, drugs were probably more important than sex in distinguishing between mainstream youth and the counter-culture. Nevertheless, the link between 'free love' and the counter-culture is important in two ways. First, the counter-culture not only rejected traditional sexual morality, but sensationalized that rejection in explicit, even outrageous ways. 'We must live together and take the pornography out of sex,' proclaimed one Rochdale resident. 'Go out and find someone to ball; if you can't [,] come home and ball yourself.'[85] Amid discussions of free love and communal sex, the idea of premarital virginity took on a rather quaint air. The deliberately outrageous rhetoric of 'balling for the hell of it' and the widely circulated pictures of 'hippies' in various states of undress at rock concerts were always exaggerated depictions of youth. Yet they were part of the process of moving youth sexuality from a covert to an overt activity.

The sexual revolution then is not primarily about 'promiscuity' or even about the number of people engaging in premarital sex. It is about the redefinition of social values and the collapse of postwar notions of the sexually appropriate and socially acceptable. As one researcher concluded, though statistics indicated a rise in premarital sexual activity, 'the real revolution has been a revolution of openness.'[86] Rhetoric and imagery are as important as actions in defining the sexual revolution. The aggressive, explicit sexual rhetoric of the 1960s was a means of shocking outside society. Paul Krassner's imagery of Lyndon Johnson performing necrophilia on John Kennedy's corpse, the chanting of four-letter words, the explicitness of musicals like *Hair* and *Oh Calcutta!* were obvious examples of sexual shock politics.[87] The double standard did not disappear, but it did diminish. Different expectations for dress and language collapsed, initially on campuses and then beyond. Women now swore in the company of men. They were no longer expected to dress more primly or behave more prissily than boys. Formal dating etiquette, from opening doors to corsages, took a place similar to that of the good suit or formal dress. Most didn't use it at all, and, for those who did, it was a rare thing, dusted off for that special occasion.

Sexuality also redefined itself. The obsession of the post-war years with images of masculinity and femininity gave way to a much more relaxed and androgynous style of fashion and behaviour. That was part of what made it rebellious. Those androgynous styles, from the skinny 'Twiggy' look to long hair on men, were now the very soul of youthful erotic imagery.[88] Those who did not understand this were irrelevant.

Old taboos had been under challenge for some time. The sexual revolution was, in fact, the culmination of a process dating back to the 1920s. Modernist emphases on the importance of sex and the 'emancipated' woman taught that sexual activity was desirable, not only for procreation, but for pleasure and self-adjustment. It was only in the 1960s, however, that the constraints upon this modernist view finally gave way. The Pill separated sex from conception to a degree previously impossible, while the power of the baby boom made it relatively easy to shrug off social taboos against sex outside of marriage. Traditional notions of proper sexual etiquette and sexual behaviour had collapsed, as with so many other things, in the face of youthful insistence upon authenticity, spontaneity, and, not least, rejection of traditional arbiters of taste and behaviour. That was something to be decided by the peer group.

The sexual revolution separated the baby-boomers from predecessor generations. As children, Canadian baby-boomers lived in a world in which certain social verities seemed inalterable. Sex was reserved for marriage. Marriage was permanent and based upon a division of labour between the male working outside and the female inside the home. Children were the central purpose of marriage, and there were usually two to four of those. By the beginning of the 1970s, many of the old verities had become uncertain. The collapse of the cult of virginity meant that relationship between sex and marriage was much more blurred than it had been previously. Divorce meant that marriage was no longer the permanent institution it had been. The decline in the birth rate created many childless or single-child families.[89] The process of adolescence and resulting independence creates a disjunction between childhood and adulthood for all generations. In the case of the baby boom, however, the break was greater, and the gulf more awesome. Social values of homogeneity, respectability, and security had yielded to forces of individualism, fragmentation, and pluralism. In the world of personal relations, orthodoxy had become heterodoxy.

IN FALL 1967, THERE WAS A SMALL BUT significant revolution in the offices of SUPA. Some of the most important women in the movement issued a manifesto. Unlike much SUPA material, this one was directed not outward but inward, at the New Left itself. The sexual revolution was desirable, the writers said, but it only raised more fundamental issues. 'The submissive role of women in the sexual act is inseparable from the values taught to people about how to treat one another ... Woman is the object; man is the subject. Women are screwed; men do the screwing.' If the sexual revolution is to be meaningful, the manifesto continued, change had to be more basic than the mere abolition of the cult of virginity. 'Sexual liberation creates the possibility for people to unlearn those social roles which act to preserve an alienating society.'

Citing black activist Stokely Carmichael's insulting phrase that 'the only position for a woman in the SNCC is prone,' these SUPA members accused the New Left of having perpetuated inequality within its own ranks. Women, they charged, had been relegated to two undesirable roles. The first was to act as a surrogate mother or housewife, providing a 'homey atmosphere' for the tired male radical, returning after the day on the picket line. The second was as 'typers of letters and distributors of leaflets,' a traditional secretarial role. Such roles made a mockery of the New Left and, 'until the male chauvinists of the movement understand the concept of liberation in relation to women, the most exploited members of any society, they will be voicing political lies.'[90] These women had just declared 53 per cent of society to be the victims of Western democratic oppression.

The 'second wave' of the women's movement, as it is sometimes known, has an uncertain relation to the history of the baby-boomers in the 1960s. For one thing, the renewed interest in women's rights was as much a product of the activities of older women as it was an offshoot of the politics of youth. For another, 'women's liberation' came late to the 1960s, and most of the impact of the changing attitudes towards women belongs to the 1970s or after. Still, the movement is important to this history for two reasons. First, the changing relationship between the sexes provides another of the great breaks in social structure that mark the pre– and post–baby boom eras. Second, the movement itself may have begun among pre-boomer adults, but the ideology and attitudes of modern feminism owes much to the mood of the 1960s.

The idea of the 'second wave' comes from the belief that women's progress in Canada has been marked by two great challenges to the status quo. The first phase, sometimes termed 'maternal feminism,' arose in the late nineteenth century and challenged Victorian notions of women's proper place. This merged into the suffrage movement and is often seen as receding with the achievement of the vote at the end of the First World War. Thereafter the profile of the women's movement ebbed and flowed, but at no time after 1920 did the women's movement have the high profile that it had gained in the pre–First World War era. The years after the Second World War were, at least on the surface, especially tranquil. The cult of domesticity emphasized the special family role of women and discouraged campaigns that questioned that role. Besides, as the magazines and experts liked to remind people, women were already equal. The goal, though, was really to achieve a workable balance between domesticity and equality, with domesticity taking the pre-eminent position.

Obviously this balance had little to do with equality. Still, to say that there was inequality doesn't explain why the 'second phase' arose when it did. Inequality has been a long-term historical reality between men and women. Rather, beneath the domestic calm, powerful social changes were occurring during the 1950s. Many of those forces which shaped the baby boom as a generation also raised questions about the traditional image of male–female relations. Those questions remained unanswered, and sometimes unarticulated, until the turbulence of the 1960s created both the opportunity and the ideological framework within which the domesticity of the previous decade could be challenged.

Revolutions, as the old historical argument goes, are not the result of oppression but of rising expectations. Certainly girls born in the decade after the war grew up in a world of rising expectations. In this sense they were classic baby-boomers. They were expected to do more and go farther, both by their parents and by themselves, than any previous generation. This child-centred commitment meant that, in spite of gender roles, girls as well as boys were furnished with the means to get ahead. As was discussed earlier, high-school completion became the new educational standard after the war. By the mid-1950s university enrolment began to head upward. What is striking in both these changes is the relative position of females. Traditionally it was assumed that females left school earlier than males on average because education was economically less necessary for a prospective housewife and mother. This also tended to mean that, on average, women married men who had more formal education than they did. Such a disparity reinforced traditional assumptions about males as head of the household.[91]

After the war, though, women began to stay in school longer and longer. The number of girls finishing high school rose dramatically between 1945 and 1960. Even more significant for the future were changes at the post-secondary level. In 1950 approximately 3,700 women graduated from university. By 1963 that number had tripled, and by 1970 it had gone up sevenfold. Most important, as figure 10.2 shows, female enrolment in post-secondary education rose much faster than its male counterpart after 1955. By the time the first baby-boomers began to graduate at the end of the 1960s, the number of female graduates fell just short of two-thirds of the number of males.[92] By the 1960s women accounted for approximately half the undergraduates in Arts faculties.[93]

These numbers are essential in understanding the development of the second wave of feminism. First, they are at least indirect evidence that in many households the desire to do your best by your children was a powerful counter to the biases of the age. Second, it is direct evidence that the situation of women was changing dramatically in a short period of time. Those born after the war were better educated than any previous generation of Canadian women. There was also less educational disparity between them and their male counterparts than in any previous generation. The very fact that they were better educated and had higher expectations explains much about the demands that were about to develop.

Perhaps not surprisingly, the growing female presence in university was initially derided as a search for an upwardly mobile husband. In the mid-1960s, during initiation week at Queen's, sophomore hazers

FIGURE 10.2
Canadian University Enrolment by Sex, 1955–1969

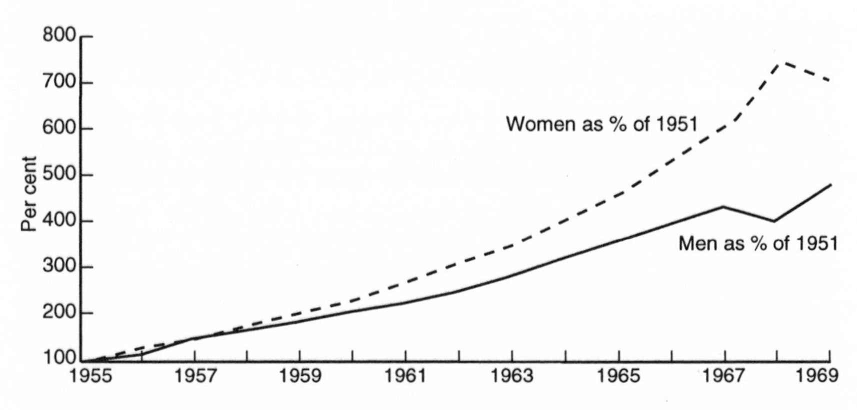

Source: Dominion Bureau of Statistics, *Survey of Higher Education, 1968–1969* (Ottawa 1969), table 14

used to chide female 'freshettes' for seeking their 'Mrs' degree. By the latter part of the decade, however, such attitudes were, like hazings, increasingly anachronistic. Whatever individual reasons brought a woman to campus, women as a group were very much like the men who came to campus at the same time. Prosperity meant that future career concerns were less significant than the actual experience of university life. The peer group remained important, even paramount, and that peer group was, as we have seen, changing campus institutions in dramatic fashion. Aside from professional faculties like Engineering, women were no longer an exotic presence on campus. They were central to the both the organizational structure of student life and to the politics of the decade.

As this was happening the cult of domesticity began to unravel. Veronica Strong-Boag has argued that, by the later 1950s, many suburban housewives were disillusioned with the 'home dreams' that had been the hallmark of their generation.[94] Even for those who were relatively content, the dreams of domesticity and security that had seemed so promising in 1945 did not have as much appeal to daughters born in affluent times. Newly forming families began to modify the vision of what marriage and home meant. This happened in two ways. First, in both Canada and the United States, the early 1960s brought a decline in the birth rate. As figure 10.3 shows, the crude birth rate peaked in Canada in 1957 at 28.2 births for every thousand women. For the next

FIGURE 10.3
Canadian Crude Birth Rate, 1955–1967

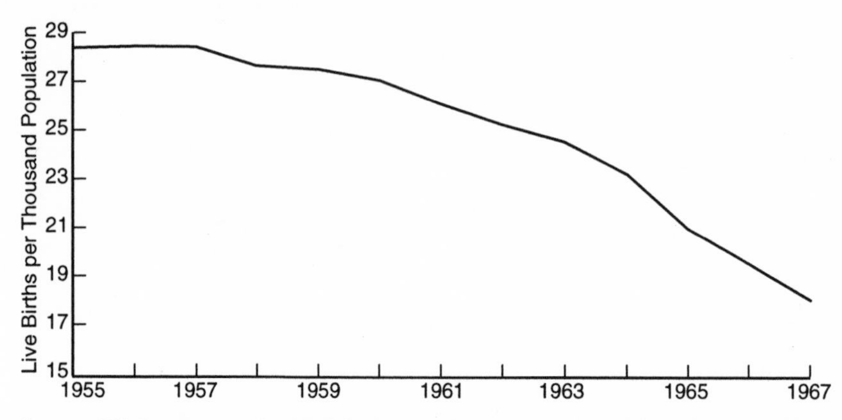

Source: F.H. Leacy, ed., *Historical Statistics of Canada*, 2d ed. (Ottawa 1983), table B4

few years, the decline was slight and, given a rising population, the actual numbers of children born in a year actually increased through the late 1950s. By the early 1960s, however, both numbers and birth rate went into freefall. By 1965 the birth rate was back down to wartime levels, and by the centennial it was the lowest ever recorded. A new generation of families was having fewer children and having them later. The great baby boom was over.

This, in turn, made it possible for women to abandon the career patterns that had been traditional in the postwar years. Through the 1960s, the career profile of women began to change. Aided by an affluent economy, the percentage of women in the paid labour force went steadily upward. Equally important, women were staying in the labour force longer. In the mid-1950s only 23 per cent of women aged twenty-five to forty-four, prime child-rearing age, worked outside the home. By the mid-1960s, the figure was about one-third and by the mid-1970s nearly one-half. A growing economy and higher levels of education also meant that the number of professional women was increasing rapidly.[95] By 1971, as the first wave of baby-boomers were leaving university, more than a third of the total labour force was female.

These changes created tensions.[96] As more women sought a different life from those of their mothers, they encountered an uncomprehending and condescending response. Now that it was no longer hedged by domesticity, notions of equality proved delusory. The women responded. As early as 1963 American Betty Friedan raised questions about the idealized and unrealistic image of women that had developed in the world of postwar suburbia.[97] Friedan's book was widely read north of the border and influenced many. Still, Canada's own version of the second wave opened in typically Canadian fashion. The government appointed a royal commission. As we have seen with the CYC, the Pearson government was relatively receptive to the currents of change that were sweeping the nation. Thus, when various groups of women began to lobby for government action on behalf of women, the government responded.[98] In 1967 it appointed the Royal Commission on the Status of Women. By the time the Commission reported in 1970, its attack on the 'exaggerated view of the child-rearing functions' of women and the cult of motherhood made it clear that the 1950s were gone.[99]

The forces reacting against the domesticity of the 1950s were many and complex. Their full story has yet to be written. Some, such as the rising expectations of the younger generation, were directly related to the experience of the baby boom. Others, such as the early political efforts, belonged to another generation. In all cases, however, the 'second wave' of the women's movement fit baby-boom sensibilities. The women born after the war had, as much as the men, felt themselves part of a privileged and historically important generation. They had entered college in record numbers, and their non-university counterparts had an unparalleled presence in the work-force. The sexual revolution was already challenging many of the traditional notions about women's nature. The impulses towards security and stability, which had seemed so important in 1945, were at a low ebb in the 1960s. Once the issue of women's role was raised, therefore, it is hardly surprising that women would turn their attention to the issue.

As the 1967 SUPA manifesto indicates, for many, the women's issue arose from personal experience. As early as 1965, women in the American New Left began to complain about the discrepancy between the rhetoric of equality and the reality of their role. At a radical conference in Michigan, recounted one observer, the 'women made peanut butter, waited on tables, cleaned up, got laid.'[100] They had practically no presence on the executive or in policy formation. Through 1965 and 1966, however, various groups of women increasingly challenged their subordinate role in the movement and, at the same time, raised the issue of women's place in society at large. By 1967 resolutions of the SDS were calling for the formation of 'women's liberation workshops and projects.'[101]

In Canada the rise of women's liberation as a New Left issue lagged a year or two behind. Though there are ephemeral early references to women's concerns, the SUPA manifesto of 1967 seems to have been the first attempt to set out the problem of the relationship of men and women in terms of the broad ideology of the movement. By then the notion of women's liberation was in the air, transmitted, as with so much else in the baby boom's culture, by the ever curious media. Across campuses the issue of women's liberation became a common topic of discussion in the final years of the decade, and women's-liberation groups were proclaimed in cities as disparate as Regina, Thunder Bay, and Halifax.[102] Initially many of these were short-lived. Widespread national organization of a new generation of women activists is more a feature of the 1970s than the 1960s. Still, by 1969, there do seem to have been ongoing, active, youth-based women's-liberation movements in Vancouver, Toronto, and Montreal.[103] In Toronto, as an example, the active women's liberation movement was soon joined, or opposed, by a series of spin-off groups, each seeking to assert their own specific perspective on the nature of change.[104] Before long the various movements began to garner national attention, often using the guerrilla-theatre tactics typical of the decade. Simon Fraser, for example, nominated a women's-liberationist as its candidate for the national university beauty contest. The subsequent disruptions, rhetoric, and controversy did much to bring women's issues to public attention.[105] At the University of Toronto, 1970 and 1971 saw major battles, and eventual victory, over the issue of a campus daycare.[106]

Initially campus newspapers, edited mainly by men, treated the new cause with a mixture of condescension and mistrust.[107] This is hardly surprising. For the first time the idealism of the baby boom was being turned upon itself. Moreover, some of the anger and bitterness of the early women's liberation movement was aimed directly at the sexual revolution. These were, after all, young adults still trying to define emotional relationships and doing so in a period in which moral values were changing and in which both idealism and romanticism placed a heavy premium upon personal relationships. The issue of equality and personality were thus naturally associated. 'When our personal relationships, particularly among man and woman, become imperialism of the self, in which the other person is to be viewed as a love object, or merely an object,' then real humanity is impossible.[108] Equality, in other words, became a precondition for true love. 'Thus in their precarious (political) situation, women cannot afford the luxury of spontaneous love. It is much too dangerous. The love and approval of men is all-important. To love thoughtlessly before one has ensured return commitment would endanger that approval.'[109]

Divisive though the rise of women's liberation was, the movement was very much a natural extension of the experience of the baby boom. The new generation of leaders that emerged at the end of the 1960s had often cut their teeth on other New Left activities. This can be seen in the ideology of the movement. The feminism of the 1960s owed more to contemporary reform movements than to earlier efforts at women's reform. Material well-being and political power merged with slippery notions of self-fulfilment, personal authenticity, and action.[110] As with other 1960s movements, the ideology was eclectic. Marx could be employed, as could Marcuse, Camus, or any of the other icons of the decade. To these male reference points were added names like Friedan, Steinem, de Beauvoir, and Millet.[111] Organizational tactics were based on the experience of the decade. Direct action, vociferous lobbying, and fractious internal debate tied the movement to the age in which it emerged. Women's liberation also may have been a relative latecomer to the causes of the decade, but it has proven one of the most powerful and enduring. A quarter-century later, it has established itself as perhaps the pre-eminent political issue of the baby-boomers' lives.

THE HIGH-SCHOOL KIDS LINING UP against the walls of the gym in 1965 had no idea of the upheavals that would mark their relationships with the opposite sex over the next few years. Unlike any recent generation, these children would ultimately decide that virginity was not a moral issue at all. First birth control, and then legalized abortion, would change the relationship between sexual activity and procreation. The 'home dreams' of the girls, or the dreams the girls were supposed to have, were becoming more complex and involved combinations of home and career to a degree unparalleled in modern history. In good baby-boom fashion, their quest for family and home was thus qualified by the search for personal fulfilment and meaning. Even before they reached adulthood, however, rising divorce rates and falling birth rates testified that the world in which they had grown up was disappearing. Had they known all of this as they stood waiting in that gym, the irony is that the walk across the dance floor would still have seemed much more frightening than the momentous changes that confronted them. Such is the nature of youth.

11

The End of the Sixties, 1968–1973

Ultimately all the strands of the sixties were linked by the generation that defined them. The adolescence of the baby boom was shaped by a strong current of romantic idealism. Though issues of alienation are relevant, the most potent force of the mid-sixties was the belief that personal and social improvement was clear and attainable. Get in touch with people and with your own emotions. Discover humanity. Involve the people politically and their innate sense of justice would come to the fore. The energy of youth would serve as a catalyst to overcome the stale and the shallow materialism that encrusted modern democracy. Much of the support for youth in the first years of political and cultural rebellion revolved around the premise that the protesters were 'young idealists,' as one journalist put it in 1964.[1] 'Mankind today has the knowledge that resources exist to eliminate poverty, illiteracy and disease,' wrote the Company of Young Canadians two years later.[2] All was possible – including personal redemption and social salvation.

By 1968 the power of youth seemed to be everywhere. In France the long quest for a student–worker alliance came into being, at least temporarily, and it nearly toppled the government. The nation was shut down, and students effectively controlled large parts of the Left Bank for weeks. Across the United States, new waves of campus protest erupted. Columbia University in New York came to a standstill in the spring as students struck. The picture of activist Mark Rudd, sitting at the president's desk, feet up, cigar in mouth, seemed a perfect symbol of the power of youth and disruption of the old order.[3] In far away Czechoslovakia, youth was a powerful element in the movement of that country towards a more liberal and open society.

Even in relatively tame Canada, the CYC and CUS were garnering front-page news coverage, while dozens of campuses had radical student governments, newspapers, or both. The 1968–9 academic year opened with several indications that the turbulence was only going to increase. Peter Warrian, outgoing president of the CUS, began the term by warning that the 'institution [of the university] was acting in violence' and that students might respond in kind.[4] Even previously peaceful places now were caught up in the chaos. At the University of New Brunswick, for example, the library had to be closed because students were protesting a new type of library card. The resultant 'Strax Affair' paralysed the campus for months.[5] Indeed, across Canada, the year was perhaps the most tumultuous in the history of a tumultuous decade.

Cultural politics were just as lively. Established bands like the Beatles, the Rolling Stones, and the Who were at the height of their musical power. Newer groups like the Doors and Pink Floyd ensured that the rock revolution kept its edge. The two years from mid-1967 to mid-1969 were remarkable even by the high musical standards of the 1960s. In that period rock established itself as an art form and continued its central role in the youth revolution. In the summer of 1967 The Beatles released their best album, *Sgt Pepper's Lonely Hearts Club Band.* Over the next months the energy continued. The Doors appeared on *Ed Sullivan* in September. Pink Floyd toured North America. The rock musical *Hair* appeared on Broadway, with its controversial celebration of hippie values and even more controversial nude scene. After an appropriate time it arrived in Toronto and Montreal – another cultural export from the youth revolution south of the border. Steppenwolf's single 'Born to Be Wild' added a new anthem to the youth revolution. The Rolling Stones' landmark album *Beggar's Banquet* appeared halfway through 1968.[6] In Canada the Guess Who released their biggest hit to date in 'Shakin' All Over,' while the Band, an American group made up of 'four Canadians and a southerner,' released its first album.[7]

Yet within five years the 'movement' was gone and the sixties were but a memory. For though youth had asserted its power to an unprecedented degree, all was not possible. Already, by the end of the decade, optimism and idealism were being obscured, if not eclipsed. Romanticism was being edged out by nihilism, and the ubiquitous capitalist culture had proven it could market beads, jeans, and even drugs if there was a profit to be made. By 1975, with the front edge of the baby boom approaching the magic age of thirty, the 'youth revolution' was over, though other revolutions endured and prospered.

SOMETIMES, AT THE VERY HEIGHT OF ITS influence and at the very centre of a movement, there are incidents that, at least in hindsight, hint of imminent decline. So it was with the youth revolution. Rock and roll, moving from triumph to triumph, had remained central to the youth culture of the decade. Increasingly it had become a symbol of the power and influence of youth.

François Ricard employs a metaphor that perfectly captures the mood of the times. Rock, he said, was a religion for the baby boom. Rock concerts were temples in which people gave witness of their faith and participated in the emotional uplift of a communal spiritual event. The faithful gathered to see and be seen and, most of all, enjoy 'their affiliation with something larger and more powerful than themselves.'[8] The ultimate event, the grand pilgrimage of the religious spirit, emerged only towards the end of the decade – the multi-day massed rock festival. The power and passion of rock and roll exhibited at these grand end-of-decade gatherings also hinted, however, at an emerging mood of chaos and decay.

The giant rock festival was a recent phenomenon. Of course music has always been a communal event, a celebration not only of the artists, but of social response to the artist's work. This had been recognized in the jazz and folk festivals that had dotted Canada and the United States. For rock it had been different. Its evolution as a stage medium, its need for amplifiers and crowd control, had confined it to rigidly controlled situations. Bands used an auditorium or, if you were a British supergroup, a stadium, with an opening act or two and then the headliners. People went for the concert and went home again. Two or three hours of frenzy and it was over.

That changed in June 1967 with the Monterey Pop Festival. The idea was to take the spirit behind events like the Newport Folk Festival and transport to the increasingly mature medium of rock. It was a tremendous success. Held over three days, the festival attracted some 50,000 people, and such bands as the Jimi Hendrix Experience, the Who, and the Byrds.[9] Just as important, the event was quickly mythologized as part of the 'new' lifestyle of the sixties. Major American magazines carried articles on the 'hippie heaven,' while a film, entitled simply *Monterey Pop*, transmitted the message across the continent. In many venues it was consciously twinned with a film on the annual convention of U.S. police chiefs in Las Vegas. The contrast between the two worlds could thus be made all the more explicit.

Almost immediately rock festivals became the order of the day. Promoters hoped to cash in on the vast audiences. Youth wanted the chance to participate in a vast gathering of their peers. Sometimes the venues were wrong, as at the June 1968 concert in Zurich, Switzerland, where police freely clubbed performers and audience alike. Still, the notion of the mega-event was growing. Concerts at Newport, California, in August 1968, and Miami, Florida, in December, each attracted an estimated 100,000 people. In the first half of 1969, even these numbers were dwarfed by the 150,000 who attended the second Newport Festival. Canada, too, was moving into the festival era. Unfortunate disruptions by bikers ruined the fairly small-scale Aldergrove, BC, festival in the spring, but in June some 50,000 attended the Toronto Rock Festival to hear such groups as the Band; Steppenwolf; and Blood, Sweat and Tears.[10]

The huge numbers attracted to these events were the source of headaches for police and potential profits for organizers. Most of all, though, they symbolized the power of rock and the power of the young. Who else but youth, after all, could bring out a quarter of a million people to memorialize a musician? Yet that is what happened at the Rolling Stones' Hyde Park memorial concert for Brian Jones in July 1969. The macabre reason for the event only added to its meaning. Ricard's religious metaphor takes on special significance on this occasion.

Of all the pilgrimages of rock, however, none is more holy nor held more reverently as a sacred memory than the one in early August 1969 to Yasgur's farm in upstate New York. The Woodstock rock festival, billed as 'three days of peace, love and music,' is undoubtedly the most famous musical event of the 1960s, if not the entire century.[11] The fame it achieved was only marginally related to the music, in spite of the impressive array of bands that played.[12] Instead, Woodstock became a mark of the generation or, more accurately, of what the generation would like to be.

From the beginning those involved were conscious of the symbolism of the event. Commentator after commentator connected the Woodstock Festival to generational values and power. Early in the concert one announcer proclaimed to the gathered believers that 'the people are going to read about you tomorrow ... All over the world.' An organizer referred to the site as 'the second-largest city in New York' and singer Arlo Guthrie announced to the audience that 'I was rapping to the fuzz ... The New York State Thruway is closed ... Yeh, far out.' The message was clear. The strength of the youth movement was, as one commentator noted, 'epical, biblical' in its proportions. Woodstock was symbolic of peace, harmony, and communality. 'There are no police!' exclaimed one organizer. 'The kids were wonderful,' commented the hapless owner of the farm, Max Yasgur. 'Nobody can blame the kids.' One of the organizers, who faced tremendous potential losses when the ticketing system fell apart, held a flower in his hand and intoned rapturously that 'this is really beautiful, man ... It has nothing to do with money.'[13]

The myth was sanctioned by the media and quickly spread across the continent. Canadian writer Jack Batten, who dissented from the Woodstock legend, complained that 'newspapers, magazines, television and deep thinkers tumbled after one another to hail the triumph of the great event, and it was hard to separate *Time* from *Rolling Stone*, the authoritative rock magazine, in the ecstasy both registered.'[14] The notion of the Woodstock generation or, even more expressive, the 'Woodstock nation,' entered the language as a further assertion of the notion of an autonomous youth subculture contained within the larger society.[15] Woodstock, then, was an event that was claimed by a generation as a symbol of their own transformative ability. In the words of the musical *Hair*, this was the 'dawning of the age of Aquarius.'

In retrospect, though, Woodstock is more of a twilight than a dawn. Indeed, much of the rhetoric may have been an attempt to regain the optimism that had existed far back in the summer of 1967. Observers at the time and since have been unanimous in concluding that the mood had darkened by 1969. Promises of utopia were being supplanted by fears of Armageddon. The Czechoslovakian spring of 1968 was crushed by Russian tanks in August. The youth-inspired overthrow of Lyndon Johnson was countered by the violence and chaos of the Democratic convention late that same summer. The assassination of Robert Kennedy and Martin Luther King, the success of the Tet offensive by the North Vietnamese and the election of Richard Nixon, the Charles Manson murders – all shook earlier assumptions about the 'age of Aquarius' through 1968 and 1969.

Then, at the very end of the latter year, all of these foreboding signs were pulled together by sacrilege in the temple. Only five months after Woodstock's glorious success came the disastrous rock concert at Altamont Speedway in California. The choice of site was a bad one, and the decision to use the notorious Hell's Angels as security guards stupid. The unruly crowd scenes and the murder at the foot of the stage mocked the image of peace and love.[16] As a piece in the *Georgia*

Straight said, 'America is now up for grabs.' Until that day the counter-culture and the radicals had grooved on their sense of distinctiveness and separateness. They were immune from history. 'But at Altamont we were the mother culture. The locust generation came to consume crumbs from the hands of the entertainment industry we helped to create.'[17]

Woodstock and Altamont symbolize the change of mood and mark the beginning of the end of the 1960s. The fact that the two events occurred almost simultaneously demonstrates the contradictory forces at work by the end of the decade. The twilight of the sixties is a complex mixture of retreat, disillusionment, and adaptation. In part the 'movement' died from without. The liberal-capitalist system was more flexible and more insistent upon its survival than many critics had assumed. Mainstream society increasingly challenged the youth movement's political critique while absorbing much of the politically charged symbolism of music, dress, sex, and even drugs. Part of the change was also internal to the baby boom. As the mood darkened, the unity of youth was put to the test and, not surprisingly, more traditional fault lines of class, ideology, gender, and ethnicity began to appear. Thus, for a complex of reasons, the generation lost its sense of unity and optimism.

This is why Woodstock and Altamont have retained such a central place in the imagination of the baby boom. Music, as has been argued earlier, was central to the generation's sense of uniqueness. The journey from utopia to failure symbolized by these two events has since stood as a metaphor for the failure of the counter-culture. Woodstock stands for the hopes and dreams of a new age – the summer of love, Haight-Ashbury, the optimism of the LSD trippers and marijuana smokers. Altamont represents the reality that came to pass – the rise of violence in the drug culture, the exploitation of the hippies, the sexual revolution's failure to bring personal happiness, speed, religious cults, and the horror of a Charles Manson. People prefer to remember Woodstock, but they cannot forget its immediate aftermath.

YOUTH POLITICS OF THE LATE SIXTIES and early seventies followed a path that paralleled the course of youth culture. The mood went from optimism and hope to darkness with an edge of violence. Factionalism grew within the New Left, and mainstream society stepped up its efforts to repress the more extreme elements. There was a great deal of noise and protest that continued through the early 1970s. As the president of the University of Toronto sarcastically put it, these years remained 'drenched in the jargon of the new left.'[18] Yet, in retrospect, a mixture of disillusionment and integration is as much the trend of the 'counter-politics' of the age as of the counter-culture. Extreme elements would ultimately find themselves attacked by society and disowned by the baby boom. Yet much of the style and ideology of the New Left would adapt itself to mainstream politics. Integration into the mainstream was thus as much a part of the story as was failure or retreat.

The turning-point in the world of student politics in Canada occurred the same year as Woodstock and Altamont. On 11 February 1969, the radical politics of civil disobedience and direct action crossed over the line to violence. Like Altamont, this event changed the baby boom's sense of itself and adult society's perception of the young generation. Like Altamont as well, this event symbolized wider trends within youth politics and foreshadowed the end of the 1960s era.

It is fitting that an event of such significance took place in Montreal. Throughout the 1960s the city was politically charged. The enthusiasm of the Quiet Revolution had turned uglier in recent years as the FLQ preached (and acted) a violent revolution in the name of Quebec independence. Youth generally were caught up in the issue of separatism. The UGEQ had pioneered the notion of the student as 'paid intellectual worker' and was radical in rhetoric and separatist in orientation. Radicals like Stanley Gray had damned McGill as an English fortress in the midst of a French nation. The question of French at McGill, and then of Gray's role as a lecturer on campus, was still being battled out at the beginning of 1969.[19] Yet the issue which was to dominate the year and destroy much of the support for 'the movement' occurred neither at McGill nor among the student separatists at the Université de Montréal. In fact, it really had nothing to do with Quebec at all.

On 29 January 1969, a special committee convened at Sir George Williams University.[20] It was supposed to hear testimony on allegations of racism levelled against a professor in the Biology department. Racism was perhaps the most loaded charge that could be laid in the 1960s, and it was especially explosive at Sir George, which had a significant number of West Indian students. To make matters worse, the issue had been festering for the past year, exacerbated by an indecisive administration and increasingly radical demands on the part of some students. Meetings and demonstrations, inflamed rhetoric, and radical politics dominated the campus through fall 1968 and into 1969. 'Get the Motherfuckers' and similar slogans had dotted campus walls and radical speeches for the previous few months. As was often the case in the 1960s, the small number of true radicals enjoyed considerable, if intermittent, support from liberal students and faculty.

The recent presence in town of American radicals like Black Panther Bobby Seale and 'black power' activist Stokely Carmichael had heightened the tension. So too had the resignation of the president of the university. The student council of Sir George Williams had complained of the investigating committee's membership, as had the representative of black students. Just a few weeks before, a Science Council meeting had ended in a near riot. The press, the students, and the hapless professors on the committee anticipated something interesting might happen when hearings reconvened. They were right.

The meeting never began. Student demonstrators 'surged on the stage' and disrupted the session. They then moved on to occupy the faculty club (a favourite target in demonstrations) and, more unusually, the computer centre.[21] For the next several days the familiar routine of heady rhetoric, futile negotiations, and the boredom of the sit-in preoccupied both protesters and police. Then, on 11 February, events took an unexpected turn. Angry students, responding to a recent rumour, broke into a nearby cafeteria and ransacked it. The police arrived, and students in the computer centre started throwing computer tapes and punch cards out of the ninth-floor window. Somebody set a fire and, by the time the police cleared the building, the computer centre was destroyed. Damage was estimated at $2 million, and several faculty members lost valuable research projects. On Mackay Street, nine floors below, the thousands of punch cards thrown out the window gave the appearance of a new blanket of snow.

Until that day the Canadian student movement had avoided violence. Demonstrations, sit-ins, and protests had, in the civil-rights tradition, employed non-violence as both a tactic and a public-relations weapon. The occasional broken window or scuffle notwithstanding, accusations of violence had more likely been directed at police than at students. Certainly the non-violent tactics of the Canadian student movement had been central to the support it received from other youth, the media, and adults in left-of-centre parties.

Much of the goodwill evaporated in the shower of punch cards on the night of 11 February. Across the country there was shock. Not surprisingly, the mainstream press condemned the destruction. *La Presse* referred to a 'gang of hooligans' and the *Montreal Star* called the action 'indefensible.' The Winnipeg *Free Press* warned that 'violence will not be tolerated' in Canadian society. The Calgary *Herald* was even tougher, terming the students 'thugs,' 'hooligans,' and 'rampaging criminals,' and demanding jail sentences.[22] In Parliament, MPs focused on the foreign students involved and called for tougher immigration restrictions.[23]

Such a reaction was to be expected. More significant was the impact of the events at Sir George Williams on campus dynamics across the nation. Student radicals had always needed a large and sympathetic body of moderates if they were to succeed. In this, the baby boom's sense of generational identification and the common youth culture of the decade had been important. The radicals were the 'us' against the adult 'them.' This did not always translate into mass support, but it did mean that student radicals received the benefit of the doubt from much of the campus body, and certainly from activists like newspaper editors and campus politicians.

The majority of students, though, were not willing to condone violence. In the wake of the computer riot, student governments across the country dissociated themselves from the incident.[24] At Sir George Williams itself, the student government criticized the violence, and student volunteers raised money to repair the damage in the computer centre.[25] Even the exceptions tended to emphasize the rule. When a group of radicals at Toronto attempted to justify the Sir George incident, they were booed by fellow students.[26] Only the UGEQ, the separatist-leaning francophone student body, defended the Sir George group, blaming the violence on the police and administration.[27]

Part of the reaction to the Sir George Williams incident seems to have had little to do with the Canadian protest scene. In the previous year or so, television and magazines had regularly beamed sensational images of violent youth from whatever American city or campus was in the news at the time. There, as one ex-radical noted, the New Left had begun to practise 'the politics of extremity.' Turning its back on the effort to win over broad liberal opinion, the movement 'set out to dig its own trenches, or grave.'[28] New groups like the Weathermen openly preached violence, calling on people to 'Bring the war home!' This was a movement, said one of its own pamphlets, 'conceived in battle and willing to die in battle.' In early 1970 Weathermen would be killed in a New York townhouse while trying to construct a pipe-bomb, thus bringing a grim reality to their own prediction.[29]

The strong Canadian reaction was attributable in part to the fear that

American extremism was moving north of the border. Just a week before the Sir George destruction, University of California president Clark Kerr was prevented from speaking at the Royal Ontario Museum by the radical Toronto Student Movement.[30] Civil disobedience had also edged towards intimidation at the Dow Chemical protests on the Toronto campus a few months earlier. Throughout Quebec there was considerable sympathy among students for the revolutionary FLQ. Simon Fraser was, as was discussed earlier, barely functioning, with student occupations moving from civil disobedience to active disruption.

As liberals, adult and student, focused on the possibility of recurrent violence, their attitude towards protest began to change. As was noted in chapter 7, civil disobedience had been legitimized by the civil-rights movement of the early 1960s. Marches in Selma or Montgomery gave moral authority to later marches in Washington, Berkeley, Toronto, or Vancouver. Breaking the law was also legitimized by the willingness of figures like Martin Luther King and early anti-war protesters to accept arrest and jail. As one SUPA member had put it in 1965, 'radical non-violence was a way of dealing with the dilemma of structural change vs. acceptable means.'[31] Passive resistance was very much a part of the Western Christian heritage – bearing witness against evil, martyrdom, moral righteousness over force. It was also, of course, less threatening. Thus the anti-war movement, the causes espoused by the New Left, the protests on campus were aided both by recent events and by the association with a residual element of basic Western values.

Violence broke the pact. For the moderate sympathizer it clouded the moral lines. Who was the martyr at Sir George Williams and who the victim? Was Clark Kerr not the victim in Toronto, and were not the protesters undermining basic Western values of free speech? For authorities, of course, the message was also sinister. Rebellion was dangerous and disruptive.[32] It could not be tolerated in the same way as marches or vigils. Violence, in other words, begat reaction. Sometimes this was an intended part of New Left policy, hoping to expose the true nature of the fascist state. It was naïve, however. In a test of force the state would inevitably win, as the fate of the Weathermen and the tragedy at Kent State the next year would reveal. In the meantime the radical Left slowly lost the sympathy of the many youth who, for all their rhetoric and styles, were still imbued with the liberal-democratic values of their upbringing.

Critics of the New Left were quick to focus on the growing violence and disruption. Through 1969 popular magazines turned their attention on the dangerous elements of the New Left. The academic community also began to respond. American George F. Kennan, though hardly a darling of the young, did have academic credentials. His *Democracy and the Student Left* viciously attacked the 'screaming tantrums' of the student movement.[33] Respected sociologist Lewis Feuer dismissed student protest as a psychologically driven rebellion against parental authority. Their 'example of violence and contempt for American society, their disruption of peaceful election debates and speeches, their intimidation of the majority, their disregard of political ethics' hardly made the student activists a group worthy of loyalty.[34] The next year trendy journalist Tom Wolfe satirized the 'nostalgie de la boue' which led American liberals to romanticize the 'primitive, exotic and romantic' side of violent protest.[35] In Canada, *Saturday Night,* obviously hostile to the New Left, provided a handy outlet for criticism. Mordecai Richler, well-known author and protagonist, mocked the pretensions of the young trendy academic.[36] Robert Fulford raised serious questions about truth, fad, and relative versus absolute truth.[37] Fulford was joined by a growing reaction on the part of intellectuals, including leading academics like Toronto's Northrop Frye.[38]

Most significant, though, was the increasingly critical tone of Canada's traditional Left. In 1969 and 1970, several veterans of the Left began to take on the student movement. At a speech in Saskatchewan, one of the members of the original CCF braintrust, Graham Spry, vehemently attacked the totalitarian tendencies of student radicals. Academic and anarchist George Woodcock concluded that these students of the New Left represented, not the ultimate ideal of the postwar era, but its betrayal. Publishing in *Saturday Night,* and subsequently in *Canadian Forum,* Woodcock dissociated himself from what he saw as the growing intolerance of student radicalism. The events at Simon Fraser, Sir George Williams, and elsewhere, he said, revealed a movement that 'pretends to be libertarian but is in action authoritarian and in prospect totalitarian.' Most controversially, he reminded readers that the Nazis began as a movement of the young and disaffected. Reviewing recent events and the tone of New Left meetings, he concluded that 'I am forced – reluctantly, as a radical and a libertarian – to admit the existence of fascistic possibilities among contemporary student movements.'[39] The Old Left had turned the rhetoric of the New Left upon itself.

THE CLASH BETWEEN THE STUDENT RADICALS and their opponents was played out most forcefully on university campuses. Many critics of the New Left concluded from the Sir George Williams incident that weakness encouraged extremism, and possibly violence. Newspapers blamed the 'vacillation of the administration' at Sir George Williams and demanded that university administrations get their house in order.[40] Even an article in the left-wing *Canadian Dimension* argued that excessive liberalism on the part of faculty and administrators opened the way for an extremist minority.[41] The demands being sent to university administrations now were not for reform but for order. 'It is incumbent on authorities administering institutions of higher learning to send disruptive students packing before they succeed in making trouble.'[42]

Once again, this backlash had one eye focused south of the border. Beginning with the Columbia University strike of 1968, the situation on American campuses had been growing more unpredictable and violent. Through 1968 and 1969, places like San Francisco State, Berkeley (as always), Harvard, and Stanford were disrupted by strikes and occupations. At Cornell, advocates of 'black power' openly carried guns during the occupation of a building. As one participant recounts, in that one academic year 'there were well over a hundred politically inspired campus bombings, and incidents of arson nationwide ... In the spring of 1969 alone, three hundred colleges and universities, holding a third of American students, saw sizable demonstrations, a quarter of them marked by strikes or building takeovers.'[43] Bombs killed a worker in one incident. A visitor was shot and killed during a demonstration during the wars over Berkeley's People's Park. The campuses were headed down a road of apocalypse and repression that would culminate in 1970 at Kent State, where four students were killed and nine wounded when National Guardsmen opened fire on protesters.

When demonstrations had first appeared in the mid-sixties, university administrations were surprised and uncertain. They either tried ineffectual repression, which only generated mass support, or vacillated, which turned the initiative over to the protesters. By the end of the decade, however, administrations had put a great deal of effort into the problem of student unrest. Presidential conferences and *University Affairs* seemed filled with little else by the turn of the decade. What they learned, by trial and error, was how to separate what John Deutsch, the principal of Queen's, condemned as the 'intolerant and arrogant voices of a small band of nihilists' from the broad band of reform-minded students. He concluded that the key to administrative success and campus peace 'lies in carefully and speedily heeding the second and refusing to be bullied by the first.'[44] Claude Bissell, president of Canada's largest university, agreed. Much of the student movement was positive, he said, but not all. One minority, he said, was attached to a 'feverish dogmatism, a conviction of correctness that is reminiscent of the Chinese revolution.'[45] Like Deutsch, Bissell felt that the trick was to ensure that the positive aspects of the student movement were separated from the extremes.

Such a strategy implied a degree of accommodation to ensure the cooperation of the 'average' student. *In loco parentis* was rapidly dismantled across the country in order to reduce potential points of friction between the university and the student. 'The university administration,' as one York student put it, 'like the state, has no business in the bedrooms of the campus.'[46] At the same time administrations rapidly ceded the principle of direct student involvement in the governance of the institution. Student representation on even the most senior committees of the university became normal by the early 1970s.[47] Most controversially, a number of universities revamped their curriculum to respond to the demands of the decade. More 'relevant' courses were introduced, and old structures were loosened. In many instances the honours program effectively disappeared in the name of anti-élitism.[48]

The other side of the response was discipline. Administrators began, individually and through bodies like the Association of Universities and Colleges of Canada (AUCC), to develop policies on student protest. Occasionally, as at the University of Saskatchewan, the response bordered on the paranoid with a full-time 'informer' to ferret out student plans for disruption.[49] More often, however, the focus was on procedure. Here, too, the responses varied. Sometimes, as in those enunciated by Old Leftist Escott Reid of Glendon College, they were liberal.[50] In other cases they were more restrictive and forceful. By 1969 or 1970, though, a clear pattern had developed. Protest was acceptable. Disruption was not. Attempts to prevent speakers from being heard or classes being attended would be met by discipline and, if necessary, the use of police. One of the clearest examples of the changing mood came in the summer of 1969, when the Council of University Presidents of Universities of Ontario (CUPUO) endorsed a series of disciplinary principles that included the immediate use of police to end disruption.[51]

The combination of concessions and discipline on the part of the university was a deliberate attempt, as Bissell and Deutsch noted, to drive a wedge between the radical activists and the main student body. This wedge was also driven, however, by the New Left itself. In the later 1960s, the confrontational style became entrenched. The debates that broke up SUPA and the increasing acrimony within campus groups indicate that the Canadian student movement was pulled between the original open-ended reformism of the earlier years and the new, darker, mood of the end of the decade. Yet the more that the New Left became radicalized, the farther it removed itself from the main student body. In that sense it unwittingly reinforced administrative desires to separate the generational sense of identity from radical leadership.

Symbolic of the apocalyptic politics of the era were the final death throes of the last great umbrella organization of student power, the Canadian Union of Students. For when that death finally came, after years of increasingly grievous and often self-inflicted injury, the unusual thing was the part activist students took in ensuring its demise.

The death struggle for the CUS came at the University of Toronto. Toronto not only was Canada's largest university but had a very high profile as a premier institution, both for undergraduate and for graduate education. During the decade it expanded in absolute terms more rapidly than any other Canadian university. In 1955 there had been 11,000 students on the single St. George campus. By 1968 there were 24,000 students spread among St. George, Erindale, and Scarborough.[52] That population was, moreover, becoming more diversified in class, outlook, and ethnicity, matching the changing nature of the city around the campuses. Much of the size and many of the differences were, however, harnessed within the college system. Trinity, St Michael's, Victoria, and others each retained elements of their ethnic, religious, and ideological traditions.

In the formative years of student protest during the mid-sixties, the University of Toronto was relatively peaceful. There were active youth politics, of course. Rochdale came out of the university system, and many SUPA members had ties with the campus. Yorkville was just down the street, and the 'beats' and 'hippies' that successively caused so much consternation to City Council were often current or recent university students. David DePoe, for example, went directly from an uninspired career as a Toronto student to his life as Yorkville's CYC volunteer and 'super-hippie.' It was a common pattern. Still, as a whole, the Toronto campus faced none of the early upsets and battles that characterized places like McGill, or the Université de Montréal, much less Simon Fraser. The traditions of the college system, the sheer size of the university as a whole, and the relative conservatism of a significant element of the student body seemed to absorb the radical and experimental elements of mid-1960s political and cultural effervescence.

The ability to avoid disruption may also have had to do with the style of student politics. For all the ideological differences that existed, student–administration relationships remained genteel. Robert Rae, to give one example, was one of the foremost student presences on campus until he departed for graduate education overseas. Rae himself, though far left of his administrative opponents, came from the same class and spoke the same language they did. His father had been ambassador to Mexico and, even more pertinently, a graduate of University College. Dressed neatly and with only a hint of long hair, the younger Rae was the respectable radical, a man who was bound to go far. President Claude Bissell referred to him as having 'a talent for easy public discourse, and, unlike almost all his contemporary radicals, a lively sense of humour.' Generally, as Bissell also noted, the student government through the end of the 1967–8 academic year was dominated by people who 'preferred discussion and compromise to violence and intractability.'[53]

Then it all began to fall apart. By 1969 the New Left on campus increasingly moved from traditional student institutions to direct politics. Such easily recognizable bodies as the Student Administrative Council competed with fast-emerging and amorphous organizations. The rhetoric escalated and the style changed. Bissell complained that the 'entente cordiale' between student and administration was broken. From the other side, a younger group of student radicals believed that the structure of governance was sufficiently corrupt that it had to be brought down, using, if need be, the 'politics of extremity.'[54] Nor, given the climate of the times, were they willing to be bound by any old-fashioned rules of procedure or civility.

The mood throughout the 1969–70 academic year was extremely political. The tone was set early by the *Varsity*, under editor Brian Johnson. It began the academic term by filling all of its first ten pages with articles on student politics. Warnings of local 'counter-violence' by the administration mixed with pieces on the CUS and wire-service articles on the famous People's Park at Berkeley.[55] Local issues were thus linked to the national and international youth revolution, a theme that continued through the next several issues. The activism of the paper was matched by events around the city. One month after the new term began, Glendon College, a branch campus of York University, held a 'Year of the Barricades' conference with such New Left celebrities as Karl Deutsch Wolff, from Germany; Jim Harding, from SFU; and Stanley Gray, from McGill.[56] The events of the previous winter at Sir George Williams and at the Royal Ontario Museum still echoed. The recent report of the CUPUO became a local issue as Bissell sought to restructure the internal disciplinary system, known as 'CAPUT.' Everything indicated that this was likely to be anything but a normal year of student politics at Canada's largest university.

What happened over the next few months was often a seemingly disconnected series of incidents, threats, debates, and compromises. Still, out of all the activity, a certain pattern prevailed. On the one side were student radicals. As was typical, the campus New Left was made up of a series of disparate and competing organizations and ideologies. Andy Wernick, himself a student radical, catalogued the multitude of groups in an article early in the term. It was a sort of student primer to campus politics of the Left.[57] The protest groups ranged across the entire left-wing spectrum, from the New Democratic Youth ('not really on the left at all') to the Maoist Internationalists ('three quarters of them are functionally insane'). The force to be reckoned with, however, was a group known as the New Left Caucus (NLC).

The NLC quickly grabbed centre stage in the fall of 1969 with a series of dramatic protests. Orientation of first-year students was matched by a series of counter-orientations. The traditional freshman dinner at Hart House was disrupted with shouts of 'power to the people' and warnings that 'orientations are simply muzak which serves to smother the tensions generated by the process of registration into a repressive system.'[58] As Wernick said, this movement was 'fast growing and centre stage.'[59] It would play an important role in events on campus over the next few months.

The NLC was an offshoot of the Toronto Student Movement (TSM), which had been involved in the Kerr incident the year before. Though its membership ranged in age, it was composed largely of baby-boom students, and the style of its membership ('freaks with long hair') as well as its style of decision making ('collective ... roughly along the lines of the Red Guards')[60] incorporated the broad themes of youth culture of the 1960s. Likewise, its ideology was typical of the New Left as it had evolved by the end of the decade. Though it thought of itself as Marxist in a general way, it was also influenced by the ideas of Mao, Fanon, Marcuse, and others. Its most striking departure from pure Marxism, as well as from earlier New Left movements, however, was its adoption of the rising issue of women's liberation, a source of some dissension and a partial reason for the collapse of the earlier TSM.[61]

The NLC was typical of the evolution of New Left politics in another way. Its style was explicitly confrontational, rejecting the 'parliamentary road to socialism' and calling for a 'revolutionary student movement.' There was an apocalyptic edge to its rhetoric and style. The crisis of modern society was at hand, and the niceties which underpinned the old order had to be thrown over. In this the NLC reflected parallel currents south of the border. There is no indication that the NLC ever contemplated the extremism of movements like the Weathermen, but in the disruptions, shouts of 'power to the people,' and sense that the apocalypse was near, this group was very much a part of the times.

In spite of the tough talk from the CUPUO over the summer, the administration was, in fact, uncertain about its own strength. Controversy and disruption continued through the fall, and at one point the president was forced to publicly recant his own tough line and to disassociate from CUPUO's promise to prevent disruptions on campus.[62] By 1969 the mood on campuses was so polarized, and even paranoid, that administrators feared that attempts to enforce rules would shut the campus down. They could talk tough, but they still saw this new incarnation of youth as a strange and unpredictable force.

If the administration was uncertain, the traditional structures of university government were in near collapse. Earlier examples at Sir George Williams and Simon Fraser had already demonstrated that student governments were ill-equipped to cope with polarized communities and crisis situations. Toronto in late 1969 confirmed the point. Members had such diverse views as to the appropriate role for student government, not to mention its goals, that meetings of council quickly collapsed into pointless recrimination. After battling back and forth on discipline, the CUS, and other issues, one frustrated member of the Student Council was overheard to lament: 'If this is reported the way it happened we'll all look like idiots.' The eavesdropping student reporter used the comment as the title of the subsequent article on the meeting.[63]

It is against this background of destabilized institutions, numerous activist factions, and considerable political consciousness that the final battle over a national student organization unfolded. The CUS was, by 1969, fighting for survival. As mentioned in chapter 9, the francophone universities, Alberta, McGill, and some others had already withdrawn. Now it faced a referendum on Canada's largest campus and, as Martin Loney, the new CUS president, admitted, defeat at Toronto would kill the organization. This was why the CUS devoted much of its annual meeting in 1969 to discussing ways and means to win over the hearts of the students. The CUS Executive hoped that it could cobble together two potent forces – the official student government and a coalition of left-wing activists. Contacts were made with local student representatives. The Student Administrative Council was, on the whole, supportive, but there was also dissent. Perhaps something of the schizophrenia of the campus came through when Council decided to vote $1,000 for a pro-CUS campaign. It then turned around and voted $500 for an anti-CUS campaign.[64]

When the CUS came to town to defend itself, it expected to face hostility from conservative students. That had been the pattern elsewhere for an organization that had moved from service to active politics. That was true, but only part of the truth. Surprisingly, the NLC, the most prominent New Left organization on campus, joined the engineers, law students, and other professional faculties to defeat the notion of a national union of students. Over the next few weeks, therefore, Toronto was treated to a series of scenes that seemed to make more sense in the psychedelic world of Rochdale than in a referendum on the future of the national student organization. Martin Loney came to town from the troubles at Simon Fraser to appeal to moderates and conservatives on campus. He was, he said, a pacifist 'who advocates compromise as a means of change.' At the same time, the CUS attempted to appear more relevant by publishing the first and last issue of what it termed a 'National Supplement.' The rhetoric there certainly didn't sound quite as moderate as Loney's. Articles such as 'The Liberal Tongue Lashing and Its Backlash,' 'Repression on Campus,' and 'Exploitation in the Alberta Beet Fields' continued the political protest which had caused the organization so much controversy in recent years.[65] In the meantime the NLC used all of the excessive rhetoric of the era to condemn the CUS as a liberal-bourgeois body. In the course of debate the shifting nature of the New Left became apparent. Old radicals like Steven Langdon, a former Student Administrative Council president, became moderates, urging continued support of the CUS.

In the midst of such confused alliances, the CUS never had a chance. By a 2–1 vote, the student body voted to pull out of the CUS. On the same day Dalhousie students reached the same decision. The organization was fatally wounded and would disband by spring 1970.[66] The body which had attempted to speak both for the students of Canada and for the New Left found such a bridge was impossible. As Howard Adelman perceptively noted a few months later, 'CUS was caught in the tension between the self-interested, inherently inegalitarian role of university education, and a social conscience which taught them to cry out against this inequity.'[67]

The irony is not that students rejected a politicized organization but that the New Left helped them to do so. The fact that the NLC (and others) sought to defeat the CUS says much about the ideological infighting that had come to mark the radical scene by the late 1960s.[68] As one participant commented in retrospect, such a position was understandable only in light of the 'apocalyptic' rhetoric of the time.[69] The crisis must be hastened. The bourgeois and the weak-minded must be exposed. In the process, however, realism went out the window. The defeat of the CUS destroyed the one national network that could unite the campus revolution. It might not have survived even if the entire New Left had supported it, but the factionalism speaks to the hubris of the age. The unstoppable revolution was turning on itself.

The collapse of the CUS is just one example of growing factionalism in the New Left. Only two years before, SUPA had been torn apart by ideological discord. By 1969 the CYC was a shadow of what had been. Reports later that year stated that the head of the Quebec wing was a supporter of the terrorist FLQ. For Pierre Trudeau this was the final straw, and in the spring of 1970 Alan Clarke was out as director and the new board had a much more moderate hue than its predecessor. In the meantime one of the founders of the organization echoed an increasingly familiar refrain. The goals of the CYC, complained Duncan Edmonds, 'were altered by the New Left group which gained control in 1966.' The result over the next three years was a 'morass of sterile ideological debate.'[70]

Thus, by the beginning of 1970, the great national movements were either gone or on their way out. This is not to say that campus politics suddenly quieted down in 1970. The next two or three years would see ongoing protests and considerable student activism. The pattern was changing, though. The issues were increasingly local, often without national coordination or context. Instead the coordination was increasingly on the administration's side. At the Association of Universities and Colleges of Canada (AUCC), senior officials continued to hammer home the mixture of accommodation and suppression. The momentum was shifting away from campus-based activism and, indeed, away from the belief that students were the basis of social change. The Left, for its part, looked increasingly back to the working class. The rest of the student body began to move on to other things. From 1969 on, the use of police increased and, even more significantly, the amount of time elapsed before police were brought in decreased markedly. By 1973 the number of incidents of protest occupations sank into insignificance.[71]

IN THE WAKE OF THE DEFEAT OF THE CUS, Toronto activist Steven Langdon reflected upon the significance of what happened. Langdon had supported the CUS but, he said, the movement had been full of contradictions – unable to overcome local fiefdoms and uncertain about its place on the political spectrum. In the end he gave the impression that it deserved to die. The question, though, was what came next. The best answer for Langdon was to abandon student exclusivism and the factionalism of the more radical Left. The alternative, he said, was to work within existing structures and, specifically, within the New Democratic Party. Here, he said, there was the possibility of translating idealism into action.[72]

The idea of a link with the NDP was not new. Throughout the 1960s, the NDP, as 'the' main left-wing party in Canada, had felt both the benefits and the pressures of the New Left. Naturally, the party was sympathetic to this new generation of reformers and tried to make room for it within existing structures. Youth wings, in particular, were often campus-based and sympathetic to New Left issues. Yet the integration of the New Left with traditional democratic socialism was not without problems. From about 1965 on, the party spent a great deal of energy trying to reconcile the perspective of the traditional rural and blue-collar constituencies with that of urban, middle-class youth.

The heterodox New Left was not amenable to party discipline, was impatient for results, and was often at odds with the large blue-collar wing of the party. The openness of the New Left also provided popular staging-grounds for radical groups bent on infiltration, most commonly Trotskyites in English Canada and separatists in Quebec.[73] A series of constituency brush-fires between youth wings and the New Left, on the one side, and party stalwarts, on the other, had become a common scene by the latter half of the decade. Urban constituencies in British Columbia and Ontario were especially vulnerable. The expulsion of a group known as the 'Ottawa Five' in 1967, for example, caused embarrassment and uncertainty in the Ontario party. 'The NDP should be proud of the Ottawa Five; they have an impressive record of service to the party and also the anti–Vietnam-war movement.'[74] Their agenda was also considerably to the left of the NDP's.

These were mere skirmishes, though, compared with events after 1968. In the 1968 election, the NDP failed to gain substantially in either seats or popular vote. This created an apparent contradiction for the party. Everywhere people seemed to be talking in terms of reform and change. Yet the voters had migrated to the Liberals. In particular, there was a common assumption that Trudeau had captured the youth vote with his 'swinging' image and a devoted popular press.[75]

The youth wing of the party charged that the NDP had lost touch with the aspirations and attitudes of the young. What youth wanted, according to this analysis, was a meaningful left-wing movement, not one dependent upon big unions and forever trying to convince the middle-aged voter that the party was 'safe.' There were also specific issues, especially Vietnam. Many youth felt the NDP's policy on Vietnam, though critical of the United States, was far too compromising. A 1966 *Bulletin* of the youth-dominated 'Socialist caucus' of the party complained that federal leader Tommy Douglas had 'done nothing to bring opposition to the war sharply before the public.'[76] By 1968 the youth wing was determined to assert its interests over those of the party.

The other major issue was Canadian nationalism. The question of how to preserve Canadian sovereignty in the face of Canada's powerful neighbour had been an intermittent concern since the later 1950s. Every federal government from 1956 on had, in one form or another, been forced to deal with the issue, however reluctantly. The later part of the 1960s, however, saw a strong growth in concern about the overriding American presence in the economy. A 1967 poll, for instance, indicated that 60 per cent of the population thought foreign ownership could endanger political independence. A plurality (47 per cent) thought foreign control of Canadian industry was an issue of major importance.[77]

As was discussed in chapter 7, there was an especially strong fusion between Canadian nationalism and youth, including, though not exclusively, radical youth. There were several reasons for this. American foreign policy seemed increasingly disagreeable, given the decline of the Cold War and the quagmire in Vietnam. Likewise, the civil-rights movement, later urban riots, and the plague of assassinations which were a feature of the sixties detracted from the notion that America was a democracy to emulate. The Left also had two additional reasons to be attracted to the issue of nationalism. First, they (as with certain conservative thinkers) saw a link between independence and socialism or, to put in negative terms, between Americanization and the dominance of liberalism. 'I am anti-American,' concluded one young writer in 1967, 'because I oppose the basic foundations upon which American society rests, the moral and philosophical foundations of the liberal system of individualism.'[78] Second, like the issue of Vietnam, nationalism was potentially attractive to youth who were otherwise not committed to the NDP.

When joined, nationalism and New Left radicalism provided a powerful force. By the end of the decade, the two themes had been increasingly linked in the minds of a number of student groups, academics, and urban, middle-class NDP supporters. For these individuals, the Left had to be brought into the new age almost as much as society as a whole. Nationalism had to be stressed. Radicalization was necessary. The result was the birth of a youth-intellectual crusade known by the unlikely name of the 'Waffle movement.'

A full history of the Waffle movement is beyond the scope of this book. Still, the insurgency is instructive for several reasons. Most important, Waffle demonstrates the link that had formed between issues of generation and other aspects of Canadian politics. Indeed, though Waffle and other groups within the party ostensibly debated ideology and policy, the issue of which class and which generation would control the party was also significant. The Wafflers were middle class, urban, and unconnected to the world of smokestacks and assembly lines. One poll indicated that the bulk of Wafflers were, in order, students, academics, and teachers.

Most of all, though, Wafflers represented the political divide of generations. Some 50 per cent of identified Waffle supporters at the 1971 leadership convention were under the age of thirty, compared with fewer than 13 per cent of non-Wafflers. One thirty-year-old Waffle supporter complained that 'as an older person I find myself uncomfortable and out of place,'[79] On the other side was the older blue-collar unionist. Often pro-American, socially conservative, and with no university education, this traditional urban working-class member was uncomfortable with the politics of radicalism and arrogance brought from campus to meeting hall.[80]

The Waffle originated in the manifesto of a group of Ontario NDPers urging the party to adopt both a more socialist platform and a more stridently nationalist tone.[81] The rhetoric and goals of the 'Manifesto for an Independent Socialist Canada' was very much in tune with the mood of the new radicalism of the 1960s. First and foremost, it was nationalist, but in a particularly anti-American way. 'The American empire is the central reality for Canadians. It is an empire characterized by militarism abroad and racism at home.' A later poll indicated that 96 per cent of Wafflers wanted to nationalize foreign-owned resource industries, for example, compared with only 25 per cent of other NDPers.[82] It also reflected postwar concerns about technology, participatory democracy, and alienation. 'Today, sheer size combined with modern technology further exaggerates man's sense of impotence. A socialist transformation of society will return man to his sense of humanity ... But a socialist democracy implies man's control of his immediate environment as well, and in any strategy for building socialism, community democracy is as vital as the struggle for electoral success.'[83]

This was a vision that owed little to the old union–agrarian links of the Canadian Left and instead looked to the rhetoric and community action of the New Left. Thus, for example, at the 1969 national convention of the NDP, the Waffle pushed issues of anti-war protest, community-based projects reminiscent of SUPA, women's liberation, and self-determination for Quebec. Manifestos were released, and 'non-negotiable' demands were laid before the party. All the time party leadership remained uncertain, and union leadership increasingly restive, in the face of this brash product of the 1960s.

By 1971 the movement turned into something of a campus crusade, reminiscent of the Eugene McCarthy campaign for the presidency in the United States three years earlier. The NDP was in the midst of a leadership race, and Waffle put forward its own candidate, James Laxer. Laxer, a historian, was very much a man in the spirit of the 1960s. His own political teeth had been cut in student politics. At the same time, he firmly believed that Canadian student radicals were, on their own, derivative of their American counterparts. To be relevant, the student Left had to become a voice for Canadian independence.[84]

Then, with an articulate leader, operating skilfully in urban constituencies and especially around campuses, the Wafflers captured many of delegate seats. As momentum built, many became convinced that this was a chance to translate the mood of the 1960s into real power. It is a reflection of the times that such a radical vision came close to victory. Laxer proved to be the only serious alternative to long-time party member David Lewis. It took four ballots before the Waffle was finally fended off. Then, as their candidate headed to the platform to congratulate Lewis, the young delegates took up the chant 'power to the people.'[85]

Lewis had been instrumental in expelling the Communists from the CCF after the Second World War. He was a tough party in-fighter and far removed from the academic idealism of Waffle. Over the next months, the Waffle and the mainline party clashed repeatedly. The battle was most intense in Ontario, where Lewis's son Stephen was party leader. After a series of messy constituency fights leading up to the 1971 Ontario election, Stephen Lewis openly criticized Waffle. In return Waffle members jeered him at a meeting in St Catharines.[86] All of this was too much for the powerful union leaders, who soon began to assert their own clout within the party. Through 1971 and into 1972, the Ontario party seemed to be on the edge of destruction, not from without but within. 'I, too, am a socialist,' Lewis grumbled, 'who wished to fight for a free Canada ... but I want to fight without the Waffle forever an encumbrance around my neck.'[87] At its June 1972 convention, the party voted to expel those who insisted on remaining members of Waffle. After some delay and recrimination, the party got its wish. The more radical Wafflers left to form a short-lived party. Others accepted the discipline of party organization and went on to work within the mainline party. The Old Left had tamed the barbarians!

Many were critical of the NDP for its failure to live up to its radical origins. Cy Gonick wrote in *Canadian Dimension* of the 'dull conservatism' of the leadership of the party.[88] 'In its endless search for respectability and electoral success,' wrote historian Michael Cross in 1973, 'Canadian social democracy has ended as a tail of the Liberal Party in Parliament.'[89] On the other hand, the party leadership dismissed Waffle as an academically based flight of fancy. The real significance of Waffle, however, may be as a transition between the politics of the street and that of the ballot box. The high hopes and ultimate defeat of Waffle provided a dose of reality to youth interested in reform. The ability of the party to assert control stands as a proxy for what was happening in society generally through the early 1970s. For, if the NDP was unwilling to accept 'the revolution,' then society was certainly an unlikely convert. The great revolution was just not going to happen, and the end of that notion, however vaguely held, may be the real end of the 1960s.

Yet the Waffle movement was also a bridge. Having shed their most romantic and radical elements, many other New Leftists remained in the NDP. Especially in Ontario and British Columbia, they would accentuate the intellectual, urban, middle-class side of the party. David Lewis was succeeded by Ed Broadbent, former university lecturer and a short-time member of the Waffle. Steven Langdon fulfilled his own prediction by moving into the party and being elected to the federal Parliament. By the 1990s the Ontario government would be headed for a term by a former University of Toronto student activist, Bob Rae. As a whole, the Ontario NDP government was as much urban professional and intellectual as blue collar or agrarian, an issue that became very apparent in the sharp divisions over the so-called social contract.

Waffle may also reflect a general trend of the later 1960s and early 1970s. The rise of the 'three wise men' in the Liberal party, and especially the leadership of Pierre Trudeau, made that party attractive for younger university-educated Canadians of less radical inclinations than the Wafflers. 'Trudeaumania' was a transient phenomenon, and Trudeau would never meet the expectations of reformers, but he did transcend the cultural gap between generations. Polls taken before the Liberal leadership convention among 'young Canadians' indicated an overwhelming preference for Trudeau.[90] As one enthusiastic young journalist gushed, 'the prospect of Pierre Elliott Trudeau becoming Prime Minister of Canada, to someone of my age and inclinations ... is the most exciting single thing that could happen to this country.' He was young (at least in appearance), 'modish,' and, most of all, 'the intellectual as activist.'[91] Here was a man that appeared to be cognizant of modern style, dress, and rhetoric. The fact that, in October 1970, he unleashed the full force of the state against the FLQ does not really distract from the trend. For here was, at a more serious level, the lesson that had been preached by university administrations over the past year or so: Reform was acceptable, but anybody moving beyond acceptable limits would face an immediate and harsh response.

OPEN THE PAGES OF, SAY, *Georgia Straight* and *Sports Illustrated* in 1968. The cultural divide is obvious. Clothes, demeanour, and, most of all, hair separates the counter-cultural world of rock and 'jock.' Moreover, the symbolism would have been clear to all the readers. The clothes and hair were more than just the accident of fashion. They were shorthand for a way of life, an attitude towards the 'system.' The shorthand would also have been confirmed in the language of the two magazines. The former talks the rhetoric of alienation and rebellion. The latter talks of competition and money. Open the same two magazines in 1973. Bright bell bottoms adorn the golfers. Black basketball players sport Afro haircuts. *Georgia Straight*, for its part, has become more commercial – more an arts-and-entertainment magazine than a rebellious expression of the counter-culture. The arrival of Disco, and the 'Glam' rock of Garry Glitter or even David (Ziggy Stardust) Bowie, indicates that rock had evolved to a new and somewhat less elemental form. 'The late sixties notion of rock-culture as pop-culture was coming to an end.'[92]

The narrowing of the gap between the world of the counter-culture and the world of sports is symbolic of wider changes. Through the early to mid-1970s, the culture of youthful rebellion and the adult mainstream drew together. This holds whether one looks at dope, sexual attitudes, style, or music. Rock and roll, for example, was now a respectable adult medium. After all, the teenagers of Elvis's day were now well into their thirties. The same was true of the politics of style. This was an age that celebrated youth, and it is hardly surprising that, after initial cries of outrage, the adult world began to emulate their younger (and more numerous) counterparts. Canada's prime minister now had hair that would have been considered outrageous on a twenty-year-old just a few years earlier. Suits had bell-bottom pants and were worn with wide paisley ties. All of this made it hard to maintain clothing as a political symbol. For younger boomers moving into the rebellious world of adolescence, it would take the nihilism of the Sex Pistols and punk rock to obtain at least a modicum of reaction from a society that had seen so much in recent years.

Dope would never be accepted by the mainstream in the same way as clothes or music. In spite of various calls to legalize marijuana, drugs remained illegal, and arrest levels remained high. Even here, though, the divide was not as great as it had been. The mainstream, for its part, gave up on its futile quest to have youth believe that marijuana was the same as speed or heroin. Instead a new accommodation was reached. Enforcement agencies relaxed their attitude towards 'soft drugs,' and the university and young-adult boomers backed away from earlier wide-open enthusiasm for all drug experimentation. Cocaine, a trendy drug of the 1970s, remained contested ground, but the accommodation generally held.

This is not to say that the world of the 1970s dismissed the 1960s as if it had never occurred. A great deal had changed. In some cases, as in the women's movement, environmentalism, and gay rights, issues raised in the 1960s gained momentum. In other instances, issues ceased to be controversial simply because they had been accepted by society as a whole – premarital sex being one obvious example, and rock music another. Both these examples, though, are evidence that the 1970s were different in that the issues were no longer defined by the baby boom. Older Canadians picked up notions that originally been identified with youth, and youth found that maybe there were those over thirty who could be trusted after all.

The mingling of politics and culture also had to do with the mingling of generations. By the mid-1970s the front edge of the baby-boomers were in their early thirties. Even for those who had stayed around university and graduate school, the realities of the adult world – marriage, jobs, and children – were now a part of daily life. As one anonymous student radical of the sixties replied when I asked why he ceased to be active in the seventies, 'It was time to get a job.'

That realization was part of the natural course of the life cycle. It was accelerated, however, by coincidence. Throughout their childhood and adolescence, the baby-boomers had lived in a time of remarkable affluence and growth. Now, just as they approached the adult world, the long era of economic prosperity came to an end. In 1970 and 1971 unemployment began to rise. By 1972 economists were talking about 'stagflation' to refer to the theoretical impossibility of slow growth, high unemployment, and high inflation which plagued Canada. Unemployment climbed from 4.7 per cent in 1969 to 6.3 per cent in 1972. More significant, among young males unemployment stood at 11.6 per cent by the latter year, more than twice what it had been five years earlier.[93] Inflation, which went up 38 per cent in the four years between 1971 and 1975, threatened to put large-ticket items like houses out of reach. Many boomers began to understand at least a little of the desire for a steady job, a home, and material well-being that had so influenced their parents.

By this time, at any rate, the great generation was well and truly divided. The older edges had merged – a few communes aside – into the world of work and family, albeit in somewhat different forms from the work and families of their parents. The younger boomers went through adolescence in a much more uncertain economy and without the spotlight of their older siblings. Demographically the baby boom continued to be a clear bulge of population. Economically it continued to pose difficult questions for society. Culturally, though, the image of the generation had become fuzzy. The baby boom had grown up.

Epilogue: A World without Limits

Concluding the story of a generation that is at the dominant point in its life cycle is an intimidating task. What, after all, can be said when the story is not yet over? What firm statements can be made about the significance of a life under way? One temptation is to conclude with anodyne noises about 'no firm conclusion being possible.' Yet, that is untrue. For, in some very fundamental ways, the world of the baby boom of the 1950s and 1960s was unique, and that uniqueness disappeared sometime during the 1970s. It will not return.

To link the 1950s and the 1960s so directly is unorthodox. Those two decades are the great divide, the 'geologic fault' in the baby-boomers' youth. Much of the story of the 1960s, after all, is one of youth reacting against the world of their childhood – suburbia, conformity, and domesticity. In their reaction many of them concluded that the flaws in Western society were not incidental but purposeful. The dark forces of technocracy, the establishment, and reactionary thinking perpetuated injustice amid democracy, and poverty amid plenty. The youth rebellion rejected the earlier rationalist sensibilities and emphasized a romantic idealism. The power of youth, as well as, some might say, the indulgence of authority, ensured that youth rebellion preoccupied society as a whole. This is the standard picture – the 1960s as rebellion against the 1950s; the baby boom as breaking free (for better or worse, depending on the point of view) from the confines of the domestic world.

In this book I have argued that there are elements of truth in this view but, as well, that many things connect the 1950s to the 1960s. Most obviously, there was the baby boom itself. Parents and professionals came out of the war asserting that the first postwar children were special. Aspirations built through years of scarcity and disruption were transferred to home and to children. The world of suburbia and the world of television reinforced the message given by parents and teachers. Soon the children picked up the clues. They learned something of the power they had as a group. When they decided that Davy Crockett hats or Barbie dolls were essential personal possessions, the fad swept the continent. Nothing here was conscious on the part of the children. They just lived in a world where they, collectively, if not individually, counted for a great deal.

This sense of being special provides the first link between the 1950s and the 1960s. By the latter decade, of course, the baby-boomers themselves were claiming a special historical destiny. They would convert the lessons of the parents into practice and convert the material prosperity of the Western world into something both widely distributed and closely linked to personal well-being. Slogans abounded. They were the 'Woodstock generation,' 'the revolution,' 'the counterculture.' Beneath it all, though, they were fulfilling their destiny as the generation that would create something new and better.

Also linking the 1950s to the 1960s was the size of the baby boom. The impact of the generation on the demography of Canadian society was immense. In 1966 half the population of Canada was under the age of twenty-one! Twenty years earlier the comparable figure was 37 per cent, and twenty years later it would be only 29 per cent. These numbers explain something of the obsession of Canada with youth in the 1950s and 1960s. The older cohorts were overwhelmed. For a period of twenty to twenty-five years, not only was there demographic imbalance, but that imbalance tilted the values and politics of the Canadian nation towards the values and politics of Canadian youth.

Finally, there was the economic affluence of the postwar years. This has been discussed at some length as a feature shaping the role and purpose of the baby boom. The long cycle of prosperity and growth after the war, though, is a crucial signpost in Canadian social history. Before 1945, children and youth grew up amid economic uncertainty and disruption. After 1972, it was true, things were far better than in the 1930s or 1940s but compared with the era that had just ended, the economy seemed once again to have entered turbulent times. Inflation ran upward to double digits, pushing housing and other large-ticket items out of sight for many of the young. Unemployment reached levels unheard of since the Depression. Worst of all for the younger baby-boomers, the workforce was filled by their slightly older peers.

In between is the exception. In the twenty-five years from the beginning of the baby boom until the early 1970s, the Canadian GNP increased more than threefold, even after the effects of inflation have been removed.[1] This allowed the standard of living of the average Canadian to double in the same period. In this sense there is little to differentiate the 1950s and 1960s, for in both decades prosperity and more or less continuous improvement in the standard of living was the norm; recession the relatively short-lived exception.

Of course, to children, or even adolescents, job figures and per-capita income mean little. Continuous affluence and confidence in the future of the economy, though, show in people's daily lives. Things came to the family. Technology and a rising standard of living meant that material well-being improved considerably – gas or oil heating, a car, maybe a second car later, a television, multiple radios, and a larger house were all part of the expectations. David Potter, the American historian, has speculated on the psychological implications of affluence on the postwar generation.[2] Even if we avoid personal psychology, however, one speculation is fairly safe: To those growing up in these years, the Western world seemed to have almost endless ability to produce goods and to supply wants. Much of the faith in the future of the children and, a little later, the student insistence that all should share in the cornucopia, is surely related to this belief in the tremendous productivity of Western society. This was a materially blessed generation but, more than that, to the young all the evidence was that such material blessings were more or less automatic.

The youthful nature of the population, the sense that a 'special generation' was growing to adulthood, and the prosperity of these years led to the most fundamentally unifying force of all. From the end of the war until the 1970s, Canadians believed in their own ability to make their personal and collective lives better. For both parents and children, the new world of the postwar era was one without limits. The individual might experience restrictions, but the potential of society to change, to improve, to build, to get better seemed almost infinite. Gallup polls revealed Canadians to be, 'staunchly optimistic.' At one point, at the beginning of the 1960s, an amazing 95 per cent of Canadians considered themselves happy, the highest percentage of any country polled. As a poll in 1962 concluded, 'Canadians are not only cheerier than most other countries in their hopes for the future but a close second to the U.S.A. in several household possessions.'[3]

The sense of the raw potential of Canada, and of its people, was a legacy of the war and a part of the yearning for a better world. Yet the idea was successfully transmitted from 1945 through the 1960s – reinforced by rising standards of living and considerable economic growth. In the 1950s, of course, the enthusiasm for the future often displayed itself as an almost naïve interest in gadgets and technology – even the technology of chrome fins and electric swizzle sticks. In the 1960s, the sense of potential more often concentrated on the spirit of the people (especially the young people) and sought to tie technology to personal growth. 'If junk consumption decreased,' wrote one reporter in the underground press in 1970, 'the work week will some day average ten hours.'[4]

Even the distinction between 1950s technology and 1960s romanticism may overstate the difference between the two decades. After all, as I have argued throughout this book, people in the 1950s were tremendously concerned with the inner spirit. The works of Freud and other psychologists were consumed avidly in the quest to understand the mysterious balance that creates the harmonious human being. In the 1960s the techniques changed. The fact that the spirit was dressed up in Freudian terms in the 1950s and paraded as spontaneity or authenticity, or even as LSD, in the 1960s doesn't change the fact that both decades were searching for personal well-being. The baby boom's emphasis on the human spirit flows in a direct line from their parents' belief in the fragile nature of the human consciousness.

Finally, both the 1950s and 1960s drew sharp lines between youth and adult society. The fears of juvenile delinquency, dating back to the Second World War, the rise of rock and roll, and, most of all, the powerful baby boom accentuated the differences between the world of the adults and that of the children. This reached its peak, of course, in the 1960s, when youth not only demanded independence but asserted the primacy of their own culture and fashion. The 1950s were filiocentric. The 1960s were dominated by the issues and tastes of the young.

It is hard to carry any of these points of unity very far into the 1970s. As was discussed above, the great growth cycle in the economy was coming to an uncertain end. The unstoppable 'youth revolution' was increasingly met by the determination of the liberal-capitalist system to maintain its own existence. The counter-culture found that utopia wasn't quite so easily maintained as had seemed the case in Haight-Ashbury or Yorkville in 1967. Violence, greed, and drug addiction shattered the naïve idealism of the earlier years.

Most of all, though, the generation was no longer unified. In the

1960s both the proponents and detractors of the 'youth revolution' acted as though a permanent line had been drawn through history. Those born before a magic date were, in the majority, people with traditional sensibilities. Those born after, whatever the exceptions, would develop into a growing force for change. René Lévesque of the Parti Québécois, to give one example, predicted the inevitable triumph of separatism because young people were more prone to separatism than were the old. And, he said, there were new young people being added every day. Such statements implied two things: that every new baby born was a recruit for an essentially baby-boom view of the world, and that the baby-boomers would forever demonstrate young and reformist tendencies. Neither prediction was correct.

First, though many causes of the 1990s have roots in the concerns of the 1960s – environmentalism and feminism come to mind as examples – the generation has not assumed a permanently radical stance on society, politics, or any other issue.[5] Traditional adult concerns about career, family, status, and security have become more important as time has gone on. The generation yielded its idealism and romanticism to pragmatism and realism. Those who, a quarter of a century ago, believed all things were possible approach the end of the century with a not-inconsiderable amount of gloom.[6] Even more obvious, not every baby born since about 1945 has identified with the baby boom. As mentioned in the introduction, later boomers and the famous Generation Xers have felt little attraction for the romantic idealism of the 1960s.

All of this meant that the 'youth cult' of the 1960s did not hold. As baby-boomers aged, so too did society, psychologically and physically. For the one thing that held constant was the imbalance in age cohorts. As figure 12.1 indicates, a significant benchmark was established in 1986, when, for the first time since the end of the baby boom, the number of Canadians under the magic age of thirty were now in a minority. In recent years most of the writing on the baby boom has had to do with age rather than youth, pensions rather than education.[7] In that sense the baby boom remains constant. It takes society's concerns with it through the life cycle. The growing conservatism of the 1980s and 1990s may have as much to do with the age of the population as with the level of government deficits.

The most important change, though, may not be demographic, though it is related, or economic, though it is related as well. Instead, it is psychological. Faith in the future and in the limitless potential for

FIGURE 12.1
Ratio of Canadians under Thirty to Those over Thirty

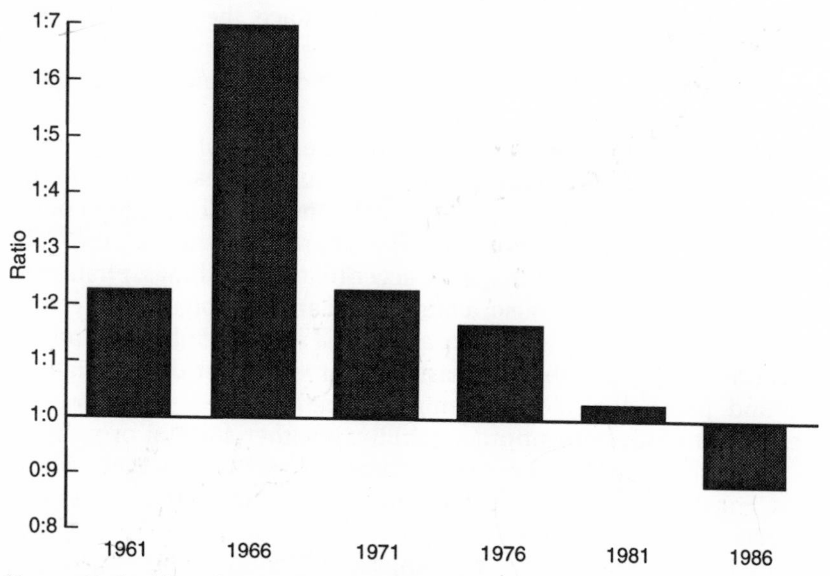

Source: Derived from *Canada Year Book*, 1963–88

change has collapsed, replaced by a more modest sense of limits, or by an even more restrictive cynicism. Over the twenty years after 1970, limits appeared on a previously unlimited horizon. Indeed, the apocalyptic rhetoric of the end of the 1960s marked a transition point for an era and for a generation. The expectations altered and narrowed. The idea that there would be a 'revolution' faded, and the notion of a grand movement divided into various subsidiary causes, labelled in a more cynical age 'special-interest groups.' The baby-boom generation is now in control but seems uncertain it can really make any sort of difference.

Was everything ephemeral, then? Does the youth of the baby boom have any longer-term historical significance? Did the great changes of the 1950s and 1960s lead anywhere? Common sense would say yes. The legacy of these decades is everywhere, and in many instances has spread from the baby boom to become universal within Canadian society. The continuing enthusiasm for self-help, consciousness raising, awareness, and popular psychology in general has connections to the spirit of both the 1950s and the 1960s. Likewise, notions of class have been challenged by different visions of social structure. The most significant social debates of the last two decades turn on sensibilities raised by the baby boom through the 1960s. Race, the place of women and of other unequal or marginalized groups, environmentalism, and many other issues remain at the forefront of discussion. None of them was important before 1960.

As well, the changes undergone during the youth of the baby boom have had an enduring effect. Most consequentially, the life cycle of the baby boom marks the swing of the social pendulum from a high point of orthodoxy to one of heterodoxy. The Depression, the war, the Cold War, and the new-found prosperity accentuated two things. First, people wanted security – a house, a family, and an unambiguous direction in life. The family was the vehicle, and social values reinforced notions of security by placing the emphasis on home, gender differentiation, job, and psychological well-being. A need for security, however, doesn't rest easily with unpredictability, whether societal or individual. Similarly, the political climate of the Cold War discouraged radical ideas. For these reasons the second mark of the postwar era was conformity.

Occasionally writers have challenged this notion, pointing to the beatnik movement or other signs of dissent. Of course there was dissent and there were differences, even wild eccentrics. Still, any examination of the social structures of the years before 1960 and those after 1970 or so reveals startling differences. Diversity in values, in personal style, and in social structures is much more a mark of recent years. Heterodoxy is everywhere – family structures, sexual values, job market, immigration rules and, from that, ethnic make-up. Even at the most mundane levels of dress, one need only observe the catwalk parade of a city street and compare it with any photograph of the 1950s to see a visible example of diversification.

Fashion in this case is but a symbol of something more profound. A fundamental shift took place between the end of the war and the 1970s. In the earlier period the assumption was that social rules and social conventions existed for a larger purpose. Those who did not fit in should change their habits, their dress, or their values. This was the essence of William Whyte's famous 'organization man.' For those that could not 'adjust' (such as those of different skin colour), society preached tolerance but didn't expect real equality. For those who didn't even try, there was scorn or worse.

For the baby-boomers the perspective was different. Though they began life in this postwar world, they were the children of affluence. They were also the post-Holocaust generation, taught that authority must be held up to moral judgment. They were the Spock and pop-psychology generation, taught that personal well-being was an inner force rather than a mere matter of food, clothing, and peace. They entered their teens as the emphasis on security and conformity began to wear thin. Generalizations must be made with care but, on balance, the baby boom grew up believing more than their parents had that personal emotional and psychic satisfaction was central to life. If society didn't meet the needs, then society should adjust. Certainly deference to authority and to established rules has never been a part of the baby boom's generational character. If a person or a group does not fit into society, then the assumption is that society must adjust its perspective. The generation that always felt it belonged has taken on as a fundamental social value the notion that belonging matters.

The generation, then, has had a significant impact, not just on institutions which continually adjust to demographic imperatives, but on social values. The changes are likely to echo long after the last baby-boomer has departed the scene. It is not a contradiction, though, to say that the main impact of the generation for change lies in its past rather than its future or present. Indeed, the most striking thing about the story of the baby-boomers is that their great historical moment came before most of them were twenty-one. The generation that took so much pride in its youth now looks back with a degree of nostalgia to the time when all things lay before it and all things seemed possible.

Notes

Preface

1 Herbert Moller, 'Youth as a Force in the Modern World,' *Comparative Studies in Society and History. An International Quarterly* 10 (April 1968), 254
2 Landon Jones, *Great Expectations. America and the Baby Boom Generation* (New York 1980), 3
3 McLuhan to Philip and Molly Deane, 15 December 1967, in Matie Molinaro, Corinne McLuhan, and William Toye, eds., *Letters of Marshall McLuhan* (Toronto 1987), 348
4 Nicholas von Hoffman, *We Are the People Our Parents Warned Us Against* (Chicago 1968)
5 Anthony Esler, *Generations in History: An Introduction to the Concept* (n.p. 1982), 44
6 The statement is by Robert Wohl and is cited by William Strauss and Neil Howe in *Generations: The History of America's Future* (New York 1991), 19.
7 Karl Mannheim, *Essays on the Sociology of Knowledge* (London 1952), 303
8 François Ricard, in *La Génération lyrique. Essai sur la vie et l'oeuvre des premiers nés du baby-boom* (Montreal 1992), makes the same distinction between early and late baby-boomers in his discussion of Quebec youth in these years.

1: Home and Family at Mid-Century

1 Charles had written a well-known study of the demography of the United Kingdom: *The Twilight of Parenthood* (London 1934). For a discussion of Charles in the Britain see Jane Lewis, *The Politics of Motherhood: Child and Maternal Welfare in England, 1900–1939* (London 1980), 38–9.

2 Enid Charles, *The Changing Size of the Family in Canada,* Census Monograph no. 1 (Ottawa 1948), 33
3 The main sources for these general figures on the baby boom come from F.H. Leacy, ed., *Historical Statistics of Canada,* 2d ed. (Ottawa 1983) [hereinafter *Historical Statistics of Canada*], Tables B1–14; Wolfgang Illing, *Population, Family, Household and Labour Force Growth to the 1980s,* Economic Council of Canada Study no. 19 (Ottawa 1967); Jacques Henripin, *Trends and Factors of Fertility* (Ottawa 1961); and *Canada Year Book,* 1947–60.
4 Henripin, *Trends and Factors,* 313, table 11.1
5 Eric R. Adams, 'Born to Mr and Mrs Canada 300,000 Babies,' *Maclean's,* 15 May 1947, 22+. As an example of child-oriented stories see 'No Home Should Be Without One,' ibid., 1 June 1948, 9+.
6 Sun Life advertisement, *Saturday Night,* 14 June 1947, 31
7 See, for example, Ruth MacLachlan Frank, MD, 'A Note to Brides: Don't Delay Parenthood,' *Chatelaine,* May 1946, 29+.
8 Henry Bowman, *Marriage for Moderns,* 3d ed. (Toronto 1954), 490, and Clifford Adams, 'How to Keep Your Mate,' *Maclean's,* 1 February 1946, 32.
9 *Maclean's,* 15 June 1945, front cover; 15 October 1945, inside back cover
10 'Morning,' *Chatelaine,* June 1945, 26
11 Adele White, 'When That Man's Home Again,' ibid., February 1945, 23
12 Community Silverware ad, 'Back Home for Keeps,' *Star Weekly Magazine,* 6 October 1945, 32
13 That is, those born between 1910 and 1925
14 C.P. Stacey, *Arms, Men and Governments: The War Policies of Canada, 1939–1945* (Ottawa 1970), 48, 66
15 *Historical Statistics of Canada,* tables B75–81
16 This phenomenon was also present in the United States. See Elaine Tyler May, *Homeward Bound: American Families in the Cold War Era* (New York 1988), 60
17 Ruth Roach Pierson, in '*They're Still Women after All': The Second World War and Canadian Womanhood* (Toronto 1986), details the experience of women in wartime work.
18 Privy Council of Canada, *Canadian War Orders and Regulations, 1942* (Ottawa 1943), Department of Munitions and Supply, Transit Controller, 31 October 1942, Transit Order 3-B
19 Maud Ferguson, 'Wartime Living in Canada,' *Canadian Affairs* 1/4 (15 June 1943), 5
20 National Archives of Canada [hereinafter NAC], Records of the Canadian Youth Commission (MG 28, I 11), vol. 42, file 6: 'Report of the City Council's

Survey Committee on Housing Conditions in Toronto, 1942–3,' 27–8. The definition of 'overcrowding' was more than one person per room in an apartment or house. See also, in the same file, Triangle Forum Club, 'A Brief to the Canadian Youth Commission on the Importance of an Adequate Housing Program in Canada' (April 1944).

21 See advertisement in *Saturday Night*, 10 March 1945, 44. On the state of housing crisis at end of war see NAC, Arthur McNamara to W.C. Clark, 22 May 1945, Records of the Department of Finance, vol. 3980, Folder 'Housing.'

22 Canadian Youth Commission, *Youth, Marriage and Family* (Toronto 1948), 42

23 *Star Weekly Magazine*, 10 November 1945, 6

24 John Sirjmaki, 'Culture Configurations in the American Family,' A*merican Journal of Sociology* 53 (1947–8), 464–70. See also May, *Homeward Bound*, 9–10.

25 Henry Bowman, 'How Can You Tell If It Is Love?,' in Morris Fishbein, *Successful Marriage: A Modern Guide to Love, Sex, and Family Life* (Garden City, NY, 1955), 5–6. See also his *Marriage for Moderns* (Toronto 1948).

26 Hilda Holland, ed., *Why Are You Single?* (New York 1949), vii, ix

27 Judson Landis and Mary Landis, *Building a Successful Marriage*, 2d ed. (Englewood Cliffs, NJ, 1953), 48. This social attitude was confirmed by a study done in 1957. See Gerald Gurin, Joseph Veroff, and Sheila Field, *Americans View Their Mental Health* (New York 1960), 117.

28 Ad for Listerine mouthwash, *Star Weekly Magazine*, 8 September 1945

29 Paul Ernst, 'No Time to Waste,' *Chatelaine*, May 1945, 6; Nell Young, 'Don't Break My Heart,' ibid., November 1948, 27

30 *Chatelaine*, September 1945, 2; A.B. McKillop, *Matters of Mind: The University in Ontario, 1791–1951* (Toronto 1994), 555

31 NAC, Records of the Canadian Youth Commission (MG 28, I 11), vol. 72, manuscript by G. Watson, 'This Is Youth Getting Down to a Career,' 98

32 Theodore Reck, 'The Chip on the Shoulder,' in Holland, ed., *Why Are You Single?*, 10

33 Jean and Eugene Benge, *Win Your Man and Keep Him* (Chicago 1948); cited in May, *Homeward Bound*, 102

34 Theodore Reck, 'The Marriage Shyness of the Male,' in Holland, ed., *Why Are You Single?*, 25, 29

35 Watson, 'This Is Youth Getting Down to a Career,' 86–7

36 Abraham Stone,' Celibate Facts and Fancies,' in Holland, ed., *Why Are You Single?*, 42

37 Bowman, *Marriage for Moderns*, 68

38 Doug Owram, *The Government Generation: Canadian Intellectuals and the State, 1900–1945* (Toronto 1986), 293–4
39 Ibid., 290–2
40 'The Great American Boom,' *Star Weekly Magazine*, 27 July 1946
41 Canada, Department of Finance, *Quarterly Review*, June 1989 reference tables
42 On the economy generally see Robert Bothwell, Ian Drummond, and John English, *Canada since 1945: Power, Politics, and Provincialism*, rev. ed. (Toronto 1989), 15–21; and Kenneth Norrie and Doug Owram, *A History of the Canadian Economy* (Toronto 1991), ch. 20.
43 *Historical Statistics of Canada*, tables B1–14, documents crude birth rate.
44 Z.E. Zsigmond and C.J. Wenaas, *Enrolment in Educational Institutions by Province, 1951–52 to 1980–81*, Economic Council of Canada Staff Study no. 25 (Ottawa 1970), 11
45 *Historical Statistics of Canada*, table W20
46 Jacques Henripin argues that the baby boom was in reality a marriage boom. See his *Trends and Factors of Fertility in Canada*, 335–7.
47 *Historical Statistics of Canada*, tables B75–81
48 Daniel Kubat and David Thornton, *A Statistical Profile of Canadian Society* (Toronto 1974), table H6
49 Peter Ward, *Courtship, Love and Marriage in the Nineteenth Century* (Toronto 1990), provides a good overview of marriage expectations and their changes over the period before 1914.
50 Paula Fass, *The Damned and the Beautiful: American Youth in the 1920s* (New York 1977), also argues that the modern but specialized family was a creation of the 1920s. On fertility, family size, and so on see Henripin, *Trends and Factors of Fertility in Canada*, 28–30.
51 John Levy and Ruth Munroe, *The Happy Family* (New York 1959; 1st ed. 1938), 43
52 On Freudianism in North America, see ch. 2.
53 The classic of this sort of study is Robert Lynd Staughton, *Middletown: A Study in Contemporary American Culture* (New York 1929).
54 Veronica Strong-Boag, 'Intruders in the Nursery: Child Care Professionals Reshape the Years One to Five, 1920–1940,' in Joy Parr, ed., *Childhood and Family in Canadian History* (Toronto 1982), 160–78. For a full study of the attempt to professionalize motherhood see the British study by Jane Lewis, *The Politics of Motherhood* (Montreal and Kingston 1980).
55 'Proceedings of the First Annual Meeting of the National Conference on Family Relations,' *Journal of Marriage and the Family* 1/1 (January 1939), 30–3

56 Beth Bailey, *From Front Porch to Back Seat: Courtship in Twentieth-Century America* (Baltimore 1988), 131–3

57 Ibid., 122

58 NAC, Records of the Canadian Youth Commission, vol. 42, file 7: 'Report of the Halifax Regional Youth Conference,' 1944

59 The next few paragraphs attempt to draw a composite picture of the advice given by marriage manuals such as Henry Bowman's, *Marriage for Moderns*; Judson Landis and Mary Landis's, *Building a Successful Marriage*; John Levy and Ruth Munroe's, *The Happy Family*; Norman Hines's, *Your Marriage* (New York 1955); and Morris Fishbein's, *Successful Marriage: A Modern Guide to Love, Sex and Family Life* (Garden City, NY, 1955); by family texts such as Joseph Kirk Folsom's, *The Family and Democratic Society* (New York 1944), and B.R. Jordan, M.L. Ziller, and J.F. Brown Brown's *Home and Family* (New York 1936); and by the studies of the Canadian Youth Commission, especially *Youth, Marriage and Family* and Mary Vicker's 'I Learned to Live with a Man,' *Chatelaine*, March 1950, 63.

60 The experts also saw sexual activity as something improvable by science. Thus, in 1948, the *International Journal of Sexology* was founded in the United States.

61 Veronica Strong-Boag, 'Home Dreams: Women and the Suburban Experiment in Canada, 1945–60,' *Canadian Historical Review* 62/4 (December 1991), 476. Note also the comment by Elaine Tyler May (*Homeward Bound*, 56) to the effect that the two striking characteristics of the 1950s family were a degree of equality and a separation of roles.

62 *Annual Report of the Civil Service Commission for 1935* (Ottawa 1935), 12

63 Bowman, *Marriage for Moderns*, 320

64 Levy and Munroe, *The Happy Family*, 59

65 Anonymous, 'My Marriage Was a War Casualty,' *Chatelaine*, December 1945, 60

66 Delys Kirk, 'Home the Hero,' *Star Weekly Magazine*, 20 October 1945

67 On the origins of the film see Joseph C. Goulden, *The Best Years, 1945–1950* (New York 1976), 4–5.

68 Frank Flaherty, 'Rehabilitation,' *Canadian Affairs* 1/7 (1 August 1943), 1. See also Robert England, *Discharged: A Commentary on Civil Re-establishment of Veterans in Canada* (Toronto 1943).

69 Terry Copp and Bill McAndrew, *Battle Exhaustion: Soldiers and Psychiatrists in the Canadian Army, 1939–1945* (Montreal and Kingston 1990)

70 Major-General G.B. Chisholm, 'Psychological Adjustment of Soldiers to Army and to Civilian Life,' *American Journal of Psychiatry* 101 (1944–5), 300–2. See also Brigadier J.C. Meakins, 'The Returning Serviceman and His

Problems,' *Canadian Medical Association Journal* 51/3 (September 1944), 195–202; D. Ewen Cameron, 'The Reintegration of the War Veteran in Industry,' *Canadian Medical Association Journal* 51/3 (September 1944), 202–6.

71 Barry Broadfoot, *The Veterans' Years* (Vancouver 1985), 38–9

72 On sex and the armies overseas see John Costello, *Virtue under Fire: How World War 2 Changed Our Social and Sexual Attitudes* (Boston 1985), chs. 13–15.

73 Canada, Privy Council, *Canadian War Orders and Regulations, 1942* (Ottawa 1943), Transit Order 3-B. See also May, *Homeward Bound,* 76–8, on the generally similar American response.

74 'Teenage Special: Looking Ahead to Your Job,' *Chatelaine,* May 1945, 13

75 Velia Ercole, 'Woman Set Free,' *Chatelaine,* October 1945, 6. For a real-life version of this attitude see May, *Homeward Bound,* 81.

76 Elizabeth Hawes, 'Women Will Not Go Back in the Kitchen,' *Star Weekly Magazine,* 8 December 1945, and Katherine Kent, 'Dames at Desks,' *Maclean's,* 15 January 1945, 10–11

77 See the interviews with working women by the Canadian Youth Commission, printed as Appendix B in its *Youth, Marriage and Family,* 214–19.

78 Margaret Francis, 'Nostalgia,' *Chatelaine,* November 1946, 16. See also Douglas MacFarlane, 'Operation Civvy,' *Maclean's,* 1 April 1946, 20.

79 Ruth Fenisong, 'The Job,' *Star Weekly Magazine,* 2 February 1946, 1

80 *Historical Statistics of Canada,* tables B75–81. See, for contemporary comment, A. Foster, 'Poets Sing of Great Loves But the Divorce Courts Are Crowded,' *Saturday Night,* 23 February 1946, 28–9.

81 Alison Prentice, Paula Bourne, Gail Cuthbert Brandt, Beth Light, Wendy Mitchinson, and Naomi Black, *Canadian Women: A History* (Toronto 1988), table A.14, 422

82 Sidney Katz, 'Why Women Are Going Out to Work,' *Maclean's,* 15 May 1951, 7–9+

2: Babies

1 Paul Popinoe, 'First Aid for the Family,' *Maclean's,* 1 May 1947, 19+, 45

2 F.H. Leacy, ed., *Historical Statistics of Canada,* 2d ed. (Ottawa 1983), table B14

3 Eric R. Adams, 'Born to Mr and Mrs Canada 300,000 Babies,' *Maclean's,* 15 May 1947, 22+

4 Gallup Organization, *Public Opinion, 1935–1971,* Poll, 10 March 1957: 'Most popular names for the years 1946–1956,' 1473. Note that this is a U.S. poll.

5 Veronica Strong-Boag, 'Intruders in the Nursery: Child Care Professionals Reshape the Years One to Five, 1920–1940,' in Joy Parr, ed., *Childhood and Family in Canadian History* (Toronto 1982), discusses the earlier phases of this professionalization. Note the comment about the postwar dependence upon child-care expertise of one upper-middle-class Toronto community in John R. Seeley, R. Alexander Sim, and E.W. Loosley, *Crestwood Heights: A Study of the Culture of Suburban Life* (Toronto 1956), 194.

6 Landon Jones, *Great Expectations: America and the Baby Boom Generation* (New York 1980), 54

7 *Alberta Home and School Association News*, November-December 1955, 1, contains the listing of programs mentioned above.

8 See, on this issue, Jay Mechling, 'Advice to Historians on Advice to Mothers,' *Journal of Social History* 9 (Fall 1975), 44–63.

9 On the problem of the historian and the implication of social conventions see Beth Bailey, *From Front Porch to Back Seat: Courtship in Twentieth-Century America* (Baltimore 1988), 4; on the postwar regard for experts see Elaine Tyler May, *Homeward Bound: American Families in the Cold War* (New York 1988), 26

10 John Cleverly and D.C. Philips, *Visions of Childhood: Influential Models from Locke to Spock* (New York 1986), and Mary Cable, '*Little Darlings': A History of Child Rearing in America* (New York 1972), provide two brief and readable overviews of child rearing over the last three centuries. Neil Sutherland, *Children in English Canadian Society: Framing the Twentieth Century Consensus* (Toronto 1976), provides a Canadian perspective on the previous century.

11 Edwards cited in Arnold Gesell and Frances Ilg, *Infant and Child Care in the Culture of Today: The Guidance of Development in Home and Nursery School* (New York 1943), 287. Wesley cited in Cleverly and Philips, *Visions of Childhood*, 29

12 Cable, '*Little Darlings*,' 165–6. For a relatively late example of this attitude see Province of Ontario, Department of Health, *The Baby* (Toronto 1943), 45.

13 John B. Watson, *Psychological Care of Infant and Child* (New York 1928)

14 Helen MacMurchy, *How to Take Care of Baby* (Ottawa 1931)

15 Cited in Jane Lewis, *The Politics of Motherhood: Child and Maternal Welfare in England, 1900–1939* (London 1980), 92. The poem is from 1923.

16 Franz G. Alexander and S. Selesnick, *The History of Psychiatry* (New York 1966), Part III: 'The Freudian Age'

17 See David J. Murray, *A History of Western Psychology*, 2d ed. (Englewood Cliffs, NJ, 1988); A.A. Roback, *A History of American Psychology* (New York 1964), and J.A.C. Brown, *Freud and the Post-Freudians* (London 1961), 2.

18 Brown, *Freud and the Post-Freudians,* 2

19 Albert R. Gilgen, *American Psychology since World War II* (Westport, CT, 1982), 41–4

20 William O'Neill, *Coming Apart: An Informal History of America in the 1960s* (Toronto 1971), 203

21 Anna Freud, 'The Psycholanalytic Study of Infantile Feeding Problems,' in *The Writings of Anna Freud* (New York 1973; originally published in 1946), vol. 2, 39–59, 'Infants without Families: Reports on the Hamstead Nurseries 1939–1945,' in ibid., vol 3.

22 On Spock's training, see Benjamin Spock and Mary Morgan, *Spock on Spock: A Memoir of Growing Up with the Century* (New York 1985), chs. 8 and 9. See also Michael Sulman, 'The Humanization of the American Child: Benjamin Spock as a Popularizer of Psychoanalytic Thought,' *Journal of the History of the Behavioral Sciences* 9 (1983), 258–65.

23 Erik H. Erikson, *Childhood and Society* (New York 1950), 360

24 Edith Steils, 'Analysis of Psychogenic Constipation in a Two Year Old,' *The Psychoanalytic Study of the Child* 3 (1948–9), 227–52; M. Wulff, 'The Problem of Neurotic Manifestations in Children of Pre-Oedipal Age,' ibid., 6 (1951), 169–79; Thomas Petty, 'The Tragedy of Humpty Dumpty,' ibid., 8 (1953), 404–12

25 See B.K. Sandwell, 'Brock Chisholm vs Santa Claus,' *Saturday Night,* 22 December 1945, 10, and Mary Lowry Ross, 'Yes, Virginia, There Is Such a Thing as a Psychiatrist,' in ibid., 6 December 1945, 10.

26 Jocelyn B. Motyer Raymond, *The Nursery World of Dr. Blatz* (Toronto 1991)

27 W.E. Blatz, *Understanding the Young Child,* 2d ed. (London 1951), vii

28 Ibid., ix–xi

29 Canadian Youth Commission, *Youth, Marriage and Family* (Toronto 1948), 145

30 Alice Payne Hackett and James Henry Burke, *80 Years of Best Sellers, 1895–1975* (New York 1977). These sales figures are for the United States. Reports and comments in the Canadian magazines and press lead to the impression that big American sellers were also generally big Canadian sellers.

31 Ruth Honderich, 'Psychiatric Services in Community Chest,' *Saturday Night,* 27 September 1947, 16. See also Lister Sinclair, 'How Freud Changed Your Life,' *Maclean's,* 15 November 1950, 8–9+.

32 Earle Birney, 'Masters of the Id,' *Saturday Night,* 11 October 1947, 41; Pierre Berton, 'Phooey on Freud,' *Maclean's,* 1 May 1949, 60+

33 Cited in Cyril Levitt, *Children of Privilege: Student Revolt in the Sixties* (Toronto 1984), 15

34 This description of the trend towards environmentalism rests generally upon Hamilton Cravens's, *The Triumph of Evolution: The Heredity–Environment Controversy, 1900–1941* (Baltimore 1988).
35 Angus McLaren, *Our Own Master Race: Eugenics in Canada, 1885–1945* (Toronto 1990), deals with the eugenics movement in Canada.
36 Blatz, *Understanding the Young Child*, 36
37 Anna Freud, 'Infants without Families,' 662
38 Wini Breines, *Free, White and Miserable: Growing Up Female in the Fifties* (Boston 1992), 42
39 John Dollard, 'Do We Have a Science of Child Rearing,' in *The Family in a Democratic Society* (New York 1949), 52
40 Richard Jenkins, 'How Behavior Problems and Juvenile Delinquency Result from Inadequate Marital Adjustment,' in Morris Fishbein, ed., *Successful Marriage: A Modern Guide to Love, Sex and Family Life* (Garden City, NY, 1955), 381. See, for a practically identical statement, Ernest Groves, Ednal Skinner, and Sadie J. Swanson, *The Family and Its Relationships*, 3d ed. (Chicago 1953), 239–40.
41 J.T. Phair and N.R. Speirs, *Good Health Today* (Toronto 1960), 323–4
42 Christine Beasley, *Democracy in the Home* (New York 1954), 38. For a nice summary of the attitudes towards toilet training and other key events of early childhood, see Helen Leland Witmer and Ruth Kotinsky, *Personality in the Making: The Fact Finding Report of the Midcentury White House Conference on Children and Youth* (New York 1952), 11–19.
43 W.W. Bauer, MD, 'Children Are So Annoying,' *Maclean's*, 15 March 1947, 65
44 National Film Board *The Feeling of Rejection*, 1947, National Sound and Film Archives, 01VCV 8401 068-2
45 J.D. Ketchum, 'The Prude Is Father to the Pervert,' *Maclean's*, 15 January 1948, 9
46 Blatz, *Understanding the Young Child*, 81. See, as a good example of this type of literature in a popular magazine, Fritz Kahn, 'Let Your Child Grow Up,' *Maclean's*, 1 July 1949, 15+.
47 Philip Wylie, *Generation of Vipers* (New York 1942). See, for example, Erikson, *Childhood and Society*, 247–83.
48 Canadian Youth Commission, *Youth, Marriage and Family*, 72; Witmer and Kotinsky, *Personality in the Making*, 198–200
49 David M. Potter, *People of Plenty: Economic Abundance and the American Character* (Chicago 1954), 201–2
50 Christine Olden, 'Notes on Child Rearing in America,' *The Psychoanalytic Study of the Child* 7 (1953), 387–92, 388–9

51 Blatz, *Understanding the Young Child*, 17; Beasley, *Democracy in the Home*, 46
52 Raymond, *The Nursery World of Dr. Blatz*, 81–2
53 Brock Chisholm, 'Nine Ways to Stop Wars,' *Chatelaine*, July 1948, 36; Marjorie Lee-Joseph and Nanette Kramer, 'Are You the Perfect Mother?,' *Star Weekly Magazine*, 19 January 1946, 11
54 In part this was a reaction against the artificial strictures of Watson on cuddling. See John Levy and Ruth Munroe, *The Happy Family* (Toronto 1959), 272.
55 Lee-Joseph and Kramer, 'Are You the Perfect Mother?,' 11
56 Evelyn Millis Duvall, *Family Living*, rev. ed. (New York 1955; 1st edition 1950), 324–5
57 Cable, '*Little Darlings*,' 183
58 Erich Fromm, *Escape from Freedom* (New York 1941)
59 Bowman, *Marriage for Moderns* (1948 edition), 337
60 Byrne Hope Saunders, Editorial, *Chatelaine*, August 1948, 1
61 Canadian Youth Commission, *Youth, Marriage and Family*, 1
62 Judson Landis and Mary Landis, *Building a Successful Marriage*, 2d ed. (Englewood Cliffs, NJ, 1953), 37
63 Saunders, Editorial, 1
64 Groves, Skinner, and Swanson, *The Family and Its Relationships*, 188. See also, on budgeting, C. Wesley Topping, 'How to Stay Married,' *Chatelaine*, February 1946, 11.
65 Sidney Gruenberg, *The Many Lives of Modern Women: A Guide to Happiness in Her Complex Role* (New York 1952), 240
66 Beasley, *Democracy in the Home*, 72
67 Canadian Youth Commission, *Youth, Marriage and Family*, 15–19; J. Roby Kidd, 'External Influences Bringing about Changes in Family Life,' in Canadian Home and School, *Canadian Family Study* (n.p., n.d.), 15–16
68 Ibid., 27
69 Beasley, *Democracy in the Home*, xiv
70 J.D. Ketchum, 'The Family: Changing Patterns in Industrial Society,' in Canadian Home and School, *Canadian Family Study*, 18
71 Blatz, *Understanding the Young Child*, 9; see also William Blatz, 'The Nagging Evil,' *Chatelaine*, February 1946, 69–70.
72 Joseph Kirk Folsom, *The Family and Democratic Society* (New York 1943), especially 234–51 and 350–64
73 Beasley, *Democracy in the Home*, 37
74 Blatz, *Understanding the Young Child*, 268; S.R. Laycock, 'Parents Are Such Problems,' *Maclean's*, 15 October 1946, 13

75 Max Braithwaite, 'The Family Is Here to Stay,' *Chatelaine*, September 1951, 112
76 Benjamin Spock, *The Common Sense Book of Baby and Child Care* [hereinafter *Common Sense*] (New York 1946), 3–4
77 Gesell and Ilg, *Infant and Child in the Culture of Today*. Note also Spock's recommendation of their work: Spock, *Common Sense*, 145.
78 Spock, *Common Sense*, 20, 26, 195–6, 336
79 Interestingly, a close comparison of the 1946 edition of Spock's work with the updated version, *Baby and Child Care* (New York 1976), indicates a more explicit use of Freudian terms in the later edition.
80 Spock and Morgan, *Spock on Spock*, 135–7
81 National Film Board, *Why Tommy Won't Eat*, National Sound and Film Archives, V18306 028
82 Fritz Kahn, 'Let Your Child Grow Up,' *Maclean's*, 1 July 1949, 46. See the similar message in Fritz Kahn, 'Are You an Oedipus?' in Holland, ed., *Why Are You Single?*, 157.
83 A.T.M. Wilson, 'The Family: The Changing Patterns in an Industrial Society,' in Canadian Home and School, *Canadian Family Study*, 19–23, 20
84 Nancy Pottishman Weiss, 'Mother, The Invention of Necessity: Dr Benjamin Spock's *Baby and Child Care*,' *American Quarterly* (1977), 519–46
85 Blatz, *Understanding the Young Child*, 258
86 May, *Homeward Bound*, 10–11
87 Adele White, 'Let's Abolish Those Atom Bomb Blues,' *Chatelaine*, January 1950, 6

3: Safe in the Hands of Mother Suburbia: Home and Community, 1950–1965

1 The suburban advertisement appeared in the Toronto *Telegram*, 1 June 1956. The house design is drawn from a contest held in *Chatelaine*, February 1952. See as well the very similar house in 'Canada's House of the Year,' *Canadian Home Journal*, August 1954, 9–13. The cost reflects early to mid-1950s prices in the area surrounding Toronto, as do the down-payments and interest rates. The citations come from a reporter for the *New York Times*, 15 January 1950: see Ralph G. Martin, 'Life in the New Suburbia,' reprinted in Louis H. Massotti and Jeffery K. Hadden, eds., *Suburbia in Transition* (New York 1974), 14.
2 One of the most famous suburban studies is a Canadian one: John Seeley, R. Alexander Sim, and E.W. Loosley, *Crestwood Heights: A Study in the Culture of Suburban Life* (Toronto 1956).

3 John Gray, 'Why Live in the Suburbs?,' *Maclean's*, 1 September 1954, 7; *Time* (Canada edition), 20 June 1960, front cover
4 Robert Fishman, *Bourgeois Utopias: The Rise and Fall of Suburbia* (New York 1987), 182
5 Dominion Bureau of Statistics, *Census of Canada, 1961*, vol. 99-526, 4–5
6 John Miron, *Housing in Postwar Canada: Demographic Change, Household Formation, and Housing Demand* (Montreal and Kingston 1988), 199
7 Ibid., table 47
8 Central Mortgage and Housing Corporation, *Review of Housing in Canada* (Ottawa 1958), III-1
9 The CMHC estimated the average house size to be 1,100 square feet and the average lot frontage to be 50 feet. See ibid., VI-6.
10 Fishman, *Bourgeois Utopias*, 20–33
11 Kenneth T. Jackson, *Crabgrass Frontier: The Suburbanization of the United States* (New York 1985), 56
12 Fishman, *Bourgeois Utopias*, 34
13 Ibid., chs. 2 and 3
14 On the North American suburbs and their relationship to transportation see Jackson, *Crabgrass Frontier*.
15 Michael Simpson, *Thomas Adams and the Modern Planning Movement: Britain, Canada and the United States, 1900–1940* (London 1985), ch. 2. Note that Adams spent several years in Canada, where his ideas had considerable influence among turn-of-the-century progressives.
16 Robert Fishman, *Urban Utopias in the Twentieth Century: Ebenezer Howard, Frank Lloyd Wright and Corbusier* (New York 1977)
17 Christopher Lasch, *Haven in a Heartless World* (New York 1977)
18 The best description of a pre-war suburban development is John Weaver's 'From Land Assembly to Social Maturity: The Suburban Life of Westdale, Ontario, 1911–1951,' *Social History* 11 (1978), 411–40.
19 William Whyte, Jr, *The Organization Man* (New York 1956), 342
20 S.D. Clark, *The Suburban Society* (Toronto 1966), 53–4; Scott Donaldson, *The Suburban Myth* (New York 1969), 15
21 V. Joseph Kosta, *Planning for Residential Subdivisions* (Winnipeg 1954), 39. See also John Caulfield Smith, 'Too Many Like This. Not Enough Like This,' *Chatelaine*, June 1949, 14.
22 Irene E. McDermott and Florence William Nicholas, *Homemaking for Teenagers, Book Two* (Peoria 1962), 69. Note that this book was approved for school use in at least Alberta, British Columbia, and Ontario.
23 Evelyn Craw Matthews, 'A Place to Play,' *Chatelaine*, May 1946, 25

24 Kate Ellen Rogers, *The Modern House U.S.A: Its Design and Decoration* (New York 1955), 31
25 H. Fliess, 'The Social Aspects of Town Planning,' Royal Architectural Institute of Canada, *Journal* [hereinafter RAIC *Journal*] 24/5 (May 1947), 167
26 'Escape to the Greenbelt,' *Newsweek*, 4 August 1952, 32–3
27 Metropolitan Toronto Planning Board, *The Official Plan of the Metropolitan Toronto Planning Area* (Toronto 1959), plate 7: 'History of Urban Development'
28 Jean-Claude Marsan, *Montreal in Evolution* (Montreal and Kingston 1981); *Census of Canada, 1941*, vol. 9, 'Housing,' table 4a
29 See, for example, Map E-18 of Edmonton (1948), or F24 of Calgary, in the William Wonders Map Collection, University of Alberta Map Library.
30 Fishman, *Bourgeois Utopias*, 190–201
31 Metropolitan Toronto Planning Board, *The Official Plan of Metropolitan Toronto Planning Area, 1959*, 47; see also plate 15.
32 Jackson, *Crabgrass Frontier*, 181
33 A spot check was done of the Toronto *Telegram*, Vancouver *Province*, *Edmonton Journal*, and *Winnipeg Free Press* for intermittent periods from 1946 to 1956. Though there are occasional exceptions, the full panoply of integrated development, show homes, and hoopla doesn't begin until the early 1950s and isn't a standard part of suburban marketing until the middle of the decade.
34 Doucet and John Weaver, *Housing the North American City* (Montreal and Kingston 1991) 128
35 Blair Fraser, 'Houses, Houses, Where Are the Houses?,' *Maclean's*, 1 March 1949, 7+
36 Jackson, *Crabgrass Frontier*, 234–7; Joseph C. Goulden, *The Best Years, 1945–1950* (New York 1976), 138–9; John T. Liell, '4000 Houses a Year,' *Architectural Forum*, April 1949, 98–106; James Dugan, 'We Live in the World's Most Famous House,' *Maclean's*, 1 May 1952; David Halberstam, *The Fifties* (New York 1991), ch. 9
37 On Levittown see Harold L. Wattel, 'Levittown: A Suburban Community,' in William Dobriner, ed., *The Suburban Community* (New York 1958), 287–313, and Jackson, *Crabgrass Frontier*, 234–8.
38 Halberstam, *The Fifties*, 135
39 '700 Sales in 4 Weeks,' *Architectural Forum*, September 1951, 207
40 CMHC, *Housing in Canada: 1945 to 1986. An Overview and Lessons Learned* (Ottawa 1986), 23; John Caulfield Smith, 'What's for Building,' *Maclean's*, 1 August 1946, 12+
41 Vancouver *Province*, 18 August 1950, 31

42 Toronto *Telegram*, 15 May 1954, 3

43 Ibid., 1 June 1956, 4; 2 June 1956, 31

44 For a good example of this, see Metropolitan Toronto Archives, Minutes of the Toronto and Suburban Planning Board, October 1946 to August 1953, Minute of 4 December 1946, as well as the general attempt to formulate policies through the 1946–8 period.

45 '8659 Students Set New School Record,' Vancouver *Province*, 6 September 1950, 3

46 British Columbia, Department of Municipal Affairs, *Municipal Statistics for the Year Ended December 31st* (Victoria 1951–61)

47 E.G. Faludi, 'Homes of Today – Slums of Tomorrow,' *Maclean's*, 1 March 1950, 22–3+. See also H. Peter Oberlander, 'New Towns – An Approach to Urban Reconstruction,' RAIC *Journal* 24/6 (June 1947), 199–211.

48 Christopher Milligan, 'Thorncrest Village: A Community in Transition,' BA thesis, Ryerson Polytechnical Institute, 1985, 8–11

49 Jonathon Sewell, 'Don Mills: E.P. Taylor and Canada's First Corporate Suburb,' in James Lorimer, ed., *The Second City Book* (Toronto 1977), 18–30; 'Business Builds a City,' *Architectural Forum*, June 1954, 147–52; S.D. Clark, *The Suburban Society* (Toronto 1961)

50 Doucet and Weaver, *Housing the North American City*, 519–20

51 John Robarts Map Library, University of Toronto, Don Mills Development Ltd, 'Master Plan of Don Mills.' On Don Mills, see Sewell, 'Don Mills.'

52 'Business Builds a City,' 150

53 Doucet and Weaver, *Housing the North American City*, 135

54 Marsan, *Montreal in Evolution*, 322

55 Thus, for example, 86 per cent of Scarborough's dwellings in 1961 were single-family detached; in contrast, only 25 per cent of houses in the suburb of St Laurent, in Montreal, were: *Census of Canada 1961*, Series CT 95-516-95-538

56 Clark, *Suburban Society*, 9

57 Ontario Department of Municipal Affairs, *Ontario Planning Newsletter* 2/9 (November 1955), 1–4

58 Ibid. 2/2 (February 1955), 3

59 Clark, *Suburban Society*, 20–1

60 Metropolitan Toronto Archives, Toronto and Suburban Planning Board Minutes, Meeting of 2 July 1952; Metropolitan Toronto Planing Board, Box 1: Meeting of 4 May 1954

61 Metropolitan Toronto Archives, Metro Toronto Planning Board Minutes, Box 1. See for example meetings of 4 October 1953, and 20 June, 22 August and 25 November 1954.

62 Arthur M. Lower, *Canadians in the Making* (Toronto 1958), 424. On the American love affair with the automobile in the postwar years see William O'Neill, *American High: The Years of Confidence, 1945–1960* (New York 1986), 29–33. The best study of the social history of the automobile is James J. Flink, *The Car Culture* (Cambridge, MA, 1975). See also Christopher Finch, *Highways to Heaven: The Autobiography of America* (New York 1992).

63 F.H. Leacy, ed., *Historical Statistics of Canada,* 2d ed. (Ottawa 1983), tables T-147–94

64 *Statistical Abstracts of the United States* (Washington, DC, 1955), 214

65 Gordon Campbell, 'An Analysis of Highway Finance and Road User Imposts in Canada,' PhD thesis, Purdue University 1956, 59

66 Province of Quebec, *Annuaire du Québec 1968–9* (Quebec 1970), 677. Canada, Dominion Bureau of Statistics, *Household Facilities and Equipment, May 1960* (Ottawa 1960)

67 *Maclean's,* 1 December 1946, 42–3

68 Jackson, *Crabgrass Frontier,* 182–5

69 Thomas Hine, *Populuxe* (New York 1986), 56

70 Gray, 'Why Live in the Suburbs?,' 7. See also, for the frontier metaphor, 'Life among the Pioneers,' *Saturday Evening Post,* 30 April 1960, 21

71 R. Miron, *Housing in Postwar Canada,* 183–7

72 Ibid.

73 By 1971, 40 per cent of Canadian households had clothes dryers and 13 per cent had dishwashers: *Census of Canada, 1971,* Series CT 93-734-93-742, 'Housing'

74 Doucet and Weaver, *Housing the North American City,* 314

75 The suburbs were Burnaby, near Vancouver; Scarborough, in Toronto; Calgary SW; a section of Dartmouth identified by census tract 22; west Ottawa; Burlington and Pointe Claire, near Montreal; and St Laurent: *Census of Canada, 1961,* Series CT 95-516-95-538

76 Frederick Elkin, *The Family in Canada* (Ottawa 1964), 21, notes the convergence in family size. The 1961 census showed a range from 3.5 per family in British Columbia to 4.2 in Quebec, for the original nine provinces. Newfoundland stood apart, with 4.7.

77 Typical housing design can be seen in the 'Canada Housing Design Council 1958 Awards: Report of the National Jury,' RAIC *Journal* 35 (June 1958), 230–4. All nine awards were given to bungalows, and none of the houses was more than 1,500 square feet in size.

78 Catherine Fraser, 'Course in Home Decorating,' *Chatelaine,* May 1952, 77

79 Arthur J. Pulos, *The American Design Adventure, 1945–1970* (Boston 1988), 2–37
80 William J. Hennessey and Eliza Dornin Hennessey, *Modern Furnishings for the Home* (New York 1956), 13–15. See also *House and Garden's Complete Guide for Interior Decoration* (New York 1953).
81 John Caulfield Smith, 'Welcome in Today's Accent,' *Chatelaine*, April 1946, 19; 'Pitfalls in Floor Plans,' *Architectural Forum*, October 1951, 198–202
82 'House with Young Ideas,' *Chatelaine*, June 1946, 13
83 Ad for Dominion Linoleum, *Chatelaine*, March 1953, 64
84 *Star Weekly Magazine*, 7 September 1946, 3
85 This depiction is developed from pictures in various home-decorating magazines in the 1950s as well as advertisements. See also National Archives of Canada, PA111483: 'Modern Canadian Kitchen 1956,' and PA 11484: 'Modern Canadian Living Room, 1957.'
86 'Don't Be a Color Coward,' *House and Garden*, February 1950, 120–1; Doris McCubben, 'Give Your House a Splash of Colour,' *Chatelaine*, March 1952, 6–7; 'The Colourful House,' *Maclean's*, 1 January 1947
87 Advertisement inside front cover, *Maclean's*, 1 August 1951; inside front cover, 1 March 1953; 1 May 1954, 8. Advertisement for Inernational Harvester Refrigerators, *Canadian Home Journal*, August 1954, 59
88 John Caulfield Smith, 'Add Colour to Your Life,' *Chatelaine*, August 1950, 15; ad for Pittsburgh Paints, *Maclean's*, 16 April 1955
89 Catherine Fraser, 'Home Decorating Course,' *Chatelaine*, July 1952, 19
90 Advertisement, *Maclean's*, 15 September 1951, 31
91 Hine, *Populuxe*, 5
92 Whyte, *The Organization Man*; John Keats, *The Crack in the Picture Window* (Boston 1956). See on the view of the suburbs Margaret Marsh, 'Reconsidering the Suburbs: An Exploration of Suburban Historiography,' *Pennsylvania Magazine of History and Biography* 112/4 (October 1988), 579–605, and Lewis Mumford, *The City in History* (New York 1961), 494
93 Clark, *Suburban Society*, 37
94 Doris McCubbin, 'Everyone Loves to Live in Wildwood,' *Chatelaine*, May 1955, 12, 46–8
95 Whyte, *Organization Man*, 298
96 Doucet and Weaver, *Building the North American City*, 112–16
97 Clark, *Suburban Society*, 86, 90
98 *Census of Canada, 1961*, Series CT 95-516-95-538
99 The one exception was St Laurent.

100 Whyte, *The Organization Man,* 320

101 Clark, *Suburban Society,* 190; Sidonie Gruenberg, 'Homogenized Children of the New Suburbia,' *New York Times Magazine,* 19 September 1954, 14+

102 For a contemporary view see 'Some Drawbacks of Suburban Life,' *Science Digest* 37/1 (January 1955), 33.

103 Donaldson, *The Suburban Myth,* 125; Veronica Strong-Boag, 'Home Dreams: Women and the Suburban Experience in Canada, 1945–1960,' *Canadian Historical Review* 72/4 (December 1991), 471–504

104 Mumford, *The City in History,* 494–5, goes even farther, arguing that the life of the child dominated all ages in the suburbs because the suburbs were geared to recreation and play. 'This was not merely a child-centred environment: it was based on a childish view of the world in which reality was sacrificed to the pleasure principle.'

4: Consuming Leisure: Play in an Era of Affluence, 1950–1965

1 Advertisement for Kiddicraft Toys, *Maclean's,* 1 September 1953, 89

2 Neil Sutherland, *Children in English-Canadian Society: Framing the Twentieth-Century Consensus* (Toronto 1976), 20

3 Evelyn Craw Matthews, 'A Place to Play,' *Chatelaine,* May 1946, 25. From south of the border see the material by the White House Committee on Children and Youth, especially August Hecksher, 'The New Leisure,' in Eli Ginzberg, ed., *The Nation's Children,* Vol. 1: *The Family and Social Change* (New York 1960), 227–47.

4 See Joseph Kirk Folsom, *The Family and Democratic Society* (New York 1943), 173–4

5 W. Bauer, MD, 'Children Are So Annoying,' *Maclean's,* 15 March 1947, 65

6 Robert H. Bremner, 'Families, Children and Social Change,' in Robert Bremner and Gary Reichard, eds., *Reshaping American Society and Institutions, 1945–1960* (Columbia, OH, 1982), 7

7 To be precise the mortality rate per thousand declined from 5.5 (1931–5) to 1.7 (1951–5) for ages one to four and from 2.2 (1926–30) to 0.7 (1951–5). F.H. Leacy, ed., *Historical Statistics of Canada,* 2d ed. (Ottawa 1983), tables B23–34

8 For a history of polio see John R. Paul, *A History of Poliomyelitis* (New Haven, CT, 1971)

9 Ibid., 1–4

10 Dominion Bureau of Statistics [DBS], *Vital Statistics* (Catalogue 84-202), for 1950, table 58; 1952, tables 24, 27; 1953, table 27

11 Winnipeg schools, for example, delayed opening in September 1953 as a

result of the epidemic. See Province of Manitoba, *Report of the Department of Education for 1954,* 36, 106.

12 Paul, *A History of Poliolymelitis,* 426–9, 436

13 DBS, *Vital Statistics,* 1965, table D9. There was one death, a middle-aged adult.

14 Erik Barnouw, *Tube of Plenty: The Evolution of American Television* (New York 1975), ch. 2

15 Ibid., 99

16 For a full history of early Canadian television see Paul Rutherford, *When Television Was Young: Primetime Canada, 1952–1967* (Toronto 1990).

17 See as examples J. Crosbie, 'Television Is Ready; It Will Need Actors, Writers, Producers,' *Saturday Night,* 21 July 1945, 19; Pierre Berton, 'Make Way for the One-Eyed Monster,' *Maclean's,* 1 June 1949, 56–7.

18 R.B. Fraser, 'Why They Won't Let You Have Television,' *Maclean's,* 15 January 1949, 38–9; Frank W. Peers, *The Public Eye: Television and the Politics of Canadian Broadcasting* (Toronto 1979), 6–19

19 Rutherford, *When Television Was Young,* 47–9

20 *Canada Year Book, 1960,* 903–4

21 The 1952 price comes from Rutherford, *When Television Was Young,* 50. The 1956 prices from advertisements in the Vancouver *Province,* 2 May 1956

22 DBS, *Household Facilities and Equipment* (catalogue 64-202) (Ottawa 1954–60), table 25

23 *Canada Year Book, 1960,* 901–2

24 See as an early example Max Rosenfeld, 'How TV Is Changing Your Life,' *Maclean's,* 1 December 1954, 34–5+, and the comment of the Toronto Women's Teachers Association that TV would cause children to lose their desire to read.

25 For a strong attack on McLuhan see Rutherford, *When Television Was Young,* 26–38.

26 The runs of shows and their characters are drawn from Tim Brooks and Earl Marsh, *The Complete Directory to Prime Time Network TV Shows, 1946–Present,* rev. ed. (New York 1981). The television schedules and material on Canadian stations was researched by David Kales, who worked patiently through TV guides from 1955 to 1960 for selected cities.

27 John Webster Grant, *The Church in the Canadian Era* (Toronto 1972), 168

28 Hours were gradually extended. By 1959 CFPL London was broadcasting by 10:30 A.M. weekdays. On the other hand, CHCH in Hamilton still began programming at noon. Not until well into the 1960s was early-morning programming standard.

29 These were the scheduled programs for the 1959 season on CBLT in Toronto. Other CBC stations, programming was essentially similar.
30 Hal Himmelstein, *Television Myth and the American Mind* (Toronto 1984), 88
31 *The Plouffe Family* was a partial exception, but this show about a traditional French-Canadian family was initially created for francophones, and its ethnic role in English Canada was secondary.
32 Steven Mintz and Susan Kellogg, *Domestic Revolutions: A Social History of American Family Life* (London 1988), 192
33 On the history of Disney enterprises in this period see Bob Thomas, *Walt Disney: An American Original* (New York 1976), and Christopher Fince, *The Art of Walt Disney: From Mickey Mouse to the Magic Kingdom* (New York 1973).
34 Benjamin Spock, *The Common Sense Book of Baby and Child Care* (New York 1946), 320
35 *Chatelaine*, April 1946, 23
36 DBS, *Canned Foods* (catalogue 32-211) for relevant years
37 The examples are all taken from *Eaton's Fall-Winter Catalogue* for 1952–3. The actual citation is from the 1946–7 catalogue, 109.
38 'Canadians Top Toy Buyers Because Kids So Plentiful,' *Financial Post*, 8 March 1958, 28. See also 'Toys ... $30,000,000 Business,' *Monetary Times*, August 1953, 20–4.
39 *Maclean's*, 1 December 1951, 6–10
40 Paula Fass, *The Damned and the Beautiful: American Youth in the 1920s* (New York 1977), 231
41 Ibid., 227
42 Changed to *Walt Disney Presents* in 1958: Brooks and Marsh, *The Complete Directory to Prime Time Network TV Shows*, 806
43 Thomas, *Walt Disney: An American Original*, 250–8
44 The three were no. 4, by Bill Hayes; no. 27, by Fess Parker; and no. 28, by Tennessee Ernie Ford. See Bruce Pollock, *When Rock Was Young: A Nostalgic View of the Top 50 Era* (New York 1981), 195–6.
45 Rutherford, *When Television Was Young*, 46–8
46 'Imported Hero Makes Good,' *Financial Post*, 9 July 1955, 21
47 Landon Jones, *Great Expectations* (New York 1980), 51
48 'Hoop Boom Spirals Linear Poly Sales,' *Canadian Plastics*, October 1958, 32–3
49 Thomas Hine, *Populuxe* (New York 1986), 5–6
50 Paul Dickson, *Timelines* (Don Mills 1990), 115
51 David Potter, *People of Plenty: Economic Abundance and the American Character* (Chicago 1954), ch. 9

52 Carl Berger, *Science, God and Nature in Victorian Canada* (Toronto 1983), 34–7
53 See G.R. Searle, *The Quest for National Efficiency* (Oxford 1971).
54 William Whyte, Jr, *The Organization Man* (New York 1956), 7
55 Murray Ross, *The Y.M.C.A. in Canada: The Chronicle of a Century* (Toronto 1951)
56 Tim Jeal, *Baden-Powell* (London 1989), 377–82. The citation is from Baden-Powell's first pamphlet on Scouts.
57 Though Baden-Powell's vision of feminity was much more hardy than was traditional in the pre-war era. See Jeal, *Baden-Powell*, 468–71.
58 E.M. Duvall and R. Havighurst, 'Is Youth Lost in the Wilds of Suburbia?,' *National Parent–Teacher* (January 1958), 10–12; Sidonie Gruenberg, 'Homogenized Children of the New Suburbia,' *New York Times Magazine*, 19 September 1954, 14+
59 Girl Guides of Canada, *The Commissioner's Handbook for 1960* (Toronto 1960), 13, 16
60 Girl Guides of Canada, *The Brownie Handbook, 1958* (Toronto 1958), 1. In the 1960s the wording was changed to: 'A Brownie is cheerful and obedient. A Brownie thinks of other people before herself.' See Girl Guides of Canada, *Policy, Organization and Rules, 1966* (Toronto 1966), vi.
61 Figures from Boy Scout Association, *Annual Reports*, 1958–67 (Ottawa); Girl Guides of Canada, *Annual Reports*, 1952–63 (Toronto)
62 Boy Scouts of Canada, *Annual Report for 1958*, 2
63 Alberta Girl Guide Headquarters, 'Reports of Annual Meetings of the Alberta Girl Guides Association,' 1948–60.
64 Girl Guides of Canada, *Commissioner's Handbook, 1960*, 14
65 W.A.H. Filer, 'Report of the Programme Committee,' in *Annual Report of the Girl Guides of Canada, 1964*, 12
66 Annual reports of the Girl Guides and Boy Scouts for relevant years
67 'Address by L.S. St. Laurent: The Gray Foundation Lectureship, January 13, 1947,' in R.A. Mackay, ed., *Canadian Foreign Policy, 1945–1954* (Toronto 1971), 392
68 George Pidgeon, 'The Church Should Enter the Doors,' United Church *Observer*, 1 January 1955, 3. Hugh Crozier, 'So Little for the Character,' United Church *Observer*, 1 January 1955; Province of Ontario, *Report of the Royal Commission on Education* [The Hope Commission], *1950* (Toronto 1951), 126–7. By the end of the decade the view that religion should be in the schools was under attack. See B. Barrett, 'Keep Religion in the Schools,' *Saturday Night*, 19 December 1959.
69 *Canadian Churchman*, 15 May 1953, 351

70 *The Gallup Poll: Public Opinion, 1935–1971*, vol 1: *1935–1948*, 698. Survey dated 9 January 1948
71 Reginald Bibby, *Fragmented Gods: The Poverty and Potential of Religion in Canada* (Toronto 1987), 11
72 Ibid., 11–12. On church attendance in the 1950s see the Canadian Institute of Public Opinion, *Gallup Poll of Canada*, 18 April 1960, which shows public responses concerning recent church attendance for 1955, 1957, and 1960.
73 From 1946 to 1956 percentages increased. From 1956 to 1961 there was a small decline, though the 1961 percentage remain higher than that in 1946: Bibby, *Fragmented Gods*, 15; John Stackhouse, 'The Protestant Experience in Canada since 1945,' in G.A. Rawlyk, ed., *The Canadian Protestant Experience, 1760–1990* (Burlington, Ont., 1990), 206.
74 Alfred Harris, 'New Faith or Old Fear,' *Saturday Night*, 10 May 1958, 10–11, 10
75 A.C. Forrest, 'Religious Revival in Suburbia,' *Saturday Night*, 13 December 1952, 11+. See also Stewart Crysdale, *The Changing Church in Canada* (Toronto 1965), and George Morrison, 'The Student Ministry in the Suburban Area,' United Church *Observer*, 15 February 1955.
76 'Observations,' United Church *Observer*, 15 January 1957, 5
77 Presbyterian Church of Canada, 'General Board of Missions Report for 1953,' *The Acts and Proceedings of the Eightieth General Assembly of the Presbyterian Church in Canada* (Toronto 1954), 201
78 John Webster Grant, *The Church in the Canadian Era* (Toronto 1972), 160
79 Right Rev. G.F. Gower, 'The State of the Church,' *Yearbook of the Anglican Church of Canada, 1959*, 18
80 See for example A.C. Forrest, 'Religious Revival; in Suburbia,' *Saturday Night*, 15 December 1952; Emil Fackenheim, 'The Current "Religious Revival": Is It Genuine?' *Canadian Forum*, March 1956, 269–70; D.J. Wilson, 'Is It Only a Bull Market on Religion,' *Canadian Business*, October 1950, 42–3+; H.H. Walsh, *The Christian Church in Canada* (Toronto 1956), 341.
81 Bibby, *Fragmented Gods*, 12–13
82 Forrest, 'Religious Revival in Suburbia,' 11
83 'This Is the House of God,' *Canadian Churchman*, 19 June 1952
84 'Is It a Great Church?' United Church *Observer*, 15 January 1956, 9–10
85 Harris, 'New Faith or Old Fear,' 51
86 Fackenheim, 'The Current "Religious Revival"'; Scott Donaldson, *The Suburban Myth* (New York, 1969), 139–40
87 'The Cover Picture,' *Canadian Churchman*, 16 January 1958, 26
88 Editorial, in ibid., 2 October 1958, 322
89 'Planning for the Future,' in ibid., 6 October 1955

90 United Church *Observer*, 15 April 1955, 12
91 S.R. Laycock, column in *Canadian Churchman*, 21 April 1955, 188
92 Bibby, *Fragmented Gods*, ch. 6
93 Pierre Berton, *The Comfortable Pew: A Critical Look at the Church in the New Age* (Toronto 1965); William Kilbourn, ed., *The Restless Church: A Response to the Comfortable Pew* (Toronto 1966)
94 United Church *Annual Reports*, 1961–70
95 Roland Marchand, 'Visons of Classlessness, Quests for Dominion: American Popular Culture, 1945–1960,' in Richard Bremner and Gary Reichard, eds., *Reshaping America: Society and Institutions, 1945–1960* (Columbus, OH, 1982), 165–6
96 Norman Ryder, 'The Cohort as a Concept in the Study of Social Change,' *American Sociological Review* 30 (1965); Jones, *Great Expectations*, 90–1

5: School Days, 1952–1965

1 Kindergarten was far from universal in the early 1950s.
2 F.H. Leacy, ed., *Historical Statistics of Canada*, 2d ed. (Ottawa 1983), table W-48
3 Ibid., table W-68
4 H.L. Campbell, *Curriculum Trends in Canadian Education* (Toronto 1952), 35
5 Figures from *Canada Year Book, 1933* (Ottawa 1934), 970; Leacy, ed., *Historical Statistics of Canada*, tables W61–80; and Wolfgang Illing and Zoltan Zsigmond, *Enrolment in Schools and Universities, 1951–2 to 1975–6*, Economic Council of Canada Study No. 20 (Ottawa 1967), Appendix A
6 'A Multi-Million Dollar Job for Construction,' *Financial Post*, 19 February 1955, 66. See also the warning issued by the chief superintendent of education for Quebec in Province of Quebec, *Report of the Superintendent of Education, 1952* (Quebec 1952), xiii.
7 For these studies see C.F. Goulson, 'An Historical Survey of Royal Commission and Other Major Governmental Inquiries into Education,' PhD thesis, Unversity of Toronto, 1966. My thanks as well to David Kales, who compiled a summary of the contents of the war and immediate postwar royal commissions for this project.
8 Canada, *Report of the Royal Commission on Dominion–Provincial Relations* (Ottawa 1940), 63
9 Province of Ontario, *Report of the Minister of Education* (Toronto 1949), 5–8
10 Ontario, *Report of the Royal Commission on Education* (Toronto 1950) [hereinafter cited as Hope Commission], 19

11 Illing and Zsigmond, *Enrolment in Schools and Universities, 1951–2 to 1975–6,* Appendix table B1
12 Ibid. See, for one view of the evolution of this change, Charles E. Phillips, *Public Secondary Education in Canada* (Toronto 1956).
13 Province of Manitoba, *Report of the Department of Education for the Year Ending June 30, 1956* (Winnipeg 1957) 10
14 Campbell, *Curriculum Trends,* 38
15 J.G. Althouse, 'Implications of the New Curriculum' (speech given 1950), in his *Addresses* (Toronto 1958), 141. See also C.C. Goldring, 'Today's Secondary School Students,' in *Education: A Collection of Essays on Canadian Education.* Vol. 2: *1956–1958* (Toronto 1959), 9–12
16 Hope Commission, 19
17 Illing and Zsigmond, *Enrolment in Schools and Universities, 1951–2 to 1975–6* , Appendix A
18 These figures are derived from ibid., appendices.
19 Province of Manitoba, *Report of the Department of Education for the Year Ending June 30, 1955* (Winnipeg 1956), 11
20 'The Huge Demand for New Schools,' *Financial Post,* 18 February 1956, 52
21 Illing and Zsigmond, *Enrolment in Schools and Universities, 1951–2 to 1975–6* , Appendix A
22 British Columbia, *Public Schools of British Columbia: Annual Report for 1952–3* (Victoria 1953), 69
23 Alberta, *Report of the Royal Commission on Education* (Edmonton 1959), 3
24 J.G. Althouse, 'Significant Trends in Education,' *University of Toronto Quarterly,* February 1956, 155–66
25 J. Bascom St John, *Spotlight on Canadian Education* (Toronto 1959), 103
26 Alberta, *Report of the Royal Commission on Education,* 36; Nova Scotia, *Annual Report of the Superintendent of Education for 1951* (Halifax 1951), vii
27 Dominion Bureau of Statistics [DBS] *Census of Canada, 1951,* vol. 4, table 4
28 Canada and Newfoundland Educational Association, *Trends in Education, 1944: A Survey of Current Educational Developments in the Nine Provinces of Canada and Newfoundland* (Toronto 1944), 5–9. See also Province of Nova Scotia, *Royal Commission on Provincial Development and Rehabilitation* (Halifax 1944); Manitoba, *Report of the Special Select Committee of the Manitoba Legislative Assembly on Education* (Winnipeg 1945).
29 See, for example, British Columbia, *Public Schools of British Columbia, Annual Report, 1948,* 30; Nova Scotia, *Annual Report of the Superintendent of Education for 1949,* ix; Ontario, *Annual Report of the Minister of Educa-*

tion, 1951 (Toronto 1951), 4. On pupil–teacher ratio see Robert M. Stamp, *The Schools of Ontario, 1876–1976* (Toronto 1982), Appendix 3.

30 Province of Manitoba, *Report of the Department of Education for the Year Ending June 30, 1957*, 11

31 'Report on an Emergency Training Scheme for Teachers for Public and Separate Schools of Ontario, dated December 2, 1949,' Hope Commission, Appendix, 601

32 There were also recruitment committees set up by concerned interest groups. See Public Archives of Alberta, Accession 67.80: 'The Records of the Alberta Education Council.'

33 Province of British Columbia, *Public Schools of the Province of British Columbia: Annual Report for 1954–55* (Vancouver 1955), 39.

34 Ontario, *Annual Report of the Minister of Education, 1953*, 14

35 Quebec, *Report of the Superintendent of Education for 1952*, xvii

36 Manitoba, *Report of the Department of Education, 1954*, 37

37 Hope Commission, 559–60

38 Ontario, *Annual Report of the Minister of Education, 1954*, 56

39 J. Bascom St John, *Spotlight on Canadian Education*, 72

40 Ontario, *Annual Report of the Minister of Education, 1953*, 13

41 Alberta, *Report of the Royal Commission on Education*, 174–5

42 Alberta, *Journals of the Legislative Assembly*, vol. 62 (Edmonton 1954), 8

43 'Emergency Teacher Training Act, *Statutes of Alberta, 1954*, ch. 26

44 Alberta, *Report of the Royal Commission on Education*, 175–6

45 Ontario, *Annual Report of the Minister of Education, 1952*, 2

46 'The Huge Demand for New Schools,' *Financial Post*, 18 February 1956, 52+

47 'This Changing Canada: How Many Billions for Schools?,' *Canadian Business*, July 1955, 36–8

48 Ontario, *Annual Report of the Minister of Education, 1954*, 5–6

49 'The Huge Demand for New Schools'

50 J.E. Parsons, 'Daylight on Tomorrow's Modern Schools,' *Saturday Night*, 6 December 1949, 10; John Caulfield Smith, 'Little Red Is Now Long and Beautiful,' *Saturday Night*, 13 December 1952, 10

51 Eric R. Arthur, 'School Design: A New Look at Old Problems,' RAIC *Journal*, February 1960, 61–70; Parsons, 'Daylight on Tomorrow's Schools,' 10. A survey of blueprints in Alberta during this period indicates that, though there was no single plan, there was great standardization. Plans, once approved, were used and reused. For example, a plan for a medium-sized Roman Catholic elementary school developed in the late 1950s was used in Coaldale, Taber, Provost, and Picture Butte: see Public Archives of Alberta, Records of the Department of Education, Accession 76.485 and 77.32.

52 Gordon S. Adamson, 'Design, Construction, Layout, Decoration and Services,' in Canadian Conference on Education, *Addresses and Proceedings* (Ottawa 1958), 117–26, 122

53 British Columbia, *Public Schools of the Province of British Columbia: Annual Report for 1954–55*, 60, 67, 74, 75, 77, 82, 85, 90, 92, 96, 108

54 Leacy, ed., *Historical Statistics of Canada*, Series H-188–96. My thanks to David Kales for his research on the issue of school amalgamations.

55 Alberta, *Report of the Royal Commission on Education* 76

56 Canada and Newfoundland Educational Association, *Report of the Survey Committee Appointed to Ascertain the Chief Educational Needs of the Dominion of Canada* (Ottawa 1943), 1–13

57 Quebec, *Annual Report of the Superintendent of Education for the Province of Quebec, 1950–1*, xxiii

58 Stamp, *Schools of Ontario*, 74–6, 106–7

59 Alberta, *Report of the Legislative Committee Appointed to Make a Comprehensive Survey and Study of Education in the Rural Districts of Alberta* (Edmonton 1935)

60 British Columbia, Department of Education, *School Finance in British Columbia* (Victoria 1935); Nova Scotia, Department of Education, *Report of the Committee on the Larger School Unit* (Halifax 1939); New Brunswick, Department of Education, *The Plenderleith Report* (Fredericton 1937)

61 Province of Saskatchewan, *Report of the Minister of Education for 1948* (Regina 1948), 11

62 Bascom St John, *Spotlight on Canadian Education*, 5

63 Stamp, *Schools of Ontario*, 98

64 John Dewey, *The School and Society* (New York 1899); *Democracy and Education* (New York 1916)

65 R.S. Patterson, 'Progressive Education: Impetus to Educational Change in Alberta and Saskatchewan,' in Howard Palmer and Donald Smith, eds., *The New Provinces: Alberta and Saskatchewan* (Vancouver 1980), 194–220

66 Quebec, *Report of the Chief Superintendent of Education*, 1952, ix

67 H.E. Smith, 'The New Education in Alberta,' *The School*, 1940, 187

68 See Campbell Ross, 'The Neatby Debate and Conservative Thought in Canada,' PhD, University of Alberta, 1989

69 Hilda Neatby, *So Little for the Mind* (Toronto 1953), 238. On the book's success see Ross, 'The Neatby Debate,' 1.

70 Eugene Forsey, 'Canadian Schools Greatest Needs – Money or Brains?' *Saturday Night*, 29 March 1958, 10–11, 11

71 Quebec, *Report of the Superintendent of Education*, 1950–1, x

72 Neatby, *So Little for the Mind*, 11

73 J.G. Althouse, *Structures and Aims of Education* (Toronto 1950), 50
74 Charles Phillips, *Public Secondary Education in Canada* (Toronto 1956), 64
75 H.L. Campbell, *Curriculum Trends in Canadian Education* (Toronto 1952), 44
76 Ibid., 100
77 R.J. Love, 'Where Do We Go from Here?' in *Education: A Collection of Essays, on Canadian Education.* Vol. 3: *1958–1960* (Toronto 1960), 23
78 J.G. Althouse, 'Implications of the New Curriculum,' in his *Addresses,* 123–30, 124
79 J.G. Althouse, *Structures and Aims of Education* (Toronto n.d.), 52
80 Hope Commission, 161
81 Ibid., 95
82 Love, 'Where Do We Go from Here?,' 22
83 Hope Commission, 95
84 See for example Gerald Craig and Beatrice Hurley, *Discovering with Science* (Toronto 1959), 23–4, 254.
85 Alberta, Department of Education, *Interim Senior High School Curriculum Guide for English 10. English 33* (Edmonton 1965)
86 Alberta, Department of Education, School Book Branch, *Price List and Requisition Form (1959)* (Edmonton 1959). See also Department of Education, School Book Branch, *Enterprise Activities for Elementary Schools in the Province of Alberta* (Edmonton 1961). For Ontario see Ontario, Department of Education, *Text Books Approved or Recommended for Use in Elementary Schools,* issued annually. See also the 'Ontario Textbook Catalogue, 1846–1970,' compiled by Marian Press and Susan Adams, R.W.B. Jackson Library, Ontario Institute for Studies in Edmonton.
87 Hope Commission, 38. See also 130.
88 J.T. Phair and N.R. Speers, *Good Health Today* (Toronto 1960), 110
89 W.W. Charters, Dean Smiley, and Ruth Strang, *Health Secrets* (New York 1947), 69
90 Irene McDermott and Florence Nicholas, *Homemaking for Teenagers* (Peoria 1956), vol. 2, 650
91 Alberta, Department of Education, *Senior High School Handbook,* 1961–2, 5
92 McDermott and Nicholas, *Homemaking for Teenagers,* vol. 2, 680
93 Phair and Speers, *Good Health Today,* 47
94 Ibid., 126
95 McDermott and Nicholas, *Homemaking for Teenagers,* vol. 2, 674
96 Helen Shocter, Gladys Jenkins, and W.W. Bauer, *Into Your Teens* (Toronto 1952), 124–5

97 Province of Alberta, *Junior High Curriculum Guide for Home Economics*, 1961

98 Canadian Institute of Public Opinion, *Gallup Poll*, 18 June 1960

99 H.B. Neatby, *William Lyon Mackenzie King*, vol. 3 (Toronto 1976), 304–5

100 Dorothy Baruch and Elizabeth Montgomery, *The Girl Next Door* (Chicago 1946)

101 Max Braithwaite and R.S. Lambert, *We Live in Ontario* (Toronto 1957), 220

102 Province of Alberta, Department of Education, *Junior High School Guide for Social Studies and Language* (September 1958)

103 D. Baker and J.M. Brown, *Civics and Citizenship: A Sourcebook for Schools* (Toronto 1961). This is an aid designed to be used with the book *Community Economics*.

104 Alberta, Department of Education, *Junior High School Guide for Social Studies* (September 1958), 5–6

105 Quebec, *Report of the Chief Superintendent for 1952–3*, xi

106 Ibid., 53

107 Government of Quebec, *First Report of the Minister of Education* (Quebec 1965), 15–16, 45,

108 On Quebec baby-boomers and the Quiet Revolution see François Ricard, *The Lyric Generation: The Life and Times of the Baby Boomers*, trans. by Donald Winkler (Toronto 1994), 95–103.

109 W.W. Brown and Dorothy Baruch, *From Eight to Nine, Teacher's Edition* (Chicago 1959)

110 Hope Commission, 109

111 Phillips, *Public Secondary Education in Canada*, 68–9. Phillips's theories about relevance are brought home by any teacher's manual from the post-war years. See, for example, *The Ginn Basic Readers' Manual for Teaching the Sixth Reader* (Toronto 1961), 9.

6: The Fifties and the Cult of the Teenager

1 Elaine Tyler May, *Homeward Bound: American Families in the Cold War* (New York 1988), 9

2 David Halberstam, *The Fifties* (New York 1993), ch. 22

3 For a general history of youth see Peter Gillis, *Youth and History: Tradition and Change in European Age Relations, 1770–Present* (New York 1974).

4 James Gilbert, *Cycle of Outrage: America's Reaction to the Juvenile Delinquent in the 1950s* (New York 1986), 4. He uses the term 'episodic' to describe short-term forces affecting the image of youth. His term seems most appropriate here, though it is a congruent usage rather than identi-

cal. See also John Modell, *Into One's Own: From Youth to Adulthood in the United States, 1920–1975* (Berkeley, CA, 1989)

5 Gillis, *Youth and History*, 133

6 The standard biography is D. Ross, *Stanley Hall: The Psychologist as Prophet* (Chicago 1972). On the creation of the 'scientific fact' of adolescence see Harry Hendrick, *Age, Class and the Male Youth Problem, 1880–1920* (Oxford 1990), 84–5. On Hall and Freud's visit to America in 1909 see William Strauss and Neill Howe, *Generations: The History of America's Future, 1584 to 2069* (New York 1991), 223.

7 G. Stanley Hall, *Adolescence: Its Psychology and Its Relations to Physiology, Anthropology, Sociology, Sex, Crime, Religion and Education*, 2 vols. (New York 1911)

8 Mortimer Herbert Appley, 'G. Stanley Hall: Vow on Mount Owen,' in Stewart Hulse and Bert Green, Jr, eds., *One Hundred Years of Psychological Research in America: G. Stanley Hall and the Johns Hopkins Tradition* (Baltimore 1986), 5–6

9 Rolf Muus, 'The Philosophical and Historical Roots of Theories of Adolescence,' in Rolf Muus, ed., *Adolescent Behavior and Society*, 2d ed. (New York 1975), 22

10 Hall, *Adolescence*, vol. 1, 266, 267, 279–82

11 Kenneth Kenniston, 'Youth: A "New" Stage of Life,' in Muus, ed., *Adolescent Behavior*, 43. Harry Hendrick, *Images of Youth* (Oxford 1990), ch. 4, looks in detail at the influence of Hall in Great Britain.

12 For a discussion of the changing literary image of the adolescent see W. Tasker Witham, *The Adolescent in the American Novel, 1920–1960* (New York 1964).

13 Gillis, *Youth and History*, 117

14 The idea of adolescence was reinforced by the notion of an almost inevitable parent–child conflict as youth sought independence. See Kingsley Davis, 'The Sociology of Parent–Youth Conflict,' *American Sociological Review* 5 (August 1940), 523–35.

15 *Canada Year Book, 1930*, 124

16 Paula Fass, *The Damned and the Beautiful: American Youth in the 1920s* (New York 1977). For a controversial attempt to define dominant and recessive generations see Strauss and Howe, *Generations*, ch. 4.

17 The proportion of Canadians aged ten to twenty-four rose from 27.7 per cent at the beginning of the 1920s to 29.2 per cent a decade later: F.H. Leacy, ed., *Historical Statistics of Canada*, 2d ed. (Ottawa 1983), tables A78–93.

18 Linda Ambrose, 'The Canadian Youth Commission: Planning for Youth and

Social Welfare in the Postwar Era,' PhD thesis, University of Waterloo, 1992, 11, 18–19

19 Frederick Elkin and William Westley, 'The Myth of Adolescent Culture,' *American Sociological Review* 20 (1955), 680–4

20 Tasker Witham, *The Adolescent in the American Novel, 1920–1960*, especially 86–98, 247–8

21 On the origins of this issue see Jeff Keshen, 'Wartime Jitters: Canada's Delinquency Scare and Its Consequences,' unpublished paper, University of Alberta, 1994. See also Gilbert, *Cycle of Outrage*, ch. 4, 'The Great Fear.'

22 Frank Musgrove, *Youth and Social Order* (London 1964), 34

23 Susan E. Houston, 'Victorian Origins of Juvenile Delinquency: A Canadian Experience,' *History of Education Quarterly* 11 (1972), 254–82

24 This summary is drawn from Houston, 'Victorian Origins,' and John Hagan and Jeffery Leon, 'Rediscovering Delinquency: Social History, Political Ideology and the Sociology of Law,' *American Sociological Review* 42 (August 1977), 587–98. See also Dorothy Chunn, *From Punishment to Doing Good: Family Courts and Socialized Justice in Ontario, 1880–1940* (Toronto 1992).

25 This notion also applied to the mentally handicapped.

26 National Archives of Canada [NAC], Records of the Canadian Youth Commission, vol. 42, contains several briefs which raise the issue of family separation and the children. See also vol. 43, file 9, Memorandum of the Family Life Committee, 'War and the Family.' Keshen, 'Wartime Jitters,' 3–4, 7

27 *Historical Statistics of Canada*, tables B1–14; Keshen, 'Wartime Jitters,' 12–13

28 Gerald Zoffer, 'Underworld Evil Breeds Juvenile Delinquency,' *Saturday Night*, 12 January 1946, 6–7, 6

29 NAC, Records of the Canadian Youth Commission, vol. 43, file 13, 'Commission Canadienne de La Jeunesse: Rapport sur la famille,' 9 April 1945. For the United States see R.A. Tesseneer and L.N. Tesseneer, 'Review of the Literature on School Drop-Outs,' *Bulletin of the National Association of Secondary School Principals* 42 (May 1958), 141–53

30 Pierre Berton, 'The Beaney Gang,' *Maclean's*, 15 December 1948, 14

31 Dominion Bureau of Statistics, *Annual Report of Juvenile Delinquents for the Years, 1935–1950*, catalogue 85-202

32 Gallup Organization, *Public Opinion, 1935–1971*, vol. 1: *1935–1948*, 20 April 1946 and 2 April 1949. See as typical examples, Gwenyth Barrington, 'This Is a Prostitute,' *Maclean's*, 1 October 1948, 12+, and Lotta Dempsey, 'What Are the Causes of Juvenile Delinquency?,' *Chatelaine*, June 1946, 10–11+.

33 Gilbert, *Cycle of Outrage*, 43–62

34 Thomas Doherty, *Teenagers and Teenpics: The Juvenilization of American Movies in the 1950s* (Boston 1988), ch. 5

35 Wolfgang M. Illing and Zoltan E. Zsigmond, *Enrolment in Schools and Universities, 1951–2 to 1975–6* (Ottawa, Economic Council of Canada Staff Study No. 20, 1967), Appendix table B-2

36 See for example 'Teenaged Bulge,' *Financial Post*, 10 September 1960, 9, and 'Tips on Selling to a Teenager,' *Financial Post*, 2 July 1960, 10. By 1959 *Life* estimated the U.S. teenage market to be almost $10 billion a year. See Wini Breneis, *Young, White and Miserable: Growing Up Female in the Fifties* (Boston 1992), 92

37 Doherty, *Teenagers and Teenpics*, 45; Breneis, *Young, White and Miserable*, 94. For a discussion of the nature of culture in the United States in these years see T.J. Jackson Lears, 'The Concept of Cultural Hegemony,' *American Historical Review* 90 (1985), 567–93.

38 For typical examples of 'adult' values see *Seventeen*, October 1957, 18, announcing its own production by Enid Haupt, *Seventeen Book of Young Living*. See, on the more general issue, Kirk Monteverde, *Teen Magazine: Communication of Values* (Boston 1975), 6.

39 Typical of the focus on the teenager in learned as well as popular literature was Ernest A. Smith, *American Youth Culture: Group Life in Teenage Society* (New York 1962).

40 As examples of the interest in Dean and Brando see 'Marlon Brando Speaks to You,' *Seventeen*, March 1956, 19–20, and 'James Dean: Bigger Than Life,' ibid., July 1957, 59. Dean also had a movie made about him, *The James Dean Story* (1957).

41 *Eaton's Fall–Winter Catalogue for 1960*, 284

42 Beth Bailey, *Front Porch to Back Seat: Courtship in Twentieth-Century America* (Baltimore 1988), 50

43 Claudia Hatch, 'The Heart of the Matter,' *Seventeen*, February 1956, 91

44 Canadian Institute of Public Opinion, 12 October 1963 poll, indicated that 79 per cent of adults disapproved of teenagers going steady.

45 Bailey, *Front Porch to Back Seat*, 50–2

46 Rene Konig, *The Restless Image: A Sociology of Fashion* (London 1973). The Wolfe quote is from the introduction.

47 Elizabeth Ewing, *History of Twentieth Century Fashion* (London 1975), 177–9; Jane Dorner, *Fashion in the Forties and Fifties* (Shepperton 1975), 'Teenage Rock'

48 This material is drawn from Eaton's catalogues for 1957 to 1961, *Seventeen* for 1956–60, and a random perusal of high-school year books in the late

1950s and early 1960s. See also the two works cited in note 47, above, which give more general fashion trends of these years.

49 Attendance figures from Dominion Bureau of Statistics [DBS], *Motion Picture Theatres, Exhibitors and Distributors,* catalogue 63-207A, 1950–60

50 On the production codes see Murray Schumach, *The Face on the Cutting Room Floor: The Story of Movie and Television Censorship* (New York 1964). On the operation of one Canadian censor see Don Wetherall with Irene Kmet, *Useful Pleasures: The Shaping of Leisure in Alberta, 1896–1945* (Edmonton 1990), 262–8.

51 DBS, *Motion Picture Theatres,* 1950–60

52 For a quick overview of the epic movies from this era see Derek Elley, *The Epic Film: Myths and History* (London 1984).

53 The best analysis of this is Doherty, *Teenagers and Teenpics.* The citation on Smell-O-Vision is on p. 28.

54 For a listing of teen movies see ibid., 'Selected Filmography,' 245–61.

55 *International Motion Picture Almanac, 1958* (New York 1958), 13A. See also 'Teen-Age Movie Going Habits,' *Motion Picture Herald,* 16 May 1959.

56 DBS, *Motion Picture Theatres,* 1950–60. There were no drive-in theatres in Quebec. For those who want real detail there is also the *International Motion Picture Almanac, 1958,* which lists the location of every drive-in in Canada (615–18).

57 Vancouver *Province,* 7 May 1953, 14

58 DBS, *Motion Picture Theatres,* 1954, 1955, 1956

59 Ed Ward, Geoffrey Stokes, and Ken Tucker, *Rock of Ages: The Rolling Stone History of Rock & Roll* (New York 1986), 105, 129–30, 175–7, indicate that strong police and parental resistance was persistent through the first years of rock and roll.

60 These hits are taken from *Billboard Magazine* and were compiled for me by David Kales.

61 DBS, 'Household Facilities,' catalogue 64-202, September 1953, table 25

62 Ibid., May 1959, table 28

63 Michael Schiffer, *The Portable Radio in American Life* (Tuscon 1991), 209. On Canada see 'Transistor Radios for Your Pocket,' *Financial Post,* 29 August 1959, 45.

64 DBS, *Manufactures of Household TV and Radios,* catalogue 43-205, 1964, table 14

65 Ward, Stokes, and Tucker, *Rock of Ages,* ch. 4

66 'Sh-Boom! The Crazy Career of the Crew-Cuts,' *Maclean's,* 1 November 1954, 26–7+

67 *The Blackboard Jungle* (Metro-Goldwyn-Mayer 1955). Directed by S. Brooks

68 For the timeline of rock and roll's evolution see Rolling Stone, *Rock Almanac: The Chronicles of Rock and Roll* (New York 1983).
69 Paul Rutherford, *When Television Was Young: Primetime Canada, 1952–1967* (Toronto 1990), 196–8
70 'Diana' was the Number 16 hit of 1957. See Gary Theroux and Bob Gilbert, *The Top Ten, 1956–Present* (New York 1982)
71 Rolling Stone, *Rock Almanac*, 21. See also *Life Magazine*, 18 April 1955, 7, for a calmer but also critical assessment of the meaning of rock and roll.
72 Barbara Moon, 'What You Don't Need to Know about Rock 'n' Roll,' *Maclean's*, 7 July 1956, 12–13+
73 Gilbert, *Cycle of Outrage*, 13
74 Doherty, *Teenagers and Teenpics*, 188
75 Ward, Stokes, and Tucker, *Rock of Ages*, 163
76 Bruce Cook, *The Beat Generation* (New York 1971), 10
77 Paul Goodman, *Growing Up Absurd: Problems of Youth in an Organized System* (New York 1960), 12

7: The Arrival of the Sixties

1 Peter Collier and David Horowitz, *Destructive Generation: Second Thoughts about the 60s* (Toronto 1989), 15
2 William Strauss and Neil Howe, *Generations* (New York 1991), 71; see also Anthony Esler, *Generations in History: An Introduction to the Concept* (n.p. 1982), 44
3 Esler, *Generations in History*, 44
4 According to one retrospective poll done in the United States, the favourite year with which to begin 'the sixties' was 1964. See Rex Weiner and Dianne Stillman, *Woodstock Census: The Nationwide Survey of the Sixties Generation* (New York 1979), 35.
5 François Ricard, *The Lyric Generation: The Life and Times of the Baby Boomers* (Toronto 1994), 107
6 Robert Bothwell, Ian Drummond, and John English, *Canada since 1945: Power, Politics, and Provincialism*, rev. ed. (Toronto 1989), 149
7 Cited in John Lewis Gaddis, *Strategies of Containment: A Critical Appraisal of American National Security Policy* (Toronto 1982), 131
8 Walter Lafeber, *America, Russia and the Cold War, 1945–1990* (New York 1990), 217–19
9 This material is drawn from David Horowitz, *From Yalta to Vietnam* (Harmondsworth 1967) and Lafeber, *America, Russia and the Cold War, 1945–1990*. Both are revisionist accounts, Horowitz's more so than Lafeber's, and

themselves reflect the changed perspective on the Cold War that has occurred since 1960.

10 For a detailed study of Cuba in the Kennedy years see Michael R. Beschloss, *The Crisis Years: Kennedy and Khrushchev, 1960–1963* (New York 1991), 90–117, 412–596. For a reaction immediately after the fact see Karl E. Meyer and Tad Szulc, *The Cuban Invasion: The Chronicle of a Disaster* (New York 1962).

11 'Hate Running Loose Hits Out at Nixons,' *Life*, 26 May 1958, 32–8. See also Stephen Ambrose, *Nixon: The Education of a Politician, 1913–1962* (New York 1987), 472–8, 481–2.

12 Ernest Levos, 'The War for Men's Minds: The Canadian Perspective on Foreign Policy in Asia, 1945–1957,' PhD thesis, University of Alberta, 1991

13 J. Ghent, 'Canada, the United States and the Cuban Missile Crisis,' *Pacific Historical Review* 1979, 165–79

14 National Archives of Canada [NAC], Records of the Canadian Union of Students, vol. 7, file 906–0: Memo dated June 1966. See also vol. 7, file – September: 'Resolutions of the 30th Congress,' 3–9 September 1966, 38–9.

15 Kennedy is reported to have said after his state visit to Ottawa, 'I didn't think he was a son of a bitch ... I thought he was a prick': Beschloss, *The Crisis Years*, 163.

16 See Bothwell, Drummond, and English, *Canada since 1945*, 234–6; George Grant, *Lament for a Nation: The Defeat of Canadian Nationalism* (Toronto 1965); Pierre Berton, *Maclean's*, 6 April 1963, 62; Ramsay Cook, 'Foreign Policy and the Election: An Uncertain Trumpet,' *International Journal* (Summer 1963), 374–80.

17 Edward Morgan, *The 60s Experience: Hard Lessons about Modern America* (Philadelphia 1991), 111–12

18 McMaster University, Special Collections, CUCND-SUPA Archives, Box 1: Gary Moffat, Introduction, *History of the Canadian Peace Movement until 1969*, 147

19 Bothwell, Drummond, and English, *Canada since 1945*, 241

20 Michael S. Cross, ed., *The Decline and Fall of a Good Idea: CCF–NDP Manifestos, 1932–1969* (Toronto 1974), 40

21 There are many histories and memoirs of the anti-segregation movement in the South. See on the early years Aldon D. Morris, *Origins of the Civil Rights Movement* (New York 1984). See also William H. Chafe, 'The Civil Rights Revolution, 1945–1960: The Gods Bring Thread to Webs Begun,' in Robert Bremner and Gary Richard, eds., *Reshaping America: Society and Institutions, 1945–1960* (Columbus, OH, 1982), 69–100, 71–93. Morgan, *The*

Sixties Experience, 35–86, looks at the ongoing relationship between civil rights and other sixties movements.

22 Chafe, 'Civil Rights Revolution,' 93–4

23 Province of Alberta, Department of Education, *Junior High School Guide for Social Studies* (adopted September 1958), 132

24 See, for example, the article 'We Have Bigotry All Right – But No Alabamas,' *Maclean's*, 17 April 1965, 4.

25 None of this denies the fact that many individuals held racist ideas.

26 Milton Viorst, *Fire in the Streets: America in the 1960s* (New York 1979), 104

27 Malcolm Reid, *The Shouting Signpainters* (Toronto 1972), 33

28 Pierre Vallières, *Nègres blanc d'Amérique: Autobiographie précoce d'un 'terroriste' québécois* (Montreal 1968). An English translation appeared in 1971 under the title *White Niggers of America.*

29 Todd Gitlin, *The Sixties: Years of Hope, Days of Rage* (New York 1987), 348, 350

30 Tom Wolfe, *Radical Chic and Mau-Mauing the Flak Catchers* (New York 1970), 8. See also Don Schance, *The Panther Paradox: A Liberal's Dilemma* (New York 1970), 226–8.

31 Gitlin, *The Sixties*, 348

32 Pamphlet, 'For an Independent Socialist Canada,' sponsored by Dave Barrett, John Conway et al. (undated but *circa* 1969). Private collection of D. Kales

33 Stewart Goodings, 'Microcosm of Biculturalism,' *Saturday Night*, April 1964, 25

34 *Ubyssey*, 2 March 1965, 4

35 S.F. Wise and R.C. Brown, *Canada Views the United States; Nineteenth-Century Political Attitudes* (Toronto 1967); Carl Berger, *A Sense of Power: Studies in the Ideas of Nineteenth-Century Imperialism* (Toronto 1970), ch. 6.

36 McMaster University, Special Collections, CUCND–SUPA Archives, Box 2: Peter [Boothroyd?] to Nancy, 14 April 1965

37 Ibid., Box 5: 'Canada in the Twentieth Century and the Future of Man,' 21

38 Kari Levitt, *Silent Surrender; The American Economic Empire in Canada* (Toronto 1970), gives one of the classic statements of this view.

39 Cyril Levitt, *Children of Privilege: Student Revolt in the Sixties* (Toronto 1984), 33–4

40 Department of Finance, *Quarterly Economic Review*, June 1989, annual reference tables

41 F.H. Leacy, ed., *Historical Statistics of Canada*, 2d ed. (Ottawa 1983), tables D175–7

42 Christopher Freeman, 'Prometheus Unbound,' *Futures*, October 1984

43 John Sterman, 'Caught by the Long Wave,' *Globe and Mail*, 20 February 1993, B4
44 Canadian Institute of Public Opinion, *Gallup Poll of Canada*, 4 April and 12 December 1959; 27 January, 24 February, and 4 June 1960
45 Ibid., 20 April 1960 and 15 February 1961. There was an interesting exception in the case of working women: see ibid., 14 June 1961. Obviously the emphasis on the family and on distinct gender roles was still strong.
46 Levitt, *Children of Privilege*, 15
47 DBS, *A Graphic Presentation of Canadian Education* (Ottawa 1961; catalogue 81-515), 27. For the problems of instability in the 1940s and 1950s in one university see Michael Hayden, *Seeking a Balance: University of Saskatchewan, 1907–1982* (Vancouver 1983), 214–15
48 *Historical Statistics of Canada*, tables W-342 and W-475
49 Claude Bissell, 'Internal University Government,' *Proceedings of the Association of College and Universities of Canada*, 1966, 68
50 Paul Axelrod, *Scholars and Dollars: Politics, Economics and the Universities of Ontario, 1945–1980* (Toronto 1982)
51 Claude Bissell, *Halfway Up Parnassus: A Personal Account of the University of Toronto, 1932–1971* (Toronto 1974), 16
52 Jacques Barzun, *The House of Intellect* (New York 1959). Note that the 'house' Barzun refers to is the process of thought on intellectual matters.
53 C.F. Fraser, 'The Crisis in the Arts, Letters and Sciences,' *Dalhousie Review*, April 1950, 35
54 Helen Horowitz, *Campus Life: Undergraduate Cultures from the End of the Eighteenth Century to the Present* (Chicago 1987). As Paul Axelrod notes, however, the emphasis on the exceptional rather than the normal tends to overdramatize the incidence of rebellion: see Paul Axelrod, *Making of the Middle Class: student life in English Canada during the thirties* (Montreal and Kingston 1990), 190.
55 See Keith Walden, 'Hazes, Hustles, Scraps and Stunts: Initiations at the University of Toronto, 1880–1925,' in Paul Axelrod and John Reid, eds., *Youth, University and Canadian Society* (Montreal 1989), 94–121.
56 Axelrod, *Scholars and Dollars*, 101
57 Hayden, *Seeking a Balance*, 216
58 W. Keith Wilkinson, 'Residence Culture: A Descriptive Study,' PhD thesis, University of Alberta, Department of Educational Psychology, 1966, 90
59 Detailed histories of student life are just beginning to emerge in Canada. For a range of studies see the articles by Brian McKillop, James Pitsula, and Judith Fingard in Paul Axelrod and John G. Reid, eds., *Youth University and Canadian Society* (Montreal and Kingston 1989).

60 E.F. Sheffield, 'Canadian University and College Enrolment,' *Proceedings of the National Conference of Canadian Universities for 1955*; George Croskery and Gerald Nason, eds., *Canadian Conference on Education. Addresses and Proceedings* (Ottawa 1958), 210. See also S.E. Smith, 'Crisis Ahead in Our Universities,' *Financial Post*, 22 January 1955, 60. On the efforts of the NCUU to generate publicity see Robin Harris, *A History of Higher Education in Canada* (Toronto 1976), 460.
61 Cited in Axelrod, *Scholars and Dollars*, 85
62 Canadian Institute of Public Opinion, *The Gallup Poll of Canada*, 29 June 1963. By 1963 the figure had shifted dramatically
63 M. Long, 'Competing with Russia in the Schools,' *Canadian Comment*, November 1957
64 Gordon Bertram, *The Contribution of Education to Economic Growth*, Economic Council of Canada Staff Study No. 12 (Ottawa 1966), 55–63. See also David Dodge, *Returns to Investment in University Training: The Case of Canadian Accountants, Engineers and Scientists* (Industrial Relations Centre, Queen's University 1972)
65 Clark Kerr, *The Uses of the University* (Cambridge, MA, 1963), 8
66 Ibid., 43, 26
67 H.B. Neatby, 'Visions and Revisions: The View from the Presidents' Offices of Ontario Universities since the Second World War,' *CHA Historical Papers*, 1988, 3–4
68 Barzun, *The House of Intellect*, 89, 95
69 Neatby, 'Visions and Revisions,' 1–15
70 Wolfgang M. Illing and Zoltan E. Zsigmond, *Enrolment in Schools and Universities, 1951–2 to 1975–6*. Economic Council of Canada Staff Study no. 20, (Ottawa 1967), table 4.7
71 J.A. Corry, 'Presidential Address,' *Proceedings of the Association of College and Universities of Canada*, 1965, 42
72 E.F. Sheffield, 'University Development: The Past Five Years and the Next Ten,' in Davidson Dunton and Dorothy Patterson, eds., *Canada's Universities in a New Age* (Ottawa 1962), 19, and J.J. Deutsch, 'Comments,' ibid., 25. Deutsch was referring particularly to the staffing problem.
73 *Report of the Board of Governors of the University of Alberta*, 1968–9
74 DBS, 'Survey of Higher Education' (catalogue 81-204), relevant years.
75 *Historical Statistics of Canada*, 2d ed., table W532
76 DBS, *A Graphic Presentation of Canadian Education* (Ottawa 1961; catalogue 81-515), 26
77 *Canada Year Book, 1959*, 395; *1969*, 378
78 'Professor Shortage Gets Worse,' *Financial Post*, 22 July 1957, 1, 16; 'How

Well Are Our Teachers Prepared,' in DBS, *A Graphic Presentation of Canadian Education*, 22–3

79 AUCC, *Proceedings*, 1966, 48

80 Claude Bissell, 'The Problems and Opportunities of Canadian Universities,' in Dunton and Patterson, eds., *Canada's Universities in a New Age*

81 Levitt, *Children of Affluence*, 34

82 Fass, *The Damned and the Beautiful*, 149; Helen Lefkowotz Horowitz, *Campus Life: Undergraduate Cultures from the End of the Eighteenth Century to the Present* (Chicago 1987), 49–55.

8: 'Hope I Die Before I Get Old': The Rise of the Counter-Culture, 1963–1968

1 McMaster University, SUPA Papers, Box 5: Mimeograph entitled 'Canada in the Twentieth Century and the Future of Man,' 4

2 'The New Learning,' *Maclean's*, May 1969, 68

3 '34,000 Beatle Fans Pay $100,000 to Hear Themselves,' *Toronto Daily Star*, 7 September 1964, 2. See, in the same edition, '200 Girls Swoon in Battle of the Beatles,' 1, and Nathan Cohen, 'With the Beatles,' 18.

4 Douglas Fetherling, *Travels by Night: A Memoir of the Sixties* (Toronto 1994), 134

5 David Sharpe, *Rochdale: The Runaway College* (Toronto 1987), 239–40

6 Ibid., 261

7 According to William O'Neill, this statement was supposedly first used during the Berkeley free-speech protest by Jack Weinberg: William O'Neill, *Coming Apart: An Informal History of America in the 1960s* (Toronto 1971), 279

8 Lewis Yablonski, *The Hippie Trip* (New York 1968)

9 'Our Schools Produce Lobotomized Dolts,' *Gateway*, 16 January 1970, C-2

10 Ed Ward, Geoffrey Stokes, and Ken Tucker, *Rock of Ages: The Rolling Stone History of Rock & Roll* (New York 1986), 209

11 Jon Pareles and Patricia Romanowski, *The Rolling Stone Encyclopedia of Rock and Roll* (New York 1983), 97, and *The Rolling Stone Rock Almanac: The Chronicles of Rock and Roll* (New York 1983) 65, 68

12 Paul Goodman, *Growing Up Absurd: Problems of Youth in the Organized System* (New York 1960), 47

13 'Backstage with the Beatniks,' *Maclean's*, 11 April 1959, 3

14 Bruce Pollock, *In Their Own Words* (New York 1975), 'Newport Generation, 1961–1965,' in R. Serge Denisoff, *Sing a Song of Social Significance* (Bowling Green 1983), 110–17. See also O'Neill, *Coming Apart*, 235.

15 Ward, Stokes, and Tucker, *Rock of Ages*, 261

16 Pareles and Romanowski, *The Rolling Stone Enyclopedia*, 329

17 Ian Sclanders, 'Hello Toronto – My How You've Changed,' *Maclean's*, 6 February 1965, 18–21
18 Morris Dickstein, *Gates of Eden: American Culture in the Sixties* (New York 1977), 185. This is confirmed in the responses to a poll done on the sixties. See Rex Weiner and Deanne Stillman, *Woodstock Census* (New York 1979), 69–70.
19 O'Neill, *Coming Apart*, 233
20 See, among others, Hunter Davies, *The Beatles*, rev. ed. (New York 1978). Ward, Stokes, and Tucker, *Rock of Ages*, ch. 15
21 'Beatlemania,' *Newsweek*, 18 November 1963, 23–4; 'New Madness,' *Time*, 15 November 1963
22 Ward, Stokes, and Tucker, *Rock of Ages*, 266
23 'Britain's Shocking Teenage Gangs,' *Toronto Daily Star*, 2 July 1964, 61. Appropriately enough, it was a British rock group, the Who, that sought to depict the mod–rocker phenomenon, in the 1979 movie *Quadrophenia*.
24 As the peer-group sense of alienation became better developed, moves were made to reunite the generation. By the late 1960s there was a fascination and sense of loose comradeship with bikers that helps explain the Stones' use of Hell's Angels at Altamont.
25 Don Newlands and Jack Batten, 'Hawks, Chicks and a Swinging Nest,' *Maclean's*, 20 March 1965, 23
26 'The Hairy Ones,' *Toronto Daily Star*, 6 July 1964, 40
27 O'Neill, *Coming Apart*, 249
28 Ibid., 259; 'What the Beatles Have Done to Hair,' *Look*, 29 December 1964
29 See, for example, 'You Can't Keep a Good Mini-skirt Down,' *Edmonton Journal*, 23 September 1967, 56
30 Jon Ruddy, 'Where Did You Go? School? What Did You Learn? Don't!' *Maclean's*, 19 November 1966, 9–11+, s7
31 Jon Ruddy, 'Stop the World, They Want to Get Off,' *Maclean's*, 1 November 1965, 51
32 'Long Hairs Take 'Trip' – Right Out of Courtroom,' *Edmonton Journal*, 5 October 1967, 1
33 Helen Horowitz, *Campus Life: Undergraduate Cultures from the Eighteenth Century to the Present* (Chicago 1988), 228
34 Paul A. Carter, *Another Part of the Fifties* (New York 1983), 96–8
35 Female teenager calling a Vancouver talk show in 1966. Cited in Simma Holt, *Sex and the Teenage Revolution* (Toronto 1967), 17
36 Peter Gzowski, 'How You Going to Keep Them Down on the Farm after They've Said F*** You,' *Saturday Night*, May 1969, 29–31
37 Holt, *Sex and the Teenage Revolution*, 43

38 'Why the Beatles Click,' *Maclean's*, January 1967, 66. See also 'Science Looks at Beatlemania,' *Science Digest*, May 1964, 24–6
39 Pareles and Romanowski, *Rolling Stone Rock Almanac*, 97. See also, on the blending of rock, folk, and politics, Myrna Kostash, *Long Way from Home* (Toronto 1980), 109, and Dickstein, *Gates of Eden*, 188.
40 Anthony Scaduto, *Bob Dylan: An Intimate Biography* (New York 1973), 205
41 Dickstein, *Gates of Eden*, 197
42 'Pot Addictive Claims Drug Fuzz,' *Ubyssey*, 4 February 1965, 2
43 Emily Murphy, *The Black Candle* (Toronto 1922), 332–3. This is a quote from the Los Angeles police chief.
44 *Statutes of Canada*, 7–8, Edward VII, 1908, C5: 'An Act to prohibit the importation, manufacture, sale of opium for other than medical purposes.' For the updated version see *Revised Statutes of Canada, 1952*, vol. 3, ch. 201: 'An Act respecting opium and narcotic drugs.'
45 Royal Canadian Mounted Police, *Law and Order in Canadian Democracy*, rev. ed. (Ottawa 1952), 194
46 *Interim Report of the Commission of Inquiry into the Non-Medical Use of Drugs* (Ottawa 1973; hereinafter LeDain Commission), 369
47 Canada, *Annual Report of the Royal Canadian Mounted Police, 1962–3*, 20–1. See also, LeDain Commission, 307.
48 LeDain Commission, 308
49 'Background,' *Maclean's*, 20 November 1965, 64
50 On the media attention on drugs see David Lewis Stein, 'The Growing Accceptability of a "Harmless" Drug,' *Maclean's*, 4 January 1964, 14–15+. For a relatively early discussion of the merits of pot see Al Horst, 'Argument,' *Ubyssey*, 12 February 1965, pf2; 'LSD as Safe as Aspirin – Hoffer,' *Varsity*, 25 September 1967, 3
51 'UBC Co-ed Charged in Drug Raid,' *Ubyssey*, 20 November 1964, 1
52 LeDain Commission, 159
53 Ibid., 161–6. On the history of marijuana usage see Brian Inglis, *The Forbidden Game: A Social History of Drugs* (New York 1975), ch. 7.
54 Ruddy, 'Stop the World, They Want to Get Off,' 22. See also Kostash, *Long Way from Home*, 114–15; Al Horst, 'Argument,' *Ubyssey*, 12 February 1965, pf2
55 Sidney Katz, 'My Twelve Hours as a Madman,' *Maclean's*, 1 October 1953, 9–13. Albert Hoffman, *LSD: My Problem Child* (New York 1980), 58–9, refers to the Katz experiment.
56 Abraham Hoffer, 'The Confrontation between the Psychedelic Experience and Society,' *Canadian Dimension* 4/5 (Summer 1967), 5–7. For a report on

some of the experiments see Muriel Clements, 'New Hope for Alcoholics,' *Saturday Night*, 4 July 1959, 14–15, and LeDain Commission, 127–30.

57 The best study of the bizarre history of this bizarre drug is Martin A. Lee and Bruce Shlain, *Acid Dreams: The CIA, LSD and the Sixties Rebellion* (New York 1985). See also LeDain Commission, *Interim Report*, 127–56.

58 Interview with T. Weckowizc, October 1990. Professor Weckowizc was in Saskatchewan and worked with the LSD team in the 1950s.

59 Lee and Shlain, *Acid Dreams*, 28–9

60 Ibid., 71,

61 Ibid., 77–89

62 Michael Starks, *Cocaine Fiends and Reefer Madness* (New York 1982), 106

63 Pareles and Romanowski, *Rolling Stone Encyclopedia of Rock and Roll*, 165; Scaduto, *Bob Dylan*, 204

64 Tom Wolfe, *Electric Kool-Aid Acid Test* (New York 1968). The book had gone through twelve printings by 1972.

65 *Canada Year Book*, 1969, 428; *1970–1*, 513

66 The major periodicals in the United States began to notice drugs on campus in 1966. See *Life*, 9 September 1966; *Newsweek*, 2 May 1966.

67 *Gateway*, 23 November 1966, 8

68 *Ubyssey*, 16 March 1967, 8

69 LeDain Commission, *Interim Report*, 495

70 *Annual Report of the Commissioner of the Royal Canadian Mounted Police*, 1966, 44

71 Regina vs Hartley and McCallum; cited in LeDain Commission, *Interim Report*, 398. See also Holt, *Sex and the Teenage Revolution*, 78.

72 David Lewis Stein, 'The Growing Acceptability of a "Harmless" Narcotic,' *Maclean's*, 4 January 1964, 14–15

73 *Gateway*, 21 November 1969, 1

74 Lee and Shain, *Acid Dreams*, 154–6

75 One American survey found that of those who considered themselves 'involved in the sixties,' about 42 per cent took amphetamines at least occasionally. The comparable figure for marijuana was 80 per cent and for LSD 47 per cent. See Weiner and Stillman, *Woodstock Census*, 117.

76 See LeDain Commission, *Interim Report*, Appendix B, for letters from various exponents and opponents of drug use. See also 'The Girl Who Came Back, *Gateway*, 9 September 1968, 5, and John Reid, 'Suicide in Slow Motion,' *Canadian Welfare* 1969, reprinted in Norman Sheffe, ed., *Youth Today* (Toronto 1970), 23–6.

77 'Two Kinds of Drugs,' *Guerilla*, March 1971, 16

78 Sheila Gormley, *Drugs and the Canadian Scene* (Toronto 1970), 65. See also

Weiner and Stillman, *Woodstock Census*, 122–3; Ron Verzuh, *Underground Times: Canada's Flower-Child Revolutionaries* (Toronto 1989), 29; M. Johnson, 'Society Screwing Its Youth,' *Gateway*, 31 October 1969, 4.

79 University of Alberta Archives, Accession 84–54, Box 1: N. Mehra, 'The Residence Student: A Study of Opinions and Reactions,' University of Alberta Office of Research and Planning, 1971, 68

80 Nechama Tec, 'Some Aspects of High School Status and Differential Involvement with Mirihuana: A Study of Suburban Teenagers,' in Rolf E. Muus, ed., *Adolescent Behavior and Society: A Book of Readings* (New York 1971), 583

81 Accurate figures on drug usage are difficult to obtain. These estimates are from the LeDain Commission, Appendix E. See also Gormley, *Drugs and the Canadian Scene*, 61.

82 'The psychological distance between activists and audience must be smaller than between audience and target': Edward Morgan, *The Sixties Experience* (Philadelphia 1991), 31. Gormley, *Drugs and the Canadian Scene*, 25

83 McMaster University, Special Collections, Radical Archives, Box 3, Canadian University Press File: Martin Nicolaus, 'The Contradictions of Advanced Capitalist Society and Its Revolution' (Radical Education Department, undated), 8

84 H.G. Schenk, *The Mind of the European Romantics* (London 1966). Note that he refers to the romantic era as 'the era of youth par excellence' (6).

85 On the dominance of technology see Thomas P. Hughes, *American Genesis: A Century of Invention and Technological Enthusiasm* (New York 1989).

86 Ibid., 5

87 Morgan, *The Sixties Experience*, 170–1; Dickstein, *Gates of Eden*, 61–2

88 'No Place. Interview with Greg Sorbara,' *Carleton*, 16 February 1968, 2. One of the most pro-technology reform organizations was the Company of Young Canadians. See National Archives of Canada [NAC], Records of the Company of Young Canadians, vol. 2, file 103–3: 'Draft of Terms of Reference of Company of Young Canadians,' 16 June 1966, and P. Findlay to Allan Clarke, 11 July 1967.

89 Bill King, 'The Sun's Gonna Shine,' *Guerilla*, 3 July 1970, 6

90 Cited in Dickstein, *Gates of Eden*, 60

91 Morgan, *The Sixties Experience*, 173

92 Goodman, *Growing Up Absurd*, 10–11

93 William Cameron, 'Portrait of a Super-Hippie,' *Star Weekly Magazine*, 23 September 1967, 2

94 Bob Cruise, 'Love Labored. Sunshine Turns On,' *Ubyssey*, 30 September 1966, 13
95 'You, Me and Liberation: Notes from Conversations with Bob McArthur, Jim Brophy, Ray James,' *Guerilla*, 1 August 1970, 9
96 'Baby It's Dead Outside,' *Gateway*, 16 March 1967, 3. Originally from the student newspaper of Boston University.
97 'Easter Be-In,' *Georgia Straight*, 11 April 1969, 9
98 John Fekete and Elly Alboim, 'Identity and Anxiety,' *McGill Daily*, 11 October 1966, 1
99 Jim Christie, 'Beyond the Spectacle,' *Guerilla*, 1 June 1970
100 Ken Lester, 'Sorting It All Out,' *Georgia Straight*, 28 May 1969, 16
101 Timothy Leary, 'Manifesto,' *Guerilla*, 19 October 1970, 20
102 McMaster University Special Collections, SUPA Papers, Box 5: 'Canada in the Twentieth Century and the Future of Man,' notes on a Conference in Ottawa, June 1967
103 Melody Killian, ' A Love Letter,' *Georgia Straight*, 4 April 1969, 13
104 'Drop Dead Pat,' *Ubyssey*, 10 March 1967, 4
105 George P. Grant, had been concerned with this issue from the mid-fifities. See his 'Man in the Atomic Age,' *Text of Addresses Delivered at the Twenty-Fourth Couchiching Conference* (Toronto: Canadian Institute of Public Affairs 1958), 39–45. This was followed by elaborations in *Lament for a Nation* (Toronto 1965) and *Technology and Empire: Perspectives on North America* (Toronto 1969). On Grant see Joan E. O'Donovan, *George Grant and the Twilight of Justice* (Toronto 1984), and William Christian, *George Grant: A Biography* (Toronto 1993),
106 Dickstein, *Gates of Eden*, 21
107 Sharpe, *Rochdale*, 41
108 Morgan, *The Sixties Experience*, 92
109 Weiner and Stillman, *Woodstock Census*, 79
110 For a listing of Number one (U.S. and U.K.) songs see Pareles and Romanowski, *Rolling Stone Rock Almanac*. For a discussion of music see Bruce Pollock, *When the Music Mattered: Rock in the 1960s* (New York 1983).
111 Fetherling, *Travels by Night*, 89
112 O'Neill, *Coming Apart*, 258
113 Ibid., 254–5
114 Lee and Shain, *Acid Dreams*, 108
115 Satsvarupa dasa Goswami, *Planting the Seed: New York City, 1965–1966* (Los Angeles 1980), 5–8
116 Cited in Sharpe, *Rochdale*, 57

117 McMaster University, Special Collections, Radical Archives, Box 6, File 'Rochdale': *Rochdale Image Nation*, undated (sometime in 1969)
118 Letter to the Editor, *Georgia Straight*, 25 April 1969, 2
119 Gormley, *Drugs and the Canadian Scene*, 25
120 National Film Archives, 76-6-77, 78, National Film Board, *Flowers on a One-Way Street* (Robin Spry Producer)
121 For a report on Yorkville from a sympathetic point of view see National Archives of Canada, Records of the Company of Young Canadians, vol. 9, file 108-3: Memo from Alan Clarke to J.S. Hodgson, 4 October 1967.
122 City of Toronto, Municipal Reference Library, Vertical file Collection, Subject 'Yorkville,' has an excellent set of newspaper clippings on the Yorkville controversy. Many of the individual newspaper citations below are drawn from that file.
123 Vertical File, *Toronto Telegram*, 17 April 1967
124 Vertical File, *Globe and Mail*, 11 May 1967. Province of Ontario, Report of the Select Committee on Youth, 1967 (cited in *Globe and Mail*, 7 April 1967)
125 Metropolitan Toronto Library, 'Biographical Scrapbook,' vol. 55, 59–69
126 NAC, Records of the Company of Young Canadians (RG116), vol. 4, file 103-6-2: Alan Clarke to Lester Pearson, 4 January 1967. See also vol. 9, file 108-3: Jerry Gambil to Alan Clarke, 20 September 1967, which details DePoe's history with the CYC
127 DePoe Interview on CITY TV, Toronto, Fall 1994
128 NAC, Lester Pearson Papers, vol. 149, file 553-2, Douglas Ward to Members CYC, 4 January 1967
129 *Star Weekly Magazine*, 23 September 1967, 2
130 Vertical File, *Globe and Mail*, 22 June 1967. See also *Toronto Daily Star*, 27 June and 18 July 1967.
131 For a chronology of the Yorkville controversy see NAC, Records of the Company of Young Canadians, vol. 9, file 108-3: Alan Clarke to J.S. Hodgson, 4 October 1967. On the 'riot' in August see Vertical File, *Toronto Daily Star*, 21 August 1967.
132 Barbara G. Myerhoff, 'The Revolution as a Trip: Symbol and Paradox,' in Philip G. Albach and Robert S. Laufer, eds., *The New Pilgrims: Youth Protest in Transition* (New York 1972), 251–66, looks at the issue of ritual and symbol in student protest.
133 NFB, *Flowers on a One-Way Street*
134 Vertical File, *Toronto Telegram*, 4 August 1967
135 Metropolitan Toronto Library, Biographical Scrapbook, vol. 55, 65

136 'Lampy's in the Limelight Down at City Hall Again,' *Toronto Daily Star*, 7 December 1967, 7
137 NFB, *Flowers on a One-Way Street*
138 Cameron, 'Portrait of a Super-Hippie,' 6
139 NFB, *Flowers on a One-Way Street*
140 'Hippies Hold Love-In,' *Globe and Mail*, 21 August 1967, 15
141 Cameron, 'Portrait of a Super-Hippie,' 2

9: Youth Radicalism in the Sixties

1 National Archives of Canada [NAC], Records of the Company of Young Canadians, vol. 2, file 103-3-1: Memorandum by Stewart Goodings, July 1966
2 Alan Walker, 'The Revolt on Campus,' *Star Weekly Magazine*, 13 January 1968, 1
3 D.C. Williams, 'The Nature of the Contemporary University,' *Proceedings of the Associations of Colleges and Universities of Canada for 1968*, 106
4 Edward Morgan, *The Sixties Experience: Hard Lessons about Modern America* (Philadelphia 1991), 31
5 Gary Moffatt, *A History of the Peace Movement in Canada* (n.p., n.d.) 41. See also McMaster University, SUPA Papers, Box 14: Dimitri Roussopoulous 'Some Notes on Reconstituting SUPA.' He says that it was always the intention of the CUCND to move beyond single-issue politics.
6 Morgan, *The Sixties Experience*, 94
7 James Harding, 'An Ethical Movement in Search of an Analysis: The Student Union for Peace Action in Canada,' *Our Generation* 3/4 (May 1966), 20–39
8 Cyrill Levitt, *Children of Privilege: Student Revolt in the Sixties* (Toronto 1984), 40
9 Moffatt, *History of the Peace Movement*, 41
10 This was a theme that recurred in several interviews with activists of the 1960s. As many of them noted, the Student Christian Movement was often their first involvement in campus politics, though usually not their last.
11 Thomas Socknat, *Witness against War: Pacifism in Canada, 1900–1945* (Toronto 1981); Richard Allen, *The Social Passion* (Toronto 1970)
12 Editorial 'Berkeley,' *Ubyssey*, 27 May 1965
13 George R. Vickers, *The Formation of the New Left: The Early Years* (Lexington, MA, 1975), 66–71
14 Students for a Democratic Society, *The Port Huron Statement* (New York 1964), 3, 62

15 On the north–south connection see McMaster University, SUPA Papers, Box 2, file 'Toronto Office Correspondence, 1964–1965.' See also a critique of the Americanism of the student Left in James Laxer, 'The Student Movement and Canadian Independence,' *Canadian Dimension* Survival Kit, No. 3: *Canadian Nationalism* (n.p. 1970), 1–9
16 Ibid., Box 2: 'Minutes of CUCND/SUPA Membership Conference,' 28 December 1964 to 1 January 1965
17 On the McNaught quote see *Our Generation* 3/4 (May 1966), 3. For the CYC comment see NAC, Records of the Company of Young Canadians, vol. 2, file 103-3-1: Memo by Stewart Goodings, July 1966.
18 Peter Gzowski, 'The Righteous Crusaders of the New Left,' *Maclean's*, 15 November 1965, 19
19 *Our Generation* 3/4 (May 1966), inside front cover
20 McMaster University, SUPA Papers, Box 2: 'The Worklist,' 26 February 1966, which gives a list of student contacts across the country
21 Moffatt, *History of the Peace Movement*, 44. For Alinsky's theories see Saul Alinsky, *Reveille for Radicals* (Chicago 1946). See also McMaster University, SUPA Papers, Box 14: Myrna Wood and Michael Rowan, 'Notes on the Nationalization of Saul Alinsky,' and Box 14: Judi Berenstein, 'Psychedelic Organizing,' undated.
22 See McMaster University, SUPA Papers, Box 14: Brenda Dineen, Harry Kpoyto, and Carol Oleniuk, 'A Contribution to the Prepatory Discussion for the Goderich Conference on the Future Direction and Structure of the New Left,' 2. As they say, the Vietnam War has 'undoubtedly been the major radicalizing factor in recent years.' See also McMaster University, Radical Archives, Box 1: Canadian Student Days of Protest, Progress Report no. 1, 26 September 1966.
23 McMaster University, SUPA Papers, Box 14: Judi Berenstein, 'Psychedelic Organizing,' 5
24 On the various activities of the SUPA see Harding, 'An Ethical Movement,' 22–4. For some examples of campus activity see SUPA advertisement in *McGill Daily*, 25 February 1966, 11
25 NAC, Records of the Company of Young Canadians, vol. 1, file 353.2: *SUPA Newsletter* 3/2 (December 1966), 'Report from Carleton'
26 Interview with Stewart Goodings, 8 January 1992
27 NAC, Pearson Papers, vol. 148, file 535.2: J.S. Hodgson to J.A. Smith, 8 August 1967
28 NAC, Records of the Company of Young Canadians, vol. 9, file 108-3: J.D. Edmonds to Paul Hellyer, 14 May 1965
29 Ibid., vol. 2, file 103-3-1: Press Release of June 1965

30 Ibid., vol. 1, file 100-4: 'Story for Canadian Embassy in Oslo on the Company of Young Canadians' (undated memo)
31 Ibid., vol. 2, file 103-3-1: Stewart Goodings to J.E.G. Hardy, 10 January 1966
32 Ibid., 'Draft of Terms of Reference of Company of Young Canadians,' 16 June 1966. See also file 103-3-2: 'Draft of Volunteer Guide,' 31 December 1967, and Pearson Papers, vol. 148: J.D. Ward to Pearson, 15 December 1966; Records of the Canadian Union of Students, vol. 7: C.A.S. Hynam, 'What Is Community Development?' (broadcast on CKUA Radio, Edmonton, 26 October 1965).
33 Ibid., vol. 42, file B-2-1: Talk by Stewart Goodings at Innis College, Toronto, undated (sometime in 1966 or 1967). See also file 103-3-7: Herbert Beaudry, 'Toward a Definition of the Company of Young Canadians,' August 1967.
34 Interview with Stewart Goodings, 8 January 1992. Goodings sees the influence as positive but for a more negative assessment see letter to the editor by Duncan Edmonds, *Toronto Daily Star*, 5 January 1970, 7
35 McMaster University, SUPA Papers, Box 14: Memo by Jim Harding, 'Cash-in or Drop-Out: The Effects of the CYC,' undated (sometime in 1966). See also NAC, CYC Papers, vol. 9, file 110-C10: Mimeograph of 'Article Written by James Laxer for Canadian University Press,' 21 February 1966.
36 Frank Trumpane column, Toronto *Telegram*, 31 August 1967. NAC, Pearson Papers, vol. 148: Mrs Jack Gogel to Richard O'Hagen, 1 May 1966
37 NAC, Pearson Papers, vol. 149, file 353.2: Joey Smallwood to Lester Pearson, 16 February 1967
38 Ibid., Ruth Watson to John Matheson, 28 August 1967
39 See for example CBC interview of Alan Clarke by Tom Gould, 24 August 1967. Clarke refuses to admit any mistakes and defends David DePoe and Lynn Curtis. A transcript of the interview is in NAC, Pearson Papers, vol. 148, file 353.2. See also ibid., Clarke to Hodgson, 4 October 1967.
40 NAC, Records of the Company of Young Canadians, vol. 4, file 103-6-2: Alan Clarke to Lester Pearson, 4 January 1967
41 Interview with Richard Price, April 1993
42 'Regina Manifesto' (1933). Cited in Michael Cross, *The Decline and Fall of a Good Idea: CCF–NDP Manifestos, 1932–1969* (Toronto 1974), 19
43 Norman Penner, *The Canadian Left: A Critical Analysis* (Scarborough, ON, 1977), ch. 5
44 David Lewis, *The Good Fight: Political Memoirs, 1909–1958* (Toronto 1981), 323–4
45 'The new left – two views,' *Peak*, 25 January 1967. See also the comment about the conservatism of American communism: Conference notes in

McMaster University, Special Collections, CUCND-SUPA Papers, Box 5: 'Twentieth Century Canada and the Future of Man,' 18.

46 Stanley Ryerson, *The Founding of Canada: Beginnings to 1815* (Toronto 1963); *Unequal Union; Confederation and the Roots of Conflict in the Canadas* (Toronto 1968). C.B. Macpherson, *The Political Theory of Possessive Individualism: Hobbes to Locke* (Oxford 1962), and many others

47 Neil Nevitte, Herman Bakvis, and Roger Gibbins, 'The Ideological Contours of "New Politics" in Canada; Policy, Mobilization and Partisan Support,' *Canadian Journal of Political Science* 22 (September 1989), 475–503

48 Marcel Rioux, 'Youth in the Contemporary World and in Quebec,' *Our Generation* 3/4 (May 1966), 9

49 The citation is from a socialist-separatist magazine *Parti pris.* Cited in Malcolm Reid, *The Shouting Signpainters* (Toronto 1972), 29–30

50 Harding, 'An Ethical Movement in Search of an Analysis,' 26. See also McMaster University, SUPA Papers, Box 5: 'Canada in the Twentieth Century and the Future of Man,' 16.

51 Alan Walker, 'Student Power,' *Star Weekly Magazine,* 13 January 1968, 4

52 Ken Lester, 'Sorting it Out,' *Georgia Straight,* 28 May 1969, 17

53 McMaster University, SUPA Papers, Box 5: 'Canada in the Twentieth Century and the Future of Man,' 6

54 Ibid., Roebuck to members of the New Left Committee, 21 October 1967

55 Arthur Waskow, 'The New Student Movement,' *Our Generation,* May 1966, 52

56 McMaster University, SUPA Papers, Box 5: 'Canada in the Twentieth Century and the Future of Man,' 20

57 Dimitri Roussoupolous, 'Towards a Revolutionary Youth Movement and an Extra-Parliamentary Opposition in Canada,' in Dimitri Roussoupolous, ed., *The New Left in Canada* (Montreal 1970), 146

58 NAC, Pearson Papers, vol. 148: 'A Draft Statement of Aims and Principles of the Company of Young Canadians ... July 25, 1966,' 2; Reid, *Shouting Signpainters,* 36–8

59 Jim Harding, 'Adolescence, Personalism and SUPA,' *SUPA Newsletter* 3/2 (December 1966), 2

60 NAC, Records of the Company of Young Canadians, vol. 3, file 103-3-7: 'Aims and Principles Adopted by the Provisional Council, July 25 1966'

61 Ibid., vol. 2, file 103-3-1: Untitled mimeograph of speech of Stewart Goodings, July 1966

62 'Theory and Practice must go Hand in Hand,' *Gateway,* 4 October 1968, C-3

63 James Harding, 'The N.D.P., The Regina Manifesto and the New Left,' *Canadian Dimension,* November–December 1966, 18, 19

64 Waskow, 'The New Student Movement,' 59
65 Morris Dickstein, *Gates of Eden: American Culture in the Sixties* (New York, 1977), 70
66 Herbert Marcuse, *One-Dimensional Man: Studies in the Ideology of Advanced Industrial Society* (Boston 1964), 26. See also 'The Functionalization,' *McGill Daily*, 28 November 1966, 4. Marcuse's early work on psychology was *Eros and Civilization: A Philosophical Inquiry into Freud* (Boston 1955).
67 Jerry Rubin, *Do It: Scenarios of Revolution* (New York 1970), 116
68 See on this Sharon Yandle, 'On Being Social Deviants,' *Peak*, 15 February 1967, 12.
69 McMaster University, SUPA Papers, Box 5: James Harding to 'Other Frustrated Radicals,' 13 April 1967
70 McMaster University, SUPA Papers, Box 1: Ste Calixte Federal Council Meeting, 'Minutes, September 10, 1965'
71 The words are those of Beverly Taylor. She was involved in the CYC after dropping out of the University of Victoria. Desmond Hill, 'Just Want to Be Happy says Angry Young Woman,' *Victoria Times*, 24 January 1967
72 Kenneth Kenniston, *Young Radicals: Notes on Committed Youth* (New York 1968), 23
73 McMaster University, SUPA Papers, Box 5: Don [McKelvey?] to Comrades, 19 April 1967
74 Ibid., Box 2: John [Conway?] to Peter Boothroyd, 25 August 1964
75 Ibid: James Harding to 'Other Frustrated Radicals,' 13 April 1967
76 Ibid., Box 14: Memo 'On the Reconstruction of a New Left Organization in Canada,' undated (late 1967)
77 Sue Helwig, 'SUPA Disbands ... Admits Stagnation,' *Varsity*, 24 September 1967, 5
78 Ken Long, 'Committee for Provocation,' *SUPA Newsletter* 3/2 (December 1966), 21
79 NAC, Records of the Canadian Union of Students, vol. 7: CUS *Bulletin* 902-0 (7 June 1966)
80 Todd Gitlin, *The Sixties* (New York 1987), 237
81 Melody Killian, 'A Love Letter,' *Georgia Straight*, 4 April 1969, 13
82 'The Bright Side of Leadership,' *Ubyssey*, 20 October 1964, 5
83 Jean Bazin, 'Address on CUS Matters,' *Proceedings of the Association of Colleges and Universities of Canada*, 1964
84 'French Universities Out,' *Ubyssey*, 15 September 1964, 1
85 Daniel Latouche, 'Student Councils Are Dead Ducks,' *McGill Daily*, 4 November 1966, 8; Terry Morley, 'Student Syndicalism. A New Concept in

Student Government,' *Gateway,* 29 January 1965, 5 (originally in Dalhousie *Gazette).* See also Philip Stratford, 'Quebec Fever and Youth,' *Saturday Night,* September 1965, 25–6

86 National Archives of Canada, Records of the Canadian Union of Students, vol. 7: 'President's Report, 1965–66,' 15–17

87 Latouche, 'Student Councils Are Dead Ducks,' 8

88 Interview with Richard Price, 11 May 1993

89 Elly Alboim and John Skinner, 'Halifax in Retrospect,' *McGill Daily,* 19 September 1966, 5. For the records of the meeting see NAC, Records of the Canadian Union of Students, vol. 7: 'Resolutions of the Thirtieth Congress of the Canadian Union of Students,' 3–9 September 1966.

90 *CUS Bulletin,* 1 February 1966. NAC, Records of the Canadian Union of Students, vol. 6: 'To Board of Directors, February 10, 1966,' and attachments, gives a good idea of the changing mood of the CUS at that early date. See also 'CUS Congress Reports,' Ubyssey, 19 September 1967, 8.

91 'Today's University a Hoax,' *CUS Bulletin,* March 1966

92 See for example 'CUS and Us,' *Ubyssey,* 15 October 1964, 4.

93 On the background see 'Left Fights Right on CUS Policy,' *Ubyssey,* 13 September 1966, 1. On the withdrawal see Brian Campbell, 'The West Gave Birth to a New Student Movement,' *Gateway,* 22 November 1968, C4–C5.

94 'CUS, UGEQ, or Neither? Council Calls for Referendum,' *McGill Daily,* 14 October 1966, 1; Arnold Aberman, 'Report: The CUS Congress,' ibid., 19 October 1966, 5

95 'CUS Survey Reveals Higher Costs, Higher Tuition Fees No Surprise, *Gateway,* 6 October 1964, 1; 'Students Walk Out Over Fees,' *Ubyssey,* 2 February 1965, 1

96 AUCC, *Financing Higher Education in Canada* [Bladen Report] (Toronto 1965)

97 See 'We Were Concerned,' *Ubyssey,* 28 October 1965, 1, and *Proceedings of the Association of Colleges and Universities for 1965,* 34.

98 NAC, Records of the Canadian Union of Students, vol. 7: Ken Drushka, 'Bladen Report: How to Finance Higher Education without Actually Rocking the Boat'

99 Harvey Shepherd, 'Education – Privilege of Rich?,' *Varsity* (reprinted in *Gateway,* 5 February 1965. The second citation is from 'We Deserve What We Get,' *Gateway,* 2 March 1965, 2.

100 Student Council of Glendon College, 'The University Is for the People,' September 1968; reprinted in Tim and Julyan Reid, *Student Power and the Canadian Campus* (Toronto 1969), 83

101 'His Honors Degree Didn't Mean a Thing,' *Gateway,* 13 September 1968, 5

102 Peter Boothroyd, 'Don't Give Us Degrees, Give Us an Education,' *Gateway*, 10 October 1968, 5

103 Matt Cohen, 'Ties that Bind: The Changing U and Society,' *Gateway*, 6 December 1968, C3; 'The Trouble Is ... You Pay for the University – They Run It,' *Georgia Straight*, 12 September 1969, 2

104 Simon Fraser University Archives [SFUA], RG8/16, Box 1-4, file 5/2: Memo by Jim Harding, 'Education Needs Freedom,' undated (probably 1967). Stanley Gray, Lecture at the 1968 Couchiching Conference, in Gordon McCaffrey, ed., *The U.S. and Us* (Toronto 1968), 143

105 Boothroyd, 'Don't Give Us Degrees ...,' 5

106 Peter Boothroyd, 'Abolish Degrees – Students Will Learn Anyway,' *Gateway*, 18 October 1968, 5

107 Jerry Farber, *The Student as Nigger: Essays and Stories* (North Hollywood 1969), Preface

108 'Jerry Farber, 'The Student as Nigger,' *Gateway*, 29 March 1969, 4–5

109 'The Road to Fascism on Campus,' *McGill Daily*, 28 September 1966, 1, and 'Lapierre Claims Students Are "installed in apathy,"' ibid., 29 September 1966, 1

110 McMaster University, SUPA Papers, Box 14: Don Roebuck, 'Notes on Campus Organizing'

111 John Searle, 'A Foolproof Scenario for Student Revolts,' from SFU Archives RG8/16, Box 1, file 6/2. This is a repint from *New York Times Magazine*, 29 December 1968

112 'The Barricade Crumbled,' *Silhouette*, 18 September 1970, 1, recounts the events of the previous year. Laurel Limpur, 'Why I Sat In,' and Paul McCrae and Sherry Brydson, 'Dow Sit-in Freezes Out as Demonstrators Picket Campus Interviews,' *Varsity*, 22 November 1967, 1

113 *Ubyssey*, 2 March 1965, 4

114 'Participation,' *Ubyssey*, 14 October 1966, 4

115 'Double-Whammy Put on *Daily*,' *McGill Daily*, 3 November 1966, 1, and subsequent issues deal with that year's crisis.

116 *Free Peak*, 7 July 1966, 1

117 Gitlin, *The Sixties*, 249–56

118 Patricia Jasen, 'In Pursuit of Human Values: The Student Critique of the Arts Curriculum in the 1960s,' in Paul Axelrod and John Reid, eds., *Youth University and Canadian Society: Essays on the Social History of Higher Education* (Montreal and Kingston 1989), 247–74, provides and excellent summary of the movement to restructure the Arts curriculum.

119 Administrative irresolution was prominently singled out in some of the most dramatic confrontations of the decade. See, for the United States,

Crisis at Columbia: Report of the Fact Finding Commission on the Columbia Disturbances (New York 1968), Part 1, ch. 4; Part 2, ch. 6.

120 Claude Bissell, *Halfway Up Parnassus: A Personal Account of the University of Toronto, 1932–1971* (Toronto 1974), ch. 8, gives the perspective of one of Canada's senior university administrators on the changing climate. His description of student attitudes by 1966 as 'cloudy and vaguely menacing' (126) says volumes about the changing relationship between administration and students.

121 Alan Walker, 'Student Power,' *Star Weekly Magazine*, 13 January 1968, 4, refers to SFU as having 'Canada's strongest student power pack.'

122 Donald Stainsby, 'Instant University,' *Saturday Night*, March 1964, 16

123 The comment on architectural style is from 'How an Old Boy Got Back at UBC,' *Maclean's*, 16 October 1965, 68. These phrases on the nature of educated at SFU are from 1960s calendars and are cited in Julie Healy et al., 'Orientation Supplement to SFU Calendar, 72–73,' 1. A copy of this document is in SFUA.

124 'Rally Tempers Blaze,' *Peak*, 27 October 27, 1965, 1; 'Students Botch Tow-Away,' ibid., 8 December 1965, 3; 'Students Deserve Equality,' ibid., 2 March 1966, 3; 'Belly-ache,' ibid., 9 March 1966, 4

125 'Is Universal Accessibility Henceforth Only for the Rich?,' *Peak*, 4 May 1966, 4

126 'Something Smells,' ibid., 15 June 1966, 2

127 'Thank-you,' ibid., 27 July 1966, 4. See also ibid., 22 June 1966, 1.

128 Simon Fraser, *Calendar* for 1967–8, 137

129 'Symposium Succeeds,' *Peak*, 9 November 1966, 5. See also Louis Feldhammer, 'An Anthropologist Evaluates "Black Power,"' *Canadian Dimension*, September–October 1967, 14.

130 The reference to Yandle's SUPA membership appears in Alan Walker, 'The Revolt on Campus,' *Star Weekly Magazine*, 13 January 1968, 2.

131 Sharon Yandle, 'Post-Mortem on Strike Action,' *Peak*, 5 April 1967, 14

132 On the PSA incident see ibid.

133 SFUA, RG8/16, 'Campus Crisis,' Box 2, file 5.2: Howard McCurdy to P.D. McTaggert-Cowan, 27 May 1968. 'Report on Simon Fraser University by the Special Investigating Committee of the Canadian Association of University Teachers, February 9, 1968,' in CAUT *Bulletin* 16/4 (April 1968), 4–27

134 SFUA, RG8/16, 'Campus Crisis,' Box 2, file 5/2: 'Memorandum by Martin Loney,' 30 May 1968. On the censure of the president see Jim Harding, 'The Meaning of the Censure,' *Peak*, 13 March 1968, 11.

135 Ibid., Gordon Hardy to Miss Laws, 7 December 1969

136 SFUA, RG 6/1, Box 1: Senate Minutes of 14 April 1969: Statement of Acting Academic Vice President R.R. Haering
137 *Vancouver Sun,* 22 November 1968, 1; *Time,* 6 December 1968, 14
138 SFUA, RG8/16, Box 2: Mimeograph of PSA Course Guides, 1969
139 'Trouble, Simon Fraser University,' *Georgia Straight,* 12 September 1969
140 SFUA, RG 8/16, Box 2: John Leggett to PSA Department, 29 October 1969
141 Ibid.: David Lewis to David Wallbaum, 14 April 1976

10: Sexual Revolutions and Revolutions of the Sexes, 1965–1973

1 Jacques Henripin, *Trends and Factors of Fertility in Canada* (Ottawa 1961), 145
2 Beth Bailey, *Front Porch to Back Seat: Courtship in Twentieth-Century America* (Baltimore 1988), Conclusion
3 Gloria Steinem, *Outrageous Acts and Everyday Rebellions* (New York 1983), 16.
4 *Toronto Daily Star,* 8 December 1970. Cited in Alison Prentice, Paula Bourne, Gail Cuthbert Brandt, Beth Light, Wendy Mitchinson, and Naomi Black, *Canadian Women: A History* (Toronto 1988), 349
5 Sara Evans, *Personal Politics* (New York 1979)
6 Ellie Langer, cited in Wini Breneis, *Young, White and Miserable: Growing Up Female in the Fifties* (Boston 1992), xii
7 F.H. Leacy, ed., *Historical Statistics of Canada,* 2d ed. (Ottawa 1983) tables D205–22
8 Yvonne Mathews-Klein, 'How They Saw Us: Images of Women in National Film Board Films of the 1940s and 1950s,' *Atlantis: A Women's Studies Journal* 4/3 (Spring 1979),
9 On the expected role of fathers see Benjamin Spock, *The Common Sense Book of Baby and Child Care* (New York 1946), 15, and 'Father's a Parent Too,' *Canadian Home and Gardens* (April 1952), 29–31
10 Veronica Strong-Boag, 'Home Dreams: Women and the Suburban Experiment in Canada, 1945–1960,' *Canadian Historical Review* 62 (December 1991), 471
11 See, for a flavour of the times, 'Can Women Combine the B.A. and the Baby,' *Saturday Night,* 21 February 1948, 24, and F.G. Vallee, 'The Changing Role of Women,' *Canadian Welfare,* 15 March 1961,
12 Sidney Gruenberg, *The Many Lives of Modern Woman; A Guide to Happiness in Her Complex Role* (Toronto 1952), 79
13 Canadian Home and School and Parent-Teacher Federation, *Canadian Family Study, 1957–1960* (n.p., n.d.), 26

14 Canadian Institute of Public Opinion, *Gallup Poll in Canada*, 18 June 1960
15 Sidney Katz, 'How the Mayburys Saved Their Marriage,' *Maclean's*, 15 April 1951, 22–3+, 32
16 Alberta, Department of Education, *Junior High Curriculum Guide for Home Economics* (September 1961)
17 Paul Popenoe and Dorothy Cameron Disney, *Can This Marriage Be Saved?* (New York 1960; first edition 1953), 33
18 Doug Baillie, 'The Debate Over the Liberalization of the Divorce Law in Canada, 1950–1968,' MA thesis, University of Alberta, 1994, surveys the attitudes towards divorce and the changes that occurred at both the political and the popular level.
19 *Historical Statistics of Canada*, 2nd ed., tables B79–80
20 Paul Popinoe, 'First Aid for the Family,' *Maclean's*, 1 May 1947, 19
21 Melinda McCracken, *Memories Are Made of This* (Toronto 1975), 11–12
22 Judith Stacey, *Brave New Families: Stories of Domestic Upheaval in Late Twentieth Century America* (New York 1990), 10
23 Frank Tumpane, 'Understanding Women,' *Chatelaine*, November 1950, 19
24 *Rebel without a Cause*, Warner Brothers, 1955, produced by David Weisbart
25 Sidney Katz, 'Going Steady,' *Maclean's*, 3 January 1959, 9–11+, 38
26 Margaret Mead, *Male and Female* (New York 1949), 290
27 Havelock Ellis, *An Intelligent Woman's Guide to Man-Hunting* (New York 1963), 49
28 McCracken, *Memories Are Made of This*, 93
29 Ira Le Reiss, 'Premarital Sex as Deviant Behavior: An Application of Current Approaches to Deviance,' *American Sociological Review* 35 (February 1970), 82
30 Evelyn Mills Duval, *The Art of Dating* (New York 1958), 205
31 Alfred C. Kinsey, *Sexual Behavior in the Human Male* (Philadelphia 1948); *Sexual Behavior in the Human Female* (Philadelphia 1953). See also Lotta Dempsey, 'Dr. Kinsey Talks about Women,' *Chatelaine*, August 1949, 10–11.
32 Katz, 'Going Steady,' 36–7
33 William Nicholls, 'Christians and Sex,' *Saturday Night*, January 1964, 33
34 Breneis, *Young, White and Miserable*, 87
35 Murray Schumach, *The Face on the Cutting Room Floor* (New York 1964), 45–87; Thomas Doherty, *Teenagers and Teenpics: The Juvenilization of American Movies in the 1950s* (Boston 1988), 31–3
36 John D'Emilio and Estelle B. Freedman, *Intimate Matters* (New York 1988), 281–2
37 'Why They Scissor the Films: How the Censors Decide What You Will See,' *Financial Post*, 23 July 1955, 18

38 P. Goodall, 'Sex Is Not a Sin,' *Saturday Night*, March 1963, 27; Morley Callaghan, 'Censorship: The Amateurs and the Law,' *Saturday Night*, 4 February 1956, 9–10
39 Lotta Dempsey, 'Dr. Kinsey Talks about Women,' *Chatelaine*, August 1949, 10–11
40 For a critical view from a Canadian see Robert Fulford, 'Dream World of the Sex Magazines,' *Saturday Night*, 17 March 1962, 17–20.
41 Robert Bothwell, Ian Drummond, and John English, *Canada since 1945: Power, Politics, and Provincialism*, rev. ed. (Toronto 1989), 159
42 *Lady Chatterly's Lover* was given legal acceptance in a 1962 decision of the Supreme Court. See Arnold Edinborough, 'Deviance and the Reading Public,' *Saturday Night*, 14 April 1962, 15–17.
43 William L. O'Neill, *Coming Apart: An Informal History of the 1960s* (Chicago 1971), 204–12
44 William Nicholls, 'Christians and Sex,' *Saturday Night*, January 1964, 33
45 Paul-André Linteau, René Durocher, Jean-Claude Robert, and François Ricard, *Quebec since 1930* (Toronto 1991), 479
46 'Bitter Attack Looms in House,' Vancouver *Province*, 1 February 1953. Cited in Campbell Ross, 'The Neatby Debate and Conservative Thought in Canada,' PhD thesis, University of Alberta, 1989, 181
47 Province of Alberta, *Junior High School Curriculum Guide for Health* (Edmonton 1961), 23
48 Katz, 'Going Steady,' 38. The professor, apparently from the University of Toronto, is not identified.
49 National Archives of Canada [NAC], Sound and Film Archives, *This Hour Has Seven Days*: 'Youth in Search of Morality' (1965); ibid., 'The Game,' 17 April 1966, 01V1CV 8302 104-37
50 Simma Holt, *Sex and the Teenage Revolution* (Toronto 1967), 21
51 NAC, National Sound and Film Archives, O1V1CV 8401 068
52 From a late war high of 739 deaths, syphilis mortality rates had been declining steadily. By the end of the 1950s, deaths were down to fewer than 200 annually, many of those from untreated problems incurred long before. The death rate was only one per hundred thousand by that time. See Dominion Bureau of Statistics, *Vital Statistics*, for the various years.
53 For a history of early birth-control movements in Canada see Angus McLaren and Arlene Tigar McLaren, *The Bedroom and the State: The Changing Practices and Politics of Contraception and Aboriton in Canada, 1880–1980* (Toronto 1986). In spite of its title the book really is not interested in the Pill.
54 *Historical Statistics of Canada*, 2d ed. table B3

55 Duvall, *Art of Dating*, 204
56 Cited in Breneis, *Young, White and Miserable*, 115
57 K.P. Burns, 'Adoption,' *Saturday Night*, 5 December 1950, 37+
58 On the background to the Pill see James Reed, *From Private Vice to Public Virtue: The Birth Control Movement and American Society since 1930* (New York 1978), 311–16.
59 Ibid., 323. See also Gregory Pincus, *The Control of Fertility* (New York 1965).
60 Reed, *From Private Vice to Public Virtue*, 344
61 Marjory Bracher, *SRO, Overpopulation and You* (Philadelphia 1966); Conference on Research in Family Planning, *Research in Family Planning* (Princeton 1966)
62 *Saturday Night*, 3 February 1962, front cover
63 K.M. Crocker and W.D. Stitt, 'Ovulation Inhibitors,' *Canadian Medical Association Journal* [CMAJ], 90/12 (21 March 1964), 716
64 'Low Cost Potent Infertility Pill Being Tested Here,' *Financial Post*, 18 February 1961, 8. See also W.L. Dack, 'Two Companies Lead in Birth Control Pills,' *Financial Post*, 11 May 1963, 36
65 Canadian Institute of Public Opinion, *Gallup Poll*, 15 Febuary 1961, indicated that 55 per cent of Canadians surveyed favoured birth control, compared with 28 per cent opposed.
66 Statutes of Canada, *Criminal Code Statutes Revised to 1950* (Ottawa 1951), ch. 36, S 270
67 G.P.R. Tallon, 'The Legal Implications of Non-Therapeutic Practices of Doctors,' *CMAJ* 87/5 (4 August 1962), 207–10
68 Canada, House of Commons, *Debates*, Session 1964–5, vol. 11, 11 September 1964, 7937. Speech of Joseph O'Keefe (St John's East). For an idea of groups supporting the change see the petitioners listed in ibid., 22 February 1965.
69 Christopher Tietze 'Teaching of Fertility Regulation in Medical Schools: A Survey in the United States and Canada,' *CMAJ* 94 (2 April 1966), 720
70 For comments on this south of the border see 'Rx Board Finds Pressure for Pills, But No Black Market,' *American Druggist* 154 (7 November 1966), 16
71 'New Group Bucks Birth Control Ban,' *Ubyssey*, 8 January 1965, 1
72 'Birth Control Panel Today,' *McGill Daily*, 15 November 1966, 3. See also the editorial in support of birth control: 'Our Sex Life and Yours,' ibid., 27 January 1967, 4.
73 'SAC–Birth Control Efforts Opposed,' *Varsity*, 6 October 1967, 1. The opposition referred to the discomfort of some residence deans about the idea of the student government visiting residents to discuss birth control. Actual administration resistance seems to have been very weak.

74 'At Last, At Last,' *Gateway*, 12 September 1969, 1. The information on the Wauneita Society comes from Elaine H. Chalus, 'From Friedan to Feminism: Gender and Change at the University of Alberta, 1960–1970,' an unpublished paper done for my graduate seminar in 1989.
75 Douglas Marshall, 'The Surprising Social Revolution We've Started with the Pill,' *Maclean's*, March 1967, 20+, 70
76 'York Gets the Pill,' *McGill Daily*, 13 November 1967, 2
77 Linteau et al., *Quebec since 1930*, 479; 'Quebec Swallows the Pill,' *Maclean's*, 2 May 1966, 2
78 For a time, age remained a controversial issue. That was largely removed, at least on campus, as more governments reduced the age of majority from twenty-one to eighteen.
79 'A Pill in Time Saves Nine,' *McGill Daily*, 23 January 1968, 12
80 Bailey, *Front Porch to Back Seat*, 79–90
81 Robert K. Bell and Jay B. Chaskes, 'Premarital Sexual Experience among Co-Eds, 1958, 1968,' *Journal of Marriage and the Family* 32 (1970), 81–4
82 James Teevan, 'Reference Group and Premarital Sexual Behavior,' *Journal of Marriage and the Family* 34 (1972), 283–91; Le Reiss, 'Premarital Sex as Deviant Behavior'
83 Myrna Kostash, *A Long Way from Home* (Toronto 1980), 112
84 Lewis Yablonski, *The Hippie Trip* (New York 1968)
85 David Sharpe, *Rochdale: The Runaway College* (Toronto 1987), 128
86 Isadore Rubin, 'New Sex Findings,' in Herbert Otto, ed., *The New Sexuality* (Palo Alto, CA, 1971), 38
87 The printing of the Krassner piece by various student papers led to considerable controversy. See, for the best example, the McGill battle over the issue: 'Obscene Libel Charged,' *McGill Daily*, 6 November 1967, 1, and 'McGill Daily Charged with Obsenity, *Varsity*, 8 November 1967, 1.
88 Twiggy was described as 'four straight limbs in search of a woman's body,' by one unappreciative older reporter: see 'Twiggy in America,' *Newsweek*, 10 April 1967, 62
89 By 1975 the birth rate in Canada was just over fifteen per thousand, or about 60 per cent of what the rate had been at the height of the baby boom: *Historical Statistics of Canada*, table B4.
90 Judy Bernstein, Peggy Morton, Linda Seese, and Myrna Wood, 'Sisters, Brothers, Lovers ... Listen ...'; reprinted in *Women Unite: An Anthology of the Canadian Women's Movement* (Toronto 1972), 31–40
91 F.H. Leacy, ed., *Historical Statistics of Canada*, 2d ed. (Ottawa 1983), tables W-340-1

92 Dominion Bureau of Statistics, *Survey of Higher Education, 1969–1970* (Ottawa 1971; catalogue 81-209)
93 For details on enrolment see Canada, *Report of the Royal Commission on the Status of Women* (Ottawa 1971), table 1.
94 Strong-Boag, 'Home Dreams,' 471–504
95 Alison Prentice, Paula Bourne, Gail Cuthbert Brandt, Beth Light, Wendy Mitchinson, and Naomi Black, *Canadian Women: A History* (Toronto 1988), table A.14
96 Ibid., 347
97 Betty Friedan, *The Feminine Mystique* (New York 1963)
98 Cerise Morris, '"Determination and Thoroughness": The Movement for a Royal Commission on the Status of Women in Canada,' *Atlantis* 5 (Spring 1980), 1–21
99 Canada, *Report of the Royal Commission on the Status of Women* (Ottawa 1970) 227
100 Evans, *Personal Politics*, 160
101 Ibid., 156
102 Sandra Burt, 'The Canadian Women's Movement: The Second Wave,' in Sandra Burt, Lorraine Code, and Lindsay Dorney, eds., *Changing Patterns: Women in Canada* (Toronto 1981), 89
103 See for a listing of various women's-liberation activities, including some in Canada, *Women: A Journal of Liberation*, published in Baltimore, beginning in 1969.
104 Bessie McGee, 'A Children's Garden of Women's Groups,' *Guerilla*, 31 July 1970, 2. Interview with Greg Kealey, Ottawa, February 1994. Andy Wernick, 'A Guide to the Student Left,' *Varsity*, 24 September 1969, 8–9
105 Mentioned in *Women. A Journal of Liberation* (Spring 1970), 17
106 Jill Conway, *True North: A Memoir* (Toronto 1994)
107 See, for example, 'Women's Day Prompts Discussion on Abortion, Wages,' *Gateway*, 29 January 1970, 8.
108 See McMaster University Archives, SUPA Papers, Box 14: 'Psychedelic Organizing,' undated manuscript by Judi Bernstein, 6
109 SFU Archives, RG8/16 Box 1–4, file 5/2: 'Love, Adapted from Notes Toward a Second Year,' *The Reflector*, 11 December 1970
110 Maren Lockwood Garden, *The New Feminist Movement* (New York 1974), 152–3
111 Betty Friedan, *The Feminine Mystique* (New York 1963); Simone de Beauvoir, *The Second Sex* (New York 1953); Kate Millet, *Sexual Politics* (New York 1969)

11: The End of the Sixties, 1968–1973

1 David Lewis Stein, 'The Younger Generation,' *Maclean's*, 20 June 1964, 1
2 National Archives of Canada [NAC], Records of the Company of Young Canadians, vol. 1, file 353.2: 'A Draft Statement of Aims and Principles ... July 25, 1966,' 1
3 On Columbia see *Crisis at Columbia: The Cox Commission Report* (New York 1968).
4 Geoffrey Meggs, 'Warrian Sees Danger of Violence,' *Varsity*, 30 September 1968, 3
5 John Braddock, 'Strife on Campus,' in Tim and Julyan Reid, eds., *Student Power and the Canadian Campus* (Toronto 1969), 115–25
6 Jon Pareles and Patricia Romanowski, *The Rolling Stone Rock Almanac: The Chronicles of Rock and Roll* (New York 1983), 132–46; Rita Lang Kleinfeld, *When We Were Young: A Baby Boomer Yearbook* (New York 1993), 488
7 Jon Pareles and Patricia Romanowski, *The Rolling Stone Encyclopedia of Rock and Roll* (New York 1983), 27–8
8 François Ricard, *The Lyric Generation: The Life and Times of the Baby Boomers* (Toronto 1994), 134
9 Ed Ward, Geoffrey Stokes, and Ken Tucker, *Rock of Ages: The Rolling Stone History of Rock & Roll* (New York 1986), 374
10 The summaries of these concerts are in Rolling Stone, *Rock Almanac*, 149–59
11 At the time this page is being drafted the twenty-fifth anniversary of Woodstock is approaching. The attention by mainstream media indicates its importance. The London *Times* referred to it as 'the baby boom's finest hour,' while both *Time* and *Newsweek* devoted cover stories to it.
12 The array of groups was impressive, including many of the biggest names of the late 1960s. Among those who played were Janis Joplin; Jimi Hendrix; Joe Cocker; Joan Baez; the Who; Crosby, Stills and Nash; Richie Havens; and Country Joe and the Fish.
13 *Woodstock*, a film by Michael Wadleigh (Warner Brothers 1970)
14 Jack Batten, 'Stoned on Rock, Stoned on Drugs,' *Saturday Night*, December 1969, 18
15 Rex Weiner and Deanne Stillman, *The Woodstock Nation* (New York 1979)
16 The movie of the same name captured the chaos of the concert and the fascination of the Rolling Stones with the event.
17 George Paul Csicesry, 'Stones Concert Ends It: America Now Up for Grabs,' *Georgia Straight*, 17 December 1969, 10

18 Claude Bissell, *Halfway Up Parnassus: A Personal Account of the University of Toronto, 1932–1971* (Toronto 1974), 131
19 'McGill Professor Won't Say He's Sorry,' *Toronto Daily Star*, 18 February 1969, 5
20 This recounting is from Dorothy Eber, *The Computer Party* (Montreal 1969), 78–90, and 'Countdown to a Crisis,' Ottawa *Citizen*, 11 February 1969, 7.
21 Ronald Lebel, 'The Black and White Case at Sir George Williams,' *Globe and Mail*, 12 February 1969, 7
22 'An Indefensible Act by Student Anarchists,' *Montreal Star*, 12 February 1969, 8; 'Lawlessness,' Winnipeg *Free Press*, 13 February 1969, 33; 'Jail Them,' *Calgary Herald*, 13 February 1969, 4; *La Presse*, 12 February 1969, 5
23 Canada, House of Commons, *Debates*, 1st session, 28th Parl., 13 February 1969, 5461–4
24 'Brandon Students Rap Montreal Destruction,' Winnipeg *Tribune*, 15 February 1969, 8
25 '400 Students Pitch In to Clean Up,' *Globe and Mail*, 13 February 1969, 3
26 Wells Warns Against Campus Incidents,' *Globe and Mail*, 13 February 1969, 5
27 UGEQ Supports Rioters,' *Montreal Star*, 13 February 1969, 3
28 Todd Gitlin, *The Sixties: Years of Hope, Days of Rage* (New York 1984), 285
29 Ibid., 380–408
30 'Wells Warns Against Campus Incidents,' 3
31 McMaster University, SUPA Papers, Box 2: Peter [Boothroyd?] to Nancy, 14 April 1965
32 See, as a good example of the administrative reaction, Walter Johns (president of the University of Alberta), 'The Vulnerable University,' speech at Varsity Guest Weekend, 12 February 1969; reprinted in Duncan D. Campbell, ed., *Those Tumultuous Years: The Goals of the President of the University of Alberta During the decade of the 1960s* (Edmonton 1977), 42.
33 C.F. Kennan, *Democracy and the Student Left* (Boston 1968)
34 Lewis Feuer, *The Conflict of Generations: The Character and Significance of Student Movements* (New York 1969), 491. For a Canadian review of both Kennan and Feuer see Neil Compton, 'What Do Young People Want?' *Canadian Forum*, June 1969, 51–2.
35 Tom Wolfe, *Radical Chic and Mau-Mauing the Flak Catchers* (New York 1970), 42
36 Mordecai Richler, 'A With-it Professor Proudly Wearing a Nehru Jacket Is the Equivalent of a Fat Old Woman Dressed in a Bikini,' *Saturday Night*, February 1969, 45–6

37 Robert Fulford, 'The Language of Now,' *Saturday Night,* January 1969, 21–3, 45–6

38 Northrop Frye, 'Why the Youth "Revolution" Isn't,' *Financial Post,* 7 December 1968, 13. See also Northrop Frye, 'Rapid Change Means Lowered Intellectual Sights,' *University Affairs,* December 1968, 14–15; George Woodcock, 'The Ominous Politics of the Student Left,' *Saturday Night,* July 1969, 19–22. See also his 'Notes on Academic Unrest II,' *Canadian Forum,* August 1969, 115.

39 Woodcock, 'The Ominous Politics of the Student Left,' and 'Notes on Academic Unrest II'

40 'Lawlessness,' Winnipeg *Free Press,* 13 February 1969, 33

41 G. David Sheps, 'The Apocalyptic Fires,' *Canadian Dimension,* February 1969, 6–7+

42 'Work or Get Out,' *Calgary Herald,* 17 February 1969, 4

43 Gitlin, *The Sixties,* 342–3

44 John Deutsch, 'Speech on the Occasion of His Installation as Principal of Queen's,' *University Affairs* 101/3 (December 1968), 7. For a similar position see Michael Hayden, *Seeking a Balance: The University of Saskatchewan, 1907–1982* (Vancouver 1983), 261

45 Claude Bissell, 'Freedom: Academic and Otherwise,' from his Dunning Lecture at Queen's 1969; cited in Tim Reid and Julyan Reid, eds., *Student Power and the Canadian Campus* (Toronto 1969), 126–33, 131

46 Richard Schultz, 'Anarchy Plus the Constable,' in Reid and Reid, eds., *Student Power and the Canadian Campus,* 135

47 Typical was the decision of the University of Alberta in 1968. After a series of SDU protests, the president responded by supporting a student presence on the board of governors while, at the same time, preparing to respond to student disruption. My thanks to Heather Devine for 'The Social Credit Government and Institutional Change at the University of Alberta,' unpublished paper, University of Alberta, 1994, 20–1.

48 For a detailed study of the changes in curiculum see Patricia Jasen, 'Ways of Knowing: An Intellectual History of the Liberal Arts Curriculum in Canadian Universities,' PhD thesis, Manitoba, 1987

49 Hayden, *Seeking a Balance,* 261

50 Escott Reid, 'When, If Ever, Do You Call the Cops,' in Reid and Reid, eds., *Student Power,* 101–6

51 Paul Carson, 'Universities to Adopt Counter-Violence,' *Varsity,* 22 September 1969, 1

52 For a brief commentary on the physical expansion see Bissell, *Halfway Up Parnassus,* ch. 3.

53 Ibid., 131
54 Gitlin, *The Sixties*, 285
55 Paul Carron, 'Universities to Adopt "Counter-Violence," 1; "People's Park," 6,' *Varsity*, 22 September 1969, 4
56 Ibid., 'Year of the Barricades,' 3 October 1969, 3
57 Andy Wernick, ' A Guide to the Student Left,' *Varsity*, 24 September 1969, 8–9
58 Bob Bossin Feels Out Campus Orientation,' *Varsity*, 22 September 1969, 5
59 Wernick, 'A Guide to the Student Left'
60 These quotes are Wernick's.
61 Interview with Greg Kealey, Ottawa, 17 February 1994. Kealey was a member of the NLC in 1969–70.
62 Susan Reisler, 'Discipline Committee Folds as Students Walk Out,' *Varsity*, 24 September 1969, 1; Mary Bastedo, 'SAC Votes to Issue Ultimatum to Bissell,' *Varsity*, 26 September 1969, 1
63 Geoff Megs and Paul Carson, 'If This Is Reported the Way It Happened ...,' *Varsity*, 10 October 1969, 1. See also, in same issue, 'Council Freaks Out,' 4.
64 'Council Freaks Out,' *Varsity*, 10 October 1969, 4
65 CUS, 'National Supplement,' 20–4 October 1969.
66 'Canadian Union of Students Decides to Phase Out,' *University Affairs* 10 (December 1969), 7
67 Howard Adelman, 'A Decade of Protest: Coroner's Report,' *Canadian Forum*, February 1970, 258
68 Cyrill Levitt, *Children of Privilege: Student Revolt in the Sixties* (Toronto 1984), 177, refers to the 'internal ideological strife' which afflicted the New Left, not just in Canada, but in the United States and Germany as well.
69 Interview with Greg Kealey, Ottawa, 17 February 1994
70 NAC, Records of the Company of Young Canadians, vol. 12, file 116-5, contained the information on the new board. For the citation see interview with Duncan Edmonds, *Toronto Daily Star*, 5 January 1970.
71 In order to assess this I tried to identify student 'occupations' of buildings across Canada between 1967 and 1973 as reported in student newspapers. No doubt several were missed, but those I found revealed the pattern mentioned. For the sake of uniformity I looked only at those occupations that involved non-student areas of campus. Dormitory protests and similar events were excluded. For obvious reasons I also excluded 'symbolic occupations,' where students entered a building took it over, read out demands, and left voluntarily.
72 Steve Langdon, 'Pat-A-Cake Politics,' *Varsity*, 29 October 1969, 7

73 For a general overview see Desmond Morton, *Social Democracy in Canada* (Toronto 1977), 89–98

74 Socialist Caucus Bulletin, 'Special Issue: The Ottawa NDP Expulsions,' No. 8 (January 1967)

75 Walter Stewart, 'Why Young Canadians Want a Prime Minister with Intellect and Guts,' *Star Weekly Magazine*, 16 March 1968, 2–6. A survey of people aged eighteen to thirty-five indicated that Trudeau was far ahead of other contenders, especially in Ontario.

76 John Steele, 'Caucus Report and Objectives,' NDP Socialist Caucus Bulletin No. 3 (January 1966). A copy of the bulletin exists in McMaster Library, SUPA Papers

77 Gallup poll for *Toronto Daily Star*, published in *Canadian Dimension*, March/April 1967, 18–19

78 The literature on this is vast. Practically any issue of *Canadian Dimension* between 1966 and the early 1970s will reflect this argument. The actual quote comes from John W. Warnock, 'Why I Am Anti-American,' *Canadian Dimension*, November/December 1967, 11. See as good examples of this argument: D. Drache, 'The Canadian Bourgeoisie and Its National Consciousness,' and C.W. Gonick, 'Foreign Ownership and Political Decay,' in Ian Lumsden, ed., *Close to the 49th Parallel: The Americanization of Canada* (Toronto 1970)

79 Cited in Robert Hackett, 'Waffle,' special issue of *Canadian Dimension*, October/November 1980, 20

80 This was admitted by many Wafflers. See, for example, Cy Gonick and Jack Warnock, 'Sour Winners: Notes on the NDP Convention,' *Canadian Dimension*, June 1971, 65.

81 Morton, *Social Democracy in Canada*, 92

82 'Policy Differences,' *Canadian Dimension*, November 1980, 15. This reprints the findings of a poll actually done in 1971.

83 'The Waffle Manifesto,' in Michael Cross, ed., *The Decline and Fall of a Good Idea* (Toronto 1974), 44

84 James Laxer, 'The Canadian Student Movement and Canadian Independence,' in *Canadian Dimension*, Survival Kit No. 3: *Canadian Nationalism* (n.p. 1970), 9

85 Morton, *Social Democracy*, 128

86 Ibid., 133

87 Ibid., 134

88 Cy Gonick, 'Waffling in Ontario,' *Canadian Dimension*, October/November 1970, 6

89 Cross, 'Introduction,' in *Decline and Fall of a Good Idea*, 16–17

90 Walter Stewart, 'What He Must Have: Intellect, Honesty and Guts,' *Star Weekly Magazine*, 16 March 1968, 2–6
91 Margaret Daly, 'A Realist, an Intellectual, and a Man of Action,' *Star Weekly Magazine*, 23 March 1968, 2, 6
92 Ward, Stokes, and Tucker, *Rock of Ages*, 486
93 *Historical Statistics of Canada*, tables D223–35

Epilogue: A World without Limits

1 F.H. Leacy, ed., *Historical Statistics of Canada*, 2d ed. (Ottawa 1983), table F55
2 David Potter, *People of Plenty: Economic Abundance and the American Character* (Chicago 1954), ch. 9
3 Canadian Institute of Public Opinion, *Gallup Poll*, 27 January 1960; 4 June 1960; 27 January 1962. See also the polls of 3 February and 24 February 1960.
4 Bill King, 'The Sun's Gonna Shine,' *Guerilla*, 3 July 1970, 6
5 For an example of 1960s environmentalism see F. Knefman, 'Pollution and the New Technological Order,' *Canadian Dimension*, January/February 1971, 35–8
6 *Maclean's*/CBC News Poll, 'Taking the Pulse,' *Maclean's*, 25 December 1995/1 January 1996 (double issue), 32–3
7 See, for example, David K. Foot, *Canada's Population Outlook* (Toronto 1982) and A. Romaniuc, *Fertility in Canada: From Baby Boom to Baby Bust* (Ottawa 1984).

Credits

National Archives of Canada: average Canadian housewife PA 111484; Don Mills Shopping Centre PA 129302; The Grange School PA 113292; the New Left Caucus PA 114867; Mackay Street, Montreal PA 139988; the police move in, Loyola, 1970 PA 137167

Provincial Archives of Alberta: protests against the Vietnam War J127/1

University of British Columbia, Special Collections: occupations of the UBC Faculty Club, #12648; Hare Krishna #15766

Index